Commonly Overlooked Time Savers

The following list includes commonly overlooked keyboard shortcuts and time-saving features.

Time-saver	Description
Selecting IDs	While entering transactions, you place the insertion point in an ID field and type the first few letters of the ID; Microsoft Dynamics GP displays a drop-down list that contains all IDs that match the letters you type.
Opening Lookup windows	You can place the insertion point in a field that contains a magnifying glass and press Ctrl+L to display the associated lookup window.
Keying dates	When you enter a transaction, Microsoft Dynamics GP suggests by default the system date on your computer. You can click the calendar beside the Date field to select a different date or you can place the insertion point in the date field and press + to increment the date by one day or – to decrement the date by one day. Each subsequent time you press + or -, Microsoft Dynamics GP increments or decrements the date by one day. When you type a date, you don't need to key the year if the year is the same as the system date, and you don't need to type any dashes or slashes; you can simply type the two digit month and two digit day and then tab out of the field.
Automatically navigating to the Batch window for a particular transaction	While viewing a transaction in a transaction entry window, you can navigate to the batch containing the transaction if you click the expansion arrow beside the Batch ID field. After the batch window opens, you can close the transaction entry window, which will now appear behind the Batch window, so that you can edit or delete the batch.
Mass Modify	Use the Mass Modify chart of Accounts window to easily create new accounts using information from existing accounts. You also can use this window to move, make inactive, or delete an account or a range of accounts. Choose Cards⇨Financial⇨Mass Modify.
Item Copy	Use the Item Copy window to quickly create a new item using the attributes of an existing item. Choose Cards⇨Inventory⇨Item, enter a new Item ID number, and choose Copy. When prompted, select the existing item you want to use as the foundation for the new item.
Auto Apply	Use this time-saving feature in Receivables Management and Payables Management to automatically apply credit transactions, credit memos, and returns to as many documents as possible. Choose Transactions⇨Sales⇨Apply Sales Documents or Transactions⇨Purchasing⇨Apply To.

Microsoft Dynamics GP For Dummies®

Working with Shortcuts in the Navigation Pane

Shortcuts appear in the upper part of the Navigation pane when you display your Dynamics GP Home page. Use shortcuts to quickly open frequently used windows and resources within Dynamics GP. For example, you can create one set of shortcuts to the windows you use regularly and another set for the ones you use for month-end procedures.

Default shortcuts are available to each new user created in Microsoft Dynamics GP. Any shortcuts that you move into the Startup folder start automatically when you log in to a company in Dynamics GP.

You can take the following actions regarding shortcuts and their folders:

Action	What to Do
Open a shortcut	Click the shortcut to open.
Open a shortcut in a folder	Click a folder name to expand its contents and click the shortcut to open.
Add a new shortcut folder	Right-click anywhere in the list of shortcuts and choose Add >> Folder.
Move a shortcut into a folder	Select the shortcut and drag it into a shortcut folder.
Delete a shortcut or folder	Right-Click the shortcut or folder and choose Delete.

To create a shortcut to a Dynamics GP window, open the window for which you want to add a shortcut. Then, choose File⇨Add to Shortcuts.

To create a shortcut to a Dynamics GP SmartList, right-click anywhere in the list of shortcuts in the Navigation pane and choose Add⇨Add SmartList. In the Add SmartList Favorite Shortcut window that appears, locate and select the favorite for which you want to create a shortcut; the favorite appears in the SmartList favorite field. Accept the default name or enter a new name, up to 79 characters, in the Name field. Choose Add and then choose Done.

For Dummies: Bestselling Book Series for Beginners

Microsoft Dynamics™ GP

FOR

DUMMIES®

Microsoft Dynamics™ GP

FOR DUMMIES®

by Renato Bellu

WILEY

Wiley Publishing, Inc.

Microsoft Dynamics™ GP For Dummies®

Published by
Wiley Publishing, Inc.
111 River Street
Hoboken, NJ 07030-5774

www.wiley.com

Copyright © 2008 by Wiley Publishing, Inc., Indianapolis, Indiana

Published by Wiley Publishing, Inc., Indianapolis, Indiana

Published simultaneously in Canada

For general information on our other products and services, please contact our Customer Care Department within the U.S. at 800-762-2974, outside the U.S. at 317-572-3993, or fax 317-572-4002.

For technical support, please visit www.wiley.com/techsupport.

Wiley also publishes its books in a variety of electronic formats. Some content that appears in print may not be available in electronic books.

Library of Congress Control Number 2008936351

ISBN: 978-0-470-38835-8

Manufactured in the United States of America

10 9 8 7 6 5 4 3 2 1

WILEY

About the Author

Renato Bellu has over 15 years of experience as an ERP implementation specialist focused on Dynamics GP (Great Plains), and has been the Dynamics GP "Thought Leader" for Avanade, a division of Accenture and joint venture with Microsoft, in addition to creating the first-ever Great Plains Practice for a Big 4 CPA firm, PricewaterhouseCoopers LLP. Renato has been the lead designer on some of the largest Microsoft Dynamics GP projects ever implemented, and for this work has become a recipient of the prestigious Microsoft *Pinnacle Award*. He holds certifications from Microsoft in Dynamics GP including Financials and Integration Manager, and holds a Bachelor of Science in Accounting from the University of Delaware. Today, Renato is a senior consultant with RSM McGladrey's Inner Circle and President's Club Microsoft Dynamics GP Practice based in Philadelphia. Helives in Haddonfield, New Jersey, with his wife, Marie, and daughter, Clare.

Dedication

This book is dedicated to my loving and beautiful wife, Marie, and daughter, Clare, who are my greatest source of inspiration and joy.

Author's Acknowledgments

I wish to acknowledge the following people:

My parents, Dr. Renato R. and Elena Bellu, whose guidance, support, and loving devotion has made my career possible.

Professor Clinton "Skip" White of the University of Delaware, a pioneer in the field of computerized accounting education, who inspired me to embark on a career focused on combining the disciplines of accounting and computer science.

Steve Ems, our practice leader, and the entire RSM McGladrey Dynamics team, the most brilliant, helpful, and talented group of folks I have ever had the pleasure of working with.

Hans Wulczyn, of RSM McGladrey, who served as technical editor.

Matt Wagner of Fresh Books, my literary agent, for making this project a reality.

Blair Pottenger, Wiley Project Editor, who managed this project with great aplomb.

Bob Woerner, Wiley Senior Acquisitions Editor, for giving me the opportunity to author this book.

Jenn Riggs, Wiley Copy Editor, for all the hard work on this book.

The entire Wiley team, including the graphics team for their adept work in bringing the text to life with their superb presentation skills.

And lastly, Elaine Marmel, without whom this project would not have been possible.

Publisher's Acknowledgments

We're proud of this book; please send us your comments through our online registration form located at www.dummies.com/register/.

Some of the people who helped bring this book to market include the following:

Acquisitions and Editorial

Project Editor: Blair J. Pottenger

Senior Acquisitions Editor: Bob Woerner

Copy Editor: Jennifer Riggs

Technical Editor: Hans Wulczyn

Editorial Manager: Kevin Kirschner

Editorial Assistant: Amanda Foxworth

Sr. Editorial Assistant: Cherie Case

Cartoons: Rich Tennant
 (www.the5thwave.com)

Composition Services

Project Coordinator: Erin Smith

Layout and Graphics: Stacie Brooks, Reuben W. Davis, Melissa K. Jester, Christin Swinford, Christine Williams

Proofreaders: Broccoli Information Management, Melissa Bronnenberg

Indexer: Broccoli Information Management

Publishing and Editorial for Technology Dummies

 Richard Swadley, Vice President and Executive Group Publisher

 Andy Cummings, Vice President and Publisher

 Mary Bednarek, Executive Acquisitions Director

 Mary C. Corder, Editorial Director

Publishing for Consumer Dummies

 Diane Graves Steele, Vice President and Publisher

 Joyce Pepple, Acquisitions Director

Composition Services

 Gerry Fahey, Vice President of Production Services

 Debbie Stailey, Director of Composition Services

Contents at a Glance

Table of Contents

Introduction

· ·

*L*et's face it— accounting can make anybody feel like a dummy . . . unless, of course, you're an accountant. But even accountants can glaze over when looking at an unfamiliar accounting software package. I've written *Microsoft Dynamics GP for Dummies* to help you take the mystery out of using the software so that you can focus on reaping the benefits of computerized accounting.

"What benefits?" you ask. Well, read on.

About This Book

Here's the situation: You're an accounting or bookkeeping professional who has just started working for a company that uses Microsoft Dynamics GP. Or, your organization has made the decision to move to Dynamics GP. You're already an expert in accounting and/or bookkeeping, but you need to get up to speed quickly on this unfamiliar accounting package.

Microsoft Dynamics GP For Dummies shows you how to get up to speed quickly by highlighting the most useful and practical features, dispelling the most common misconceptions, and letting you in on the best tips and tricks. This book assists you in setting up a company in which to store your accounting data and then shows you how to use Dynamics GP to pay bills, invoice customers, post information to the general ledger, produce financial reports, and who knows, maybe get a raise in the process.

Although Dynamics GP is a modular product (and you can purchase only those modules you feel you need), licensing for Dynamics GP is moving toward a per user license rather than a per module license. In the Appendix, I describe all of the modules available in Dynamics GP and I also describe the licensing plans available to you, which focus on enabling you to purchase the modules you need in common combinations.

Modules provide you with solutions that meet business needs, and, when using Dynamics GP, you work with a *series* that combines related business functions. For example, Sales series combines the functions of receivables management and invoicing.

Note: This book covers the Purchasing series, the Sales series, the Financial series, and the Inventory series. The Purchasing series includes purchase order processing, vendor invoicing, and payables management. The Sales series includes sales order processing, invoicing, and receivables management. The Financial series includes the General Ledger module and Bank Reconciliation module. The Inventory series includes the Inventory Management module.

But you don't need to worry about what's installed on your computer when you work in Dynamics GP, because you work by selecting tasks to perform that correspond to business functions such as creating an invoice for a customer or paying a vendor bill. The modules installed are transparent to you and Dynamics GP lets you work in a way that makes business sense instead of "computer" sense. You can read more about performing these task-related business functions in Part II.

What You Can Safely Ignore

The gray boxes that you see throughout the book are called sidebars. Sidebars contain extra information that you really don't *have* to know but that I thought you might find useful and interesting. So feel free to skip the sidebars.

Foolish Assumptions

I'll be honest — I had to assume some things about you to write this book. So, here's what I assume about you:

- ✔ You already know about the day-to-day stuff that you need to do financially to run your business — you know, write checks, send invoices to customers, record payments from customers, and so on. In fact, you're probably an accounting or bookkeeping professional. I *don't* assume that you know how to do any of that in Dynamics GP.

- ✔ You have a personal computer (that you know how to turn on) with Microsoft Windows XP, Windows 2000, or Windows Vista. I wrote this book using Windows Vista.

- ✔ You are a Dynamics GP user or are interesting in becoming one.

How This Book Is Organized

Every great book needs a plan. I divided this book into six parts, each made up of two to eight chapters so that you can easily find the information that you need.

Part I: Great Things with Microsoft Dynamics GP

If you're new to Dynamics GP, you probably want to read this part. I introduce you to Dynamics GP, explain how to get around in it, how to create a company, how to build an effective chart of accounts, and how to set up default information that saves you lots of time later.

Part II: Daily Entry Tasks

In this book — in this part, in fact — I cover the modules you use to do the stuff that you do on a regular basis (remember, while you work, you think business functions and user roles, not modules):

✔ In the Purchasing series, the Purchase Order and Payables Management modules to buy and pay for goods from vendors

✔ In the Sales series, the Sales Order and Receivables Management modules that you use to create sales orders and invoices for your customers as well as collect your money and identify who hasn't paid an invoice

✔ In the Financial Series, The General Ledger module where you make changes to your chart of accounts and make journal entries for transactions such as recording depreciation, and the Bank Reconciliation module to balance your check book against your bank statement

✔ In the Inventory series, the Inventory Management module, where you manage inventory items

Part III: Stuff You Do From Time to Time

In this section, I cover a variety of topics that you typically *don't* do every day. First, I show you how to close your books and print reports — after all, you put information *into* Dynamics GP, so you should be able to get it out and see the effects of your business habits.

I also show you how to use utilities and the Professional Services Tools module to find and fix data discrepancies and quickly make mass changes to your data.

Part IV: Administering & Extending Your Dynamics GP System

In this section, I show you how to easily keep your accounting information safe — a *very* important chapter. Why? Because you spend so much time putting stuff into Dynamics GP that it would be criminal to lose it just because your hard drive crashes or your office is robbed. I also show you how to modify and customize Dynamics GP to extend its functionality.

Part V: The Part of Tens

If you've ever read a *For Dummies* book before, you've seen the Part of Tens. This part contains a collection of ten-something lists. My Part of Tens includes ten common implementation pitfalls and the Top Ten most useful features in Dynamics GP.

In the Appendix, you'll find a short description of each Microsoft Dynamics GP module available, and you'll also find a description of the licensing plans available.

Icons Used in This Book

Throughout the book, you notice symbols in the margin. These symbols, or *icons,* mark important points.

This bull's eye appears next to shortcuts and tips that make your work easier.

When you see this icon, something could go wrong, so make sure that you read the paragraph. This icon warns you of common mistakes and ways to avoid them.

This icon marks any point that you want to be sure to remember. You might want to reread paragraphs that are marked with this icon.

Where to Go from Here

Just getting started with Microsoft Dynamics GP? Turn the page. Do you have a specific topic of interest? Use the Index or the Table of Contents to find the topic and turn to that page.

Part I
Great Things with Microsoft Dynamics GP

The 5th Wave   By Rich Tennant

"I bought a software program that should help
us monitor and control our spending habits, and
while I was there, I picked up a few new games,
a couple of screen savers, 4 new mousepads, this
nifty pullout keyboard cradle..."

In this part . . .

*I*f you are just getting acquainted with Microsoft Dynamics GP, this part is the place to start. In this part, you find out about common Dynamics GP lingo and how to navigate in Microsoft Dynamics Microsoft Dynamics GP. In Chapter 2, you read about creating a company, designing the Chart of Accounts, and establishing some common setup functionality.

Chapter 1

What Microsoft Dynamics GP Does Best

In This Chapter

▶ Familiarizing yourself with the Microsoft Dynamics GP window

▶ Understanding Dynamics GP terms

▶ Knowing how Dynamics GP keeps your CPA happy

Microsoft Dynamics GP is a robust accounting package that can meet the needs of any number of types of organizations. All installations of Dynamics GP have certain characteristics in common. In this chapter, I describe these common characteristics and, in the process, introduce you to Dynamics GP lingo.

Introducing Microsoft Dynamics GP

Familiarizing yourself with the Microsoft Dynamics GP window is the first order of business. You'll find it much easier to perform tasks if you know how to find them.

In Figure 1-1, you see a typical Dynamics GP opening window. Dynamics GP uses a Navigation pane down the left side of the window, similar to the one found in Microsoft Outlook. The Navigation pane enables you to, well, navigate to various places in the program. In Figure 1-1, I clicked Home in the Navigation pane.

The Home page you see in the Content pane when you open Dynamics GP on your computer might not match the one shown in Figure 1-1 because you can customize the Home page — and you can read about customizing your Dynamics GP Home page in the section "At Home with the Home Page," later in this chapter.

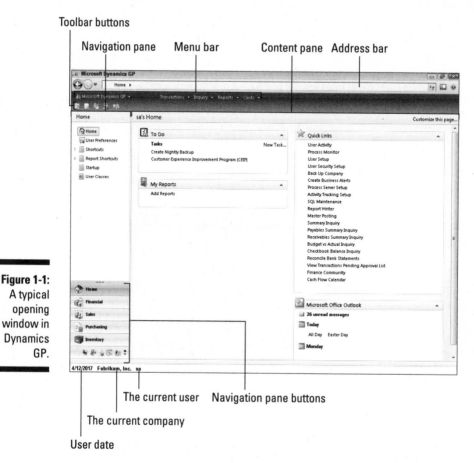

Toolbar buttons

Navigation pane   Menu bar   Content pane   Address bar

The current user   Navigation pane buttons

The current company

User date

Figure 1-1:
A typical
opening
window in
Dynamics
GP.

Along the top of the screen, you can use the Address bar to type locations within Dynamics GP and then press Enter or click the Refresh button at the right end of the Address bar to view those locations. But most people use the Menu bar, which appears just below the Address bar, and the Navigation pane to move around Dynamics GP.

Menus and toolbars

The Menu bar is actually one of several toolbars available in Dynamics GP. Its official name is the Main toolbar but it functions just like the menu bars in other programs you've used, so I'm going to call it the Menu bar. Below the Menu bar (refer to Figure 1-1) you see the Standard toolbar. If you're a "button" person, you can display any of the available toolbars by right-clicking the toolbar area to display the shortcut menu shown in Figure 1-2. From this shortcut menu, click any toolbar you want to display. If a check mark appears beside the toolbar name it's already displayed, and clicking it removes the check mark and hides that particular toolbar.

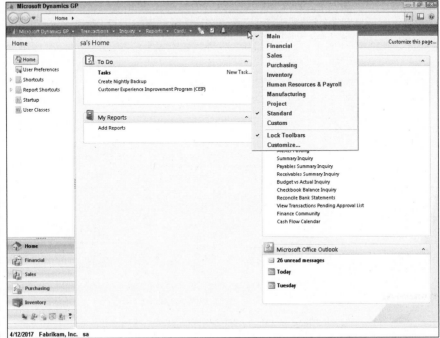

Figure 1-2:
Right-click the toolbar area to display this shortcut menu and control the visible toolbars.

The Navigation and Content panes

Let's take a moment to focus on the main portion of the window, which is divided into two parts. The Navigation pane runs down the left side of the window, and the results of clicking something in the Navigation pane appear in the Content pane on the right side of the window. In Figure 1-3, I clicked the Sales series button in the Navigation pane.

Navigation pane buttons

The buttons along the bottom portion of the Navigation pane represent series of related functions in Dynamics GP. When you click any particular Navigation pane button, lists associated with that series appear above the buttons in the Navigation pane, and the actions you can take within the series fill the Content pane on the right side of the Dynamics GP window (refer to Figure 1-3). I'll tell you more about lists in the next section, but for the time being let's focus on the buttons in the Navigation pane.

Lists for the selected series

Content pane containing actions for the selected series

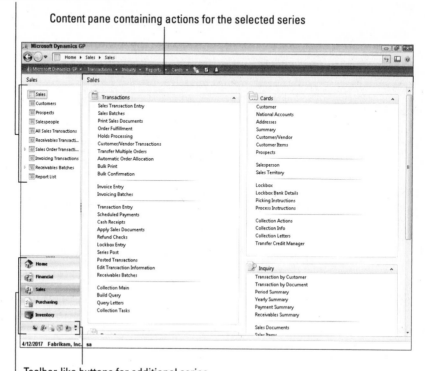

Figure 1-3:
The
Navigation
pane.

Toolbar-like buttons for additional series

Navigation pane buttons

Looking back at Figure 1-3, you see "named" buttons for Home, Financial, Sales, Purchasing, and Inventory. In addition to these named buttons, toolbar-like buttons appear at the bottom of the Navigation pane (in Figure 1-3 they appear under the named Inventory button). These toolbar-like buttons function the same way that the named buttons function — they simply represent additional series of related functions such as Human Resources and Payroll.

If you place the mouse pointer over one of the toobar-like buttons, a tool tip appears to identify the button.

You can increase or decrease the number of named buttons that appear in the Navigation pane. Click the Configure Buttons button, which is the last button in the area where the toolbar-like buttons appear. When you click the Configure Buttons button a shortcut menu appears, as shown in Figure 1-4. To display more buttons with names, click Show More Buttons. To display more toolbar-like buttons, click Show Fewer Buttons. When you show more buttons, Dynamics GP moves a toolbar-like button up and displays it as a named button. Similarly, if you show fewer buttons, Dynamics GP removes a named button but displays a toolbar-like button for it.

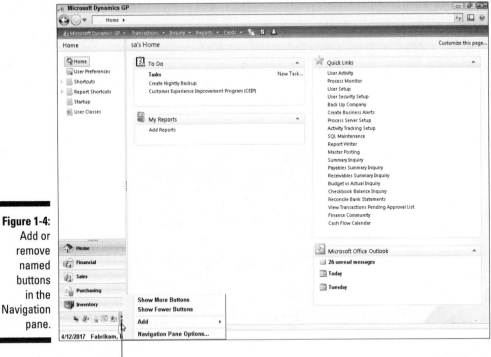

Figure 1-4:
Add or
remove
named
buttons
in the
Navigation
pane.

The Configure Buttons button

In addition to controlling how many named buttons appear, you can control the
order in which the buttons appear. You also can prevent buttons from appearing
for business functions your company doesn't use. For example, if you outsource
your payroll functions, you can prevent the HR & Payroll button from appearing.

To control the buttons that appear in the Navigation pane, right-click any
button in the Navigation pane and then click Navigation Pane Options. The
Navigation Pane Options dialog box appears (see Figure 1-5).

Remove check marks beside any button you do not want to display in the
Navigation pane by clicking the check box. To change the order of the
Navigation pane buttons, select a button in the list by clicking on it and
then clicking the Move Up or Move Down buttons. Click OK when you
finish, or click Reset to return to the defaults.

Lists

The Navigation pane also contains lists for the selected series. Using a list
you can view similar records, select one or more records, and then simultaneously perform actions for all of the selected records. For example, in the
Customers list shown in Figure 1-6, you can select multiple customer records
and then print statements for the selected customers.

Figure 1-5:
Use this dialog box to specify the buttons to display in the Navigation pane and the order in which they should appear.

Filter area

Action pane

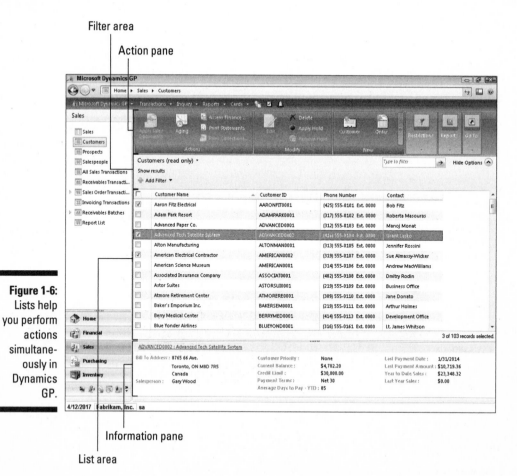

Figure 1-6:
Lists help you perform actions simultaneously in Dynamics GP.

Information pane

List area

You select the action you want to take in the Action pane of the List window. You can add filters in the Filter area. The list elements (in this example, the list elements are the customers) appear in the List area, and you select various list elements with check marks to take actions on them. The details for any list element you highlight — regardless of whether you place a check mark by the list element — appears at the bottom of the List window in the Information pane.

If you have proper security privileges, you can create list views that contain just the information you want to view. See Chapter 15 for details.

Who, when, and where you are

At the very bottom of the Dynamics GP window, the *user date* (usually the current day's date; Dynamics GP uses the date set on your computer) appears in the lower-left corner. Beside it, you see the name of the company in which you are working, and beside the company name you see the name of the user who is currently logged into the company (refer to Figure 1-1).

If you move your mouse pointer over any of these three pieces of information, you'll find that they are buttons. If you click any of these buttons, you can make changes. For example, you can change the user date by clicking the Date button. Or, you can switch companies by clicking the name of the current company; when you do, the Company Login window appears (see Figure 1-7). Select the company you want to open from the drop-down list and click OK.

The user date acts as the default date for transactions or batches you post, and depending on your report options it might be used to filter reports. The system date is merely a handy default, and you can override it when you add, edit, or post transactions.

Figure 1-7:
Use this
dialog box
to log in to
a Dynamics
GP com-
pany.

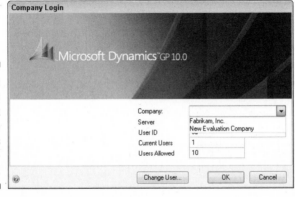

When you click the name of the currently logged in user, a dialog box very similar to the one shown in Figure 1-7 appears. You can select a server on which Dynamics GP is installed and type a User ID and password, but you have no option to select a company.

At Home with the Home Page

You can customize your Home page so that it helps you work efficiently. You can add information, reorganize the information, change the information that appears in each pane, and customize the To Do and Quick Links areas. Let's take a look at the process.

Adding to and reorganizing the Home page

In Figure 1-8, you see a typical Home page. In the Content pane, you see areas for To Do and My Reports on the left, and the Quick Links and Microsoft Office Outlook areas on the right. You can move these areas around and you can change the information that appears in some of these areas. You also can add a Metrics area that displays graphics for information that is important to you.

Let's add the Metrics area to the left side of the Content pane, below the My Reports area. Follow these steps:

1. **Click the Customize This Page link in the upper-right corner of the Home page's Content pane (refer to Figure 1-8).**

   The Customize Home Page dialog box appears (see Figure 1-9).

2. **To add the Metrics area to the Home page, select the Metrics check box.**

3. **To make the Metrics area appear on the left side of the Content pane, click Metrics in the Column 2 list and then click the arrow pointing left towards Column 1.**

   You can reorder the areas in the Content pane using the Move Up and Move Down buttons on either side of the Column 1 and Column 2 lists.

4. **Click OK.**

   Your newly modified Home page appears (see Figure 1-10).

The Customize This Page link

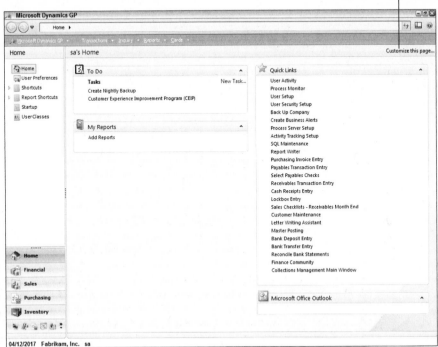

Figure 1-8:
The different areas of
the Content
pane of
a typical
Home page.

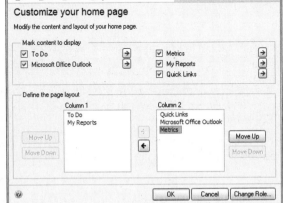

Figure 1-9:
Use this
dialog box
to customize
your Home
page.

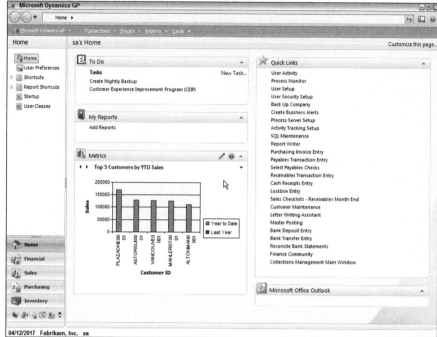

Figure 1-10:
Figure 1-10:
The Home
page after
adding the
Metrics
area.

Notice the left- and right-pointing arrows in the upper-left corner of the Metrics area of Figure 1-10? Click these buttons to display other metric charts you've selected to view. Read the next section for more on how to select metric charts to view.

Changing the details of a Home page

You can change the details that appear in any area on the Home page. For example, you can specify the metric charts you want available in the Metrics area. Move the mouse pointer into any area (I moved into the Metrics area in Figure 1-10) and buttons appear at the right edge of the area's title bar. By clicking the pencil button, you can display the details available for the area and select the ones you want to display. In Figure 1-11, you see the Metrics Details dialog box.

The appearance of a "details" dialog box changes, depending on the one you choose to view.

Suppose that you want to add the Total Purchases for the Past 12 Months chart to the Metrics you can view from your Home page. Follow these steps:

1. **In the Metrics Details dialog box, click the chart you want to add.**

   In this case, Total Purchases for the Past 12 Months.

2. **Click the Insert button.**

   To change the order of the charts you display on your Home page, use the Move Up and Move Down buttons.

3. **Click OK when you finish.**

Figure 1-11: The Metrics Details dialog box, where you select the Metrics charts you want available on your Home page.

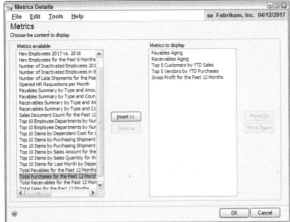

Customizing the Quick Links area

You might want to set up Quick Links to reports, macros, and data entry screens you use regularly. You follow the same basic steps as you did in the previous section for the Metrics area, but you have a few more options you can set. For example, you can add a link to a Dynamics GP window, a Dynamics GP navigation list, a Web page, or an external file or program, as shown in Figure 1-12.

You also can provide your own name for a Quick Link entry. For example, you'll find a Transaction Entry window in the Purchasing series and in the Sales series. If you add both to your Quick Link list, you'll want a way to distinguish them. In the Quick Links Details dialog box, click the entry you want to rename and then click the Modify button. The Properties box for the entry you selected appears (see Figure 1-13). In the Name box, type the name you want Dynamics GP to display in the Quick Links list and then click OK.

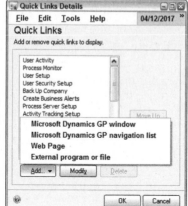

Figure 1-12:
The types of links you can add to the Quick Links list.

Figure 1-13:
In the Name box, type the name you want displayed in the Quick Links list.

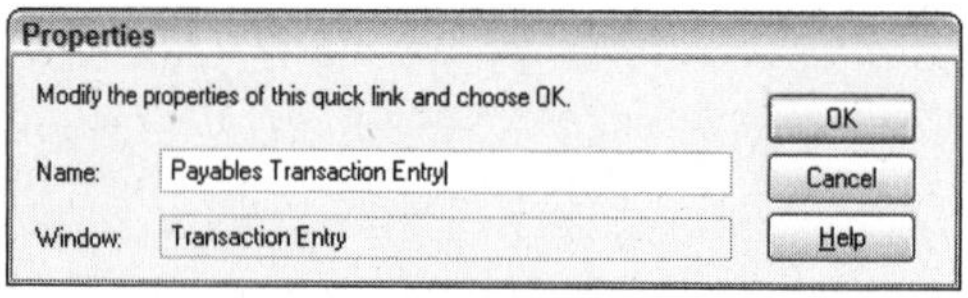

Customizing the To Do area

You can display reminders, tasks, and, if you're using the Workflow module, workflow tasks and notifications in the To Do area of the Home page. You can let Dynamics GP create reminders for you for a variety of conditions. For example, you can have Dynamics GP remind you to post various recurring batches.

Tasks may be (but are not necessarily) tied to some Dynamics GP event or window, and you can create recurring and non-recurring tasks that you can assign to yourself or someone else. For example, you can create a task to remind yourself to print monthly reports or send out customer satisfaction letters.

If you don't display reminders in the To Do area of your Home page, reminders, along with tasks that are due today or are overdue, appear in the Reminders window. The Reminders window appears automatically when you start Dynamics GP, or you can open the Reminders window by choosing Microsoft Dynamics GP⇨Reminders from the Menu bar. You also can open the Task List window by choosing Microsoft Dynamics GP⇨Task List in the Menu bar.

Familiarity Breeds Affection, Efficiency, and Productivity . . . and a Pay Raise

Dynamics GP contains certain common features that you use as you work in the product. If you click a series button in the Navigation pane, you'll see that the Content pane for each series is organized in the same manner, with headings for Cards, Transactions, Inquiry, Reports, Routines, Utilities, and Setup. In the sections that follow, I describe these common functions, along with some other common features available throughout all series in Dynamics GP.

Cards

When you store background information in Dynamics GP, you use a *card*. What do I mean by background information? Well, for example, you need to store names and addresses and other vital information about your customers and your vendors. For your chart of accounts, you need to store an account name, type, and number. You store this information on cards. Then, when you create a customer invoice or a vendor bill, Dynamics GP uses the card information to fill in this pertinent information on the invoice or bill — saving you the time you'd spend looking up and then filling in the information repeatedly. In Figure 1-14, you see a sample Customer card.

Figure 1-14:
A typical
Customer
card.

But you can set up more than just name and address information for customers and vendors; you can set up cards for other types of related information. For example, in addition to Customer cards, you can set up cards that associate a customer with the vendor you typically order from for the customer. You also can set up a card that identifies items typically ordered by a customer, and you can set up a card for each salesperson that stores his or her commission rate, address, sales territory, and sales manager, so that all sales commissions on invoices are applied to the correct salesperson and sales manager.

In Part II, I discuss more details about cards for customers, vendors, inventory items, and the General Ledger. Cards for a particular series appear in the right-side of the Dynamics GP window when you select that series in the Navigation pane. Or, you can find all of the cards that you can create by clicking Cards on the Menu bar and then pointing to the appropriate series within Dynamics GP.

Transactions

Transactions are the entries you make to record accounting events in Dynamics GP. You can enter transactions individually or in batches, and you use different windows within a series to enter individual transactions or transactions in batches. For example, you when you receive a bill from a vendor, you can use the Payables Transaction Entry window, shown in Figure 1-15, to record the individual bill and track it for payment.

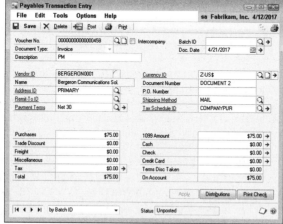

Figure 1-15: Use this window to enter an individual vendor bill.

To create a batch of vendor bills, you use the Payables Batch Entry window, shown in Figure 1-16. You can create *single-use batches,* where you simply enter a series of transactions into a batch, or you can create *recurring batches,* which are particularly useful if you enter the same transactions on some regular basis. For example, if you pay certain bills weekly, you can create a batch that contains all of those weekly bills and avoid entering those bills every week.

TIP

The recurring batch feature is especially useful to record monthly journal entries in the General Ledger. Those recurring batches can act as a checklist of closing entries.

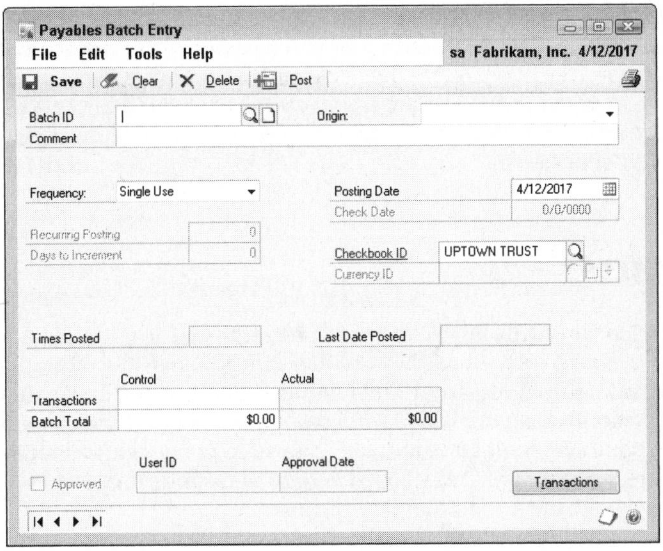

Figure 1-16:
Use this window to record a batch of vendor bills.

[Screenshot of Payables Batch Entry window]

Payables Batch Entry
File   Edit   Tools   Help   sa Fabrikam, Inc. 4/12/2017
Save   Clear   Delete   Post

Batch ID   I   Origin:
Comment

Frequency: Single Use   Posting Date   4/12/2017
                                       Check Date   0/0/0000
Recurring Posting   0
Days to Increment   0   Checkbook ID   UPTOWN TRUST
                                        Currency ID

Times Posted   Last Date Posted

              Control   Actual
Transactions
Batch Total $0.00 $0.00

              User ID   Approval Date
Approved   Transactions

Using batches is a handy way to separate work into different posting periods when you set up transactions to post by batch date. And, using the Control Totals feature of batches, you can ensure that you record all of the transactions because you provide a total number of transactions and the associated dollar amount when you set up the batch. Microsoft Dynamics GP monitors the number of transactions you subsequently record in the batch and the total dollars of each transaction; the batch totals should match the number and dollar amount total of the individual transactions in the batch.

Microsoft Dynamics GP *posts* transactions to update your company files. In Chapter 2, you read about the posting options that you can set; suffice it to say at this point that, in most cases, when you post a transaction you post it throughout the Dynamics GP system so that the transaction updates all appropriate journals and ledgers.

The way you enter transactions controls the timing associated with posting. If you enter transactions individually, you can set up your company so that Dynamics GP posts the transaction immediately, and your records are always up to date. If you enter transactions in batches, you also post them in batches. Saving a batch of transactions doesn't post the batch; you take a separate action to actually post the transactions. In general, you can edit or delete transactions in unposted batches as needed.

To make a change to a posted transaction, you need to enter another transaction that corrects the effects of the original transaction. That way, Audit Trails shows the history of each transaction and ties transactions together appropriately. You can read more about Audit Trails later in this chapter in the section "Keeping Your CPA Happy," and in Chapter 2.

Transactions available for a particular series appear in the Content pane of the Dynamics GP window when you select that series in the Navigation pane. Or, you can find all of the transactions that you can create by clicking Transactions in the Menu bar and then pointing to the appropriate series within Dynamics GP.

Inquiries

You can use inquiries in Dynamics GP to review information in a quick and efficient manner. You can view summary or detailed information and, in many cases, sort the information. For example, suppose that you'd like a quick picture that summarizes your company's outstanding receivables. On the Menu bar, you can click Inquiry⇨Sales⇨Receivables Summary to display the window shown in Figure 1-17. Then, to view your receivables picture company-wide, click the Calculate button.

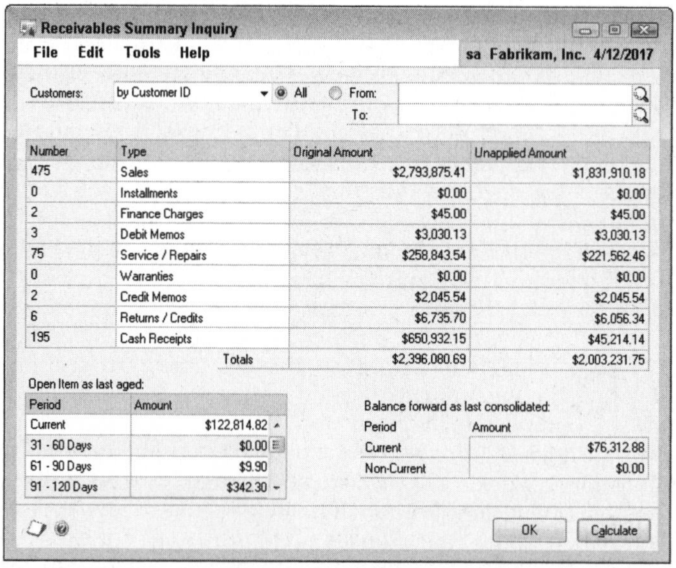

Figure 1-17:
Use an inquiry to quickly determine your company's current receivables picture.

Receivables Summary Inquiry				
File Edit Tools Help			sa Fabrikam, Inc. 4/12/2017	

Customers: by Customer ID ▼ ● All ○ From: ____ To: ____

Number	Type	Original Amount	Unapplied Amount
475	Sales	$2,793,875.41	$1,831,910.18
0	Installments	$0.00	$0.00
2	Finance Charges	$45.00	$45.00
3	Debit Memos	$3,030.13	$3,030.13
75	Service / Repairs	$258,843.54	$221,562.46
0	Warranties	$0.00	$0.00
2	Credit Memos	$2,045.54	$2,045.54
6	Returns / Credits	$6,735.70	$6,056.34
195	Cash Receipts	$650,932.15	$45,214.14
	Totals	$2,396,080.69	$2,003,231.75

Open Item as last aged:

Period	Amount
Current	$122,814.82
31 - 60 Days	$0.00
61 - 90 Days	$9.90
91 - 120 Days	$342.30

Balance forward as last consolidated:

Period	Amount
Current	$76,312.88
Non-Current	$0.00

OK   Calculate

You also can use this window to see the receivables status for a single customer.

Reports

You'll find a plethora of reports available for each series in Dynamics GP — reports that enable you to both verify and analyze company information. To view the available reports, click Reports on the Menu bar. The categories of reports appear; as you highlight a category, the reports in that category appear. See Chapter 12 for details on setting report options and printing reports.

Routines

Routines are tasks you perform on a periodic basis. For example, you can use routines to run monthly customer statements or apply finance charges to customers. To see the routines available in Dynamics GP, click Microsoft Dynamics GP on the Menu bar, and then choose Tools⇨Routines.

Utilities

Utilities help you clean up data by removing it. You also can use utilities to check and repair your data if discrepancies appear. For example, a power outage while you're using Dynamics GP can result in transactions being partially but not completely posted. You can use utilities to track down the problems. Also, some utilities save you time by allowing you to make mass changes to your data. For example, the Price List utility is a wizard that lets you copy price lists from one item to another item or a range of items. In Chapter 13, you find more information on using utilities to find and repair problems.

You can view the available utilities by going to the Menu bar and choosing Microsoft Dynamics GP⇨Tools⇨Utilities.

Setup

If you have sufficient security rights (see Chapter 14), such as the rights of a power user, and you click any series in the Navigation pane, you'll see a section in the Content pane called Setup. In that section, you'll see a list of links you can click to set up the behavior of Dynamics GP. For example, in Figure 1-18, you see the links available in the Setup area for the Sales series.

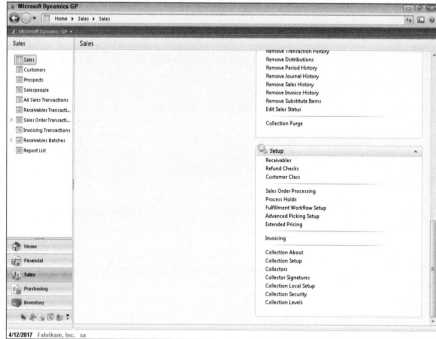

Figure 1-18:
Each series
displays
an area in
the Content
pane where
you can set
up various
aspects of
the series.

If you click each of these links, you can establish the way you want Dynamics GP to behave using the options that appear. In Figure 1-19, you see the Receivables Management Setup window, which displays the options available when you click the Receivables link in the Setup area of the Content pane.

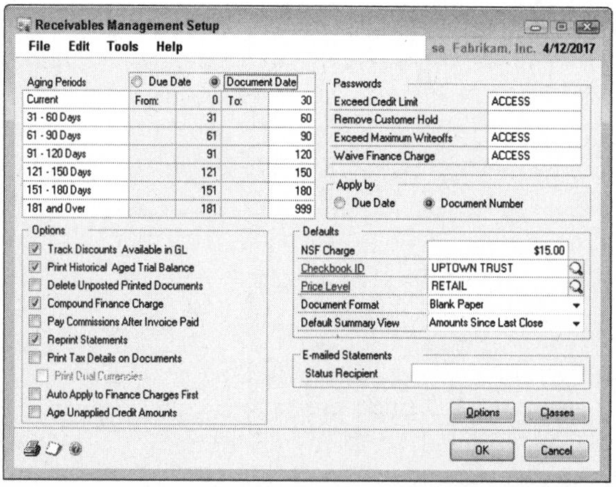

Figure 1-19:
Using Setup
windows,
you can
determine
Dynamics
GP's
behavior in
various situ-
ations.

Yellow sticky notes

In every window in Dynamics GP, next to almost every field you'll see an icon that looks like a piece of paper — and functions like a sticky note (see Figure 1-20).

The Note icon

Figure 1-20:
You can attach notes to fields in a window.

When you click any particular Note icon, a window like the one in Figure 1-21 appears; you can use this window to store free-form information.

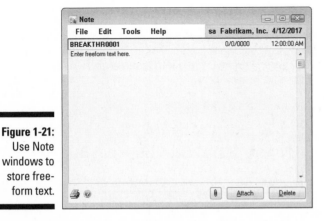

Figure 1-21:
Use Note windows to store free-form text.

Working with SmartLists

SmartLists provide you with fast, easy access to information in your Dynamics GP company. Using a SmartList query, you can quickly and easily obtain information about accounts, customers, employees, vendors, transactions, and items. You can display the results on-screen, print the information, or send it to Word or Excel. For example, suppose that you want to view all of your 1099 vendors. You can use a SmartList like the one shown in Figure 1-22 to display a list of all of your 1099 vendors.

You also can export SmartList information to an Excel or Word file.

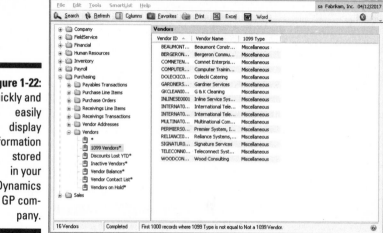

Figure 1-22: Quickly and easily display information stored in your Dynamics GP company.

SmartLists can also be used to facilitate workflow. If you assign users to monitor particular lists, you can create queues of work to be performed. Because all users, including managers, can view the SmartLists, a bottleneck in the workflow becomes immediately apparent.

SmartLists also can replace paper-based workflows that typically sit in a basket on someone's desk. For example, you can create a SmartList for Sales Orders in a certain batch named "URGENT" and then assign the shipping department to monitor this SmartList and ship those orders ahead of others.

To view the SmartList window, click Microsoft Dynamics GP⇨SmartList in the Menu bar. For more information on using SmartLists, see Chapter 12.

Reminders and tasks

Dynamics GP can create reminders for you for a variety of conditions. For example, you can have Dynamics GP remind you about overdue invoices a specified number of days past the due date. Or, you might want to create a reminder to post various recurring batches. You also can create custom reminders — reminders that you define.

The Reminders window, shown in Figure 1-23, appears automatically when you start Dynamics GP if you have reminders or tasks that are due today or overdue. Or, you can open the window by choosing Microsoft Dynamics GP➪Reminders.

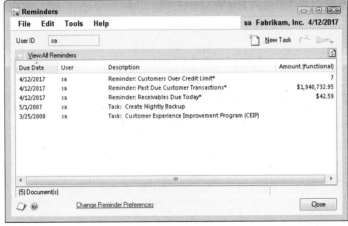

Figure 1-23:
The
Reminders
window.

The Reminders window doesn't appear if you choose to display reminders in the To Do area of your Home page. See Chapter 2 for details on customizing your Home page.

You can create tasks that you assign to yourself or someone else using Dynamics GP. Tasks appear in the Reminders window (refer to Figure 1-23) and in the Task List window, which you can open by choosing Dynamics GP➪Task List. Using either window, you can monitor or set the progress of a task.

See Chapter 15 for details on creating reminders and tasks.

Keeping Your CPA Happy

Dynamics GP contains a feature called Audit Trails that makes accountants very happy. Using the Audit Trails feature, you can trace a transaction from anywhere in your Dynamics GP company back to the location where you originally entered it. Read more about setting up the Audit Trails feature in Chapter 2.

You also can purchase the Audit Trails module, which enables you to monitor each user's activity in Dynamics GP. Using the Audit Trails module, you can view before and after snapshots of records that have changed. You can decide exactly what changes you want to track; for example, you can capture a change made to an inventory item description. The Audit Trails module notes the change, the date and time of the change, and the user who made the change.

Chapter 2

Getting Started with Microsoft Dynamics GP

In This Chapter

▶ Planning the installation of Microsoft Dynamics GP

▶ Creating a company

▶ Setting up company information

Microsoft Dynamics GP is a complex product that can meet the complex needs of a variety of different types of businesses. As such, it is not a product you simply sit down, install, and "away you go." You'll find that your implementation of Dynamics GP will be most successful if you take the time to plan the process. This planning includes both hardware and software planning, as well as planning the way your Dynamics GP company will function. You'll also probably want to plan to stagger implementation, bringing different people in your organization into the process at different points in time. If you put effort into the planning phase, you will experience a smooth and easy implementation.

If you haven't previously set up large-scale business management systems, please consider using an authorized Microsoft Dynamics partner, like me, to help you plan and complete your implementation. Yes, you can hire me if you'd like.

In addition to the planning process, I briefly discuss creating a company, and I show you how to use the Setup Checklist to establish the way your Dynamics GP company will work. The options that you choose while setting up your company depend on the needs of your organization. And, while I'd like to cover all of the possible options, I don't have enough space in this book. So, I'm going to cover areas generally needed by everyone and try to touch on some of the other areas you should consider when setting up your company.

Preparing to Install Microsoft Dynamics GP

Planning and preparation are key to getting Dynamics GP up and running quickly and efficiently. You need to plan the technical side of implementation, which addresses the hardware and software you need, and the practical side of implementation, which addresses subjects like the structure of your chart of accounts, the way you want to post transactions, and the types of roles your users fill along with the privileges in Dynamics GP that you want to assign to those roles.

As you read through the following discussion, be aware that I'm assuming that the technical people in your organization address hardware and software requirements and install Dynamics GP, and the business people handle the functional side of implementation. For a few tasks, such as security, I believe you'll find that people from both groups work together to establish the behavior of Dynamics GP.

Addressing hardware and software needs

Most people use Dynamics GP in a network environment so that multiple users can update company accounting information simultaneously. For this reason, the company data file resides on a server. The Dynamics GP company file is an SQL database that contains tables for the various types of information you store.

Because you use Dynamics GP in a network environment, client machines have different requirements than the server. And, the server has different requirements depending on how you intend to use Dynamics GP. So, let's start with the client machine.

Once you have set up your server and at least one client machine with suitable hardware and software, you can install Dynamics GP on the server and on the client machine and let the business people begin to configure the system while you finish setting up additional client machines. I suggest that you install the sample company, Fabrikam, Inc., so that the business people can test and experiment without repercussions. They also can use Fabrikam, Inc., to establish the users who will have access to your Dynamics GP company and the individual items each user can access within the company. You can copy this information from Fabrikam to your company.

Client computer requirements

To use Dynamics GP, a client machine should

✔ Use Windows Vista Business, Ultimate, or Enterprise (32-bit and 64-bit), or Windows XP Professional with Service Pack 2 (32-bit only).

✔ Contain an Intel Pentium IV 2.4 gigahertz (GHz) or higher processor.

✔ Have 800 MB or more on the system root hard drive.

✔ Have at least 512 MB of RAM; Microsoft recommends 1 GB.

✔ Contain a 100-MB Ethernet Full Duplex or 1-GB Ethernet network card.

✔ Since Dynamics GP integrates with Microsoft Office, the client machine should contain either Microsoft Office 2007, Microsoft Office 2003, or Microsoft Office XP.

✔ In addition, the client machine should contain Microsoft Internet Explorer 7 or 6 with Service Pack 1 and Adobe Reader 8.0, 7.0, or 6.0.

Server requirements

Although the requirements for the server vary depending on the way in which your organization plans to use Dynamics GP, certain elements are common to any Dynamics GP installation. For example, the server should use some edition of Windows 2003 Server for its operating system. In addition, the server will need some edition of SQL Server 2005 or 2000.

Server requirements are not cast in stone; use the suggested requirements below that best describe your organization.

If your organization is planning to use the Business Essentials edition of Dynamics GP to have 20 or fewer users process 1000 or fewer transactions daily, and import very little data, set up a dedicated server using

✔ The latest edition of Windows 2003 Server Standard, Windows 2003 Small Business Server Premium, or Windows 2003 Small Business Server Standard.

✔ The Standard or Workgroup edition of either SQL Server 2005 or SQL Server 2000.

✔ Although you can use MSDE 2000 or SQL Server 2005 Express Edition, I believe you won't be happy with performance.

✔ Either one dual-core processor or two single-core processors.

✔ A minimum of 1 GB of RAM.

✔ A 100-MB Ethernet Full Duplex or 1-GB Ethernet network card.

✔ Disks configured for SQL Server using RAID 1 for operating system and applications and RAID 5 for SQL database log and data files.

If your organization is planning to use the Advanced Management edition of Dynamics GP to have 20–60 users process 1,000–4,000 transactions daily, import data, use Terminal Services, and generate some OLAP cubes, set up a dedicated server using

✔ The latest edition of Windows 2003 Server Enterprise or Standard, X64 or X32.

✔ The Enterprise or Standard edition of either SQL Server 2005 or SQL Server 2000.

✔ Either one dual-core processor or two single-core processors.

✔ 4 GB or more of RAM.

✔ A 100-MB Ethernet Full Duplex or 1-GB Ethernet network card.

✔ Disks configured in the following way:

- RAID 1 for operating system and applications (two disks).

- RAID 1 for SQL database log files (two disks).

- RAID 5 (four disk minimum) or RAID 10 (eight disk minimum) for SQL data files.

- RAID 1 for TempDB (two disks) — optional, but recommended.

- RAID 0 for SQL backups (full disk volume and log) (two disks).

If your organization is planning to use the Advanced Management edition of Dynamics GP to have 60–100 users process more than 4,000 transactions daily, import data regularly, use Terminal Services, and generate OLAP cubes to a different machine, set up a dedicated server using

✔ The latest edition of Windows 2003 Server Enterprise, X64 or X32.

✔ The Enterprise edition of either SQL Server 2005 or SQL Server 2000 or the Standard X64 edition of SQL Server 2005.

✔ Either two dual-core processors or four single-core processors.

✔ 8 GB or more of RAM.

✔ A 1-GB Ethernet network card.

✔ Disks configured in the following way:

- RAID 1 for operating system and applications (two disks).

- RAID 1 for SQL database log files (four disks).

- RAID 10 (eight disk minimum) for SQL data files.

- RAID 1 for TempDB (four disks).

- RAID 0 for SQL backups (full disk volume and log) (two disks).

Planning your company setup

While the technical people get the computers ready, the business people can determine a great deal about how the Dynamics GP company will function. Before you begin using Dynamics GP on a daily basis, you should

✔ Create your chart of accounts.

✔ Import any existing data.

✔ Enter additional customer, vendor, item, and employee records.

✔ Enter sales tax details and schedules.

✔ Enter beginning balances.

✔ Print reports of beginning balances and master records.

✔ Back up your beginning data.

To effectively implement Dynamics GP, organizations usually choose to use an authorized Microsoft Dynamics GP Partner consulting firm that employs Dynamics consultants who typically have passed rigorous Microsoft certification exams. Partnering with a good firm who has experienced implementation specialists available is not only recommended, but is often the only practical way to get your Dynamics GP system up and running. In other words, don't try this at home, kids.

During your initial work with your consultant (before you actually buy Dynamics GP), you might receive a high-level proposal and a software demonstration that addresses the unique needs of your company. But once the project gets underway, the consultants will need to dig much deeper. Together, you and the consultants will conduct design sessions and interviews to ensure that the specific needs of your organization are addressed; the consultants will also try out different approaches in the sample company.

Before your consultants start setting up Dynamics GP, and as a result of the design sessions and interviews, your consultants should provide you with a written project plan that includes estimated hours by task along with a detailed design document that should cover the following topics:

✔ **Executive Summary and Background:** Describes why you are implementing Dynamics GP.

✔ **Expected Benefits (of the implementation):** Identifies what you should expect to gain for your pain and trouble.

✔ **Project Team Members:** Identifies team members and their expected roles.

✔ **Dynamics GP Modules List:** Identifies the modules you will be implementing and the reasons those modules are recommended.

✔ **Module-by-Module Design:** Describes how the module will be configured uniquely for your company.

✔ **Third-Party Products:** Identifies what, if any, third-party products will be implemented, why they are necessary, and how they will be configured.

- **Network Infrastructure:** Describes the workstations, the network, database, and remote connectivity needed for your implementation.

- **Data Conversion:** Identifies the information that will be imported into Dynamics GP from your old system, the level of detail and the number of prior years' worth of this information, and the tool that will be used to import the information.

- **Customizations:** Explains what, if any, customizations need to be made to the off-the-shelf Dynamics GP system to make Dynamics GP meet your company's unique requirements. If customizations are necessary, this section should identify the language or the development tools that will be used to produce the customizations, along with proposed screen shots.

- **Integrations:** Identifies what, if any, ongoing data feeds your organization requires as part of the implementation, along with the timing, direction of data flow, the technique used to start them, and the software language/program used for the integration.

- **Reporting:** Describes the modifications needed to built-in Dynamics GP reports, the reports needed in FRx Financial Report Writer, and custom reports written in Crystal Reports, SQL Reporting Services, or some other report writing tool. These descriptions should identify the selection, sorting, and grouping criteria, along with required fields.

- **Training:** Identifies the training schedule and location, including preparation needed for the training room, as well as the topics covered and the proposed training methods. For example, your consultants may recommend a "train the trainer" approach, enabling trainers in your organization to do the bulk of the training.

- **Testing:** Describes issues such as the preparation of a test environment, including creation of test companies or test database servers, as well as testing scenarios created by the users that cover typical transactions.

- **Go Live Support:** Explains how the consulting firm plans to support your company once Dynamics GP goes into production, including help desk, logging bugs or issues, and requesting change orders.

Too many times, Dynamics GP implementations fail due to a lack of detailed planning. If any of these sections does not appear in sufficient detail, speak up and ask your consultants to address your concerns.

The consulting firm should publish a detailed project plan and design document, and then hold one or more feedback meetings where you can question design decisions and suggest changes prior to the actual setup of the system.

One tool which your consultants may choose to employ is the Dynamics GP Setup Checklist. This checklist helps ensure completeness in the setup by listing all the setup tasks one typically performs during a Dynamics GP implementation. Depending on the size of your organization, a number of people might be involved in completing these tasks. Once the technical people get Dynamics GP installed on your server and one client machine and create a company, you can use the Setup Checklist window, shown in Figure 2-1, to guide you through the process and help you keep tabs on what's done and what's not done. In this chapter, I don't cover everything on the Setup Checklist — there simply isn't room.

The technical people won't stop working; they still need to complete the installation process for Dynamics GP on various client machines, and they, with input from the business people, will also probably be the ones who establish security for your Dynamics GP company. You can read about security in Chapter 14.

In the Setup Checklist window, tasks appear in the order in which you or your consultants should complete them. The Setup Guide, in the form of a Help window, appears alongside the Setup Checklist window so that you can get additional information whenever you need it.

Along the left side of the Setup Checklist window, you see the views you can set while working in the window. You can view all of the tasks assigned to you or just the ones you haven't yet completed. You also can view all tasks, as I have in the figure, or only all incomplete tasks. Finally, you can view all completed tasks. And, you can opt to display optional setup tasks and setup tasks for unregistered modules.

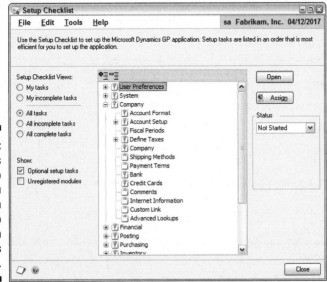

Figure 2-1: Use this window to help you through the setup process in Dynamics GP.

In the center of the Setup Checklist window, you see the list of tasks; click a plus sign beside a Setup Checklist entry to view the setup tasks for that category. In Figure 2-1, I display the tasks in the Company category. If you click the name of the category, the help information appearing in the Setup Guide window changes to describe that category (see Figure 2-2).

On the right side of the Setup Checklist window, you can assign the selected task to another user in your organization by clicking the Assign button. When you assign a task, you set the start date and the due date.

If the task is yours to complete and no plus or minus sign appears beside it in the Setup Checklist, you can click Open to open the window associated with the task and complete it. Or, you can set the task's status to one of the following: Not Started, In Progress, Complete, or Not Used. If a plus sign appears, click the plus sign to view the tasks associated with that category.

The icons beside each task reflect the status of the task.

For example, suppose that you want to set user preferences. You can use the steps that follow to set up any category in Dynamics GP:

1. **In the Menu bar, click Microsoft Dynamics GP⇨Tools⇨Setup⇨Setup Checklist.**

   The Setup Checklist window opens, along with the Setup Guide window.

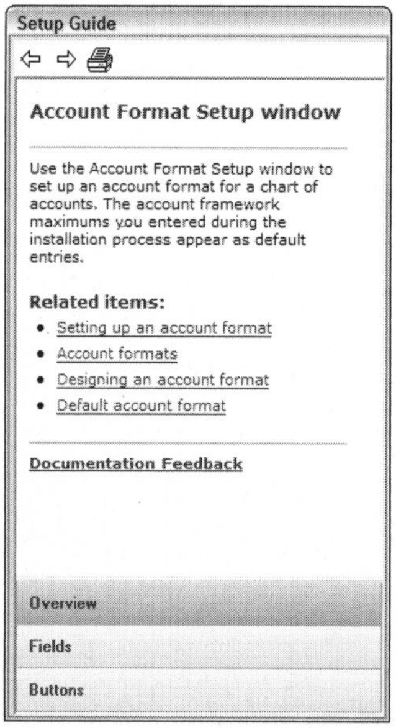

Figure 2-2:
The Setup
Guide that
appears
beside
the Setup
Checklist
window.

> **Setup Guide**
>
> ⇦ ⇨ 🖨
>
> **Account Format Setup window**
>
> Use the Account Format Setup window to set up an account format for a chart of accounts. The account framework maximums you entered during the installation process appear as default entries.
>
> **Related items:**
> - Setting up an account format
> - Account formats
> - Designing an account format
> - Default account format
>
> **Documentation Feedback**
>
> Overview
>
> Fields
>
> Buttons

2. **In the Setup Checklist window that appears (refer to Figure 2-1), click User Preferences.**

   If the Open button doesn't become available when you click a category in Step 2, click the plus sign (+) beside the category to expand the tree. Then, click the specific area you want to set up and the Open button will become available.

3. **Click Open.**

   The User Preferences dialog box appears (see Figure 2-3).

4. **Make sure that the user for which you want to set options appears in the User ID box.**

5. **Select the options you want to set. You can optionally set colors for link fields and required fields by clicking the Display button.**

   Link fields are just what they sound like — fields in windows that link to other windows; when you click a link field, Dynamics GP opens the appropriate window.

6. **Click OK.**

   Dynamics GP displays the Setup Checklist Status dialog box, in which you set the status for the task by choosing either In Progress, Complete, or Not Used. When you click OK, Dynamics GP updates the status for the task.

If, at a later date, you want to make changes to the way Dynamics GP behaves, you can redisplay the Setup Checklist and simply follow these steps again.

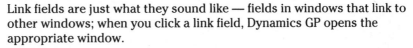

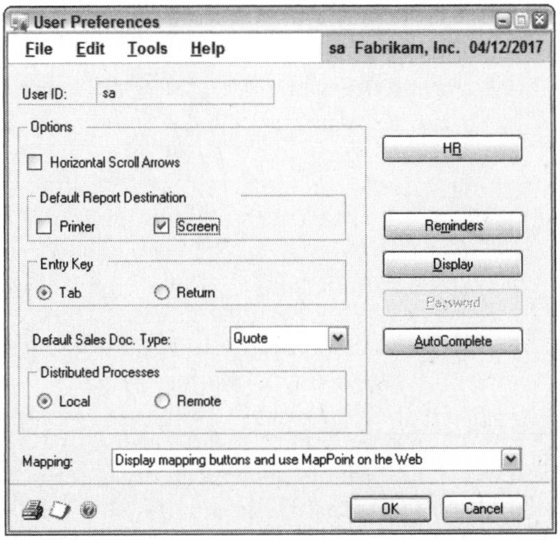

Figure 2-3:
The User Preferences dialog box.

Creating a New Company

I'm going to assume that the technical people create the Dynamics GP company your organization will use, and I'm going to assume that they follow my earlier suggestion and install the sample company, Fabrikam, Inc.

When you create your own company, you can install the default chart of accounts, shipping methods, and payment terms, unless you plan to import that information from your previous accounting system or enter it manually. If you install the default information, you can modify that information to suit your needs. And, you can copy user settings from another company.

Although you can make limited changes to the account format after setting up your chart of accounts, you must clear data from the Account Master Table and then re-enter the chart of accounts — not a tantalizing prospect, so, consider your chart of accounts format, both for present and future use, carefully before you install Dynamics GP and create the chart of accounts.

To create your company, be sure that you are logged on to the computer as the administrator and then run Dynamics GP Utilities, which you can find by choosing Start⇨Programs⇨Microsoft Dynamics⇨GP⇨GP Utilities. When prompted, log in as sa or the system administrator to ensure you have the privileges you need to create the company.

Dynamics GP Utilities acts like a wizard. As you create your company, you supply a company ID and name that Dynamics GP users can change later by choosing Microsoft Dynamics GP⇨Tools⇨Setup⇨Company⇨Company. Using the Dynamics GP Utilities wizard, set the options for which you're prompted — chart of accounts, shipping methods, payment methods, and user settings — and select a location on the server for the company data file. The account framework you select will apply to all Dynamics GP companies you create and you cannot change the framework later, although you can modify the account format to some extent; see "Setting up your chart of accounts" later in this chapter.

After Dynamics GP Utilities finishes creating the SQL tables for your company database, open Dynamics GP and provide access to the new company for users by choosing on the Menu bar Microsoft Dynamics GP⇨Tools⇨Setup⇨System⇨User Access. In the User Access Setup window that appears, select a user, select the check box beside each company to which you want this user to have access, and choose OK to save your changes.

Dynamics GP users open the company by starting Dynamics GP, supplying their user name and password, and then selecting the company. The very first time you open a company, the Select Home Page dialog box appears (see Figure 2-4). Select a role that matches the work that you typically do and click OK. Your Home page role is different from your security role and does not affect the security access you have within Dynamics GP.

Figure 2-4:
Use this
dialog box
to select
a role that
most closely
matches
the job you
perform.

Don't worry about selecting the wrong role; you can change your role later. After all, you're going to want to change your role when you get promoted. To change your role, click the Customize This Page link in the upper-right corner of the Home page. Then, click the Change Role button to redisplay the dialog box shown in Figure 2-4.

Setting up company address information

You can use the Company Setup window to enter addresses for your company. The address you enter using the steps below will appear on all documents. If your business has several locations or different departments and contacts, you can set up multiple addresses and then select the address to print on specified documents.

Follow these steps to set up company address information:

1. **On the Menu bar select Microsoft Dynamics GP➪Tools➪Setup➪ Company➪Company to open the Company Setup window (see Figure 2-5).**

2. **Enter the company's main address.**

3. **To enter addresses for additional locations, departments or contacts, click the Address button.**

   The Company Addresses Setup window appears (see Figure 2-6).

4. **In the Address ID field, enter a short name to identify the location, department, or contact.**

Figure 2-5:
Use this
window to
set up your
company's
address.

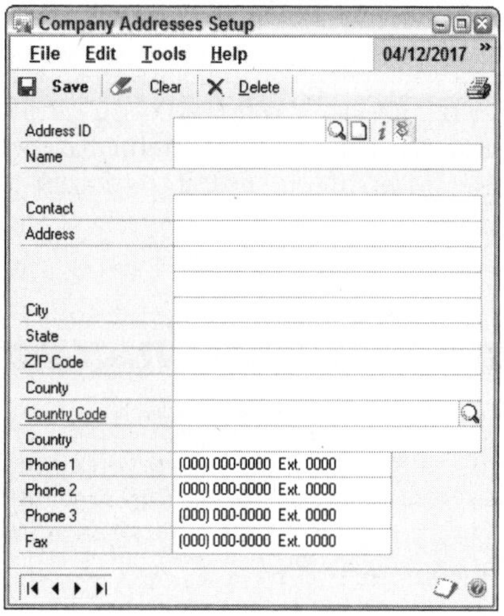

Figure 2-6:
Use this
window
to set up
additional
addresses
for your
company.

5. **Enter the address information.**

6. **Click Save to save the address.**

7. **Repeat Steps 4–6 to create additional addresses. When you finish entering addresses, click Save and then the X in the upper-right corner of the window to close it.**

8. **In the Company Setup window, choose OK to save the addresses you've entered.**

You can print a list of the addresses you set up for the company by first choosing Reports⇨Company⇨Setup. Then, in the Setup Reports window that appears, select Addresses from the Reports drop-down list.

Setting up user-defined fields for your company

You'll find two user-defined fields (User Defined 1 and User Defined 2) in the Company Setup window that you can use to store additional information about your company. You can print this information on a report by adding them to the report's layout using the Report Writer. See Chapter 12 for more information on using the Report Writer.

If your company is located in Europe, you must use the User Defined 1 field to store your country code, which is printed on value-added tax documents.

To set up these user-defined fields, from the Menu bar select Microsoft Dynamics GP⇨Tools⇨Setup⇨Company⇨Company to display the Company Setup window shown previously in Figure 2-5. Type the information you want to appear in either or both of the user-defined fields on the right side of the window, and click OK to save your changes.

Setting up Internet information for your company

You also can store Internet-related information about your company and each address you've established for your company, including an email address, the address of your Internet home page, and an FTP site address.

To set up company Internet information, follow these steps:

1. **From the Menu bar select Microsoft Dynamics GP⇨Tools⇨Setup⇨Company⇨Internet Information to open the Internet Information window shown in Figure 2-7.**

2. **Choose Company from the Select Information For drop-down list.**

3. **In the Address ID field, click the right or left arrows to select an address.**

4. **Enter Internet information in the appropriate fields.**

5. **Click Save.**

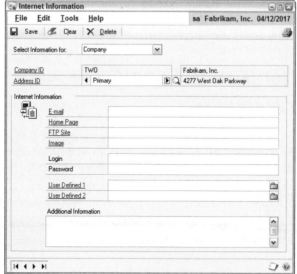

Figure 2-7:
Add
company
Internet
information
using this
window.

Reviewing Company Information

Before you begin daily use of Dynamics GP, you should review and possibly set up additional information listed on the Setup Checklist. This section covers some of the additional information you might want to set up.

Although you can use the Setup Checklist to establish all of these settings, I use the Menu bar to show you how to open these windows.

Setting up company options

Use the Company Setup Options window to enter additional company setup options. For example, you can establish how you want to separate payment distributions in this window. Select Microsoft Dynamics GP⇨Tools⇨Setup⇨ Company⇨Company to display the Company Setup window shown earlier in Figure 2-5. Then, click the Options button to display the Company Setup Options window shown in Figure 2-8 and select the options you want to include. Click OK to save your options and redisplay the Company Setup window.

In the System Setup Guide, on pages 60 and 61, you find a complete explanation of the options available in this dialog box. The System Setup Guide, along with all of the manuals for Dynamics GP, is available as a .pdf file using the Help system in Dynamics GP. Click the Help button in the upper-right corner of the Dynamics GP window and choose Printable Manuals.

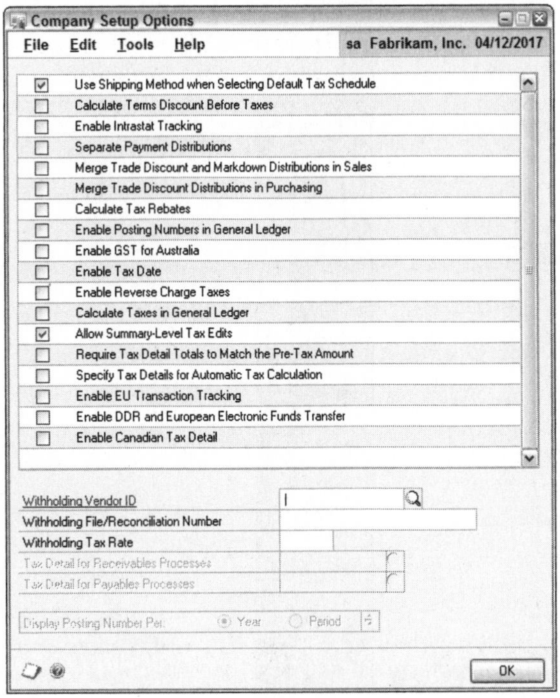

Company Setup Options — sa Fabrikam, Inc. 04/12/2017

File Edit Tools Help

☑	Use Shipping Method when Selecting Default Tax Schedule
☐	Calculate Terms Discount Before Taxes
☐	Enable Intrastat Tracking
☐	Separate Payment Distributions
☐	Merge Trade Discount and Markdown Distributions in Sales
☐	Merge Trade Discount Distributions in Purchasing
☐	Calculate Tax Rebates
☐	Enable Posting Numbers in General Ledger
☐	Enable GST for Australia
☐	Enable Tax Date
☐	Enable Reverse Charge Taxes
☐	Calculate Taxes in General Ledger
☑	Allow Summary-Level Tax Edits
☐	Require Tax Detail Totals to Match the Pre-Tax Amount
☐	Specify Tax Details for Automatic Tax Calculation
☐	Enable EU Transaction Tracking
☐	Enable DDR and European Electronic Funds Transfer
☐	Enable Canadian Tax Detail

Withholding Vendor ID

Withholding File/Reconciliation Number

Withholding Tax Rate

Tax Detail for Receivables Processes

Tax Detail for Payables Processes

Display Posting Number Per: ◉ Year ○ Period

OK

Figure 2-8:
Click the
options you
want to
enable in
your
company.

Setting up your chart of accounts

If you didn't plan to import a chart of accounts, you probably created your company using the default chart of accounts. And, when the first Dynamics GP company was created, you established an account framework and an account format. The account framework identifies the maximum length for account numbers, how many segments an account number contains, and the length of each segment. The account framework you establish provides the maximums for all Dynamics GP companies you create, and Dynamics GP imposes a limit of 66 characters and 10 segments.

Typically, setting up the account framework using 10 segments with a maximum length of six characters for each segment is usually more than enough, even for a very large enterprise. In most cases, a chart of accounts typically has between two and four segments, and length of each segment is usually no more than five characters.

Many companies assign a specific meaning to a particular segment of the account number; for example, the last segment might represent departments within your company. Or, if you use the Inventory Control module, the first segment might represent a site. On financial statements, you can sort by a particular account segment to highlight specific information.

The account format is the structure of each account in a particular company — the length of the account number, the number of segments within each account number, and the length of each segment.

If you created your company using the default chart of accounts, Dynamics GP establishes the following defaults for your account format:

- ✔ Account length of nine characters
- ✔ Three segments
- ✔ Segment 1 is three characters long
- ✔ Segment 2 is four characters long
- ✔ Segment 3 is two characters long

Although you cannot change the account framework, you can make some limited changes to the account format:

- ✔ At any time, you can lengthen one or more segments in the account format, up to the account framework maximum values you set when you installed Dynamics GP.

- ✔ If you haven't set up a chart of accounts yet or if you've entered your chart of accounts but haven't entered transactions, you can shorten one or more segments of the account format.

To shorten the format if you have set up your chart of accounts, you must clear data from the Account Master Table and then re-enter the chart of accounts — not a tantalizing prospect, so, consider your chart of accounts format, both for present and future use, carefully before you create the accounts.

To change the account format, choose Microsoft Dynamics GP➪Tools➪ Setup➪Company➪Account Format to display the Account Format Setup dialog box shown in Figure 2-9.

The account framework maximums appear in the dialog box along with the current settings for each segment; remember, you cannot change the maximum values and, if you have created accounts, you cannot shorten the account length or segment length. Make whatever changes you want and click OK to save them.

Using the Account Segment Setup window, you can provide names for your account segments that describe their purpose.

Figure 2-9:
Use this
window
to make
changes to
the account
format.

Reviewing fiscal periods

When you create a new company, Dynamics GP automatically creates default fiscal periods for you, calculating the beginning date for each period. But, you can change those fiscal periods by changing the period beginning date. At a minimum, you should verify that the default fiscal periods work for you. And, to start a new year, you need to create fiscal periods for that year. In this section, I present an overview of fiscal periods; to create fiscal periods for a new year, see Chapter 11.

Dynamics GP enables you to define up to 367 periods per year. Dynamics GP also places no limitation on the number of simultaneously open future or historical years you keep. And, each year can have a different number of periods. But, you can post transactions to all open years and one historical year.

You can change the starting and ending dates for open or historical years, but you cannot use dates that fall within the most recent historical year.

To review fiscal periods, choose Microsoft Dynamics GP⇨Tools⇨Setup⇨ Company⇨Fiscal Periods to display the Fiscal Periods Setup window (see Figure 2-10).

From the Year list box, select the year you want to review, and Dynamics GP displays the fiscal periods for the selected year.

You use this dialog box to change fiscal period dates and to create new open and historical fiscal years. You can read about this process in Chapter 11.

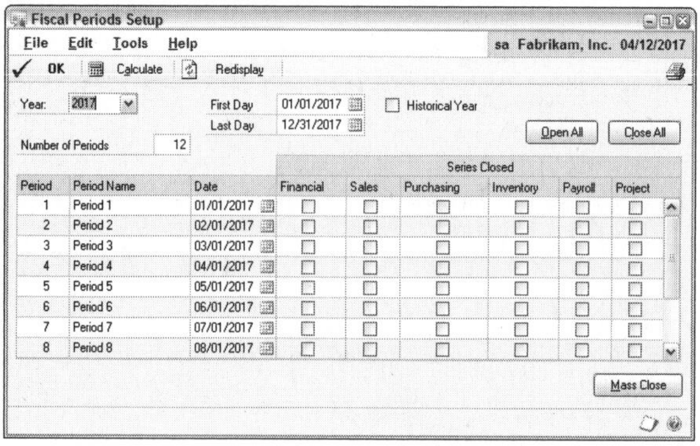

Figure 2-10:
Use this
window
to review
fiscal period
setup.

Establishing opening balances

Typically, most people don't start using Dynamics GP on the first day they start doing business, so, that means that you have some accounting information that you need to enter into Dynamics GP. For example, you might have unpaid vendor bills, unpaid customer invoices, or outstanding loans. You can import this information if you have it in electronic form, or you can enter it manually in Dynamics GP. In this section, I describe the general process to set up opening balance information.

The Integration Manager module is most often used to import information into Dynamics GP.

To represent opening balances for your Balance Sheet and Income Statement accounts, you can record journal entries. Essentially, you create journal entries that represent the balances for each year of information you want stored in Dynamics GP. For example, you might want to record five years worth of historical balances so that you can produce comparative reports that go back five years. In this case, you would create one journal entry for each historical year, enter and post the oldest year's entry first, and then close that year. Next, enter and post the second-oldest year's entry and then close that year. Continue entering journal entries in this fashion, one per year. You can record detailed journal entries from your old system or summarized monthly net changes. If you do opt to record detailed journal entries, I suggest that you store the unique journal entry number from your old system in the reference for the new Dynamics GP journal entry. That way, you will be able to cross reference each Dynamics GP journal entry back to the source in your old system.

If you import summarized net changes, then you won't be able to drill down to review details in Dynamics GP. However, if you plan only to use the information to prepare summarized comparative financial reports, you probably will not need to drill down for details.

To record information such as unpaid vendor bills or customer invoices, enter those transactions in the appropriate module, again by importing or recording the transactions manually. Make sure that you don't post these opening balance transactions through to the General Ledger — if you do, you'll overstate your Accounts Receivable and Accounts Payables balances in the General Ledger. For more information about posting, see the next section.

Setting up shipping methods and payment terms

Shipping methods describe the ways in which goods are transported between you, your vendors, and your customers. *Payment terms* describe the agreement you make with your customers and vendors regarding payment for goods or services.

When you create a new Dynamics GP company, you have the opportunity to set up default shipping methods and payment terms. You can review these terms and create additional ones if you need them.

To review or add shipping methods, choose Microsoft Dynamics GP⇨Tools⇨Setup⇨Company⇨Shipping Methods to display the Shipping Methods Setup window shown in Figure 2-11.

Figure 2-11: Use this window to review or create shipping methods.

To review existing shipping methods, use the arrows in the lower-left corner of the window. Or, print a report of existing shipping methods by choosing File⇨Print in the Shipping Methods Setup window.

To add a shipping method, enter a shipping method and description, and select Pickup if you or the purchaser picks up the goods, or select Delivery if the goods need to be delivered. Then, enter the carrier's name, account number, contact person, and phone number. Click Save to save your shipping method.

To review or add payment terms, choose Microsoft Dynamics GP⇨Tools⇨ Setup⇨Company⇨Payment Terms to display the Payment Terms Setup window shown in Figure 2-12.

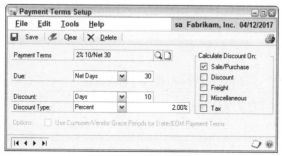

Figure 2-12:
Use this window to review or create payment terms.

You can review existing payment terms using the arrows in the lower-left corner of the window. Or, print a report of existing payment terms by choosing File⇨Print in the Payment Terms Setup window.

Create payment terms by typing the name of the payment term in the Payment Terms box. Then, use the Due list box to describe when the full amount of the payment is due.

- ✔ Select Net Days if the payment is due within a specified number of days after the invoice date; then, enter the number of days.

- ✔ Select Date if the payment is due by a particular date, and then enter the number representing the day of the month on which the payment is due. For example, if the payment is due on the 15th of the month, enter **15**.

- ✔ Select EOM if the payment is due in full by the end of the month in which the invoice was issued.

- ✔ Select Next Month if the payment is due in full by a particular date in the month following the invoice date. Then, enter the number representing the day of the month on which the payment is due. For example, if payment is due on the 10th of the month following the invoice date, enter **10**.

If you offer or receive a discount for paying earlier than the due date, use the Discount list to identify the timeframe associated with the discount:

- ✔ Select Days to describe a discount applied for payments made within a specified number of days after the invoice date. Then, enter the number of days.

- ✔ Select Date to describe a discount applied for payments made by a specified date of the month following the invoice date. Then, enter the number representing the date of the month.

✔ Select EOM to describe a discount applied for payments made by the end of the month that appears on the invoice.

Use the Discount Type field to specify whether the offer is a percentage or currency amount discount. Then, enter either the percentage or currency amount.

Finally, you can use the check boxes in the Calculate Discount On section to describe the amounts to which the discount applies.

Dynamics GP supports using a grace period that works in conjunction with payment and discount terms for both customers and vendors. You establish grace periods for customers or vendors on their respective cards, using the Customer Maintenance or Vendor Maintenance windows.

You can edit payment terms at any time, and any changes you make affect only new transactions.

Setting your posting options

You can simplify data entry if you identify posting accounts, which is the process of *matching* — also called *mapping* — the accounts in your chart of accounts to the accounts Dynamics GP uses when posting transactions. For example, you identify the account in your chart of accounts that you want Dynamics GP to use whenever a transaction affects cash. If you make these assignments, the assigned posting accounts appear by default in the various transaction entry windows, taking the guesswork out of the transaction entry process for end users.

You can identify posting accounts in three main areas: globally, on cards, and on classes. To identify posting accounts that globally affect your entire company, you use the steps that follow. For example, if all of your vendor transactions should post to one communal Accounts Payable account, you should use the steps following to identify the posting account for the communal Accounts Payable account.

However, if you want to post some vendor transactions to one accounts payable account and other vendor transactions to another accounts payable account, you can identify the proper posting account on each vendor's card. Dynamics GP will look at the vendor card and, if no posting account appears on the card, Dynamics GP will then use the global posting account.

Suppose, though, that you want to post some inventory items to an inventory account for large, expensive items, and other inventory items to another inventory account for smaller items. Dynamics GP uses *classes* as a way to enable you to organize information — customers, vendors, employees, and items — using some common characteristic. In my example, you can assign your inventory items to an appropriate class and select a posting account for the class. When you assign a posting account at the class level, Dynamics GP gives you the option to simultaneously assign the posting account to all cards included in the class. You can read more about setting up classes and assigning posting accounts to them in Chapters 3, 5, and 10.

When posting a transaction, Dynamics GP looks at the card first for a posting account and, if you didn't assign a posting account to the card — either manually or by using a class to assign a posting account to the card — Dynamics GP looks for the posting account you set for the company. During transaction posting, Dynamics GP does *not* look at posting accounts assigned to classes.

You can assign a posting account to a class as a means to create a default posting account for newly created cards or to mass-update posting account changes to cards assigned to a particular class.

To identify posting accounts, follow these steps:

1. **Select Microsoft Dynamics GP⇨Tools⇨Setup⇨Posting⇨Posting Accounts to display the Posting Accounts Setup window, shown in Figure 2-13.**

2. **Click in the Accounts column on the row of the posting account you want to assign.**

3. **Click the Lookup button in the Accounts column title.**

   Dynamics GP displays the Accounts window, in which you click an account and then click the Select button.

4. **You can repeat Steps 2 to 3 for each posting account listed in the Posting Accounts Setup window to establish default accounts.**

5. **Click OK.**

The Lookup button

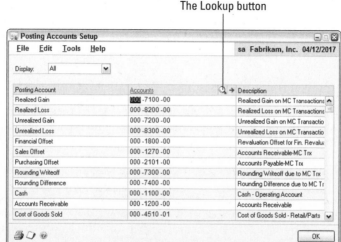

Figure 2-13: Use this window to assign posting accounts.

You also can specify posting options that control how Dynamics GP posts transactions. For example, you can control whether transactions from the Sales series automatically update the General Ledger, or whether they automatically update the Sales series but create a batch of journal entries that you can review before posting them to the General Ledger. You also can specify whether Dynamics GP should create one journal entry per transaction posted or per batch posted.

You can set different posting options for each Dynamics GP transaction window.

To set posting options, follow these steps:

1. **Select Microsoft Dynamics GP⇨Tools⇨Setup⇨Posting⇨Posting to display the Posting Setup dialog box shown in Figure 2-14.**

2. **Select a series from the Series drop-down list.**

3. **From the Origin drop-down list, select the transaction type for which you want to set posting options.**

   If you want to treat all transactions generated through the series in the same way, select All.

4. **Select the options you want to assign; I describe the options in Table 2-1 at the end of these steps.**

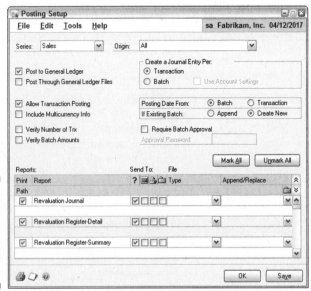

Figure 2-14: Use this window to establish posting options.

5. At the bottom of the dialog box, specify the way you want to print posting reports.

You can print reports to your screen, a printer, or one of five file formats: tab-delimited, comma-delimited, text, HTML, or Adobe PDF if you have Adobe Acrobat Writer installed on your computer. If you opt to print reports to a file, you can specify what you want Dynamics GP to do if the file already exists: append the new report to the existing report file or replace the existing report file.

6. Click OK to save your settings.

Table 2-1	Posting Options
Option	*Description*
Post to General Ledger	Check this box to create a batch of journal entries from subsidiary series transactions that you can review before you post them in the General Ledger and update your accounts.
Post Through General Ledger Files	Check this box to automatically update the General Ledger accounts with the effects of transactions from the subsidiary series. **Tip:** If you leave both the Post to General Ledger and Post Through General Ledger Files unchecked, transactions don't post in the General Ledger. You might want to set up posting this way while you enter beginning balance information in each subsidiary series.
Allow Transaction Posting	Uncheck this box to require that Dynamics GP post all transactions in a batch; check the box to be able to post transactions individually.
Include Multicurrency Info	Check this box if your organization uses Multicurrency Management to include multicurrency information in posting journals. Multicurrency information will not appear if you reprint posting journals.
Verify Number of Trx	Check this box to have Dynamics GP confirm that the number of transactions in the batch matches the number you specified when you created the batch.
Verify Batch Amounts	Check this box to have Dynamics GP confirm that the dollar amount of transactions in the batch matches the number you specified when you created the batch.

Option	Description
Create a Journal Entry Per	Select Transaction to create separate journal entries for each transaction, creating more detailed information. Select Batch and leave Use Account Settings unchecked to create one summary journal entry for an entire batch; this combination is the fastest posting method. Select Batch and check Use Account Settings to produce a mixture of detail and summary information by posting according to the specifications of each account. **Tip:** You can specify the level of posting for each account in the chart of accounts; see Chapter 8 for details. **Remember:** If you choose to summarize data during posting, the posting process may occur somewhat faster and take up less disk space than if you post in detail, but you also won't find the detailed information in the General Ledger. For that reason, many organizations choose to post everything in detail.
Posting Date From	Available only if you select Transaction in the Create a Journal Entry Per field, select Batch to assign the batch date as the posting date to all transactions in the batch, or select Transaction to assign the Transaction date as the posting date.
If Existing Batch	If you post a second batch from the same series for the same type of documents before approving an existing batch in the General Ledger, select Append to add transactions in the second batch to the first batch. Otherwise, select Create New to create a new batch.
Require Batch Approval	Check this box to post only those batches that have been approved. If you check this option, you must also supply an approval password.

Handling sales taxes

Sales tax is a fact of life. As a customer, you pay it. As a vendor, you collect it, usually for a multitude of taxing authorities — the state, the city, perhaps the county, and the list goes on. And, the rules and amounts associated with paying and collecting sales tax vary from jurisdiction to jurisdiction. In some cases, you must pay or charge different sales tax rates for a single jurisdiction, based on what you buy from the vendor or sell to the customer. So, sales taxes can be complicated.

In this section, I'm providing a basic overview of taxes, and I won't get into details regarding special tax situations outside the United States. For example, if your business operates in Australia, where you charge withholding tax, see Chapter 19 of the System Setup Guide. You can view the System Setup Guide if you click the Help button in the Dynamics GP window and then choose Printable Manuals.

To simplify the whole sales tax concept in Dynamics GP, you create two tax records. First, you create *tax detail records,* which describe each sales tax you need to pay or charge, along with its taxation rate and the taxing authority to whom you remit collected taxes. Then, after setting up each individual tax detail record, you set up *tax schedules,* which store combinations of tax detail records, and you assign tax schedules to customer, vendor, and, if appropriate, inventory cards. That way, when you create a sales transaction for a customer or a purchase transaction for a vendor, Dynamics GP automatically applies the correct sales taxes to the transaction.

Suppose, for example, that you sell something to a customer in Tampa, Florida. You need to charge Florida state tax, tax for Hillsborough County — the county containing Tampa — and the city of Tampa. To help avoid errors, Dynamics GP doesn't let you add three tax details to the customer's card. Instead, you create a tax schedule that consists of the tax detail records for Florida state tax, Hillsborough County tax, and City of Tampa tax. Then, you assign the tax schedule to the cards of customers subject to these three taxes.

Dynamics GP doesn't require that you assign tax schedules to customer, vendor, and, if appropriate, inventory cards, but doing so is a good idea. If you do, you'll then deal with sales tax in a consistent way and avoid mistakenly assigning the wrong tax schedule to a transaction.

The tax detail and schedule records I discuss in this section don't apply to freight and miscellaneous charges.

Working with tax details

When deciding what tax details to create, remember these rules of thumb:

- ✔ If you plan to sell goods or services in a jurisdiction, set up a Sales tax detail record.

- ✔ If you plan to buy goods or services in a jurisdiction, set up a Purchases tax detail record.

- ✔ Set up separate tax details for goods and services taxed at different rates in the same jurisdiction.

To set up a tax detail record, follow these steps:

1. On the Menu bar, select **Microsoft Dynamics GP**⇨**Tools**⇨**Setup**⇨ **Company**⇨**Tax Details** to display the Tax Detail Maintenance window shown in Figure 2-15.

2. Enter an ID in the Tax Detail ID field and a description for the tax detail in the Detail field.

   On reports and in windows, Dynamics GP sorts the details in alphanumeric order, so you may want to take that into consideration when providing the Tax Detail ID.

3. From the Type list, select either Sales or Purchases.

4. In the History field, select Calendar Year, Fiscal Year, or both.

   - *Calendar Year:* Tracks tax detail history by month, and this information is often required by taxing authorities.

   - *Fiscal Year:* Tracks tax detail history for each fiscal period you defined, and this information helps you print reports that accurately reflect fiscal period activity.

5. If appropriate, enter your number in the Tax ID Number field.

6. In the Account field, select the appropriate account to track taxes paid or received, such as Sales Tax Payable for Sales tax detail records and Sales Tax Expense for Purchase tax detail records.

7. From the Based On list, select a tax base to determine how Dynamics GP calculates taxes for this tax detail.

8. In the Percentage or Amount field — the field name depends on the choice you made in the Based On list in the previous step — enter the rate or amount for the tax detail.

9. From the Round list, select a method to describe the way you want Dynamics GP to round the tax amount.

Figure 2-15: Use this window to define a tax detail record.

10. **If appropriate, use the Based On Detail field to select the tax detail that serves as the foundation for the tax you are creating.**

11. **If appropriate, use the Taxable Amount Min and Max fields to enter the minimum and maximum taxable amount for this detail.**

If there is no maximum taxable amount, don't enter anything other than 0 in the maximum taxable amount field; otherwise, you risk increasing processing time when Dynamics GP calculates taxable amounts.

If you entered a minimum or maximum taxable amount, use the Include list to specify whether to calculate the tax on the full amount of the transaction or the amount within the minimum-maximum range. Also, use the Qualifiers list to specify what Dynamics GP uses when comparing the taxable minimum and maximum amounts when deciding whether to calculate the tax; the available choices depend on the selection you make in the Based On field.

12. **Select the Taxable Tax box if other taxes will be calculated on this tax.**

13. **To identify taxes on invoices, check the Print on Documents box and, in the field beside Print on Documents, enter a one-character code to identify the tax.**

The character will appear on your invoices next to each of the items taxed.

14. **Click the Address button to enter address information for the taxing authority.**

Dynamics GP displays the address for the tax detail on period-end reports for the taxing authority.

15. **Choose Save to save the tax detail.**

Creating tax schedules

When creating tax schedules, use these rules of thumb:

✔ For each jurisdiction where you plan to do business, set up a Purchases tax schedule that includes all Purchases tax details that apply to the jurisdiction and a Sales tax schedule that includes all Sales tax details that apply to the jurisdiction.

You assign Purchases tax schedules to vendor cards and Sales tax schedules to customer cards. You also can assign a default Purchases tax schedule and Sales tax schedule in the Payables Management Setup Options window and the Receivables Management Setup Options window, respectively.

✔ For each category of inventoried items that you buy or sell that is taxed at different rates in different jurisdictions, set up a single tax schedule that contains applicable tax details for all jurisdictions. Be sure to include both sales and purchases details in this tax schedule. You assign item tax schedules to item records.

✔ Set up one tax schedule for non-inventoried items, one for freight, and one for miscellaneous charges. Each tax schedule should include the tax detail records that most commonly apply. You assign each of these tax schedules to transactions, as appropriate. You assign each of these tax schedules in the Setup Options window of each appropriate module.

To create a tax schedule, follow these steps:

1. **On the Menu bar, select Microsoft Dynamics GP➪Tools➪Setup➪ Company➪Tax Schedules to open the Tax Schedule Maintenance window shown in Figure 2-16.**

2. **Use the Tax Schedule ID and Description boxes to provide information to identify the tax schedule.**

3. **In the Available Tax Detail IDs list, select the tax detail you want to add to the tax schedule.**

4. **Click the Insert button.**

   Dynamics GP adds the tax detail record to the Selected Tax Detail IDs list.

5. **Repeat Steps 3 through 4 for each tax detail record you want to include in the tax schedule.**

6. **Choose Save to save the schedule.**

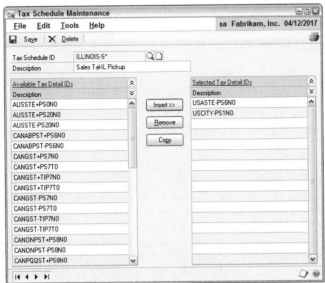

Figure 2-16:
Use this
window to
create tax
schedules.

To save time, you can copy existing tax schedules to create new ones. In the Tax Schedule Maintenance window, enter the Tax Schedule ID and Description for the new tax schedule. Then, click the Copy button. The Tax Schedule Copy dialog box appears, in which you select the ID of the tax schedule you want to copy and click OK. Dynamics GP adds the Tax Detail IDs stored in the selected tax schedule to the Selected Tax Detail IDs list of the schedule you are creating. Click Save to save the new tax schedule.

Setting company default tax schedules

After you create your tax schedules, set up default schedules for your company. Dynamics GP uses these default tax schedules if you have not assigned a tax schedule to a customer, vendor, or item.

Select Microsoft Dynamics GP➪Tools➪Setup➪Company➪Company. In the Company Setup dialog box, shown in Figure 2-17, use the Lookup buttons beside the Sales Tax Schedule field and the Purchases Tax Schedule field to select and assign default tax schedules to your company.

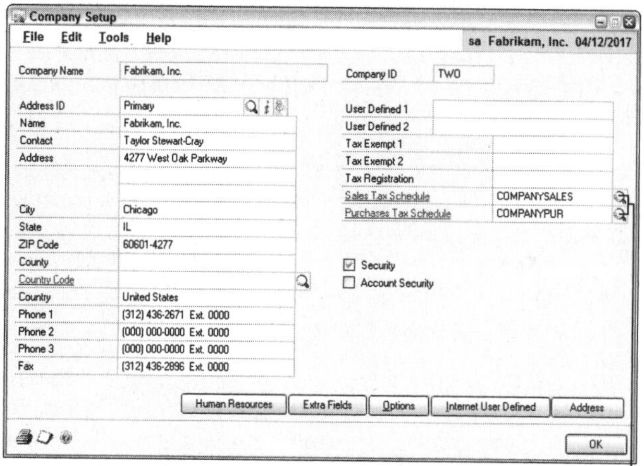

Figure 2-17:
Assign default tax schedules to your Microsoft Dynamics GP company.

Use these Lookup buttons.

Keeping tabs via the audit trail

An *audit trail* is a collection of documents that enable you to trace an accounting event back to the document that provided the basis for the accounting event. In Dynamics GP, the audit trail is a collection of records that allows you to trace a transaction from anywhere in your Dynamics GP company back to the location where you originally entered it. And, because Dynamics GP assigns both source document codes and audit trail codes to each transaction you enter and post, you should find it easy to track a transaction through your Dynamics GP company and also locate the original source document you used when you created the Dynamics GP transaction.

Don't confuse the optional Audit Trails module with the mandatory audit trail codes that Dynamics GP assigns automatically to each transaction. The Audit Trails module provides a history of users' changes to company data. For example, if a user changed the description of an inventory item, the Audit Trail module would capture the date and time of the change and the name of the user, and would store the before and after description.

Each time you post transactions, whether individually or in batches, Dynamics GP creates and prints a posting journal that contains a record of all of the transactions you posted. Source document codes and audit trail codes appear on all posting journals, and you can use the posting journals to help you track transactions based on their source document and audit trail codes.

Source document codes are general in nature and don't identify the journal in which you'll find a particular transaction, but they help you identify the type of transaction. When you set up a Dynamics GP company, the system automatically creates a number of commonly used source document codes, and you can set up additional codes using the Source Document Setup window. To display this window, select Microsoft Dynamics GP⇨Tools⇨Setup⇨Posting⇨Source Document. You can print a list of the existing codes from this window by choosing File⇨Print. Figure 2-18 shows a sample Source Document report.

You can assign source document codes to the various types of transactions using the Audit Trail Code Setup window. By making these assignments, Dynamics GP automatically assigns the same source document code to all transactions that originate from a particular window. To display the Audit Trail Code Setup window, shown in Figure 2-19, select Microsoft Dynamics GP⇨Tools⇨Setup⇨Posting⇨Audit Trail Codes.

You cannot change the audit trail codes Dynamics GP sets up when you create your company, and you cannot create new audit trail codes. But, from this window, you can change the number that Dynamics GP will assign the next time you post a particular transaction type, and you also can change the default source document code assigned to any audit trail code.

You can print a list of the audit trail codes from the Audit Trail Codes Setup window. Choose File⇨Print.

Each audit trail code consists of two parts: the prefix and the journal number. The prefix identifies the type of posting journal in which the transaction appears. For example, if you create an adjusting entry when you reconcile your bank statement, Dynamics GP posts that entry to the Cash Management Adjustments journal, which has a prefix of CMADJ. The second part of the audit trail code, the journal number, identifies the specific journal in which you'll find a particular transaction.

If you entered a transaction in a subsidiary module like the Purchasing module and posted it through the General Ledger, Dynamics GP assigns two audit trail codes to it — one for the originating module and one for the General Ledger.

Part II
Daily Entry Tasks

The 5th Wave   By Rich Tennant

"Ms. Lamont, how long have you been sending out bills listing charges for 'Freight,' 'Handling,' and 'Sales Tax,' as 'This,' 'That,' and 'The Other Thing?'"

In this part . . .

Read this part to find out how to perform the tasks most users of Microsoft Dynamics GP perform on a daily basis. Work with vendors, customers, reconciling the bank, and controlling inventory.

Chapter 3

Paying Bills

. . . .

In this chapter

▶ Setting up vendor cards

▶ Entering vouchers

▶ Writing checks

▶ Voiding transactions

. . . .

*L*et's face it — nobody likes paying bills. Yep, that old adage applies: "It's a dirty job, but somebody's gotta do it." By using the Purchasing series of Microsoft Dynamics GP, however, you can make quick work of the task while effectively managing your outstanding payables.

In this chapter, I show you how to use the Payables Management module. In Chapter 4, I cover the rest of the Purchasing series — the Purchase Order module.

Setting Up Default Information for Payables Management

To use the Payables Management module effectively, there's some setup work you should complete. For example, you should establish the aging periods you want to use; *aging periods* help you determine how long you've owed money to vendors.

Before you start setting up the Payables Management module, you should make sure that you complete the setup process for your company, as described in Chapter 2, and the General Ledger module, as described in Chapter 8. Also, complete the setup of the Multicurrency Management module if you're using it.

You use the Payables Management Setup dialog box shown in Figure 3-1 to set the majority of the options associated with the Payables Management module. You can open this dialog box by clicking Purchasing in the

Navigation pane of your Dynamics GP Home page and, in the Content pane, click Setup and then click Payables. Or, you can use the Menu bar; select Microsoft Dynamics GP⇨Tools⇨Setup⇨Purchasing⇨Payables.

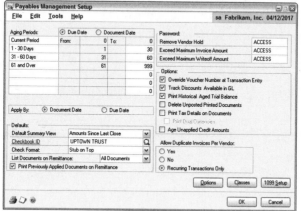

Figure 3-1:
The
Payables
Manage-
ment Setup
dialog box.

With the Payables Management Setup dialog box open, follow these steps:

1. **In the Aging Periods section, describe the aging periods you want to use.**

   Dynamics GP automatically establishes four aging periods; the buckets you see depend on whether you select Due Date or Document Date. In Figure 3-1, you see the aging periods for Due Date: the Current period, 1–30 Days, 31–60 Days, and 61 and Over. You can set up as many as seven periods of any length you choose; type a description in the first column and press Tab. With the insertion point in the last column of the Aging Periods table, type the number representing the last day of the aging period. Dynamics GP automatically fills in or adjusts the first day of the following aging period.

2. **In the Apply By section, choose to automatically apply payments to outstanding vouchers — Dynamics GP's term for vendor bills — by Document Date or by Due Date.**

   Dynamics GP tends to use the terms *invoice* and *voucher* interchangeably when referring to a bill you receive from a vendor. To keep things simple, I refer to these documents as vouchers unless an on-screen option specifically uses the term *invoice*.

   If you apply by Due Date, Dynamics GP applies payments and credits first to vouchers with the earliest due date. If you apply by Document Date, Dynamics GP applies payments and credits first to vouchers with the earliest document date.

3. **In the Default Summary View list box, select the default view you want to appear in the Vendor Yearly Summary and Vendor Yearly Summary Inquiry windows. Select**

   - *Amounts Since Last Close* to have Dynamics GP display the selected vendor's summary information since the last year-end close

   - *Fiscal Year* to have Dynamics GP display the selected vendor's summary information for the fiscal year you specify

   - *Calendar Year* to have Dynamics GP display the selected vendor's summary information for the calendar year you specify

4. **Enter the Checkbook ID from which you pay most vendors.**

   Dynamics GP displays this checkbook as the default when you create batches using the Payables Batch Entry window, but you can change the checkbook for an individual batch as needed.

   You can create a checkbook from the window that appears when you click the Checkbook ID Lookup list button or by choosing Cards⇨ Financial⇨Checkbook.

5. **From the Check Format list box, select the format that best describes the check stock you use when printing checks.**

   The choice you make here appears as the default in the Print Payables Checks and Print Payables Transaction Check windows; you read more about these windows later in this chapter.

6. **From the List Documents on Remittance list box, select the default information you want Dynamics GP to print on the remittance and on the check stub. You also can check the Print Previously Applied Documents on Remittance box.**

   A *remittance* prints on blank paper and contains the same information that appears on the check stub.

7. **In the Password section, you can assign passwords to control which Dynamics GP users have the ability to perform sensitive tasks, like removing a vendor from a Hold status.**

8. **In the Options section, you can do any of the following:**

   - Select the *Override Voucher Number at Transaction Entry* box to allow users to enter voucher numbers other than the one suggested by Dynamics GP.

   - Select the *Track Discounts Available in GL* box to post available payment terms discount amounts to a separate general ledger account.

   - Select the *Print Historical Aged Trial Balance* box to ensure that Dynamics GP keeps enough transaction history to enable you to print the Historical Aged Trial Balance report.

> • Select the *Delete Unposted Print Documents* box to permit users to delete an unposted but printed document.
>
> Allowing users to delete printed but unposted documents is generally not a good idea.
>
> • Select the *Print Tax Details on Documents* box to include tax information on all documents printed from the Payables Transaction Entry window and the Payables Transaction Entry Zoom window.
>
> • Select the *Age Unapplied Credit Amounts* to age credit amounts along with vouchers.

9. **Select an option to specify how you want to handle duplicate bills per vendor.**

   Typically, you should not allow duplicates.

10. **You can click the Options button to display the Payables Setup Options dialog box shown in Figure 3-2. Click OK when you finish setting options in this dialog box to redisplay the Payables Management Setup dialog box.**

    Using the Payables Setup Options dialog box, you can modify the default document names and codes that Dynamics GP sets up. You also can change the numbers for the next temporary Vendor ID, voucher, payment, and payment schedule. And, you can assign default tax schedules — the ones you set up when you set up your company — for purchases, freight, and miscellaneous charges that will appear in the Payables Transaction Entry window. Finally, you can set up labels for two user-defined fields that you can use to track additional information about your vendors; you can use the first user-defined field to sort most vendor reports. The user-defined fields are free-form text fields, and the names you set here will automatically appear on the SmartList and on the Vendor Card.

Figure 3-2:
The
Payables
Setup
Options
dialog box.

Payables Setup Options				sa Fabrikam, Inc. 04/12/2017
File Edit Tools Help				
Type	Description	Code	Next Voucher Number	0000000000000460
Invoice	Invoice	INV	Next Payment Number	0000000000000439
Finance Charge	Finance Charge	FIN	Next Schedule Number	SCHED00000000001
Misc Charge	Misc Charge	MIS	Tax Schedule IDs:	
Return	Return	RET	Purchase	ALL DETAILS
Credit Memo	Credit Memo	CRM	Freight	ALL DETAILS
Payment	Payment	PMT	Miscellaneous	ALL DETAILS
Schedule	Schedule	SCH		
			User-Defined 1	Type
Next Temp. Vendor ID	TEMPORARY000001		User-Defined 2	User-Defined 2
				OK

11. **Click the 1099 Setup button to display the 1099 Setup dialog box shown in Figure 3-3 and review or change the default 1099 information that Dynamics GP sets up.**

Dynamics GP enables you to produce three types of 1099's: Dividend, Interest, and Miscellaneous. Use the Tax Type list at the top of the box to view the defaults Dynamics GP established for each type of 1099.

If you start using Dynamics GP in the middle of the year, you can enter the 1099 amounts from prior periods by choosing Cards⇨Purchasing⇨ 1099 Details.

12. Click OK to redisplay the Payables Management Setup dialog box.

13. Click OK to save your settings.

Figure 3-3:
The 1099 Setup dialog box.

Setting Up Vendor Classes

Using vendor classes, you can group vendor information in ways that make sense in your business and simultaneously speed up the process of setting up your vendors. When you create a vendor class, you establish default settings for the class. For example, you identify the currency used by all vendors in the class as well as the payment terms, tax schedule, shipping method, general ledger posting accounts, and a variety of other settings. Then, you can apply these defaults to all vendors in the class — Dynamics GP refers to this process as *rolling down* the vendor class settings — instead of setting up the defaults for each vendor individually. If you set up vendor classes, setting up vendors becomes quick and easy.

Start by creating a vendor class that has the majority of the settings that you want to apply to all vendor classes. You can then use the settings for this vendor class as the foundation for subsequent vendor classes you create, saving you time when you create vendor classes.

Don't worry if a few vendors you intend to assign to the class use slightly different settings than the ones you establish for the class. You can make changes to these settings when you create the individual vendor. The idea here is to get Dynamics GP to do most of the work for you by assigning the majority of settings as defaults.

In the following steps, only the setting in Step 4 is required; all the other settings are optional.

To create a vendor class, follow these steps:

1. **Click the Purchasing series in the Navigation pane of your Home page.**

2. **Click Setup.**

3. **Click Vendor Class.**

    Dynamics GP displays the Vendor Class Setup window shown in Figure 3-4.

4. **Assign an ID to the class and provide a description.**

    Check the Default box if you want to use the settings you establish for the current vendor class as the default settings for future classes you create.

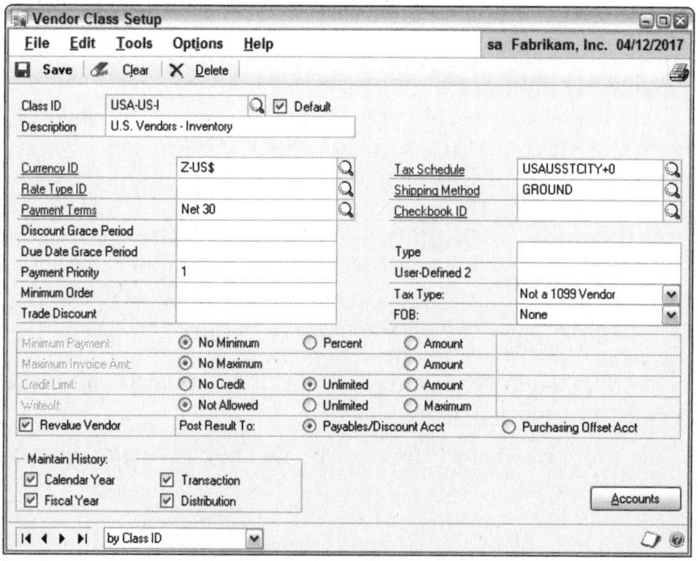

Figure 3-4:
The Vendor Class Setup window.

5. **In the center section of the window, click the Lookup button — the one that looks like a magnifying glass — beside any field to make the following selections, as they apply to most vendors in the class:**

- *Currency ID:* Select the currency used by vendors in this class. If you use the Multicurrency Management module, also use the Rate Type ID to select the rate type used by vendors in this class.

- *Payment Terms:* Select the payment terms used by vendors in this class.

- *Discount Grace Period:* Dynamics GP uses this field in conjunction with the vendor's payment terms to determine due dates. If the document date plus the number of grace period days is the same as or later than the payment terms discount date, both the discount date and the due date will move to the following month.

- *Due Date Grace Period:* Dynamics GP uses this field in conjunction with the vendor's payment terms to determine due dates. If the discount date plus the number of due date grace period days is the same as or later than the payment terms due date, the due date will move to the following month.

- *Payment Priority:* This shows how to order vouchers when paying vendors in the class. Using payment priorities, you can, for example, pay the vouchers of your most important vendors before paying vouchers for other vendors.

   For payment priorities to work properly, use the same number of characters for all priorities you use. Dynamics GP sorts the characters from left to right and numbers take priority over letters. For example, a priority of 01 is higher than a priority of A1.

- *Minimum Order:* If you also use the Purchase Order Processing module, enter the minimum amount your company must order from vendors in this class.

- *Trade Discount:* Enter the trade discount percentage offered to you by most vendors in this class.

- *Tax Schedule:* Select the tax schedule used by vendors in this class.

- *Shipping Method:* If you also use the Purchase Order Processing module, select the shipping method used by vendors in this class.

- *Checkbook ID:* Select the checkbook ID you use to pay vendors in this class.

- *Type* and *User Defined 2:* If appropriate, fill in information for the two user-defined fields.

- *Tax Type:* Select the tax type that applies to most vendors in this class.

- *FOB:* If you also use the Purchase Order Processing module, select the *freight on board* type for most vendors in this class.

6. **In the grid toward the bottom of the window, make selections as appropriate for vendors in this class:**

   - Identify the minimum payment percentage or amount, the maximum invoice amount, the credit limit, and whether Dynamics GP should write off differences between vouchers and payments.

   - Establish whether you can revalue multicurrency documents for vendors in this class and, if so, the account to which Dynamics GP should post the result.

7. **In the Maintain History section, select the type of history you want to keep for vendors in this class. Keeping history enables you to print reports about purchasing activity:**

   - Keep calendar year history if you need to print 1099's for vendors in this class.

   - Keep fiscal year history if your fiscal year does not follow the calendar year.

   - Keep transaction history to view information about paid vouchers in an inquiry window and to print the Historical Aged Trial Balance.

   If you opted to print the Historical Aged Trial Balance in the Payables Management Setup window shown earlier in Figure 3-1, Dynamics GP automatically keeps transaction history regardless of your selection in the Vendor Class Setup window.

   - Keep distribution history so that you can print the Distribution History and Check Distribution reports.

8. **Click the Accounts button to display the Vendor Class Accounts Setup dialog box shown in Figure 3-5. Use this dialog box to**

   - Identify whether to use the cash account associated with the vendor class checkbook or the one you assign to the vendor when you set up vendors as described later in this chapter in the section, "Setting Up Your Vendors."

   - Select default posting accounts for vendors in this class. Click the Lookup button in the middle of each row to assign the account number in your chart of accounts associated with the account listed in the left column. Dynamics GP automatically fills in the description you assigned to the account number.

9. **Click OK to save your selections and redisplay the Vendor Class Setup window.**

10. **Click the Save button to save your selections.**

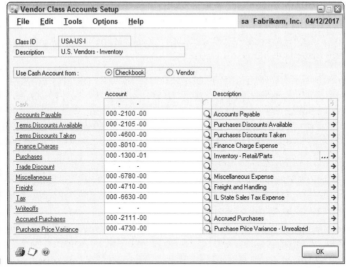

Figure 3-5:
Use this
dialog box
to establish
default
posting
accounts for
vendors in
the selected
class.

You can delete a vendor class if it becomes obsolete by displaying it in the Vendor Class Setup window shown in Figure 3-4 and clicking the Delete button. Deleting a vendor class doesn't affect the vendors assigned to the class, except that the Vendor Class ID field on the vendor card will be invalid. Before you delete a vendor class, print a Vendor List sorted by class; that way, you can see the vendors that will be affected if you delete the class. You print the Vendor List from the Reports section of the Content pane that appears when you select the Purchasing series in the Navigation pane. See Chapter 12 to learn about setting up a report to sort in a particular way.

Setting Up Your Vendors

You create vendor cards for each of the vendors with whom you do business. The vendor card stores vendor address information as well as posting account information. By assigning your vendors to a vendor class, you can have Dynamics GP automatically assign much of the information for the vendor class to the vendor.

Adding vendor cards

You add vendor cards to identify to Dynamics GP the vendors with whom you do business on a regular basis. Follow these steps:

1. **From the Menu bar, click Cards⇨Purchasing⇨Vendor to display the Vendor Maintenance window shown in Figure 3-6.**

    You also can click Purchasing in the Navigation pane and then, in the Cards section, click Vendor.

2. **In the top section of the window, type an ID for the vendor, the vendor's name, a short name to use when the full name is too long — on reports, for example —, and the name you want Dynamics GP to print on the vendor's checks. In addition, assign a vendor class if appropriate.**

    Assigning a vendor class makes setting up the vendor easier, because Dynamics GP automatically fills in default settings such as the tax schedule, shipping method, currency ID, payment terms, and posting accounts.

3. **In the middle section, fill in address and phone number information and, if appropriate, a UPS zone. If you didn't select a vendor class ID, fill in the vendor's tax schedule and shipping method. You can create multiple addresses for a vendor, as you see in the next section of this chapter, "Setting up vendor addresses."**

4. **At the bottom of the window, if the vendor uses different addresses for purchases, receiving checks, or shipping, select the address ID's.**

5. **In the Vendor Account box, you can supply the account number your vendor assigns to you.**

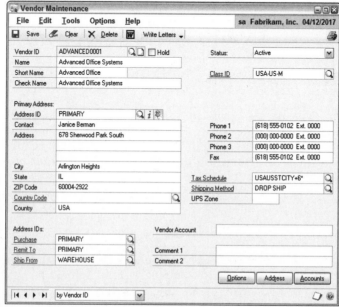

Figure 3-6: Use the Content pane to begin setting up a vendor card.

Your consultant can modify the check layout so that your account number with that vendor appears on the stub or the face of the check, helping to ensure that your payments are more likely to be applied correctly.

The two comment fields are for your use; any information you type in them appears on the Vendor Setup List. For example, Dynamics GP allows telephone extensions to be a maximum of four digits, so if the extension is longer you can enter it in one of the Comment fields.

6. **Click the Options button to display the Vendor Maintenance Options window.**

   The Vendor Maintenance Options window is identical to the Vendor Class Setup window shown earlier in Figure 3-4. See the earlier section, "Setting Up Vendor Classes," for a description of the options in this window. Click OK to redisplay the Vendor Maintenance window shown in Figure 3-6.

7. **Click the Accounts button to display the Vendor Account Maintenance window (see Figure 3-7).**

   Typically, you set most of these accounts at either the company level or the Vendor Class level, but you might want to set the Purchases account in this window. In many cases, you assign vouchers to only one expense account for a vendor, but, in some cases, you might regularly assign some purchases for a vendor to one account and other purchases to another account. Notice the ellipsis button beside the Purchases account; click this button to open the Additional Vendor Accounts window shown in Figure 3-8.

Click here to define multiple accounts for purchases.

Figure 3-7:
The Vendor
Account
Main-
tenance
window.

	Account	Description	
Vendor Account Maintenance		sa Fabrikam, Inc. 04/12/2017	
File Edit Tools Options Help			
Vendor ID	ADVANCED0001		
Name	Advanced Office Systems		
Use Cash Account From:	● Checkbook ○ Vendor		
	Account	Description	
Cash	- -		
Accounts Payable	000 -2100 -00	Accounts Payable	→
Terms Discounts Available	000 -2105 -00	Purchases Discounts Available	→
Terms Discounts Taken	000 -4600 -00	Purchases Discounts Taken	→
Finance Charges	000 -8010 -00	Finance Charge Expense	→
Purchases	500 -6150 -00	Supplies-Allocated - Consulting/Training	... →
Trade Discount	- -		→
Miscellaneous	000 -6780 -00	Miscellaneous Expense	→
Freight	500 -6500 -00	Postage/Freight - Consulting/Training	→
Tax	000 -6630 -00	IL State Sales Tax Expense	→
Writeoffs	- -		→
Accrued Purchases	000 -2111 -00	Accrued Purchases	→
Purchase Price Variance	000 -4730 -00	Purchase Price Variance - Unrealized	→
		OK	

Use this window to list all account numbers you use for the vendor. When you record vouchers from this vendor, Dynamics GP automatically filters the Lookup list to display only the accounts you list in the Additional Vendor Accounts window. If you select the Default on Trx check box, Dynamics GP automatically adds the selected account to the distribution window.

When you record a voucher, you can select any account you want; using the Additional Vendor Accounts window simply helps you quickly and easily select accounts for most vouchers from the vendor.

Click OK twice to redisplay the Vendor Maintenance window shown in Figure 3-6.

If you do not assign a vendor class or set up default accounts using the Vendor Account Maintenance window, Dynamics GP will assign, on transactions, the accounts you specified when setting up your company. See Chapter 2 for details on setting up company default posting accounts.

8. **You can click the Address button to display the Vendor Address Maintenance window, which you can read about in the next section, "Setting up vendor addresses."**

9. **Click Save to save the vendor card.**

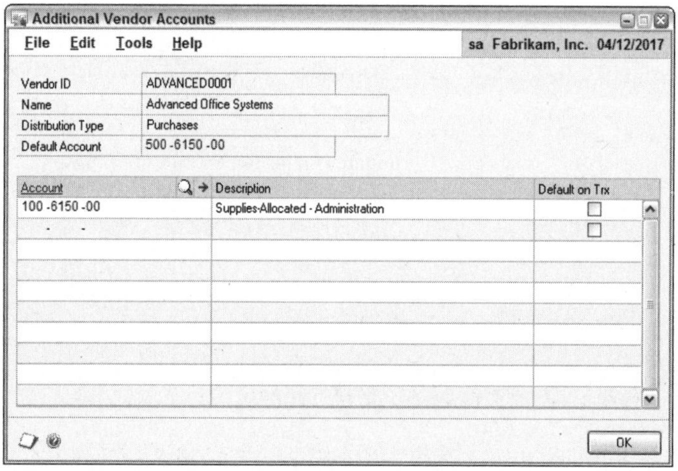

Additional Vendor Accounts				sa Fabrikam, Inc. 04/12/2017
File Edit Tools Help				

Vendor ID	ADVANCED0001
Name	Advanced Office Systems
Distribution Type	Purchases
Default Account	500 -6150 -00

Account	Description	Default on Trx
100 -6150 -00	Supplies-Allocated - Administration	☐
- -		☐

OK

Figure 3-8:
The Additional Vendor Accounts window.

Setting up vendor addresses

You might need more than one address for a vendor if you send purchase orders to one location, payments to another location, and receive shipments from a third location. Follow these steps to create an address ID other than the one you stored on the vendor's card:

1. **Choose Cards⇨Purchasing⇨Addresses or click Addresses in the Cards section of the Content pane.**

   Dynamics GP displays the Vendor Address Maintenance window (see Figure 3-9).

2. **Enter or select a Vendor ID.**

3. **In the Address ID box, type a name that describes the address, such as Primary, Warehouse, or Remit To.**

   You can click the Internet Information button — the *i* button beside the Address ID Lookup button — to display the Internet Information window and type an e-mail address, a Web site address, or an ftp site address. When you finish, click Save and then click the X in the upper-right corner of the window to close it and redisplay the Vendor Address.

4. **Supply a contact name and address, phone, and fax information.**

5. **Click Save to save the address.**

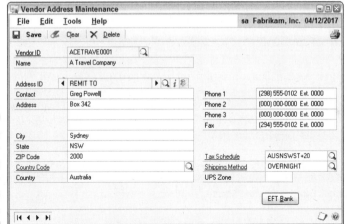

Figure 3-9:
The Vendor
Address
Main-
tenance
window.

Placing a vendor on hold

Suppose that a vendor ships you merchandise you didn't order. If you want to ensure that you don't pay the vendor's bill while you straighten out the matter, place the vendor on hold. While a vendor is *on hold,* you can't record any payments, but you can record other types of transactions.

You can place individual vouchers on hold as well. Choose Transactions⇨ Purchasing⇨Holds to display the Hold Payables Transactions window. Select the vendor to see the vouchers entered for the vendor. Then, place a check-mark in the Hold column beside the voucher you want to place on hold and click OK.

To place a vendor on hold, open the Vendor Maintenance window by choosing Cards➪Purchasing➪Vendors or, in the Content pane, under the Cards section, clicking Vendor. Click the Lookup button beside the Vendor ID field to select the vendor. Then, at the right edge of the Vendor ID field, check the Hold box. Click Save to save your settings and click the X in the upper-right corner of the window to close it.

When you don't need a vendor anymore

When you decide that you don't need a vendor anymore, you can either make the vendor inactive or you can delete the vendor.

Making a vendor inactive is the less intrusive and less permanent way of proceeding. To make a vendor inactive, open the Vendor Maintenance window by choosing Cards➪Purchasing➪Vendors and select the vendor. Then, use the Status list box to change the vendor's status to Inactive.

You may notice Temporary in the Status list; you assign this status to a vendor with whom you plan to have a . . . well . . . temporary relationship. Because the relationship won't last long, you use this status to have Dynamics GP keep minimal information about the vendor.

Deleting a vendor is a more permanent approach than setting a vendor's status to inactive. Dynamics GP won't let you delete a vendor card for any vendor with a current balance, posted and/or unposted transactions, a United States vendor with a 1099 amount for the current year, or a vendor with transactions in history.

Using utilities and reports, you can determine whether a vendor has transaction history or current year activity. See Chapter 13 for information on utilities and Chapter 12 for information on reports.

If the vendor meets the other criteria for deletion but has history, you must delete the history before deleting the vendor. You can delete a temporary vendor without removing vendor history, so, if you don't want to take the time to remove history, you can change a vendor's status to temporary and, if the vendor doesn't have a current balance or 1099 amounts for the current year, you can delete the vendor.

To delete a vendor card, choose Cards➪Purchasing➪Vendors to open the Vendor Maintenance window shown earlier in Figure 3-6. Select the ID of the vendor you want to delete, and then click the Delete button.

Entering Beginning Balances

I have to assume that you aren't just starting out in business; in fact, you've probably been in business for quite awhile. And, in that case, you probably have outstanding balances that you owe to vendors. If you recorded the vouchers for these outstanding balances in your old accounting system and intend to import information, probably with the help of an authorized Dynamics GP partner, the import process will establish your beginning balances for your vendors and you can skip this section.

If you are not planning to import these beginning balances, then you need to enter them in Dynamics GP. You enter them using Dynamics GP vouchers and, if any of the vouchers are partially paid, Dynamics GP payments. You follow the steps described in the sections that follow with one exception: You *don't* want to post these transactions to the General Ledger.

You see, the sum of the beginning balance transactions you enter for all of your vendors should equal the amount you recorded for Accounts Payable when you set up your opening balances as described in Chapter 2. Since you already established the balance of your Accounts Payable account when you set up your system, you want to record these beginning balance transactions so that they don't affect the General Ledger balance for Accounts Payable; otherwise, your Accounts Payable balance in the General Ledger will be overstated.

To avoid posting these transactions to the General Ledger, temporarily change your posting setup (see the steps below). Then, enter a beginning balance batch for outstanding vouchers; if any of these vouchers are partially paid, you can enter the original amount for the voucher and create another beginning balance batch that contains the payments you made against the partially paid vouchers. Or, you can enter just the remaining balance due on the voucher. When you finish posting these two batches, re-establish the original posting settings so that future transactions will post to the General Ledger.

To temporarily change your posting setup, follow these steps:

1. **On the Menu bar select Microsoft Dynamics GP⇨Tools⇨Setup⇨ Posting⇨Posting to open the Posting Setup window (see Figure 3-10).**

2. **From the Series list, select Purchasing.**

3. **From the Origin list, select Payables Trx Entry.**

4. **Remove the checkmark beside the Post to General Ledger check box.**

5. **Repeat Steps 3 and 4 for payments except, in Step 3, select Payment Entry.**

6. **Click OK to save the settings and close the Posting Setup window.**

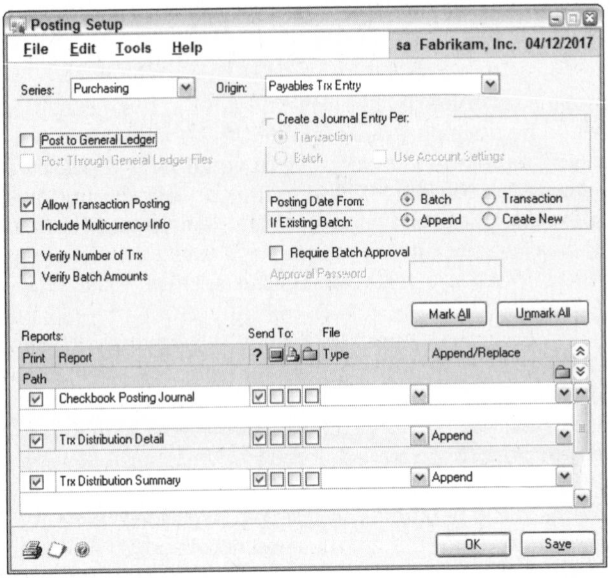

Figure 3-10:
Use this
window to
temporar-
ily change
posting
settings.

Any payables transactions that you post will not affect your General Ledger. After you create and post your beginning batch transactions using the steps in the next section, repeat the steps above to re-establish posting to the General Ledger.

In addition, before you begin your regular routine work, you might want to print an Aged Trial Balance report because, at this point, the report would provide a record of your beginning outstanding vendor balances. See Chapter 12 for details on setting up and printing reports.

Entering Payables Transactions

You can enter several different types of payables transactions. In this section, we discuss entering transactions to record vouchers and transactions to pay vouchers.

You can enter transactions individually or in batches. When you enter transactions in batches, you group similar transactions during data entry. You read about both methods in this section.

Finally, to update your company files with the information contained on a transaction, you post it. If you enter transactions individually, you post them when you enter them. However, if you enter transactions in batches, you have the option to save the batch, print a report that shows the contents of the batch, and review it before posting.

Posting to or through the General Ledger — What's the difference?

You might have noticed two options related to posting to the General Ledger. When you select the option to post *to* the General Ledger, you allow a batch from one of the other modules to update the General Ledger. Effectively, this option controls whether the updates to another module can possibly affect the General Ledger. If you select *only* this option, Dynamics GP doesn't automatically post the batch in the General Ledger; instead, the batch appears in the General Ledger, where you can review it. Then, if you want the batch to update the General Ledger, you take a second step and post it in the General Ledger. So, if you select the option to post a batch *to* the General Ledger, updating your General Ledger accounts becomes a two-step posting process that enables you to review batches before updating the General Ledger.

If you select the option to post a batch *to* the General Ledger, then you also have the choice of posting *through* General Ledger files. If you also select this second option, available only if you chose to post to the General Ledger, Dynamics GP posts the batch in the originating module and simultaneously updates the General Ledger with no additional steps on your part. Most people prefer this approach because it ensures that the General Ledger doesn't become out of balance with the subsidiary ledger. If you find a mistake in a transaction from a subsidiary ledger, don't edit the original journal entries. Instead void the transaction in the subsidiary ledger; that action will automatically generate journal entries to reverse the original journal entries.

Creating a batch

You can create two types of batches: single use batches or recurring batches. Use a *single use batch,* for example, to enter beginning balance transactions. Use a *recurring batch* if the transactions you intend to enter happen repeatedly on some consistent frequency, such as weekly or monthly. You can save time using a recurring batch because you don't need to enter the batch each time; you simply need to post it when appropriate.

You also use the technique described below to create a batch of beginning balance transactions.

To create a batch, follow these steps:

1. **On your Home page in the Transactions section of the Content pane for the Purchasing series, click Batches. Or, choose Transactions⇨ Purchasing⇨Batches.**

   The Payables Batch Entry window, shown in Figure 3-11, appears.

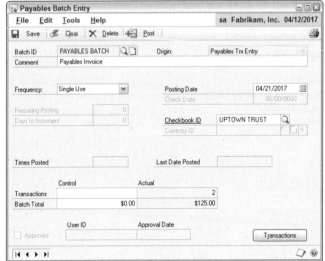

Figure 3-11:
The
Payables
Batch Entry
window.

2. **In the Batch ID field, type a number to identify the batch.**

   You can use the Batch ID more than once as long as each batch contains a different type of transaction, and you also can supply a comment to describe the batch.

3. **From the Origin list, select the type of payables transactions you plan to enter in this batch.**

   • *Payables Trx Entry* to record vouchers

   • *Computer Check* to record and print checks for vouchers

   • *Manual Payment* to record checks for vendors that you don't intend to print or to record payments made by wire transfer

4. **From the Frequency list, select a frequency for the batch, such as Single Use or Monthly.**

   If you select a recurring frequency, you can type a number in the Recurring Posting box to control the number of times the batch posts. To keep the batch available indefinitely, leave the value at 0.

5. **Enter the date you want to update the General Ledger with the batch information.**

   Dynamics GP updates Payables Management information using the date you assign to the transaction, but the Posting date is especially important if you have established your posting setup to post by batch date instead of transaction date. When you post by batch date, the date you enter in this field determines the accounting period that the expenses appear on the financial statements.

If you select Computer Check as the Origin in Step 3, enter the date you want printed on the check, the Currency ID if you use the Multicurrency Management module, and the check's file format.

6. **Select a Checkbook ID.**

7. **Optionally, in the Control column of the grid at the bottom of the window, enter the number of transactions and the total dollars you expect to enter for the batch.**

After entering the transactions, you can compare the control totals to the actual totals to make sure you have entered everything correctly. Some users add up the totals for a stack of invoices and then want to ensure that the batch total agrees to the user's total. However, most users don't bother adding control totals.

8. **Click Save to save your batch.**

To edit the batch information of an unposted batch, reopen the Payables Batch Entry window, click the Lookup button beside the Batch ID field, and select the batch ID to display the batch. Then, make your changes and click Save. To delete an unposted batch, reopen the Payable Batch Entry window, display the batch, and click the Delete button. You can't delete computer check batches with a status other than Available or A/P transaction batches containing printed checks.

In the sections that follow, you add transactions to the batch.

Entering a voucher

Each time you receive a bill from a vendor, you enter it into Dynamics GP so that Dynamics GP can help you manage your outstanding payables effectively by aging the bills according to the terms you have established. In this way, you make the best use of your cash; you don't pay your bills too early and lose the ability to take advantage of other income-earning opportunities, and you don't pay your bills too late and lose discounts or incur late fees.

You also use the steps below to create beginning balance transactions for unpaid vouchers at the time you start using Dynamics GP. I suggest you enter the beginning balance voucher transactions in one single use batch; see the preceding section for steps on creating a batch.

Optionally, use the steps in the preceding section to start a new batch of transactions. If a batch already exists, you can add this transaction to the batch by displaying the batch information in the Payables Batch Entry window shown previously in Figure 3-9 and clicking the Transactions button. Or you can add the transaction to an existing batch as you create the transaction, as I do in the following steps.

If you use the Purchase Order Processing module and you want to record a bill from a vendor that relates to a purchase order, don't use the steps in this section. Instead, see the "Receiving Stuff" section in Chapter 4.

Follow these steps to record a voucher from a vendor:

You also follow these steps to enter a vendor finance charge, miscellaneous charge, return, and credit memo.

1. **Click the Purchasing series button in the Navigation pane.**

2. **In the Transactions section of the Content pane, click Transaction Entry to open the Payables Transaction Entry window (see Figure 3-12).**

   The next available voucher ID number appears by default in the Voucher No. field.

3. **From the Document Type list, select Invoice.**

   You can optionally enter a description for the document. This description flows through to the General Ledger detail history, so it's a good idea to fill it out, especially for transactions that are something other than typical monthly bills.

4. **To assign the voucher to an existing batch, click the Lookup button beside the Batch ID field and select the batch.**

   If you select an existing batch, Dynamics GP assigns the batch posting date as the document's date. Otherwise, you can change the default document date from the user date to whatever date you want the document to update your Payables Management records.

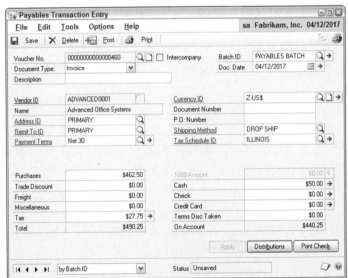

Figure 3-12: Payables Transaction Entry window.

You cannot save transactions not assigned to batches; they must be posted as you enter them, and you cannot edit them later.

5. **In the Vendor ID field, select a vendor.**

   Dynamics GP fills in the vendor's name, currency ID, default addresses, payment terms, shipping method, and tax schedule. If necessary, you can change any of these fields.

If you use multiple Remit To ID's for the same vendor, Dynamics GP creates a separate check for each Remit To ID.

6. **In the Document Number field, enter the number the vendor assigned to this transaction.**

   If the vendor doesn't assign numbers to transactions, set up your own numbering system for that vendor to assign unique numbers to transactions, since the Document Number field is required.

   If your company doesn't use the Purchase Order module but does use purchase orders and you want to match your purchase orders to vouchers, you can supply your purchase order number in the P.O. Number box. Most users ignore this field if they are using the Purchase Order module, because the Purchase Order module handles matching purchase orders to vouchers.

7. **In the Purchases field, enter the amount of the vendor's bill before freight, tax, or miscellaneous charges.**

   If you set up a trade discount for the vendor, Dynamics GP calculates the trade discount.

8. **If appropriate, enter amounts in the Freight and Miscellaneous fields.**

   I'll assume, for the moment, that you intend to pay this voucher later. Later in this chapter, in the section "Writing checks," I describe how to handle a voucher that you intend to pay immediately.

9. **If you assigned the transaction to a batch in Step 3, click the Save button. If you did not assign the transaction to a batch, click the Post button.**

See the section "Posting batches," later in this chapter, for details on posting transactions you save in a batch.

You can print an edit listing of any batch by selecting the Batch ID in the Payables Batch Entry window and then choosing File➪Print.

Editing or deleting a voucher

You can edit or delete a transaction in an unposted batch. You edit any transaction in the window where it was created; in the following example, I show you how to edit an unposted voucher, but the same process applies if you need to edit other types of transactions.

At any time before you pay a bill, you can edit the due date of a posted but unpaid voucher to change when the voucher is due by editing the transaction information. Select Transactions➪Purchasing➪Edit Transaction Information.

To edit an unposted voucher, open the Payables Transaction Entry window shown earlier in Figure 3-10 by clicking Transaction Entry in the Transactions section of the Content pane. Click the Lookup button beside the voucher number and Dynamics GP displays the Vouchers window shown in Figure 3-13; this window contains vouchers available to edit.

Click the voucher you want to edit and then click Select to display the voucher in the Payables Transaction Entry window. In that window, make any needed changes and click the Save button. To delete the voucher, click the Delete button.

If you know the number of the batch containing the voucher, you can type it in the Find By Batch ID field and limit the vouchers Dynamics GP displays to only those in the batch number you entered.

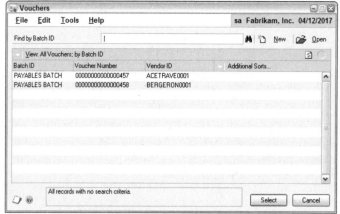

Figure 3-13: Use this window to select a voucher to edit.

Writing checks

You can pay vouchers in a few different ways. For example, suppose that the UPS guy is standing there, waiting for payment on a COD delivery. You can record a voucher that you simultaneously pay. Or, you can enter a voucher as described in the preceding section, either as a single voucher or as part of a batch, and then, when you're ready, pay vouchers.

You can print computer checks for payments or you can enter a manual check to record, say, the purchase of supplies at the local office supply store, where you sent somebody with a check. In this case, you print no check but need to record the written check.

When you record that manual check for the office supply store, enter an invoice first so that you can apply the manual check to the invoice.

Simultaneously creating a voucher and printing a check

Let's walk through the scenario where the UPS guy is waiting for a check. Dynamics GP lets you print a check, but printing the check doesn't update your company files. Because you intend to hand this check to the UPS guy, you should post it immediately after printing it. Follow these steps:

1. **Create a voucher in the Payables Transaction Entry window using Steps 1 through 7 in the preceding section.**

2. **In the Cash, Check, or Credit Card box, enter the amount you want to pay.**

   If you enter the amount in the Check field, Dynamics GP displays the Payables Check Entry dialog box shown in Figure 3-14. Select the checkbook from which you want to write the check and make sure that the Check Number field displays the number of the check you intend to use.

3. **Click OK to redisplay the Payables Transaction Entry window.**

4. **Click the Distributions button; the Payables Transaction Entry Distribution dialog box appears (see Figure 3-15).**

5. **As needed, change the distributions for the transaction and click OK to redisplay the Payables Transaction Entry Distribution window.**

   Clicking Default makes Dynamics GP redistribute the transaction using your posting account defaults. Click Change to the message that appears to let Dynamics GP update the distributions.

6. **Click Print Check to display the Print Payables Transaction Check window shown in Figure 3-16.**

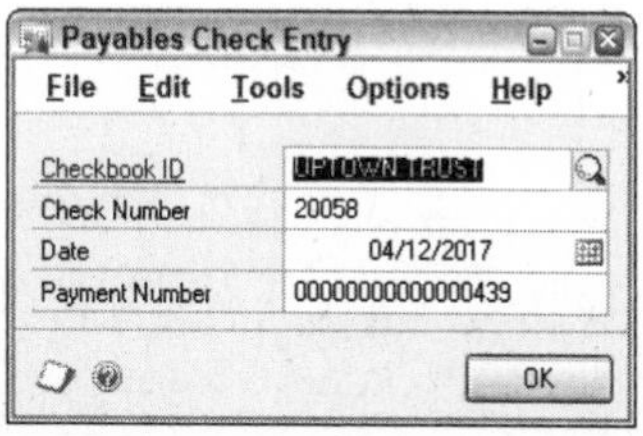

Figure 3-14: Select a checkbook.

Payables Check Entry		
File Edit Tools Options Help		
Checkbook ID	UPTOWN TRUST	
Check Number	20058	
Date	04/12/2017	
Payment Number	00000000000000439	
		OK

Figure 3-15:
The
Payables
Transaction
Entry
Distribution
dialog box.

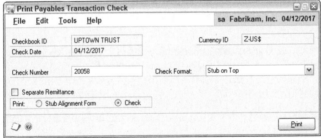

Figure 3-16:
The Print
Payables
Transaction
Check
window.

7. **Select the Separate Remittance box to print check stub information on a separate sheet of paper.**

8. **In the Print box, click Check.**

   If you want to align the check stub, select Stub Alignment Form.

9. **Click Print and select Printer in the Report Destination dialog box.**

   Dynamics GP prints the check and redisplays the Payables Transaction Entry window.

10. **Click Post.**

Recording a manual check

Now let's walk through the scenario where you wish to record the check that paid for those office supplies. In this case, you won't be printing a check, but you do need to account for the check. Follow these steps:

Use the steps that follow to create payments for partially paid beginning balance vouchers.

1. **Select Transactions⇨Purchasing⇨Manual Payments or, in the Transactions section of the Content pane, click Manual Payments.**

   Dynamics GP displays the Payables Manual Payment Entry window shown in Figure 3-17.

2. **Create or select a batch.**

   See the section "Creating a batch," earlier in this chapter, for more information.

3. **Select a Vendor ID and, if appropriate, a Currency ID.**

4. **Select a payment method.**

   Dynamics GP distributes manual payments with a Payment Method of Credit Card by debiting Accounts Payable and crediting cash. Consider the credit card company as your vendor, because you pay them for the goods and services you purchase with the card.

5. **Enter the amount of the payment and click Apply.**

   Dynamics GP displays the Apply Payables Documents window shown in Figure 3-18.

6. **Click the check box beside a voucher with an outstanding amount and click OK.**

   Dynamics GP redisplays the Payables Manual Payment Entry window.

   You can click the Auto-Apply button to automatically apply the transaction amount to as many vouchers as possible, based on the amount you're applying and the amount of the available vouchers. Note, though, that Dynamics GP only auto-applies amounts to vouchers containing the same remit-to address. Dynamics GP also takes any discount if the discount is still available and if the unapplied amount is large enough to pay off the voucher.

7. **To change account distributions for the transaction, click Distributions to open the Payables Transaction Entry Distribution window shown earlier in Figure 3-13.**

8. **Click Save to add the payment to the batch you identified in Step 2.**

You can print an edit list that contains the transactions in the batch by choosing File⇨Print in the Payables Manual Payment Entry window.

Figure 3-17:
The Payables Manual Payment Entry window.

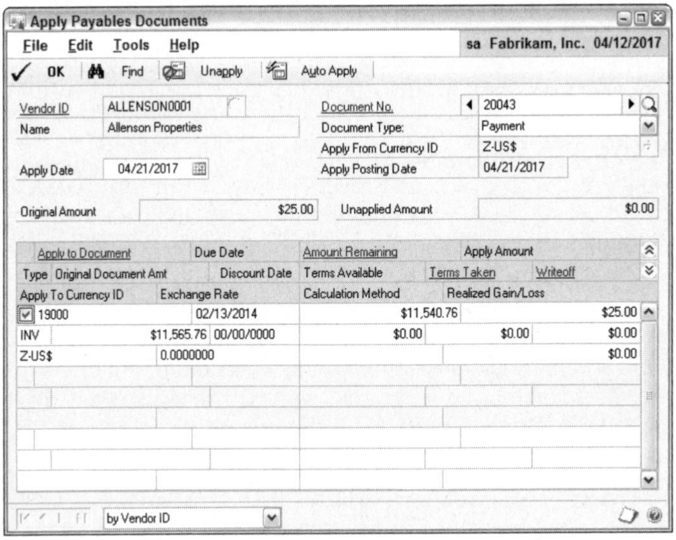

Figure 3-18:
The Apply Payables Documents window.

Printing batches of checks

Most people pay vendor bills and print batches of checks at some regular interval. Printing batches of checks typically takes less time than printing checks one at a time.

To print a batch of checks, you build a batch that contains the checks you want to print. You can select vouchers to pay based on vendor, voucher number, due date, or discount date. Because building a batch can be a lengthy process, based on the selection criteria you specify, you might want to print an Aged Trial Balance report to review unpaid vouchers before you build the batch. Once the batch is built you can edit it, adding more vendors and vouchers or deleting or partially paying the selected vouchers.

If you are only going to print a small handful of checks, you can simply enter and simultaneously print the checks using the Edit Payables Check window (choose Transactions➪Purchasing➪Edit Check).

To build a batch of computer checks, follow these steps:

1. **Select Transactions➪Purchasing➪Batches to open the Payables Batch Entry window (see Figure 3-19).**

2. **Enter a Batch ID and select Computer Check from the Origin list.**

   You can add transactions to an existing batch if you select the Batch ID here.

3. **From the Frequency list, choose Single Use.**

4. **Click the Lookup button beside the Checkbook ID box and select a checkbook to use for all checks in the batch.**

5. **Click Transactions to display the Go To window shown in Figure 3-20.**

6. **Choose Select Payables Checks to open the Select Payables Checks window (see Figure 3-21).**

7. **Use the Select Vendor ID, Select Document ID, Due Date Cutoff, and Discount Date Cutoff fields to identify the vouchers you want to include in the batch.**

Figure 3-19: The Payables Batch Entry window.

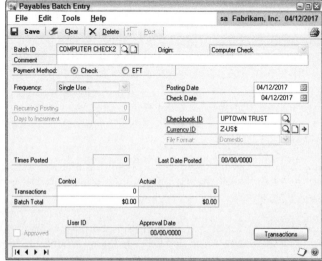

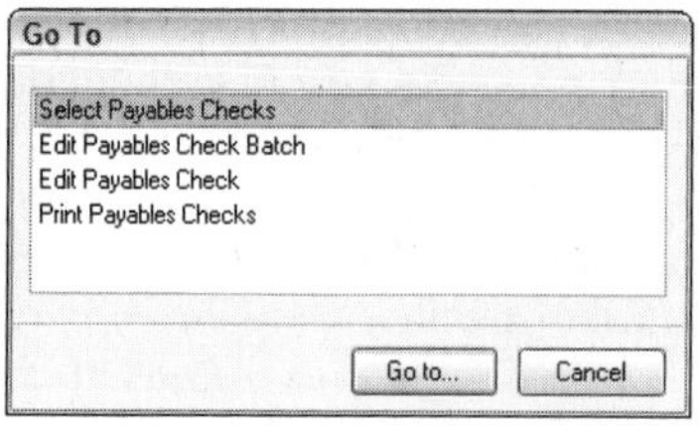

Figure 3-20:
Use this
window
to identify
the action
you want to
take.

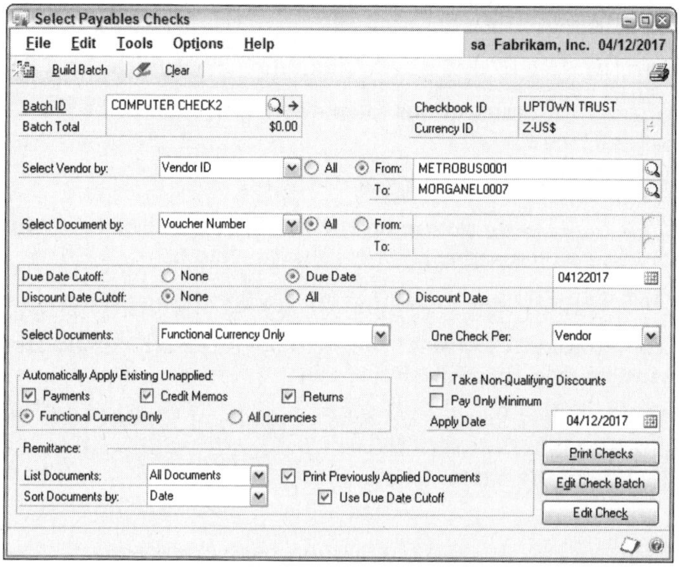

Figure 3-21:
The Select
Payables
Checks
window.

8. **Use the settings in the Automatically Apply Existing Unapplied box to identify the types of documents you want Dynamics GP to automatically apply, and you can set the Apply date.**

   Dynamics GP selects, by default, the Automatically Apply Existing Payments, Credit Memos, and Returns boxes. Most users unselect these boxes so that they can control the way Dynamics GP applies these types of transactions.

9. **Select remittance and check stub information.**

10. **At the top of the window, click Build Batch to create the batch of checks to process.**

    When Dynamics GP finishes building the batch, the total dollars in the batch appear in the Batch Total field below the Batch ID field.

The hourglass icon will not appear, so please be patient and wait for a value to appear in the Batch Total field before proceeding. After Dynamics GP finishes building the batch, Dynamics GP reverts all settings in this window to the default settings that appear when the window first opens, so, don't let that confuse you.

Before you print a batch of checks, you may want to review the checks you're about to print. You can print an edit list for the transactions in the batch from the Payables Batch Entry window. Select the batch and then choose File➪Print or click on the Printer icon in the top-right corner of this window.

Suppose that you find a check in the batch that you really don't want to print. You can remove the check from the batch if you edit the batch. If you haven't yet closed the Select Payables Checks window, you can click the Edit Check Batch button. If you have closed the Select Payables Checks window, reopen the Payables Batch Entry window as shown earlier in Figure 3-17 and select the batch containing the transaction you want to remove. Click the Transactions button and, from the Go To window shown earlier in Figure 3-18, choose Edit Payables Check Batch to display the Edit Payables Check Batch window shown in Figure 3-22.

To remove a check, scroll down the list on the left side of the window and click the vendor to whom the check would be paid. Vouchers for that vendor appear on the right side of the window. To remove one or more vouchers, deselect them from the list on the right. To remove all of the vendor's vouchers from the batch, deselect the vendor in the left column. As you deselect vouchers to pay, Dynamics GP updates the batch total and the checkbook bank balance.

You can add a voucher to the batch by selecting the vendor in the left column and the voucher in the right column.

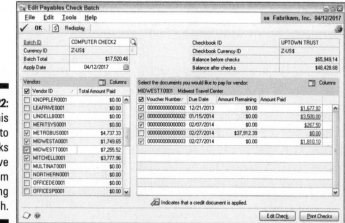

Figure 3-22: Use this window to add checks to or remove checks from an existing batch.

Posting batches

To update your data in the Payables Management module, you must post batches you enter. If you enter individual transactions, you must post them at the time that you enter them, so, the information in this section only applies to transactions entered in batches.

Before you post batches, you may want to review the transactions in them. To review batches, display the Payables Batch Entry window (choose Transactions⇨Purchasing⇨Batches). Use the Lookup button to select the batch you want to review; then click File⇨Print to print an edit list.

After you review the edit listing, you can post batches with an origin of Payables Trx Entry or Manual Payment from the Payables Batch Entry window by clicking the Post button. After the batch posts, posting journals you specified when you set up the Payables Management module will print.

To post batches with an origin of Payables Trx Entry or Manual Payment, follow these steps:

If you temporarily changed your posting options so that you could post vendor beginning balances and avoid updating the General Ledger, don't forget to change your posting options back so that Payables Management batches will update the General Ledger. See the section "Entering Beginning Balances," earlier in this chapter, for details on making the change to your posting options.

1. **From the Transactions section of the Content pane, choose Series Post to open the Purchasing Series Posting window (see Figure 3-23).**

2. **Select the batch(es) you want to post.**

Figure 3-23:
Use this
screen
to post
batches.

3. **Click the Post button.**

   Dynamics GP prints the appropriate posting journals and updates your Payables Management module files.

Voiding payables transactions

You can delete unposted payables transactions, but you cannot delete posted transactions. However, you can eliminate the effects of a posted payables transaction by voiding it. When you void a transaction, Dynamics GP generates a set of debits and credits that reverse the original effect of the transaction you choose to void.

Voiding historical transactions

The window you use to void a transaction depends on whether the transaction is an historical transaction — one that has already been paid — or an open transaction. To void an historical transaction, follow these steps:

1. **Choose Transactions⇨Purchasing⇨Void Historical Transactions to open the Void Historical Payables Transactions window shown in Figure 3-24.**

   By default, all historical transactions appear in the window, but you can use the From and To option button to select a range of Document ID numbers, or you can limit the types of documents that appear by opening the Doc Type list and selecting Return, Credit Memo, or Payment.

2. **Mark each document to void by checking the box in the Void column.**

3. **In the Void Date column, you can change the date or accept the date Dynamics GP suggests, which is the date Dynamics GP sent the transaction to bank reconciliation.**

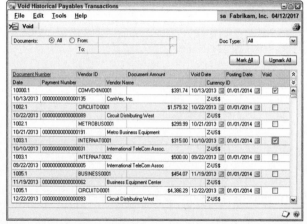

Figure 3-24:
The Void Historical Payables Transactions window.

4. **In the Posting Date column, you can change the date or accept the date Dynamics GP suggests for posting the reversing entries generated by voiding a transaction in the General Ledger.**

Often, users forget to change the posting date when voiding a transaction, and Dynamics GP then posts the reversing transactions in the General Ledger to an old period for which the books have been closed. To avoid this problem, bump up the posting date to an open financial period. In addition, the user in charge of the General Ledger module should use the Fiscal Periods Setup window (choose Tools⊅Setup⊅ Company⊅Fiscal Periods) to mark periods as closed.

To print a Void Historical Transactions Edit List to show all the documents that you marked to be voided, choosing File⊅Print.

5. **To void the marked transactions, click the Void button.**

Dynamics GP voids the transactions and prints the Void Historical Payables Transactions Posting Journal if you set up the system to print this posting journal.

Voided transactions appear and are identified by an asterisk on reports that display historical information and in the Payables Transaction Inquiry window.

After you have voided an historical transaction, Dynamics GP opens the associated voucher again. At that point, you can either pay it, or if you don't intend to pay it, you should read and follow the steps in the next section, "Voiding open transactions."

Voiding open transactions

You can void open transactions that have not been applied or are not on hold. You follow almost all the same steps to void open transactions; follow these steps:

1. **Select Transactions⊅Purchasing⊅Void Open Transactions to open the Void Open Payables Transactions window (see Figure 3-25).**

Figure 3-25: The Void Open Payables Transactions window.

Void Open Payables Transactions							
File Edit Tools Help						sa Fabrikam, Inc. 04/12/2017	
Void							
Vendor ID	ACETRAVE0001					Mark All	Unmark All
Voucher Number		Document Number	Document Amount	Void Date	Posting Date	Void	
Date	Vendor Name			Currency ID			
0000000000000017		1003	$796.03	09/17/2013	01/01/2014	☐	
09/17/2013	A Travel Company			Z-US$			
0000000000000018		1004	$605.45	10/24/2013	01/01/2014	☑	
10/24/2013	A Travel Company			Z-US$			
0000000000000019		1005	$1,906.44	11/24/2013	01/01/2014	☐	
11/24/2013	A Travel Company			Z-US$			
0000000000000020		1006	$2,158.75	12/18/2013	01/01/2014	☐	
12/18/2013	A Travel Company			Z-US$			
0000000000000302		11006	$1,054.39	01/28/2014	01/31/2014	☑	
01/28/2014	A Travel Company			Z-US$			

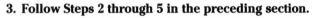

2. **Use the Lookup button beside the Vendor ID field to select a vendor.**

   Dynamics GP displays all of the open transactions for that vendor.

3. **Follow Steps 2 through 5 in the preceding section.**

If you try to mark a document that has been applied or is on hold, Dynamics GP displays a message and does not let you mark the document.

Chapter 4

Working with Purchase Orders

*P*urchase orders provide you with a great way of managing orders for inventory and non-inventory items so that nothing slips through the cracks. It isn't uncommon to place an order for goods and receive the bill separately from the shipment. In Microsoft Dynamics GP, you can post separate transactions to recognize each event or, if you receive the vendor's invoice at the same time that you receive the shipment, you can post both transactions simultaneously.

The Purchase Order Processing module (POP) works with or without the Inventory module; you can enter inventory or non-inventory items on purchase orders. POP also works with the Project Accounting module's cost categories, which you can optionally tie to items you create in the Inventory module. POP also works with the Sales Order Processing module, enabling you to create a purchase order line specifically to fulfill a special order from a customer. By linking a sales order line item to a purchase order line item, you reserve the goods for the customer's order.

Before you set up the Purchase Order Processing module, you should complete the setup process for the Payables Management module and the Inventory Control module if you are using it.

Setting Up to Use Purchase Orders

Setting up the Purchase Order module involves setting preferences for the Purchase Order module's behavior as well as establishing defaults for the module. Follow these steps to open the Purchase Order Processing Setup dialog box and set up purchase orders:

1. **On the Menu bar, select Microsoft Dynamics GP⇨Tools⇨Setup⇨ Purchasing⇨Purchase Order Processing.**

   The Purchase Order Processing Setup dialog box appears (see Figure 4-1).

2. **At the top of the dialog box, you can establish document codes and starting numbers for purchase order documents and receipt documents, and you can choose to use blank paper or a form when you print documents.**

   You can reuse a document number if you have deleted the document or removed it from history.

3. **In the Decimal Places for Non-Inventoried Items list, select the number of decimal places you want to use when displaying and entering quantity for non-inventoried items.**

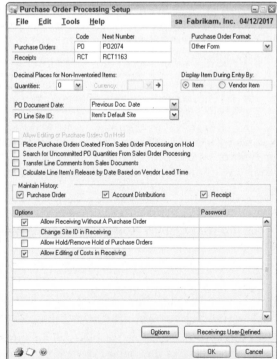

Figure 4-1: The Purchase Order Processing Setup dialog box.

4. In the Display Item During Entry By section, select an option to display the item numbers stored in Dynamics GP or the item numbers used by your vendors.

5. In the PO Document date list, specify whether to use the date from the last document or the user date as a default date each time that you open the Purchase Order Entry window.

6. In the PO Line Site ID list, specify whether to use the Site ID displayed on the previous line of the PO or the Site ID you established for the item in Dynamics GP as the default Site ID for purchase order line items.

7. Select the Place Purchase Orders Created From Sales Order Processing on Hold box if you want to review purchase orders generated during sales order processing before processing them.

If you select this option and place a Sales Order Processing line item on an existing purchase order line item, Dynamics GP will not place the purchase order on hold. And, if you've assigned a password to the Allow Hold/Remove Hold of Purchase Orders option at the bottom of this window, you will not need to enter the password when you generate purchase orders in Sales Order Processing. But, you will need the password to remove holds when you view a purchase order in the Purchase Order Entry window.

8. Select the Search for Uncommitted PO Quantities From Sales Order Processing box if you want Dynamics GP to search for uncommitted purchase order quantities when you attempt to create a link between a sales line and a purchase order.

If you don't select this box, you'll be able to create a new purchase order for the sales document, but you won't be able to link the sales line to an existing purchase order. See Chapter 6 for information about linking an item to an existing purchase order.

9. Select the Transfer Line Comments from Sales Documents box to have Dynamics GP transfer line item comments from sales documents to new purchase orders.

This option has no effect on existing purchase orders.

10. Select the Calculate Line Item's Release Date Based On Vendor Lead Time box to have Dynamics GP calculate an automatic release date for a purchase order line item by subtracting the vendor's planning lead time from the required date.

If you don't select this option, Dynamics GP doesn't calculate a release date.

If you select this box, you can use the PO Line Items to Release Report to identify purchase order line items that you should release to vendors.

11. In the Maintain History section, select the boxes of the types of purchase order history you want to keep.

12. **In the Options portion at the bottom of the dialog box, select the options you want to enable; you can assign passwords to any of the options. You can allow the following:**

    • *Allow Receiving Without A Purchase Order:* Allows users to enter line items on a shipment, shipment/invoice, or invoice receipt that don't appear on a purchase order. If you don't select this option, you won't be able to receive or invoice items that aren't associated with a purchase order.

    • *Change Site ID In Receiving:* Allows users to receive line items to locations other than the one(s) indicated on the original purchase order.

    • *Allow Hold/Remove Hold Of Purchase Orders:* Allows users to place and remove holds on new, released, or change order purchase orders for standard orders or drop shipment orders. If you select this box, Dynamics GP makes available the Allow Editing of Purchase Orders On Hold check box above the Options portion of the dialog box, which you can check to allow editing, deleting, and voiding of purchase orders on hold.

    • *Allow Editing of Costs In Receiving:* Allows users to change an item's Unit Cost and Extended Cost in the Receivings Transaction Entry window. By default, Dynamics GP calculates purchase price variances by comparing the cost posted when receiving an item with the standard cost for items.

    If you select the Allow Receiving Without a Purchase Order options, you should the select the Allow Editing Of Costs In Receiving so that you'll be able to enter costs for items without purchase orders. To control who performs these actions, you can require a password.

13. **Click Options to display the Purchase Order Processing Setup Options dialog box shown in Figure 4-2.**

14. **Use the options at the top of the box to set tax schedule defaults; when you finish, click OK to redisplay the Purchase Order Processing Setup dialog box.**

    Select Advanced to enable the options to select separate tax schedules to use for non-inventoried items, freight, and miscellaneous charges; for inventory items, Dynamics GP uses the tax schedule you choose for each item when you set up the item. Select Single to use one tax schedule for all items on all documents, even if an item is nontaxable or the vendor is tax exempt. Dynamics GP wont' calculate taxes on freight or miscellaneous charges.

    If you select Advanced, you can select Taxable to use the tax details assigned to the vendor or site, Nontaxable, or Base On Vendor to use the tax schedule assigned to the vendor's purchase address.

In the section "Automatically Generating Purchase Orders," later in this chapter, you read about the options you set at the bottom of this dialog box.

15. **At the bottom of the Purchase Order Processing Setup dialog box, you can select Receivings User-Defined to display the Receivings User-Defined Fields Setup dialog box (see Figure 4-3) and set up labels for user-defined fields, lists, and dates that you use while entering shipments and shipment/invoices. When you finish, click OK to redisplay the Purchase Order Processing Setup dialog box.**

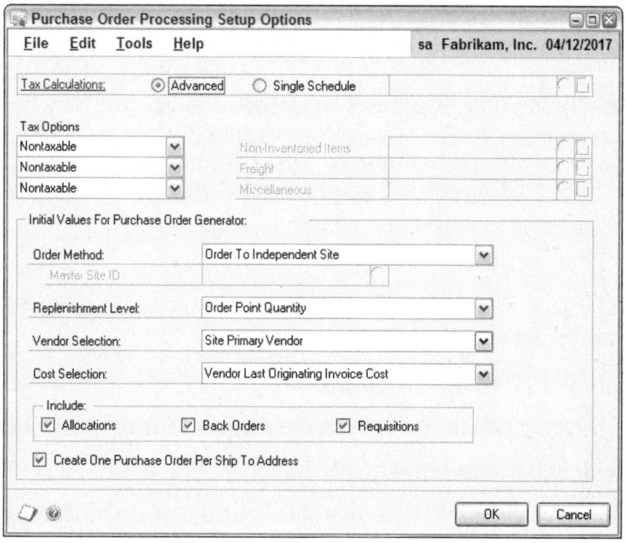

Figure 4-2: The Purchase Order Processing Setup Options dialog box.

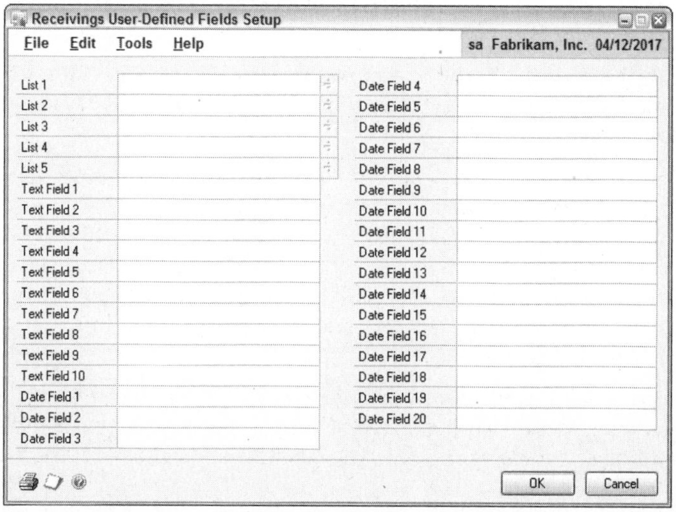

Figure 4-3: The Receivings User-Defined Fields Setup dialog box.

16. **Click OK to save your selections.**

Setting Up Buyers

If your company has several buyers working in the purchasing department, handling purchasing responsibilities, you may want to identify a buyer for each purchase order to track orders more easily. When more than one person does the buying for a company, you often find it necessary to identify the purchase orders for a particular person. By including a buyer on each purchase order, you can then print a report of purchase orders that you sort by Buyer ID.

Buyers do not have to be Dynamics GP users; they may or may not be linked to a user. If you enter a Buyer ID that you didn't assign to an existing user, Dynamics GP prompts you to either select an existing user or add a new buyer.

To set up a buyer, follow these steps:

1. **Choose Cards⇨Purchasing⇨Buyers to display the Buyer Maintenance window shown in Figure 4-4.**

2. **In the Buyer ID field, enter an ID.**

3. **In the Description field, enter a description for the buyer ID.**

4. **Choose Insert to save the buyer ID.**

   Dynamics GP displays the buyer ID in the list at the bottom of the window.

5. **Choose OK when you finish adding buyer IDs.**

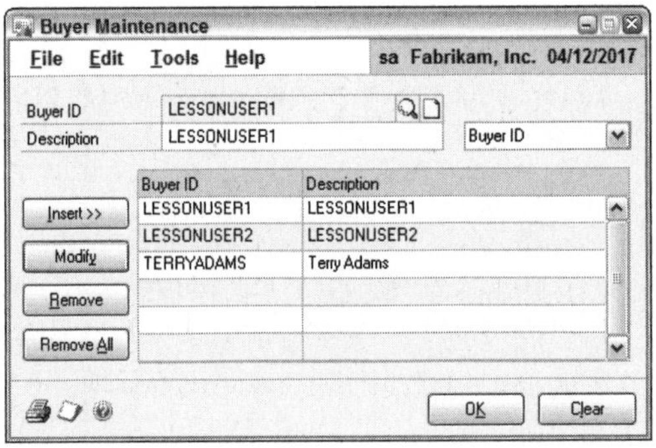

Figure 4-4:
The Buyer Maintenance window.

Buyer ID	Description
LESSONUSER1	LESSONUSER1
LESSONUSER2	LESSONUSER2
TERRYADAMS	Terry Adams

You can use the Buyer Maintenance window to modify the description for a buyer and to delete a buyer. If you delete a buyer ID that is linked to an active purchase order that isn't in history, Dynamics GP retains the buyer ID on that purchase order; in addition, Dynamics GP does not delete the associated Dynamics GP user ID.

Entering Purchase Orders

You use the Purchase Order Entry window to enter any of four different types of purchase orders:

- **Standard:** Lists the items you want delivered to your business; these items might be ones you receive into your inventory or they might be non-inventory items or services.

- **Blanket:** Lists the quantities of a single item that you want delivered to your business in a series of shipments, usually on specified dates.

- **Drop-ship:** Lists items that you want shipped directly to your customer. The vendor sends you a voucher, and you send an invoice to your customer.

- **Blanket drop-ship:** Lists the quantities of a single item that you want delivered directly to a customer in a series of shipments, usually on specific dates. The vendor sends you a voucher and you send an invoice to the customer.

Many companies only use standard purchase orders and ignore the other types.

Creating a standard purchase order

When you create a purchase order, Dynamics GP assigns the purchase order a status of "New." Later in this chapter, you read about printing the purchase order and releasing it.

To create a standard purchase order, follow these steps:

1. **Choose Transactions↔Purchasing↔Purchase Order Entry to display the Purchase Order Entry window shown in Figure 4-5.**

2. **From the Type list, choose the type of purchase order you want to create.**

3. **From the Buyer ID list, select a buyer.**

4. **Accept the default date or enter a date that Dynamics GP will use to update your purchasing records.**

Expansion button   Lookup button

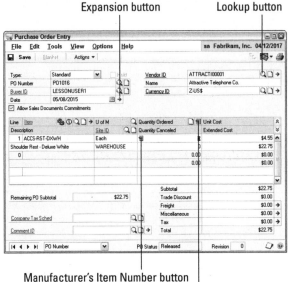

Manufacturer's Item Number button

Sales Commitments For Purchase Order button

Figure 4-5:
The
Purchase
Order Entry
window.

5. **Click the Date expansion button to display the Purchasing Date Entry window shown in Figure 4-6.**

   You can use this window to enter an expiration date for the purchase order and establish default required and promised dates for line items on the purchase order. Choose OK to redisplay the Purchase Order Entry window.

6. **Select the Allow Sales Document Commitments option to allow users to commit purchase order line items to matching sales order line items.**

   Dynamics GP displays the Link Purchase Order icon in the Quantity Ordered field beside line items with sales commitments. You can select the line item and click the Link Purchase Order icon in the Quantity Ordered heading to view, add, or delete commitments in the Sales Commitments for Purchase Order window (see Figure 4-7).

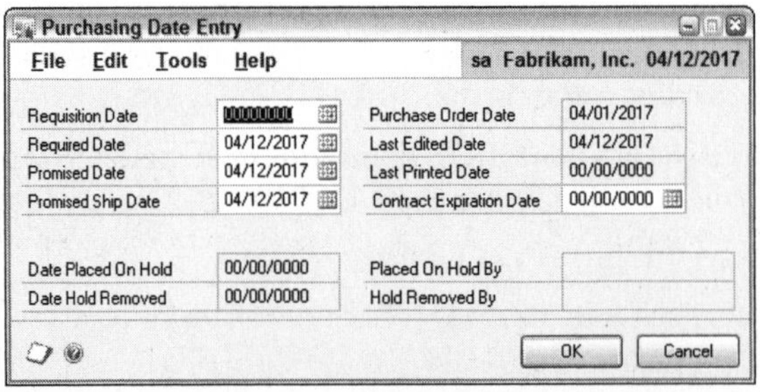

Figure 4-6:
The
Purchasing
Date Entry
window.

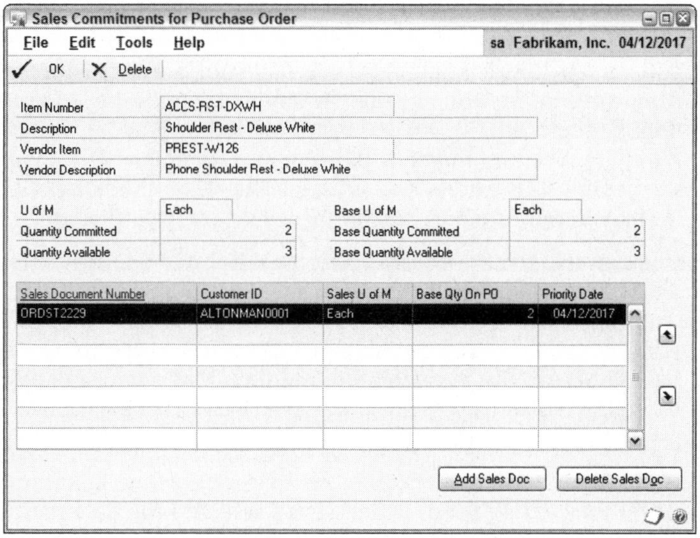

Figure 4-7:
The Sales Commitments for Purchase Order window.

When you click Add Sales Doc, Dynamics GP displays the sales documents containing orders for the item you're purchasing. Click an order and click Select to match the sales order to the selected line on your purchase order. Click OK to close the Sales Commitments for Purchase Order window and redisplay the Purchase Order Entry window (refer to Figure 4-5).

Just so you understand the flow of events, a user enters a sales order for a customer and then uses the Purchase button on the Sales Transaction entry window to generate a Purchase Order for one or more items on the Sales Order to order the goods to fulfill the customer's order.

7. **Click the Lookup button in the Vendor ID list to select the vendor from whom you order the item.**

8. **To add an item to the purchase order, click the Lookup button beside the Item column heading and select the item you want to order from the list that appears.**

   Dynamics GP displays the item's default description, unit of measure, and unit cost.

   If you don't select an existing item, Dynamics GP assumes that you are ordering a non-inventory item, and you then need to enter a description unit of measure and unit cost.

   You can click the Manufacturer's Item Number expansion button beside the Item column heading to open the Purchasing Manufacturer's Item Number Entry window and select or create a manufacturer's part number and description.

You must assign unique numbers to inventory items. In addition, when you purchase the item from a vendor, Dynamics GP also prompts you to enter a vendor item number if you have not previously ordered the item from the vendor. You can use the same number for the Dynamics GP item number and the vendor item number, or you can assign different numbers. You can toggle between your Dynamics GP item number and the vendor item number by pressing Ctrl+D or choosing Options⇨ Display Vendor Item in the Purchase Order Entry window.

9. **You can use the Purchasing Item Detail Entry window shown in Figure 4-8 to enter specific information such as the required and promised shipping dates for a line on your purchase order. To open this window, select a line on the purchase order and click the expansion button beside the Item column heading. Make your changes and then click Save to redisplay the Purchase Order Entry window.**

You can use different Release By dates for each line on a purchase order. Dynamics GP calculates the Release By Date if, in the Purchase Order Processing Setup window, you selected the Calculate Line Item's Release By Date Based on Vendor Lead Time option.

10. **In the Quantity Ordered field, enter the item quantity.**

11. **In the Unit Cost column, enter or modify the unit cost of the item.**

12. **Click the Lookup button in the Site ID field to select a site ID for the item.**

13. **Repeat Steps 8 through 12 to enter all the line items for the purchase order.**

Dynamics GP calculates taxes automatically as you enter items; you can change the tax schedule assigned to the purchase order using the Lookup button beside the Tax Schedule ID field.

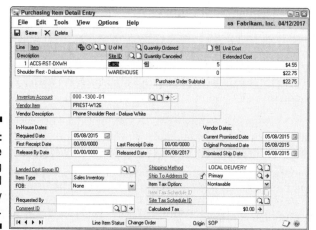

Figure 4-8: The Purchasing Item Detail Entry window.

14. **As appropriate, enter amounts for the trade discount, freight, and any miscellaneous amounts.**

    Dynamics GP automatically calculates the trade discount if you assigned a trade discount percentage to the vendor from whom you're purchasing the items.

15. **If you want to print a copy of the purchase order, choose File⇨Print.**

16. **Click Save to save the purchase order.**

Dynamics GP set the status of the purchase order you just created to "New"; you can view any purchase order's status by displaying it in the Purchase Order Entry window and noting the PO Status at the bottom of the window. The section "Editing Purchase Orders," later in this chapter, describes how to view and, if necessary, change the status of each line on a purchase order.

Creating a drop shipment purchase order

You create all purchase orders using basically the same steps — the ones outlined in the preceding section, "Creating a standard purchase order." When you create a drop shipment purchase order, you need to assign the purchase order to a customer and, immediately after you select the vendor in the Vendor ID field, Dynamics GP displays the Enter Drop-Ship Customer dialog box shown in Figure 4-9.

Figure 4-9:
The Enter Drop-Ship Customer dialog box.

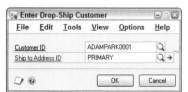

Click the Lookup button beside the Customer ID field to select the customer and then click OK; Dynamics GP redisplays the Purchase Order Entry dialog box so that you can finish filling out the purchase order.

Creating a blanket purchase order

You create blanket purchase orders in the Purchase Order Entry window using the steps in the section "Creating a standard purchase order," earlier in this chapter, and supplying some additional information along the way.

Dynamics GP handles a blanket purchase order differently than a standard or drop shipment purchase order, as you might expect. The first line item you enter for a blanket purchase order is called the *control blanket line item,* and Dynamics GP assigns the line number 0 to the control blanket line item. Dynamics GP uses this line item as the foundation of the blanket purchase order; on the control blanket line item, you enter the total amount you ultimately want shipped. Then, using the Purchasing Blanket Detail Entry window shown in Figure 4-10, you create lines for the blanket purchase order that identify the quantities and delivery dates for the individual shipments. For example, you might enter a quantity of 1,200 units on the control blanket line item and then set up twelve additional line items, each with a quantity of 100 and its own delivery date. To open the Purchasing Blanket Detail Entry window, fill in all of the Purchase Order Entry window, including the details for the control blanket line item, and then click the Blanket button in the Purchase Order Entry window.

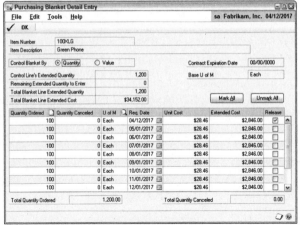

Figure 4-10:
The
Purchasing
Blanket
Detail Entry
window.

Dynamics GP doesn't include the control blanket line item in tax amounts or in the purchase order's subtotal, and the control blanket line item won't print on the purchase order. In addition, you can't receive items against the control blanket line item. If you delete the control blanket line item, Dynamics GP also deletes all blanket line items, and you cannot delete the control blanket line item if you have received items against any of the other lines on the purchase order.

A drop-ship blanket purchase order is nothing more than a combination of the drop shipment purchase order and a blanket purchase order. To create a drop-ship blanket purchase, complete the steps in the section, "Creating a standard purchase order." After you select the vendor, Dynamics GP asks for the customer ID. Then, fill in the control blanket line item, click the Blanket button, and create your individual shipments.

Automatically Generating Purchase Orders

If you specify a reorder point for an inventory item, you can automatically generate a purchase order to replenish the item. The purchase order generator analyzes inventory levels and suggests purchase order line items based on default settings and reorder levels. You can modify the suggested purchase orders before you create them.

You can set up Dynamics GP so that you automatically generate purchase order lines for only some of your inventory items; you don't need to automatically generate purchase orders for all items.

Setting up to automatically generate purchase orders

In this section, you read about establishing default reorder information that Dynamics GP applies to all items for which you intend to automatically create purchase order lines. You can change these settings for individual inventory items; see Chapter 10 for more information.

To set up default reorder information when automatically generating purchase order lines, follow these steps:

1. **On the Menu bar, select Microsoft Dynamics GP⇨Tools⇨Setup⇨ Purchasing⇨Purchase Order Processing.**

   The Purchase Order Processing Setup window appears.

2. **Click the Options button to display the Purchase Order Processing Setup Options dialog box shown in Figure 4-11.**

3. **In the Initial Values for Purchase Order Generator section, use the Order Method list box to select one of the following order methods as the default for automatically generated purchase order lines:**

   - *Order To Independent Site:* Specifies shipment of the items to the site that needs the items.

   - *Order To Master Site:* Specifies shipment of the items to a central location — called a *master site* — and subsequently distributed to other sites called *subordinate sites*.

4. **If you selected Order To Master Site in Step 3, select a master site.**

   When determining the amount to order, Dynamics GP combines demand from all subordinate sites with demand for the master site you select.

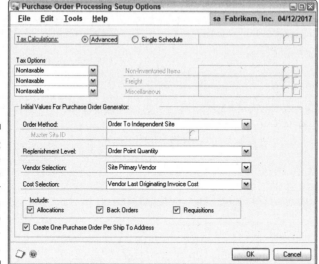

Figure 4-11:
The
Purchase
Order
Processing
Setup
Options dia-
log box.

5. **From the Replenishment Level list box, select a default replenishment level:**

   • *Order Point Quantity:* Orders the quantity that will bring available inventory up to the order point value defined for the item.

   • *Order-Up-To Level:* Orders the quantity that will bring available inventory up to the order-up-to level value defined for the item. If the order-up-to level is zero or less than the Order Point Quantity, Dynamics GP uses the Order Point Quantity.

   • *Vendor EOQ (available only if the Order Method you chose in Step 3 is Order To Independent):* Orders the economic order quantity that is defined for the item and a selected vendor.

6. **If you selected Order To Independent Site in Step 3, indicate which vendor to use for purchase orders.**

   If you chose Order to Master Site in Step 3, Dynamics GP uses the master site's vendor selection to determine the vendor.

7. **If you selected Order To Independent Site in Step 3, indicate which item cost to use for purchase orders.**

   If you chose Order to Master Site in Step 3, Dynamics GP uses the master site's cost selection to determine the cost.

8. **In the Include section, select**

   • *Allocations* to make Dynamics GP subtract the allocated quantity from the current supply when calculating the required quantity.

- *Back Orders* to make Dynamics GP subtract the back-ordered quantity from the current supply when calculating the required quantity.

- *Requisitions* to make Dynamics GP subtract the requisitioned quantity from the current supply when calculating the required quantity.

9. **Choose OK to close the window and redisplay the Purchase Order Processing Setup window.**

10. **Click OK again to close the Purchase Order Processing Setup window.**

Automatically generate purchase order lines

When you automatically generate lines for purchase orders, Dynamics GP searches through the inventory items and sites that you set up to use the Purchase Order Generator and then displays suggested purchase order lines. Follow these steps:

1. **Choose Transactions⇨Purchasing⇨Purchase Order Generator to display the Generate Suggested Purchase Orders window shown in Figure 4-12.**

2. **You can use the Restrictions section to restrict Dynamics GP's search for items to include on purchase orders.**

3. **In the Options section, you can opt to ignore subordinate sites and items with no Vendor ID.**

Figure 4-12: Use this window to establish settings for Dynamics GP to use when generating suggested purchase orders.

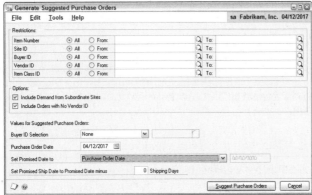

4. In the Values for Suggested Purchase Orders, you can

- Select a particular buyer.

- Establish the purchase order date.

- Establish the promised date.

- Establish the promised shipping date.

5. Click Suggest Purchase Orders.

A window appears that helps you monitor Dynamics GP's progress while searching for items to suggest. When Dynamics GP finishes, the Suggested Purchase Orders Preview window appears (see Figure 4-13).

By default, Dynamics GP marks all items in the window unless attempting to include the item on a purchase order will result in an error or a warning.

You can include items marked with a warning symbol — an exclamation point in a yellow triangle — when you generate purchase orders, but you cannot include items marked with an error symbol — a red X in a circle.

6. Remove the checkmark in the Include column beside any item for which you don't want to generate a purchase order.

7. You can change the vendor, the unit of measure, the order quantity, and the unit cost.

If you change the vendor, Dynamics GP might recalculate the quantities, promised dates, FOB, unit of measure, and the unit cost.

If you change the unit of measure, Dynamics GP doesn't automatically update the quantity, but it does recalculate the unit cost.

To view the details for a particular item, click anywhere in the item's line and then click the expansion arrow beside the Item Number column heading. Dynamics GP displays the Suggested Purchase Order Detail window.

8. Choose Generate Purchase Orders.

When Dynamics GP finishes creating the specified purchase orders, a Purchase Order Generated report appears, listing the purchase orders. Any errors appear in an error log that prints after the Purchase Order Generated report.

Dynamics GP sets the status of the purchase orders to "New"; the section "Releasing purchase orders," later in this chapter, describes how to change the status of a purchase order to "Released."

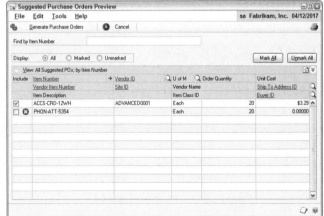

Figure 4-13:
The
Suggested
Purchase
Orders
Preview
window.

Managing Purchase Orders

After you enter purchase orders, you may want to make changes to the information. Or, you may want to use lines on one purchase order to create lines on another purchase order or to create an entire purchase order. You will also want to print purchase orders to release them to vendors so that the vendors can fill the purchase orders. Finally, you may need to remove purchase orders from Microsoft Dynamics GP because you won't be releasing them to vendors.

Viewing the status of purchase orders

Before you try to make changes to a purchase order, you should understand the statuses Microsoft Dynamics GP assigns to purchase orders, because these statuses affect the kinds of changes you can make.

The status of each purchase order appears at the bottom of the Purchase Order Entry window, in the PO Status field (see Figure 4-14).

You also can view and, in some cases, edit the status of any line on a purchase order using the Edit Purchase Order Status window shown in Figure 4-15. To display this window, choose Transactions⇨Purchasing⇨Edit Purchase Orders.

Select the purchase order you want to view. Then, in the line item section, click the Status arrows to control the amount of detail Dynamics GP displays.

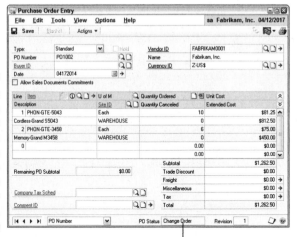

Figure 4-14: You can view the status of a purchase order in the Purchase Order Entry window.

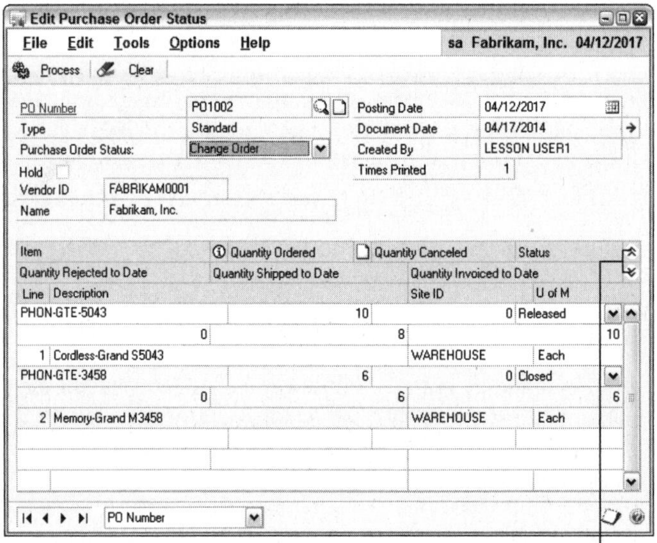

PO Status field

Figure 4-15: In the Edit Purchase Order Status window, you can view the status of each line of a purchase order.

Status arrows

Dynamics GP assigns one of six statuses to a purchase order, with the following meanings:

✔ **New:** You have entered but not sent the purchase order to a vendor. You can make any kind of change.

✔ **Released:** You have printed the purchase order and you haven't changed any lines on the purchase order.

✔ **Change Order:** You have made changes to at least one line of a purchase order that you previously released. You can manually change the status of a line from Closed or Received to Change Order.

✔ **Received:** You have accounted for, either by receiving or by canceling, the entire quantity you ordered but not yet matched the receipt to a voucher.

✔ **Closed:** You have accounted for, either by receiving or canceling, all items on the purchase order and you have matched invoices to all items you received.

✔ **Canceled:** You have canceled all line items on the purchase order.

Three of the statuses have "line item" meanings as well as "purchase order" meanings. Above, I've listed the "purchase order" meanings. When you see the Released status on a line item in the Edit Purchase Order Status window, you have released the purchase order; you may or may not have received part of the item listed on the line. When you see the Closed status on a line item in the Edit Purchase Order Status window, you have received or canceled all items on the line and matched received amounts on the line to a voucher. When you see the Canceled status on a line item in the Edit Purchase Order Status window, you haven't received any of the items listed on the line and you won't be processing anything against the line in the future.

In addition to identifying line status, you can also determine the amount remaining that you haven't yet received by subtracting the sum of the Quantity Shipped To Date and the Quantity Canceled from the Quantity Ordered.

Editing purchase orders

To edit any purchase order, you can redisplay it in the Purchase Order Entry window and make your changes. The changes you can make to a purchase order depend on its status and, possibly, the status of each line on the purchase order as well.

If the purchase order's status is New, you can make any changes to it that you want — add new lines, delete existing lines, change quantities, and so on. If the purchase order's status is Released, you can make changes; once you save the purchase order, Dynamics GP changes the status to Change Order. You also can make changes to purchase orders with a status of Change Order.

In some cases, you cannot make changes. For example, you cannot cancel a closed purchase order, and you cannot cancel the received portions of lines on a released purchase order. If you try to make changes you can't make,

Dynamics GP will display a message that explains the problem. You can then display the purchase order in the Edit Purchase Order Status window to view the status of each line and determine the changes you can make.

Canceling purchase orders

You may want to cancel all of a purchase order or some lines on a purchase. The process is simple: select Transactions⇨Purchasing⇨Purchase Order Entry to display the Purchase Order Entry window (see Figure 4-16). Select the purchase order you want to cancel or the one containing lines you want to cancel. Then, in the Quantity Canceled field on the line of the item you want to cancel, type in the quantity you want to cancel. To cancel the entire purchase order, repeat this process for all lines on the purchase order or display it in the Edit Purchase Order Status window and change its status to Canceled.

You cannot cancel items you have already received.

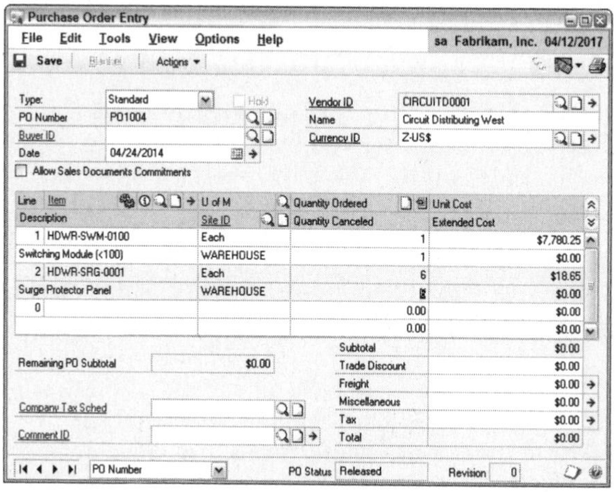

Figure 4-16:
Use the
Purchase
Order Entry
window
to cancel
items on a
purchase
order.

Copying purchase order information

It's not unusual to find that you order the same things with some regular frequency. Instead of redoing all the work involved in creating a new purchase order, you can use information on an existing purchase order to create an entirely new purchase order. You can copy any type of purchase order — standard, blanket, drop-ship, or drop-ship blanket — and Dynamics GP automatically creates another purchase order of the same type.

1. **Select Transactions⇨Purchasing⇨Purchase Order Entry to display the Purchase Order Entry window (see Figure 4-17).**

2. **Click Actions.**

3. **Click Create and Copy New PO.**

   Dynamics GP displays the Copy a Purchase Order window (see Figure 4-18).

4. **Select a purchase order to copy.**

5. **If appropriate, change the vendor, currency, and document date for the new purchase order you are creating.**

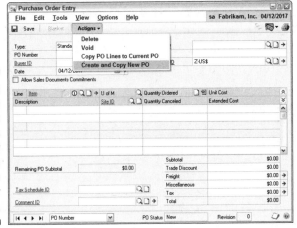

Figure 4-17:
Use the Actions menu to copy existing purchase order information.

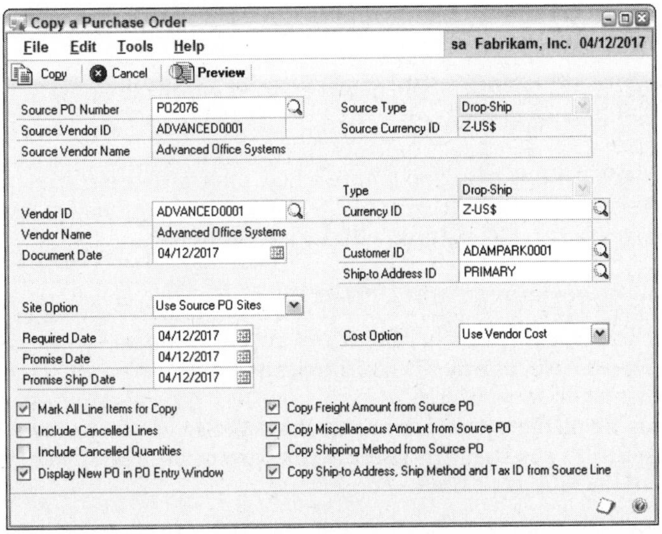

Figure 4-18:
The Copy a Purchase Order window.

6. **For drop-ship purchase orders, select a Customer ID and a Ship-to Address ID.**

7. **Make a selection from the Site Option list box.**

   If you select Use Site, select a site in the field that appears.

8. **Enter dates in the Required Date, Promise Date, and Promise Ship Date fields.**

9. **Make a selection from the Cost Option list box.**

10. **Use the check boxes at the bottom of the window to select the copy options you want to use.**

11. **To view and, if appropriate, modify lines before you copy them, click the Preview button at the top of the window to display the Preview Line Items window shown in Figure 4-19.**

    You can select specific lines to include on the new purchase order, and you can change the Order Quantity and Unit Cost. Click OK when you finish to redisplay the Copy a Purchase Order window.

Figure 4-19: The Preview Line Items window.

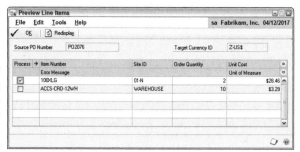

12. **Click Copy.**

    Dynamics GP displays the newly created purchase order in the Purchase Order Entry window.

The preceding steps help you create a new purchase order from an existing purchase order. You also can copy lines from one purchase order to another, using basically the same steps, with two exceptions:

✔ Before you perform Step 2, select the purchase order onto which you want to add lines, and

✔ In Step 3, Select Copy PO Lines to Current PO.

Dynamics GP displays the Copy a Purchase Order window shown earlier in Figure 4-18, and you then complete Steps 4 through 12 to select the purchase order and the line you want to copy.

Releasing purchase orders

When you release a purchase order to a vendor for fulfillment, you typically provide the vendor with a physical copy of the purchase order. Luckily, in Dynamics GP, printing the purchase order also sets the purchase order's status to "Released."

You can print and release an individual purchase order or you can print and release multiple purchase orders simultaneously. Although the steps are a little different, the general concept is the same.

To print an individual purchase order, open the Purchase Order Entry window by choosing Transactions➪Purchasing➪Purchase Order Entry. Then, select the purchase order you want to print and choose File Print. Dynamics GP displays the Purchase Order Print Options dialog box shown in Figure 4-20.

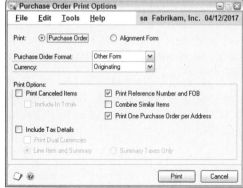

Figure 4-20: The Purchase Order Print Options dialog box.

From the Purchase Order Format list box, select to print the purchase order on blank paper or using another form.

You can choose from five different purchase order formats, but the chances are good that none of these built-in formats will look exactly the way you want your purchase orders to look. The formats can be modified using the GP Report Writer to, for example, add your company logo. Typically, your Dynamics GP consultant will modify one or more of these formats for you during your implementation.

In the Print Options section, check boxes to print canceled lines, tax details, the Reference Number you entered in the Dynamics GP Item Maintenance window, and the FOB designation. You also can opt to combine similar items; Dynamics GP considers items similar when the item number, unit of measure, originating unit cost, required date, shipping method, and address information are the same. And, you can opt to print a single purchase order even if the address and shipping methods for individual line items are different. If you choose this option, Dynamics GP prints the address and shipping method for each purchase order item on the purchase order.

Click Print to print the purchase order.

To print multiple purchase orders, you don't use the Purchase Order Entry window; instead, you use the Print Purchasing Documents window shown in Figure 4-21. You can open this window by choosing Transactions⇨Purchasing⇨Print Purchasing Documents.

At the top of the window, select Purchase Orders to indicate the type of document you want to print. From the Purchase Order Format list box, select Blank Paper or the form that has been modified to meet your needs. You can sort the order in which purchase orders print by purchase order number or Vendor ID.

In the Print Options section, you can make the same choices described above, with one addition: You can opt to reprint purchase orders you printed previously.

In the Include PO Status section, select the boxes that describe the types of purchase orders you want to print.

You can print a range of purchase orders using any one of the options listed in the Ranges list box. At the bottom of the box, you can insert or remove restrictions for selected range.

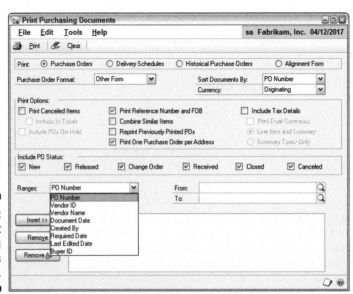

Figure 4-21: The Print Purchasing Documents window.

Click Print, and Dynamics GP prints all of the purchase orders that meet the criteria you established.

Clearing out those dusty old POs

There are three ways to "get rid" of purchase orders:

- ✔ You can delete them,
- ✔ You can void them, or
- ✔ You can remove them if they are complete.

To delete or to void . . . that is the question

You can delete or void purchase orders that you haven't printed — purchase orders with a PO Status of New — from the Purchase Order Entry window. Choose Transactions⇨Purchasing⇨Purchase Order Entry. Then, select the purchase order you want to delete, click the Actions drop-down menu, and then click Delete or Void.

You cannot delete a purchase order with a status of New if you have entered unposted receipts or vouchers.

So, when do you choose Delete and when do you choose Void? Well, if you don't care to keep any kind of record that a purchase order ever existed, you can delete it. When you delete a purchase order, Dynamics GP removes the purchase order information from the system and makes the purchase order number available for so that you can reuse it.

If you maintain history, voiding a purchase order might be a better choice. When you void a purchase order, Dynamics GP moves purchase order information to history and doesn't make purchase order numbers available for you to reuse until you remove history, if you're keeping history. If you're not keeping history, voiding removes purchase order information.

If you keep history and void purchase orders, you'll be able to determine why a purchase order number is missing or out of sequence and you can view information about voided purchase orders using the purchasing inquiry windows or by printing the Purchasing Voided Journal or the Purchase Order History Report.

Removing completed purchase orders

Completed purchase orders are ones that have a status of Closed or Canceled. You can remove closed or canceled purchase orders if you haven't yet moved them to history. To keep your company running smoothly, you should remove completed purchase orders on some regular basis. If you keep purchase order history and you remove completed purchase orders, Dynamics GP moves the completed purchase orders to history. If you don't keep history, Dynamics GP deletes completed purchase orders from your company.

Always make sure to make a backup of your company before you purge any data in Dynamics GP such as removing completed purchase orders, just in case something goes wrong and you need to restore the data.

To remove completed purchase orders, follow these steps:

1. **Select Microsoft Dynamics GP⇨Tools⇨Routines⇨Purchasing⇨Remove Completed Purchase Orders to open the Remove Completed Purchase Orders window shown in Figure 4-22.**

Figure 4-22:
The Remove
Completed
Purchase
Orders
window.

2. **From the Document Range list, select a type of range and then use the From and To boxes to enter the first and last records in the selected range.**

3. **In the Restrictions section, choose Insert to establish the range you've chosen to remove.**

You can select purchase orders to remove using multiple document ranges and associated restrictions. For example, you can set up a Purchase Order Number range (PO001 to PO1000) and a Vendor ID range (Atlas to Gardner). Each range you establish appears in the Restrictions box after you click Insert.

4. **If you want to manually select purchase orders to remove, click Restrictions.**

Dynamics GP displays the Restrict Purchasing Documents window, where you make your selections.

5. **Choose the Process button in either the Restrict purchasing Documents window or the Remove Completed Purchase Orders window.**

Dynamics GP removes the selected purchase orders and then prints the Completed PO Removal Report, which lists the purchase orders that were removed.

To delete purchase order history, select Microsoft Dynamics GP⇨Tools⇨ Utilities⇨Purchasing⇨Remove Purchasing History.

Receiving Stuff

When you order stuff using purchase orders, the stuff will arrive with or without the vendor's invoice. If the stuff arrives with the invoice, you can record the receipt and the vendor invoice simultaneously, automatically matching the shipment to the vendor invoice. If the stuff arrives separately from the vendor invoice, you record the shipment separately from the vendor invoice. And, it doesn't matter if the stuff arrives before or after the vendor invoice; you still record them separately. You use the steps in the next section to record shipments that arrive with or without the vendor's invoice. You use the steps in the section, "Recording vendor invoices without shipments," later in this chapter, to record a vendor invoice that arrives separately from a shipment.

You can enter the information in batches, as you see in the sections that follow, or as individual transactions.

Recording a receipt

You use the steps in this section to receive items against purchase order line items with a status of New, Released, Change Order, or Received. Dynamics GP updates the quantity on hand for the items received, and, if you receive an invoice, the vendor's account.

If the stuff arrives without the vendor's invoice, you use the steps in this section to record the shipment, and, when the vendor's invoice arrives, you use the steps in the next section, "Recording vendor invoices without shipments," to match the vendor's invoice to the shipment.

After these steps, you'll find some tips to help you speed up the receiving process and handle some special cases, such as receiving all items on a purchase order and receiving items from multiple purchase orders.

1. **Choose Transactions⇨Purchasing⇨Receivings Transaction Entry to display the window shown in Figure 4-23.**

The Auto-Rev button

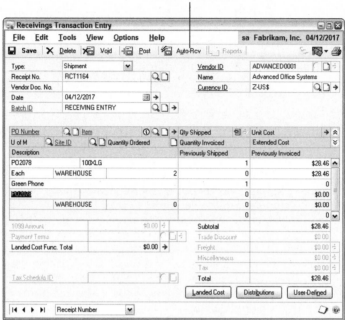

2. In the Type box, select the type of receipt you want to record:

- Select *Shipment/Invoice* if you received both merchandise and a bill from the vendor.

- Select *Shipment* if you received merchandise only with no vendor bill.

  When you receive the vendor's bill associated with the shipment, use the steps in the next section to record it and match it to the shipment receipt.

- Select *In-Transit Inventory* if you are receiving merchandise you transferred from one site to another.

3. Press Tab to let Dynamics GP insert the next available number in the Receipt No. field.

4. In the Vendor Doc. No. field, record the vendor's document number; this field is required for Shipment/Invoice transactions.

5. In the Date field, enter the receipt date.

You can assign a separate posting date for the General Ledger. Click the Date expansion button to display the Receivings Date Entry window, where you can specify different dates for the receipt date and the posting date.

If you set up posting options to post transactions recorded in the Receivings Transactions Entry window by batch posting date, Dynamics GP will use the batch date to record the associated journal entries in the General Ledger if you post the transaction as part of a batch instead of posting the transaction separately.

6. **In the Batch ID field, enter a batch number or use the Lookup button to select an existing batch.**

   Dynamics GP assigns the user date as the default batch posting date; to change the batch posting date, click the expansion button beside the Batch ID field to display the Purchasing Batch Entry window, where you can change the posting date.

7. **Use the Lookup button in the Vendor ID field to select the vendor from whom you received goods.**

8. **Click the Lookup button beside the PO Number heading to display a list of available purchase orders from the selected vendor and choose the purchase order on which the merchandise was ordered.**

   If you opted to select the Allow Receiving Without a Purchase Order option in Purchase Order Processing Setup, you can leave the PO Number field blank.

9. **Click the Lookup button beside the Item heading to display the Purchase Order Items window shown in Figure 4-24.**

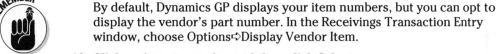

   By default, Dynamics GP displays your item numbers, but you can opt to display the vendor's part number. In the Receivings Transaction Entry window, choose Options⇨Display Vendor Item.

10. **Click an item to receive and then click Select.**

   Dynamics GP redisplays the Receivings Transaction Entry window with the item filled in.

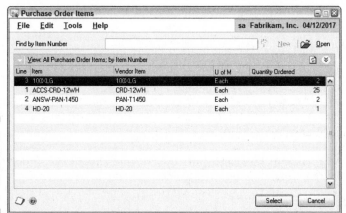

Figure 4-24: The Purchase Order Items window.

11. **Enter the quantity you received of the item.**

    Dynamics GP displays the Purchasing Lot Number Entry window or the Purchasing Serial Number Entry window if the item you select needs a lot or serial number. If you use multiple bins, you also can enter a bin number for the serial or lot number. Dynamics GP displays the Bin Quantity Entry window if you receive an item that you don't track by lot or serial numbers but requires bin information.

    Dynamics GP displays an icon in the Qty Shipped field for purchase order line items with sales commitments. Select a line item and click the button next to the Qty Shipped heading to view or prioritize commitments in the Sales Commitments for Purchase Order window.

12. **If necessary and your options in Purchase Order Processing Setup permit, you can select a Site ID other than the one specified on the purchase order to receive line items to a different location.**

    If you use multiple bins and you change the site ID, Dynamics GP replaces your previous bin selections with the default bin assigned to the new site ID. In addition, if you track the item by serial or lot numbers, Dynamics GP removes your previous lot number or serial number selections and displays the Purchasing Lot Number Entry window or the Purchasing Serial Number Entry window so that you can assign lot numbers or serial numbers.

13. **You can edit the unit cost or extended cost, if the Purchase Order Processing Setup options permit.**

14. **In the Quantity Invoiced field, enter the number of items listed on the vendor's invoice.**

    This field is not available on shipment transactions.

15. **Repeat Steps 6 through 12 to record additional receipts; repeat Steps 7 through 12 to add lines to the current receipt.**

    You can receive items from multiple purchase orders by entering or selecting a different purchase order number in a new row.

16. **Enter trade discount, freight, and miscellaneous amounts as appropriate.**

    You can choose Distributions to open the Purchasing Distribution Entry window, where you can change account distributions. And, if you use landed costs, choose Landed Cost to open the Receivings Landed Cost Apportionment Entry window, where you can add landed costs to all line items on a receipt. You can enter user-defined information for this receipt if you choose User-Defined and display the Receivings User-Defined Fields Entry window. The User-Defined fields pertain to the entire transaction, not to individual line items.

17. **Choose Save or Post.**

You cannot post the transaction in the Receivings Transaction Entry window if you entered a batch. If you entered a single receipt and opt to post it, Dynamics GP might print one or more posting journals and distribution breakdown registers; Dynamics GP prints the reports based on the options you set in the Posting Setup window.

Suppose that you receive a shipment, with or without the vendor's invoice, and the shipment completely fills an existing purchase order. To quickly receive all the lines on a purchase order, complete Steps 1 through 6 above. Then, click the Auto-Rcv button (refer to Figure 4-23) to display the Select Purchase Order dialog box shown in Figure 4-25.

Use the Lookup button to select a purchase order and click Receive All to redisplay the Receivings Transaction Entry window with all lines on the purchase order filled in as fully received. To view the details of the purchase order, you can click View Details before clicking Receive All; Dynamics GP displays the Select Purchase Order Items window shown in Figure 4-26.

Figure 4-25:
The Select Purchase Order dialog box.

Figure 4-26:
The Select Purchase Order Items window.

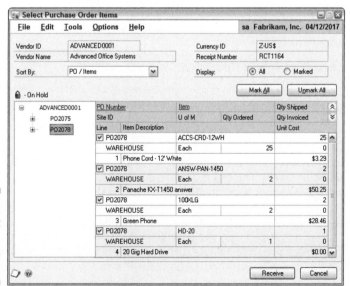

Using this window, you can simultaneously receive items from multiple purchase orders. In the left side of the window, click a purchase order; Dynamics GP displays the lines on that purchase order in the right side of the window. Click the box at the beginning of a line to include that line in the receipt.

You can sort items in this window using the Sort By list.

Finally, you can receive items that don't appear on purchase orders as long as you selected the option to permit this action in the Purchase Order Processing Setup window. You use the Receivings Transaction Entry window and the steps outlined above, but don't fill in a purchase order number in the PO Number field for items you wish to receive that didn't appear on a purchase order.

Recording vendor invoices without shipments

When the vendor's bill for a purchase order arrives separately from the stuff, enter the shipment receipt and invoice receipts separately. You can match the shipments you have already entered to the vendor bills as you enter them.

Follow these steps to enter an invoice receipt:

1. **Choose Transactions⇨Purchasing⇨Enter/Match Invoices to display the Purchasing Invoice Entry window shown in Figure 4-27.**

The Auto-Invoice button

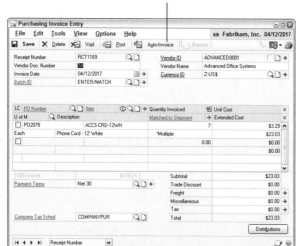

Figure 4-27: The Purchasing Invoice Entry window.

2. **In the Vendor Doc. No. field, record the vendor's document number; this field is required for Shipment/Invoice transactions.**

3. **In the Date field, enter the invoice date.**

   You can assign a separate posting date for the General Ledger. Click the Date expansion button to display the Purchasing Invoice Date Entry window, where you can specify different dates for the invoice date and the posting date.

4. **In the Batch ID field, enter a batch number or use the Lookup button to select an existing batch.**

   Dynamics GP assigns the user date as the default batch posting date; to change the batch posting date, click the expansion button beside the Batch ID field to display the Purchasing Batch Entry window, where you can change the posting date.

5. **Use the Lookup button in the Vendor ID field to select the vendor from whom you received goods.**

   You use the LC check box to record a landed cost. You don't complete Steps 6 or 7 if you check this box. Instead, you click the Lookup button in the Item heading to display the Landed Costs window, select an item, and then enter the purchase order in the Match Options window.

6. **Click the Lookup button beside the PO Number heading to display a list of available purchase orders from the selected vendor and choose the purchase order associated with the vendor's invoice.**

7. **Click the Auto-Invoice button to display the Select Purchase Order Items window shown in Figure 4-28.**

   You can select an item and provide the quantity invoiced, but that approach generally takes longer, especially when you have received several shipments for several line items.

   Dynamics GP automatically selects the items on the selected purchase order for which you have received merchandise. Dynamics GP also suggests automatically that the invoice you create should account for the total amount you have received to date.

8. **If necessary, change the value in the Qty Invoiced field.**

9. **Click Invoice.**

   Dynamics GP redisplays the Purchasing Invoice Entry window.

   If multiple shipments exist for the line item, Dynamics GP displays "Multiple" in the Matched to Shipment field. You can click the Expansion button beside the field to display the Match Shipments to Invoice window shown in Figure 4-29, which identifies the shipments to which Dynamics GP matched the invoice. Click OK to redisplay the Purchasing Invoice Entry window.

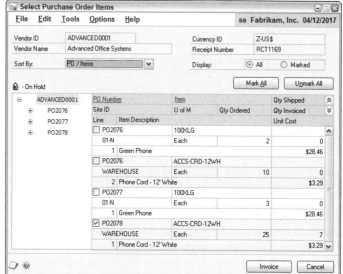

Figure 4-28:
The Select
Purchase
Order Items
window.

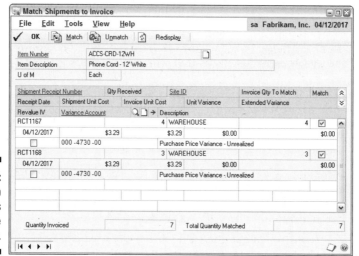

Figure 4-29:
The Match
Shipments
to Invoice
window.

If an icon appears in the Quantity Invoiced field, the line item is a
drop-ship purchase order line item with sales commitments. Select the
line item and choose the button next to the Quantity Invoiced heading
to view commitments in the Sales Commitments for Purchase Order
window.

10. **Enter trade discount, freight, and miscellaneous amounts.**

11. **To make changes to account distributions, choose Distributions to
    open the Purchasing Invoice Distribution Entry window.**

12. **Click Save.**

Posting receipts

To update your data in the Purchase Order Processing module, you must post batches you enter. If you enter individual transactions, you must post them at the time that you enter them, so, the information in this section only applies to transactions entered in batches.

Before you post batches, you may want to review the transactions in them. To review batches, display the Purchasing Batch Entry window (choose Transactions⇨Purchasing⇨Purchasing Batches). Use the Lookup button to select the batch you want to review; then, click File⇨Print to print an edit list.

After you review the edit listing, you can post batches by clicking the Post button. After the batch posts, posting journals you specified in the Posting Setup window when you set up the Purchase Order Processing module will print.

To post several batches — both Purchase Order Processing batches and Payables Management batches — at one time, follow these steps:

1. **From the Transactions section of the Content pane, choose Series Post to open the Purchasing Series Posting window (see Figure 4-30).**

2. **Select the batch(es) you want to post.**

3. **Click the Post button.**

   Dynamics GP prints the appropriate posting journals and updates your Payables Management module files.

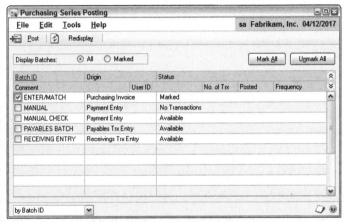

Figure 4-30: The Purchasing Series Posting window.

Chapter 5

Billing Your Customers

*Y*ou wouldn't be in business if you didn't have customers. And, as you sell goods or services to your customers, you create invoices that describe the sales. In this chapter, I describe how you can use the Receivables Management module, part of the Sales series, to create invoices for your customers and, when necessary, create and apply credit memos for customers. Depending on the needs of your business, you might want to create quotes and sales orders before creating invoices; you use the Sales Order Processing module, described in Chapter 6, to create these types of documents. Or, if your business predominantly manages projects, you can use the Project Accounting module to create invoices. Space doesn't permit me to cover the Project Accounting module in detail, but, in this chapter, I do describe how you choose the module to use to create invoices.

In Chapter 7, you can read about handling payments you receive from customers.

Knowing Where to Do the Billing

In Microsoft Dynamics GP, you can create invoices to send to customers in different ways.

Using the Receivables Management module, you can create an invoice that doesn't list products but simply lists sales dollar information; if you print this invoice, it doesn't contain any descriptive information. Companies that use customized billing systems to create invoices can use the Receivables Transaction Entry window in Dynamics GP to record sales and update Dynamics GP data for reporting purposes. You also use this window to create a variety of transactions that increase, do not affect, or decrease a customer's account balance. Read about creating these transactions in the section, "Creating Receivables Management Transactions," later in this chapter.

If you use the Sales series — both the Receivables Management module and Sales Order Processing module — and you want to create an invoice that details line items or is related to a quote or sales order, you use the method described in Chapter 6 to create the invoice.

You may notice an option for Invoice Entry among the Sales series transaction choices. This window is a throwback to a time before the Sales Order Processing module existed. Most people don't bother with the Invoice Entry window.

You also can create invoices if you use the Project Accounting module. Most people use the Project Accounting module when the bulk of the work they perform is project-oriented and they want to track revenues and expenses associated with each project or job. In situations where you work on projects, you tend to bill on some regular basis; in the Project Accounting module, you set up billing cycles that include information on billing frequency. You can assign billing cycles to customers (and projects and contracts — cards you establish in the Project Accounting module) and then generate bills for the billing cycle; you have the opportunity to specify whether to limit the bills you generate to customers, projects, and contracts assigned to the billing cycle. So, if you use the Project Accounting module, you should generate bills related to projects and contracts using the tools available in the Project Accounting module.

Establishing Receivables Management Options

To make the Receivables Management module work most efficiently, you should establish some default information. You use the Receivables Management Setup window to establish this default information, including the aging periods you want to use, how to apply documents, passwords needed to perform certain activities, and default information to save time when you create customer invoices.

Before you set up Receivables Management, be sure to finish setting up the system overall and the General Ledger.

To set default Receivables Management options, follow these steps:

1. **On the Menu bar, select Microsoft Dynamics GP⇨Tools⇨Setup⇨ Sales⇨Receivables to display the Receivables Management Setup dialog box shown in Figure 5-1.**

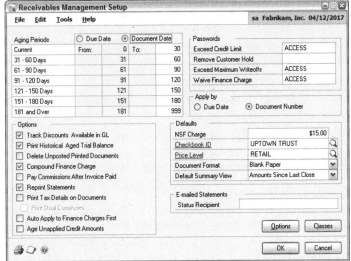

Figure 5-1:
The
Receivables
Manage-
ment Setup
dialog box.

2. **Use the Aging Periods grid in the upper-left portion of the dialog box to set up the aging periods you want to use for open item customers and specify the way you want to age documents — by Due Date or by Document Date.**

The system defines two aging periods for balance forward customers: current and non-current.

To understand the difference between aging by Document Date or by Due Date, assume you have an invoice dated May 5, with a due date of June 5, and you age documents on the end of the month. On June 30, if you opt to age by Document Date, the invoice would be 54 days old. If you opt to age by Due Date, the same invoice would be 23 days on June 30.

For open-item customers, you can establish up to seven aging periods; if you age by Document Date, you must establish at least one aging period, and if you age by Due Date, you must establish at least two aging periods. Set starting value for any aging period as one day later than the ending value of the previous period. The entry in the To field for the last period you establish must be 999.

Dynamics GP displays information for the current period and the follow-ing three aging periods you define on Aged Trial Balance reports. If you use more than four aging periods including the current period, add them to the Aged Trial Balance reports using the Report Writer.

3. In the Options section, check any of the following boxes, as appropriate:

- *Track Discounts Available in GL:* Tracks discounts separately from Accounts Receivable. If you choose this option, Dynamics GP posts the discounts to the account you assign to Terms Discounts Available in the Customer Maintenance window. If you choose not to track discounts, Dynamics GP posts the discounts available to the Accounts Receivable account, not to a separate account.

- *Print Historical Aged Trial Balance:* Retains transaction history for all customers and allows you to print the Historical Aged Trial Balance.

- *Delete Unposted Printed Documents:* Allows users to delete an unposted, printed document from the Receivables Transaction Entry window or the Receivables Batch Entry window.

- *Compound Finance Charge:* Assesses finance charges on past due finance charges. In some jurisdictions, assessing finance charges on finance charges isn't legal, so I recommend that you check with your accountant before choosing this option. If you choose this option, Dynamics GP includes unapplied finance charges as part of customer balances when you assess finance charges. If you don't choose this option, Dynamics GP excludes finance charges from customer balances when you assess finance charges.

- *Pay Commissions After Invoice:* Tracks commissions for salespeople only after customers pay invoices. If you don't choose this option, Dynamics GP treats the commission as payable as soon as you post an invoice.

- *Reprint Statements:* Allows users to reprint customer statements at any time. When you choose this option, Dynamics GP saves statement data each time you print statements, so each statement will be available for reprinting. You can then reprint a statement, but Dynamics GP marks it as a reprinted statement.

- *Print Tax Details on Documents:* Includes summary tax information on all documents printed from the Sales Transaction Entry and Sales Transaction Entry Zoom windows. If you choose this option and you're using Multicurrency Management, you also can choose Print Dual Currencies to print summary tax information in both the originating and functional currencies on sales documents that include tax details.

- *Auto Apply to Finance Charges First:* Automatically applies credit documents such as credit memos or payments to finance charge documents before invoices.

- *Age Unapplied Credit Amounts:* Ages unapplied credit amounts using the document date in relation to the aging date and your aging periods. If you age documents by Due Date and you choose this option, the due date for unapplied credit documents will be the same as the document date.

Aging *unapplied* credit amounts does not affect the way that Dynamics GP ages fully or partially applied credit documents.

4. **In the Passwords section, enter passwords to restrict the users who can**

   • Enter transactions that exceed a customer's credit limit

   • Override a "hold" previously established for a customer

   • Write off amounts that exceed the maximum amount you set for a customer

   • Waive finance charges you set for a customer

   If you leave any of the password fields blank, Microsoft Dynamics GP doesn't require a password for those activities.

5. **In the Apply By section, specify whether to apply credit memos, returns, and payments by Due Date or Document Number when you opt to apply any of these documents automatically.**

   When you apply by Due Date — the choice of most companies — Dynamics GP applies the credit memo, return, or payment to the documents with the oldest due date. This approach helps customers minimize finance charges on past due invoices. When you apply automatically by Document Number, Dynamics GP applies the credit memo, return, or payment first to sales invoices, in lowest numerical order, followed by debit memos, finance charges, and services/repairs.

6. **In the Defaults section, supply an amount for NSF Charge, the Checkbook ID, price level, document format, and default summary view you want Dynamics GP to use by default.**

7. **In the E-mailed Statements section, use the Status Recipient box to enter an e-mail address where you want Dynamics GP to send a status report on the e-mail statements generated.**

   This report lists the e-mail statements Dynamics GP sent successfully and information about any errors that might have occurred.

   In addition to printing customer statements, you also can send e-mail statements in Portable Document Format (PDF) to selected customers using any MAPI (Messaging Application Programming Interface) compliant e-mail service. You also must install Adobe Distiller or PDFWriter to send customer statements by e-mail.

8. **Choose Options to display the Receivables Setup Options dialog box shown in Figure 5-2.**

Figure 5-2:
The
Receivables
Setup
Options
dialog box.

You must use separate numbers for each document type. An alphanumeric numbering scheme gives you more flexibility to identify documents. The lookup window for document numbers doesn't display a document code, so including some alphabetic characters to indicate the document type can be helpful. Also, make sure each document number ends with digits rather than letters; otherwise, Dynamics GP will have trouble incrementing the document number.

Establish default tax schedules to save time during data entry; users can, if necessary, change the tax schedules as they create transactions.

You can set up labels for two user-defined fields that you can use to track additional information about your customers; you can use the first user-defined field to sort most customer reports. The user-defined fields are free-form text fields, and the names you set here will automatically appear on the SmartList and on the Customer Card.

Use the check boxes in the Sales History Includes section to determine whether Dynamics GP posts sales amounts, trade discount amounts, amounts charged for freight, miscellaneous charges, and tax amounts to sales history.

 9. **Choose OK to save your entries, close the Receivables Setup Options window, and redisplay the Receivables Management Setup window.**

10. **Choose OK to save your entries and close the Receivables Management Setup window.**

What Customer Classes Can Do for You

Using customer classes, you can group customer information in ways that make sense in your business; using customer classes also speeds up the process of setting up your customers. When you create a customer class, you establish default settings for the class. For example, you specify whether Dynamics GP should treat the balances of all customers in the class as open item balances or balance forward balances. For more information on Dynamics GP and open item versus balance forward balances, see the sidebar, "How Dynamics GP handles open item and balance forward balances," later in this section.

You also can identify the way you want Dynamics GP to maintain customer history as well as setting credit and transaction options. Then, you can apply these defaults to all customers in the class — Dynamics GP refers to this process as *rolling down* the customer class settings — instead of setting up the defaults for each customer individually. If you set up customer classes, setting up customers becomes quick and easy.

Start by creating a customer class that has the majority of the settings that you want to apply to all customer classes. You can then use the settings for this customer class as the foundation for subsequent customer classes you create, saving you time when you create customer classes.

Don't worry if a few customers you intend to assign to the class use slightly different settings than the ones you establish for the class. You can make changes to these settings when you create the individual customer. The idea here is to get Dynamics GP to do most of the work for you by assigning the majority of settings as defaults.

How Dynamics GP handles open item and balance forward balances

You can set up customers to maintain open item balances or balance forward balances. Dynamics GP processes certain information differently for each of the two setups. For example, for open item balance customers:

✔ You can apply payments to specific invoices.

✔ Dynamics GP saves detailed transaction information, which appears on customer statements until you remove the transactions.

✔ You can establish up to seven aging periods, and you can age accounts at any time of the month. Dynamics GP ages accounts before assessing finance charges to ensure that individual transactions are aged based on their dates.

✔ You can enter multicurrency transactions.

(continued)

(continued)

For balance forward customers:

✔ You don't apply transactions to specific invoices; instead, you apply payments to the noncurrent balance.

✔ Dynamics GP retains transaction information only for the current period; for noncurrent periods, Dynamics GP consolidates all transaction totals into an account total and brings that account total forward to the next aging period after you assess finance charges and print customer statements.

✔ You can establish only two aging periods: current and noncurrent. Dynamics GP consolidates balances when you remove paid transactions.

✔ You cannot enter multicurrency transactions.

Most companies use open item customers exclusively because they don't want to lose the detail associated with transactions beyond the current period.

In the following steps, only Step 4 is required; all the other settings are optional.

To create a customer class, follow these steps:

1. **Click the Sales series in the Navigation pane.**

2. **Click Setup.**

3. **Click Customer Class.**

   Dynamics GP displays the Customer Class Setup window shown in Figure 5-3.

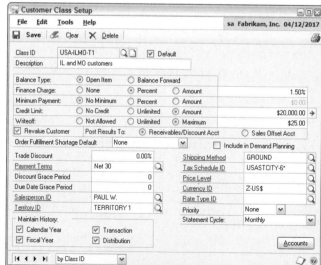

Figure 5-3: The Customer Class Setup window.

4. **Assign an ID to the class and provide a description.**

   Select the Default box if you want to use the settings you establish for the current customer class as the default settings for future classes you create.

5. **In the grid below the class description, select options for the Balance Type, Finance Charge, Minimum Payment, Credit Limit, and Write Off options as they apply to most customers in the class.**

   Use the Revalue Customer check box to establish whether you can revalue multicurrency documents for customers in this class and, if so, the account to which Dynamics GP should post the result.

6. **From the Order Fulfillment Shortage Default list, choose None, Back Order Remaining, or Cancel Remaining.**

   If you select None, you will have to handle shortages manually.

7. **In the Trade Discount field, the Payment Terms field, the discount Grace Period field, the Due Date Grace Period field, the Salesperson ID field, and the Territory ID field, set default values to appear on transactions for customers assigned to this class.**

   Dynamics GP uses the Discount Grace Period field and the Due Date Grace Period in conjunction with the customer's payment terms to determine due dates. If the document date plus the number of grace period days is the same as or later than the payment terms discount date, both the discount date and the due date will move to the following month. If the discount date plus the number of due date grace period days is the same as or later than the payment terms due date, the due date will move to the following month.

8. **In the Maintain History section, select the type of history you want to keep for customers in this class. Keeping history enables you to print reports about sales activity:**

   • Keep calendar year history if you want to print monthly and annual sales reports for customers in this class.

   • Keep fiscal year history if your fiscal year does not follow the calendar year.

   • Keep transaction history to view information about paid invoices in inquiry windows and to print the Historical Aged Trial Balance.

   If you opted to print the Historical Aged Trial Balance in the Receivables Management Setup window shown earlier in Figure 5-1, Dynamics GP automatically keeps transaction history regardless of your selection in the Customer Class Setup window.

   • Keep distribution history so that you can print the Distribution History report.

9. **In the lower-right section of the window, click the Lookup button — the one that looks like a magnifying glass — beside any field to make the following selections, as they apply to most customers in the class:**

   - Select the Shipping Method used by customers in this class.

   - Select the Tax Schedule ID used by customers in this class.

   - If you use standard pricing, select a price level — for example, wholesale or retail — to assign to customers in this class.

     See Chapter 10 for more information on standard pricing and extended pricing.

   - Select the Currency ID used by customers in this class. If you use the Multicurrency Management module, also select the rate type used by customers in this class.

10. **From the Priority list box, select a priority that you can use when you allocate items in the Sales Automatic Order Allocation window.**

11. **From the Statement Cycle list box, select the frequency with which you intend to produce statements for customers assigned to this class.**

12. **Click the Accounts button to display the Customer Class Accounts Setup dialog box shown in Figure 5-4. Use this dialog box to**

    - Identify whether to use the cash account associated with the customer class checkbook or the one you assign to the customer when you set up customers as described later in this chapter in the section, "All About the Customer Card," and

    - Select default posting accounts for customers in this class. Click the Lookup button in the middle of each row to assign the account number in your chart of accounts associated with the account listed in the left column. Dynamics GP automatically fills in the description you assigned to the account number.

13. **Click OK to save your selections and redisplay the Customer Class Setup window.**

14. **Click the Save button to save your selections.**

You can delete a customer class if it becomes obsolete by displaying it in the Customer Class Setup window shown in Figure 5-4 and clicking the Delete button. Deleting a customer class doesn't affect the customers assigned to the class, except that the Customer Class ID field on the customer card will be invalid. Before you delete a customer class, print a Customer List sorted by class; that way, you can see the customers that will be affected if you delete the class. You print the Customer List from the Reports section of the Content pane that appears when you select the Sales series in the Navigation pane. See Chapter 12 to learn about setting up a report to sort in a particular way.

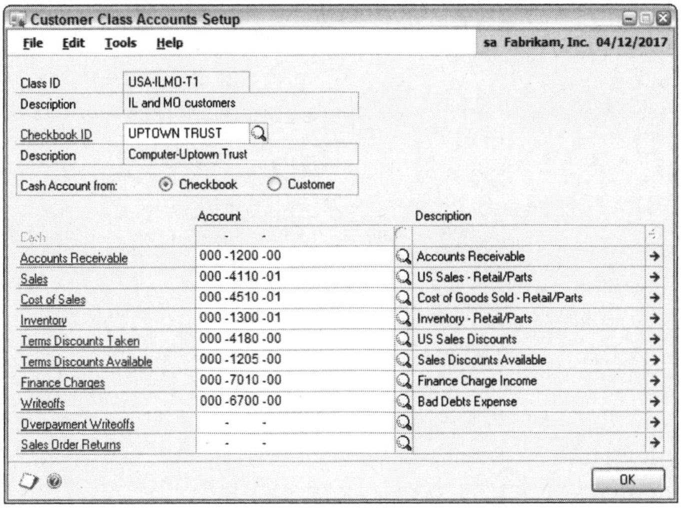

Figure 5-4:
Use this
dialog box
to establish
default
posting
accounts
for custom-
ers in the
selected
class.

	Customer Class Accounts Setup					
File	Edit	Tools	Help			sa Fabrikam, Inc. 04/12/2017

Class ID   USA-ILMO-T1
Description   IL and MO customers

Checkbook ID   UPTOWN TRUST
Description   Computer-Uptown Trust

Cash Account from: ⦿ Checkbook   ◯ Customer

	Account		Description	
Cash	- -			
Accounts Receivable	000 -1200 -00		Accounts Receivable	→
Sales	000 -4110 -01		US Sales - Retail/Parts	→
Cost of Sales	000 -4510 -01		Cost of Goods Sold - Retail/Parts	→
Inventory	000 -1300 -01		Inventory - Retail/Parts	→
Terms Discounts Taken	000 -4180 -00		US Sales Discounts	→
Terms Discounts Available	000 -1205 -00		Sales Discounts Available	→
Finance Charges	000 -7010 -00		Finance Charge Income	→
Writeoffs	000 -6700 -00		Bad Debts Expense	→
Overpayment Writeoffs	- -			→
Sales Order Returns	- - -			→

OK

All About the Customer Card

You create customer cards for each of the customers with whom you do
business. The customer card stores customer address information as well
as posting account information. By assigning your customers to a customer
class, you can have Dynamics GP automatically assign much of the information for the customer class to the customer.

When printing reports and making inquiries, Dynamics GP often displays information in Customer ID order. So, when you set up your customer cards, make
sure that your customer ID numbers use the same number of characters and
are set up consistently — that is, if you include alphabetic characters in the
number, place them in the same location within the number.

Adding customer cards

You add customer cards to identify to Dynamics GP the customers with
whom you do business on a regular basis. Follow these steps:

1. **From the Menu bar, choose Cards⇨Sales⇨Customer to display the
   Customer Maintenance window shown in Figure 5-5.**

   You also can click Sales in the Navigation pane, and, in the Cards section, click Customer.

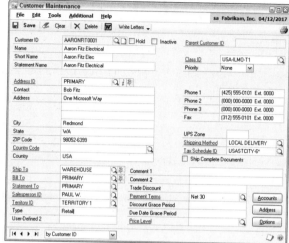

Figure 5-5:
The
Customer
Mainten-
ance
window.

2. **In the top section of the window, type an ID for the customer, the customer's name, a short name to use when the full name is too long — on reports, for example — and the name you want Dynamics GP to print on the customer's statements. In addition, assign a Parent Customer ID and a Class ID if appropriate.**

   You can read more about Parent Customer ID in the next section.

3. **Use the Priority list box to select a priority to assign to the customer; 1 is the highest priority and None is the lowest priority.**

   You can use the customer priority number when you allocate items in the Sales Automatic Order Allocation window.

4. **In the middle section, fill in address and phone number information and, if appropriate, a UPS zone. If you didn't select a customer class ID, fill in the customer's shipping method and tax schedule.**

   You can create multiple addresses for a customer, as you see in the next section of this chapter. If you use Sales Order Processing, select the Ship Complete Documents option if the customer doesn't accept partial shipments of Sales Order Processing documents.

   See Chapter 6 for more information on Sales Order Processing.

5. **At the bottom of the window, if the customer uses different addresses to receive shipments, invoices, and statements, select the address ID's.**

6. **Use the Salesperson ID and the Territory ID fields to assign the customer to a particular salesperson or territory.**

7. **Fill in appropriate information in the user-defined fields; in Figure 5-5, User-Defined 1 has been established as the Type field for customers.**

The two comment fields are for your use; any information you type in them appears on the Customer Setup List. For example, Dynamics GP allows telephone extensions to be a maximum of four digits, so if the extension is longer you can enter it in one of the Comment fields.

8. **Use the Trade Discount box to supply information about any trade discounts you offer the customer.**

If you assigned the customer to a Customer Class, Dynamics GP fills in Payment Terms, Discount Grace Period, Due Date Grace Period, and Price Level information from the class. If appropriate, you can make changes.

9. **Click the Accounts button to display the Customer Account Maintenance window.**

The Customer Account Maintenance window looks and functions exactly like the Customer Class Accounts Setup window shown earlier in Figure 5-4. See the section, "What Customer Classes Can Do for You," earlier in this chapter, for more information.

Click OK to redisplay the Customer Maintenance window shown in Figure 5-5.

If you do not assign a customer class or set up default accounts using the Customer Account Maintenance window, Dynamics GP will assign, on transactions, the accounts you specified when setting up your company. See Chapter 2 for details on setting up company default posting accounts.

10. **If you need more than one address for a customer, click the Address button to display the Customer Address Maintenance window.**

In the Address ID box, type a name that describes the address, such as Primary, Warehouse, or Billing. Supply a contact name and address, phone, and fax information, and click Save to save the address. You can use the EFT Bank button to establish electronic funds transfer information for the customer.

You can click the Internet Information button — the *i* button beside the Address ID Lookup button — to display the Internet Information window and type an e-mail address, a Web site address, or an ftp site address. When you finish, click Save and then click the X in the upper-right corner of the window to close it and redisplay the Customer Address Maintenance window.

11. **Click the Options button to display the Customer Maintenance Options window.**

Much of the Customer Maintenance Options window is identical to the Customer Class Setup window shown earlier in Figure 5-4. See the section, "Setting Up Customer Classes," earlier in this chapter, for a description of many of the options in this window. You will find, however, some additional fields in this window. For example, you can store credit card and bank information, tax exemption numbers, and the customer's tax registration number. You also can establish e-mail addresses to use to send e-mail statements. Click OK to redisplay the Customer Maintenance window shown in Figure 5-6.

12. **Click Save to save the customer card.**

Understanding the National Accounts feature

You can use the National Accounts feature to create a relationship between customers you identify. For example, suppose that you sell products to ABC Corporation, and ABC Corporation has several different stores that order separately and receive merchandise directly. Further suppose that you bill ABC Corporation for all orders placed by any of their stores. You can set up ABC Corporation as a national account and relate all of ABC Corporation's stores to the national account. Then, you can manage all of ABC Corporation's stores in a uniform way.

To distinguish between the national account customer and the customers related to the national account, Dynamics GP refers to the national account — ABC Corporation in our example — as the *parent customer*. Dynamics GP refers to all of ABC Corporation's stores as *children* or *child customers*.

Using a national account, you can opt to receive payments from child customers or only from the parent customer. You also can apply the settings you establish for the parent company for credit status, holds, and finance charges to the child customers. Dynamics GP's reports and inquiries can provide consolidated information about the activity of a national account parent customer or provide details for an individual child customer.

You use existing open item customers to create a national account, and you cannot assign a single customer to more than one national account relationship. Follow these steps to create a national account:

1. **On the Menu bar, select Cards⇨Sales⇨National Accounts to open the National Accounts Maintenance window (see Figure 5-6).**

2. **Select a parent customer ID.**

3. **Select the options you want to assign to the national account.**

4. **Click a blank line in the Child Customer ID column toward the bottom of the window and then click the Lookup button to display a list of customers. Select a customer to add it as a child customer.**

   If you select a customer that isn't an open item customer or a customer that belongs to another national account, Dynamics GP displays a message, indicating that you cannot add that customer to the national account.

   You can add a range of customers by clicking the Select Children button at the bottom of the window. Dynamics GP displays the Select Children window, where you can identify a range of customers.

5. **Click Save to save the national account.**

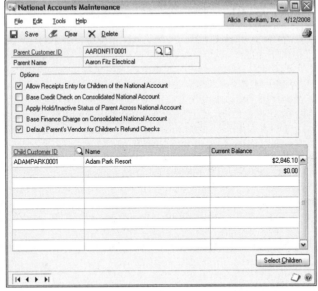

Figure 5-6:
The
National
Accounts
Mainten-
ance
window.

Placing a customer on hold

Suppose that a customer's unpaid balance is larger than the credit limit you established for that customer; you might want to place a *hold* on the customer's record to prohibit additional sales activity. Once the customer pays you, you can remove the hold.

Dynamics GP ignores the Hold option if you place a hold on a child customer of a national account and you have selected the Apply Hold/Inactive Status Of Parent Across National Account option in the National Accounts Maintenance window.

To place a customer on hold, open the Customer Maintenance window by using the Menu bar and selecting Cards⇨Sales⇨Customers or, in the Content pane, under the Cards section, clicking Customer. Click the Lookup button beside the Customer ID field to select the customer. Then, at the right edge of the Customer ID field, select the Hold box. Click Save to save your settings and click the X in the upper-right corner of the window to close it.

To remove the hold, reopen the window and remove the check from the Hold box.

When you don't need a customer anymore

When you decide that you don't need a customer anymore, you can either make the customer inactive or you can delete the customer.

Making a customer inactive is the less intrusive and less permanent way of proceeding and your only choice if you are keeping historical information for the customer. You can inactivate customers for whom no outstanding invoices exist; if you have trouble making a customer inactive, remove paid sales transactions for the customer.

You cannot inactive a parent customer ID of a national account if children of the national account have unposted or open transactions, and you selected the Apply Hold/Inactive Status of Parent Across National Account option in the National Accounts Maintenance window.

To make a customer inactive, open the Customer Maintenance window by using the Menu bar and selecting Cards⇨Sales⇨Customer and select the customer. Then, select the Inactive check box.

Deleting a customer is a more permanent approach than setting a customer's status to inactive. Dynamics GP won't let you delete a customer card for any customer

✔ With a current balance until you complete year-end closing;

✔ With posted and unposted transactions;

✔ With transactions in history; to delete this card, remove history for the customer; or

✔ That is part of a national account until you remove the customer from the national account.

To print a list of customers eligible for deleting, print a Customer Card Removal Edit List. Open the Customer Mass Delete window by using the Menu bar and selecting Utilities⇨Sales⇨Mass Delete. Then, choose File⇨Print.

To delete a customer card, use the Menu bar and select Cards⇨Sales⇨ Customers to open the Customer Maintenance window shown earlier in Figure 5-6. Select the ID of the customer you want to delete, and then click the Delete button.

Setting Up Sales Territories and Sales People

You can set up sales territories to track the way you sell your products. For example, you might set up sales territories to manage sales in geographic regions — North, South, East, and West. Using sales territories in Dynamics GP, you can track history, sales, and commissions for each territory. You also can use salespeople cards in Dynamics GP to track commissions for calendar and fiscal years.

Since you assign salespeople to territories, set up your territory cards before you set up your salespeople cards. To create a territory card, open the Sales Territory Maintenance window shown in Figure 5-7 by using the Menu bar and selecting Cards➪Sales➪Sales Territory.

Even if you don't use sales territories, set up at least one sales territory for your salespeople; otherwise, Dynamics GP won't let you post commissions.

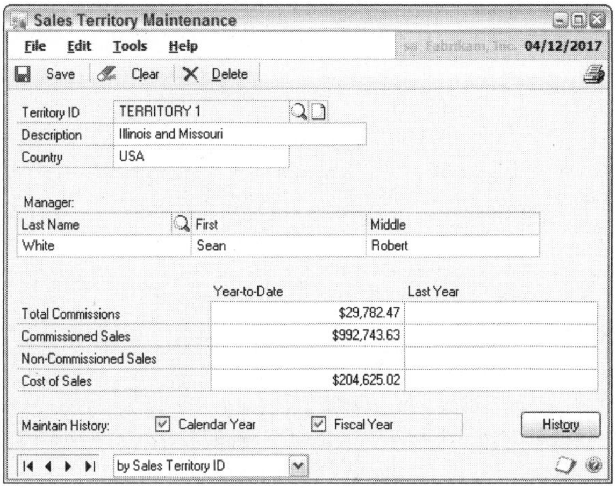

Figure 5-7:
The Sales Territory Maintenance window.

Sales Territory Maintenance		
File Edit Tools Help	sa Fabrikam, Inc. 04/12/2017	
🖫 Save ✎ Clear ✕ Delete		
Territory ID	TERRITORY 1	
Description	Illinois and Missouri	
Country	USA	
Manager:		
Last Name	First	Middle
White	Sean	Robert

	Year-to-Date	Last Year
Total Commissions	$29,782.47	
Commissioned Sales	$992,743.63	
Non-Commissioned Sales		
Cost of Sales	$204,625.02	

Maintain History: ☑ Calendar Year   ☑ Fiscal Year   History

by Sales Territory ID

Supply a Territory ID, description and the country in which the territory is located. Then, type the name of the territory manager. If you are creating your territory cards after the beginning of your year, you can supply values in the grid at the bottom of the box; as you go forward and record sales transactions, Dynamics GP updates these values automatically. Or, you can leave the balances blank and let Dynamics GP update them as you enter beginning balance and subsequent transactions. Also, decide whether you want to maintain calendar year and fiscal year history for reporting purposes. When you finish, click Save and repeat this process for each territory you want to create.

You can use the Description and the Country fields on the Sales Territory Card to group territories together for reporting purposes. For example, one of my clients uses the Country field to store the region of the country, such as Mid-Atlantic, and the Description field is used to indicate whether the territory is international or domestic. In this way, my client can produce custom sales reports using a report writer like SQL Reporting Services or Crystal Reports that shows information grouped by territory or by international or domestic location.

To create a salesperson card, follow these steps:

1. **On the Menu bar, select Cards⇨Sales⇨Salesperson.**

   Dynamics GP displays the Salesperson Maintenance window shown in Figure 5-8.

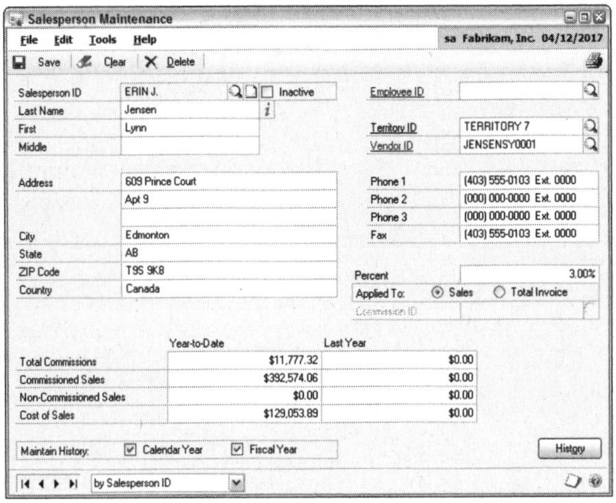

Figure 5-8:
The
Salesperson
Mainten-
ance
window.

2. **Supply a Salesperson ID and fill in the name, address, and phone number information for the salesperson.**

3. **Select a Territory ID for the salesperson.**

   If the salesperson is one of your company's employees, you can select the employee ID. If the salesperson is an independent contractor, select the salesperson's Vendor ID.

4. **In the Percent field, enter the commission percentage the salesperson earns.**

5. **If you are creating your salesperson cards after the beginning of your year, you can supply commission information in the grid at the bottom of the box; as you go forward and record sales transactions, Dynamics GP updates these values automatically.**

If you prefer, you can leave the commission information blank and, when you enter customer beginning balances, assign the salesperson to each beginning balance transaction.

6. **Decide whether you want to maintain calendar year and fiscal year history for reporting purposes. When you finish, click Save and repeat this process for each territory you want to create.**

7. **Click Save.**

Entering Customer Beginning Balances

I have to assume that you aren't just starting out in business; in fact, you've probably been in business for quite awhile. And, in that case, some of your customers probably owe you money. If you recorded the invoices for these outstanding balances in your old accounting system and intend to import information, probably with the help of an authorized Dynamics GP partner, the import process will establish your beginning balances for your customers and you can skip this section.

If you are not planning to import these beginning balances, then you need to enter them in Dynamics GP. And, you enter them the same way you enter all customer invoices as described in the next section with one exception; you *don't* want to post these transactions to the General Ledger.

You see, the sum of the beginning balance transactions you enter for all of your customers should equal the amount you recorded for Accounts Receivable when you set up your opening balances in the General Ledger as described in Chapter 2. Since you already established the balance of your Accounts Receivable account when you set up your system, you want to record these beginning balance transactions so that they don't affect the General Ledger balance for Accounts Receivable; otherwise, your Accounts Receivable balance in the General Ledger will be overstated.

To avoid posting these transactions to the General Ledger, temporarily change your posting setup. Then, for open item customers, enter a beginning balance batch for outstanding invoices. When you finish posting this batch, re-establish the original posting settings so that future transactions will post to the General Ledger.

For balance forward customers, you still change your posting setup temporarily, as outlined in the steps below. And, you still enter beginning balance transactions. However, because Dynamics GP doesn't maintain transaction detail for balance forward customers beyond the current period, you need to enter your beginning balance transactions in two batches: one containing transactions that make up the non-current period balance followed by a batch containing transactions that make up the current period balance. In between entering these two batches, you need to consolidate period balances.

You only need to consolidate period balances for balance forward customers; most companies don't use the balance forward method for aging customers because the method eliminates detail after the current period. For details on consolidating period balances, refer to the Receivables Management manual.

To temporarily change your posting setup, follow these steps:

1. **On the Menu bar, select Microsoft Dynamics GP⇨Tools⇨Setup⇨ Posting⇨Posting to open the Posting Setup window (see Figure 5-9).**

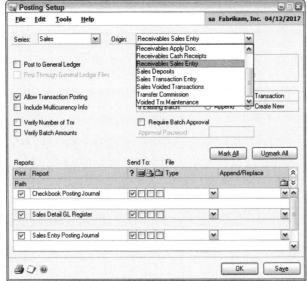

Figure 5-9: Use this window to temporarily change posting settings.

2. **From the Series list, select Sales.**

3. **From the Origin list, select Receivables Sales Entry.**

4. **Remove the check in the Post to General Ledger check box.**

To understand the difference between posting through and posting to the General Ledger, see the sidebar "Posting to or through the General Ledger — What's the difference?" in Chapter 3.

5. **Repeat Steps 3 through 4 two more times, selecting Receivables Apply Doc and then Receivables Cash Receipts from the Origin list.**

6. **Click OK to save the settings and close the Posting Setup window.**

Any receivables transactions that you post will not affect your General Ledger. After you create and post your beginning batch transactions, repeat the steps above to re-establish posting to the General Ledger.

In addition, before you begin your regular routine work, you might want to print an Aged Trial Balance report because, at this point, the report would provide a record of your beginning outstanding customer balances. See Chapter 12 for details on setting up and printing reports.

Creating Receivables Management Transactions

You use the Receivables Transaction Entry window to create a variety of sales-oriented transactions:

- ✔ *Invoices* reflect sales you made to customers and increase a customer's account balance. The invoices you create using the Receivables Transaction Entry window are summary invoices that list dollars but no other details. To prepare an invoice that lists details, use the Sales Order Processing module; see Chapter 6.

- ✔ *Finance charges* increase a customer's account balance; it is unusual to enter a finance charge since Dynamics GP automatically assesses finance charges, but, if you need to add a finance charge, use this document type.

- ✔ *Debit memos* increase a customer's account balance. You might enter a debit memo to record a charge for special handling.

- ✔ *Warranty documents* do not affect a customer's balance. You might enter a warranty document to record a service or repair covered by a manufacturer's warranty and then use this document as the foundation to bill the manufacturer. In addition, you can use the warranty to record the expense incurred by your company in offering the warranty.

- ✔ *Service/repair documents* increase a customer's account balance. You can enter a service/repair document to charge a customer for a service or repair not covered by warranty.

- ✔ *Credit memos* decrease a customer's account balance. You might issue a credit memo, for example, to reduce a freight charge.

- ✔ *Returns* decrease a customer's account balance. You can use the Return document to record a refund of a sale.

You can create an individual invoice or include the invoice as part of a batch. For details on batching documents, see Chapter 3. If you use the Receivables Batch Entry window to create a batch, you can add invoices to the batch immediately or later, by including the Batch ID when you create the transaction, as described in the steps that follow.

If you use the Sales Order Processing module and you want to record an invoice that relates to items on a sales order, don't use the steps in this section. Instead, see Chapter 6. Similarly, be aware that the effects of transactions such as credit memos and debit memos entered through the Receivables Transaction Entry window will not affect the Sales Order Processing History Tables. Therefore, your sales history reports, which typically display only transactions entered through the Sales Order Processing module, may be incomplete. For this reason, you may want to use the Sales Order Processing module to enter a Return document instead of using the Receivables Management module to enter a credit memo.

To create a Receivables Management document, follow these steps:

1. **On the Menu bar, select Transactions⇨Sales⇨Transaction Entry to display the Receivables Transaction Entry window shown in Figure 5-10.**

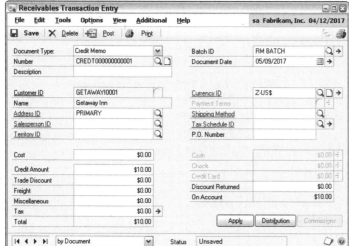

Figure 5-10:
The Receivables Transaction Entry window.

2. **From the Document Type list, choose a document type.**

   For this example, I selected Credit Memo. Dynamics GP fills in the next available document number using the information stored in the Receivables Setup Options window. You can optionally enter a description that helps identify the transaction. If you post to the General Ledger with detail, the description you provide appears as the reference in the General Ledger Transaction Entry window.

3. **In the Customer ID field, select a customer.**

   Dynamics GP fills in the customer's name, default billing Address ID, and, for Sales/Invoice, Service/Repairs, and Returns documents, the Salesperson ID, Territory ID, Currency ID, Payment Terms, Shipping Method, and Tax Schedule ID. If necessary, you can change any of these fields.

4. **In the Batch ID field, select a batch if appropriate. Use the Document Date field to enter a date for the transaction.**

If you assign the transaction to a batch, Dynamics GP updates Receivables Management information on the Document Date and, if you set up posting options to post by batch date, Dynamics GP updates the General Ledger using the batch date. You can override the batch date and set the date for the transaction to update the General Ledger by clicking the Document Date expansion button and setting a posting date.

5. **In the bottom-left side of the window, enter the transaction amounts.**

6. **For Sales/Invoice, Returns, Service/Repairs, Finance Charges, and Debit Memo documents, if the customer makes a payment at the time of the sale, use the fields on the bottom-right side of the window to record the amount.**

   Dynamics GP displays another window related to the type of payment you record, and you can enter detailed information about the payment. You also can click the Commissions button to change the commissions Dynamics GP calculates based on the way you set up the salesperson assigned to the transaction.

7. **You can click the Distribution button to display the Sales Transaction Distribution Entry window and override the default account distributions Dynamics GP makes for the transaction based on the settings stored on the customer card.**

8. **For Credit Memo and Returns documents, click the Apply button.**

   Dynamics GP displays the Apply Sales Documents window shown in Figure 5-11.

   Applying the credit memo or return is optional at this point; you can post unapplied documents and apply the credit memo or return later on using the Apply Sales Documents window (on the Menu bar, select Transactions⇨Sales⇨Apply Sales Documents).

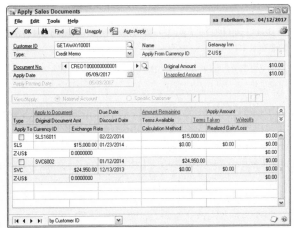

Figure 5-11: The Apply Sales Documents window.

9. **Select a document to which you want to apply the credit memo or return and then click OK to redisplay the Receivables Transaction Entry window.**

10. **You can print the document by clicking the Print button.**

    If you print, Dynamics GP automatically saves or posts the document. If you don't print, save or post the transaction.

Letter Writing Assistant

Dynamics GP's Letter Writing Assistant enables you to use customer, vendor, and employee information stored in Dynamics GP to create letters using Microsoft Word. Dynamics GP comes with predefined letter templates to create credit application acceptance letters, proposal cover letters, collection letters, letters to vendors to dispute charges, applicant offer letters, letters describing benefit summaries, and other employee memos. You also create your own letters; for example, you can create your own letter to notify your customers of an upcoming major sale.

The Letter Writing Assistant is a wizard that walks you through the process; follow these steps:

1. **On the Menu bar, select Reports⇨Letter Writing Assistant.**

    A welcome window appears; click Next.

2. **In the window that appears, choose to prepare a letter using one of the existing templates or to create your own template.**

    For this example, choose Prepare The Letters Using An Existing Letter.

3. **Click Next. Dynamics GP displays the Letter category window shown in Figure 5-12.**

4. **Select a category in the left pane; a description of the letters in the category appears in the right pane.**

    For this example, I selected Customer.

5. **Click Next to select who should receive the letter.**

    You can send the letter to all customers, vendors, or employees, active or inactive customers, vendors, or employees, or a range of customer, vendor, or employee names, ID's or those stored on a SmartList.

6. **Click Next to display the available letter templates (see Figure 5-13).**

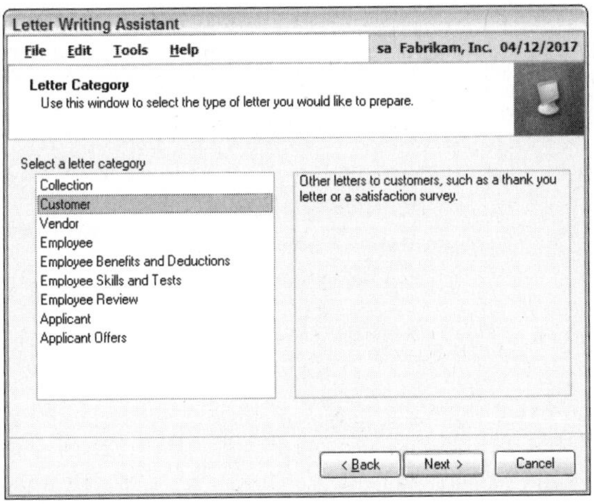

Figure 5-12:
The Letter
Category
window.

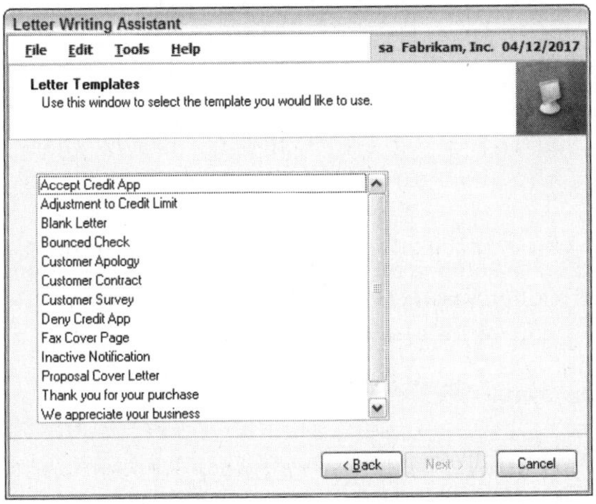

Figure 5-13:
Dynamics
GP contains
a wide
variety of
Customer
letter
templates.

7. **Select a letter template and click Next.**

   Dynamics GP displays a list confirming who should receive the letter. You can remove entries from the list by removing the check from the box beside the appropriate names.

8. **Click Next.**

   The last window of the Letter Writing Assistant appears, where you can supply the name, title, phone, and e-mail address of the sender.

9. **Click Finish.**

   Microsoft Word opens showing the letter addressed to the first recipient (see Figure 5-14). If you scroll down, you'll find one letter per page for each recipient you selected.

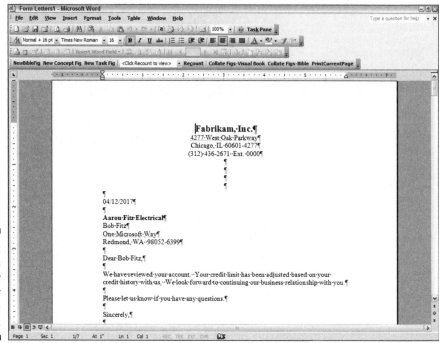

Figure 5-14:
Letters
created by
the Letter
Writing
Assistant.

You can edit the letter and make any changes you want; the changes you make do not affect your future use of the template. You can print all of the letters by clicking the Print button in Word.

You can create your own letter by choosing the Blank Letter template.

If you want to create a letter that you can use again, create your own letter template by selecting Customize The Letters By Adding New Letters Or Changing Existing Letters option in Step 2. Using this option, you can create a new letter or edit or delete an existing letter. If you create a new letter, you can start with a blank Word document or an existing Word document that you may have already created.

As you create your new letter template, you add Dynamics GP fields such as your company name and address or placeholders representing customer, vendor, or employee names and addresses wherever you want them to appear in the letter. When you finish creating the letter template, choose File⇨Save to save the letter template for future use.

Chapter 6

Using the Sales Order Processing Module

The Sales Order Processing module (SOP) helps you create sales-related documents that contain detailed information. You can prepare quotes, sales orders, fulfillment orders, invoices, back orders, and returns. In this chapter, you read about each of these types of documents, when to use them, and how to create them. I also show you how to manage SOP documents, including, for example, transferring information from a quote to a sales order and creating a purchase order using a back order.

Understanding Document Types

You can enter six types of documents using the Sales Order Processing module:

- ✔ Quotes
- ✔ Sales orders
- ✔ Fulfillment orders
- ✔ Invoices
- ✔ Back orders
- ✔ Returns

A *quote* is an estimate you prepare for a customer to detail the cost of items before your customer makes a purchase decision. You can include any type of item on a quote, regardless of whether you track it in inventory. For example, you can include labor and mileage charges. Dynamics GP automatically calculates your cost and the price to the customer. You don't post a quote because it doesn't represent a binding legal document to complete a transaction, but, if appropriate, you can transfer quote information to sales orders, invoices, or fulfillment orders. Placing inventory items on quotes never allocates quantities or reduces the available quantity.

You use a *sales order* typically when you and a customer have agreed upon the items or services you will provide. You can transfer information from a quote or a back order to a sales order, and you can transfer information on a sales order to a back order, an invoice, or a fulfillment order. You also can use information on a sales order to create a purchase order. You don't post sales orders because they don't represent a binding legal agreement to provide goods or services. But, you can use sales orders to allocate inventory, setting the item aside for that order and reducing the available quantity.

If your organization uses multiple participants to complete a sale, you can set up the Sales Order Processing module to use sales fulfillment workflow. Using *sales fulfillment workflow,* each participant completes his or her task and then passes appropriate documents to the person responsible for the next step in the process. As part of sales fulfillment workflow, you create *fulfillment orders,* which are special types of sales orders that you can track through the workflow process. At the end of the workflow process the fulfillment order becomes an invoice.

You create an *invoice* to record the sale of products or services; invoices are legally binding documents that record the prices and details of transactions. You post invoices so that Dynamics GP can update your accounts.

While creating a quote, fulfillment order, sales order or invoice, you might find that you don't currently have the items the customer wants to order; in this case, you can transfer the appropriate information to a *back order.* You don't post back orders because they aren't legally binding documents. You can create a purchase order from a back order, and, when you receive the merchandise, you can use the back order to create a sales order or an invoice.

You record a *return document* when a customer returns items you previously sold. When you post a return document, Dynamics GP decreases the customer's account balance and increases inventory quantities if appropriate.

You can't enter a return in Sales Order Processing for a drop-ship item. If a customer returns an item ordered as part of a drop shipment, enter a credit memo in Receivables Management to reduce the customer balance and a credit memo in Payables Management to reduce the balance you owe the vendor.

Setting Up Sales Order Processing Documents

For each type of document that your organization uses, you must set up at least one document ID. Think of a document ID as a template that describes the ways in which Dynamics GP handles that type of document.

But, you aren't limited to only one document ID for each type of document; you can set up and customize an unlimited number of quote, order, back order, fulfillment order, invoice, and return document ID's, and you can set up different options for each document ID. For example, you might set up separate quote ID's for your wholesale, retail, and catalog customers because you might wish to establish different default days before a quote expires.

The method you use to set up document ID's is the same for each type of document; only the options available to set vary. So, let's walk through setting up a document ID for a quote, and then I'll describe any additional options for the other types of documents.

To create a quote document ID, follow these steps:

1. **On the Menu bar, select Microsoft Dynamics GP⇨Tools⇨Setup⇨ Sales⇨Sales Order Processing.**

2. **At the bottom of the window, click the Sales Document Setup button and select Quote to display the Sales Quote Setup window shown in Figure 6-1.**

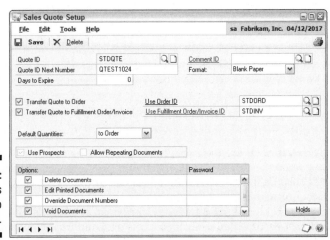

Figure 6-1: The Sales Quote Setup window.

3. Enter a quote ID and, if you want, a starting number for quotes that use this document ID as well as a Comment ID.

4. From the Format box, select the type of form you want to use for this document ID.

5. In the Days to Expire box, type a number if you want quotes created using this document ID to expire.

6. If you select the Transfer Quote to Order box, Dynamics GP allows you to convert a quote to a sales order; using the Use Order ID field, you can select the sales order document ID Dynamics GP should use when transferring this quote to a sales order.

7. You can use the Transfer Quote to Fulfillment Order/Invoice check box and the User Fulfillment Order/Invoice ID field to convert quotes to fulfillment orders and invoices if you use sales fulfillment workflow.

8. From the Default Quantities list box, indicate whether Dynamics GP should display item quantities in the Quantity to Order or Quantity to Invoice fields on the quote in the Sales Transaction Entry window.

9. Select Use Prospects if you want this document ID available for prospective customers.

10. Select Allow Repeating Documents if you want users to be able to create repeating quotes using this document ID.

11. In the Options section, you can select and set passwords for the following:

    • *Delete Documents:* This option permits users who know the password, if you set one, to delete quotes.

    • *Edit Printed Documents:* This option permits users who know the password, if you set one, to change quotes after printing them.

    • *Override Document Numbers:* This option permits users who know the password, if you set one, to change the document number that appears in the Sales Transaction Entry window.

    • *Void Documents:* This option permits users who know the password, if you set one, to void quotes.

You can click the Holds button to assign a process hold to the document ID; when you assign a process hold, Dynamics GP stops processing particular document ID's or documents.

12. Click Save to save the document ID.

To create document ID's for the other types of SOP documents, use the preceding steps, but with subtle differences:

✔ You can set the options described in Steps 3 and 4 for each type of document ID.

✔ You can set the options described in Steps 6 and 7 for quotes, sales orders, and back orders.

✔ You can set the Default Quantities option described in Step 8 for quotes and back orders.

✔ You can set the Allow Repeating Documents option described in Step 10 for quotes and sales orders.

✔ You can set all of the options described in Step 11 for each type of document ID. In addition, for the sales order, you can select and set a password for the Allow Invoicing of Unfulfilled or Partially Fulfilled Orders option. And, for the return, you can select and set a password for the Override Item Unit Cost for Returns option.

✔ For Sales Orders, you can opt to

- *Allocate* items — the process of reserving items for the order — by line item or by document and batch

- Transfer sales orders to back orders

- Use a separate fulfillment process to verify the items that are picked to fill the order

- Allow back ordered items to print on invoices

- Override the quantity to invoice with the quantity fulfilled; if you enable this option, you also can opt to enter or change information in the Qty to Back Order field and the Qty Canceled field in the Sales Order Fulfillment window

- Set a Credit Limit Hold ID

✔ For Fulfillment Order/Invoice documents, you can opt to

- Allocate items by line item or by document and batch

- Transfer fulfillment order/invoice documents to back orders

- Use a separate fulfillment process to allocate item quantities and fulfill item quantities separately

- Set a Credit Limit Hold ID

- Enable fulfillment workflow; if you select this option you can select a fulfillment workflow hold ID, opt to update the actual ship date when you confirm the shipment and click the Workflow button to set the active workflow statuses for the fulfillment order/invoice document

- Override the quantity to bill with the quantity fulfilled; if you enable this option, you also can opt to enter or change information in the Qty to Back Order field and the Qty Canceled field in the Sales Order Fulfillment window

- Update the invoice date to display the date you print the invoice in the Invoice Date field in the Sales Date Entry window

✔ For Return document ID's, you can opt to use the same sequential numbering system for Fulfillment Order/Invoice documents and Return documents.

A word about fulfillment orders

A fulfillment order is a special type of sales order in Microsoft Dynamics GP. Fulfillment orders use six different document statuses you establish through the sales fulfillment workflow feature to provide you with a structure to control typical sales processes; document statuses include typical sales processes, such as printing the picking ticket, picking goods from inventory, printing packing slips, packing and shipping the goods, and invoicing the customer. Typically, organizations in which multiple participants complete a sale may find using sales fulfillment workflow beneficial because it can help track the status of an order in the system and eliminate dependence on handwritten log books and external Excel spreadsheets. However, some organizations find that using Fulfillment Orders over-complicates the process and requires too much extra data entry. Your Dynamics GP consultant can help you determine whether fulfillment orders are right for you.

To use sales fulfillment workflow, use the Sales Fulfillment Order/Invoice Setup window to activate workflow for sales; on the Menu bar, select Microsoft Dynamics GP⇨Tools⇨Setup⇨Sales⇨Sales Order Processing; in the window that appears, click the Sales Document Setup button and choose Fulfillment Order/Invoice. Dynamics GP provides six default document statuses, but you can change them in the Sales Fulfillment Workflow Setup window; on the Menu bar, select Microsoft Dynamics GP⇨Tools⇨Setup⇨Sales⇨Fulfillment Workflow Setup.

You can create a fulfillment order in the Sales Transaction Entry window or from a quote, a back order, or an order. Because a fulfillment order is a special type of sales order, you don't post fulfillment orders; instead, you save them. And, like sales orders, you can create an invoice from a fulfillment order. Remember, posting the invoice updates the revenue, cost of goods sold, and accounts receivable accounts in the General Ledger and decreases the on hand quantity of an inventory item.

You advance the document status of a fulfillment order by simply following the steps in the sales process, confirming that items on fulfillment orders have been picked, packed, and shipped using the Sales Transaction Entry window, the Sales Order Fulfillment window, or the Sales Bulk Confirmation window; you can open any of these windows by choosing Transactions⇨Sales and then selecting the appropriate window.

To view the details about the document status for a fulfillment order, click the Document Status link in the Sales Transaction Entry window.

Occasionally, you might need to reverse the status of a document. For example, suppose that you print a picking ticket for a customer order but don't confirm the pick. Then, the customer calls to add an item to the order. In this case, reverse the document status from Status 2 to Status 1 and continue with the regular process. To reverse the status of a document, use the Edit Sales Document Status window, which enables you to move the document status back one status at a time. You cannot reverse a document status of a fulfillment order with a document status of Status 6; in this case, the fulfillment order has become an invoice. In addition, reversing document statuses does not reverse the quantity fulfilled or quantity allocated values.

Setting Up the Sales Order Processing Module

Before you set up the Sales Order Processing module, you should complete the setup of your company, of the Receivables Management module, and of the Inventory Control module.

To establish default information for Dynamics GP to use while you work in the Sales Order Processing module, follow these steps:

1. **On the Menu bar, select Microsoft Dynamics GP⇨Tools⇨Setup⇨ Sales⇨Sales Order Processing to display the Sales Order Processing Setup window shown in Figure 6-2.**

Figure 6-2: The Sales Order Processing Setup window.

2. **In the Preferences section, select the following options as appropriate:**

   - *Display Item Unit Cost:* Select this option if you want to display the unit cost of each item on the document during transaction entry. For each item, Dynamics GP displays the current cost or the standard cost of the item, depending on the inventory valuation method you assigned.

   - *Track Voided Transactions in History:* Select this option to maintain a historical record of transactions you void. If you don't select this box, Dynamics GP removes voided documents after you post and doesn't include them on reports.

     You should not reuse the document numbers of voided document numbers.

- *Calculate Kit Price Based On Component Cost:* If you're using a percent markup or percent margin pricing method and you select this option, Dynamics GP uses the current or standard cost of the kit components to calculate the total cost for the kit, and the percent markup or the percent margin of the kit.

- *Display Quantity Distribution Warning:* Select this option to have Dynamics GP display an alert message during transaction entry when you don't fully distribute the quantity ordered, invoiced, back ordered, or quoted.

- *Search For New Rates During Transfer Process:* This option affects only those who use Multicurrency Management. When you select this option, Dynamics GP determines whether to use a different exchange rate when transferring information from an existing document, such as a quote, to a new document, such as a sales order.

- *Track Master Numbers:* Select this option to track the flow of documents. Dynamics GP assigns the same master number to each subsequent document you create from an original document. This useful feature helps you maintain a trail for a document as you transfer it from one document type to another. You see, as you transfer the quote to an order or an order to an invoice, Dynamics GP assigns the document a brand new number based on the next sequence number for that document type. But, if you track master numbers, Dynamics GP assigns the same master number to the document as you transfer it through its lifecycle.

- *Prices Not Required in Price List:* Select this option if you use the Inventory Control module and you don't maintain prices for every item. When you enable this option and create a Sales Order Processing document, you can enter a price for an item that has no established price. You can limit the users who can enter prices by assigning a password.

3. **In the Data Entry Defaults section, make selections as appropriate:**

- *Quantity Shortage:* Select a method for Dynamics GP to use when you don't have enough of an item to fulfill a customer's request. Most organizations select Back Order Balance so that Dynamics GP places any shortage in quantity on back order. Since this option is just a default, you can change it on an individual line item basis as you process sales orders.

I typically advise clients not to allow users to override the quantity shortage. If you allow users to override quantity shortages, a user could post an invoice that pulls items from inventory for which no on hand quantities are available, thereby creating a negative on-hand quantity. Negative on-hand quantities are meaningless and distort your stock status.

- *Document Date:* Select the default date you want Dynamics GP to display when you open the Sales Transaction Entry window — the date from the last document you entered or the User Date.

- *Price Warning:* Select a method to alert users when Dynamics GP uses the default price for an item on a sales document instead of the default price for the customer.

  Dynamics GP determines the price of an item on a sales document using the price level for the customer in the Customer Maintenance window. If no price level is available, Dynamics GP uses the default price level in the Receivables Management Setup window. If no default price level appears in the Receivables Management Setup window, Dynamics GP uses the default price level for the item. You can opt to turn on the Extended Pricing feature, which allows for date sensitive and customer specific prices and promotional pricing; if you use this feature, it handles the pricing. The Extended Pricing feature requires more setup and maintenance and is more complicated than the regular pricing, so check with your Dynamics GP consultant to make sure you really require the extended features before you enable it.

- *Requested Ship Date:* Select the default date you want Dynamics GP to display as the requested ship date for line items in the Sales Date Entry window — Document Date or Days After Doc Date. If you select Days After Doc Date, enter the number of days after the document date that the items should be shipped.

4. **In the Document Defaults section, enter default information you want Dynamics GP to display in the Sales Transaction Entry window for the Site ID, Checkbook ID, Quote ID, Order ID, Fulfillment Order ID (if you use sales fulfillment workflow), Invoice ID, Back Order ID, and Return ID.**

If you haven't set up default documents as described in the next section, "Entering a Sales Order Processing Documents," skip Step 4 and complete these entries after you complete the next section.

5. **In the Posting Accounts From section, select an option to specify whether Dynamics GP should display, by default, the posting accounts associated with the customer or with the item as you enter transactions.**

Generally, I recommend that you select Posting Accounts from Item; that way, the Item Card will generate the General Ledger account distributions. Also, I recommend that you place each Item in an Item Class and that you set the default General Ledger accounts at the Item Class level and roll down the accounts to the individual Item Cards so that sales of different classes of inventory items can update different revenue and/or cost of goods sold accounts. Regardless of your selection, Dynamics GP uses the default accounts receivable account on the Customer Card or from your general posting setup.

6. **In the Maintain History section, select the types of history you want to maintain.**

If you select the Quote, Order, and Invoice/Return boxes, Dynamics GP retains a detailed copy of the sales document after it is transferred to another document type, voided, or posted. If you select the Account

Distributions box, Dynamics GP retains a detailed record of transaction distributions that post through the General Ledger, including the audit trail code, account, account description, debit or credit amount, and other information about each transaction.

If you opt not to maintain history, Dynamics GP deletes quotes, orders, and back orders when you transfer or void them and deletes invoices and returns when you post them. Keeping history increases the amount of disk space you need to run Dynamics GP. Periodically, you can remove history to ensure that you're keeping only the records you need (see Chapter 31 of the Microsoft Dynamics GP Sales Order Processing manual). It is generally good practice to save all the history; you can always purge history later if you start to run out of disk space, or better yet, get more disk space. Hard drive capacity has increased dramatically while hardware prices have dropped.

7. **In the Decimal Places for Non-Inventoried Items section, enter the number of decimal places you want to see when you display and enter quantity amounts for non-inventoried items.**

Before you click OK to save your options, you can click the following buttons to set additional options:

- ✔ **Sales Document Setup:** You read about setting of SOP documents in the next section, "Entering a Sales Order Processing Document."

- ✔ **User-Defined:** In the Sales User-Defined Fields Setup window that appears, you can define three list fields, two date fields, and five text fields. You also can define two text fields for prospective customers and five text fields about customer item numbers.

- ✔ **Numbers:** In the Sales Document Numbers Setup window that appears, you can establish codes and starting numbers for SOP documents, and you can identify the form on which you want to print SOP documents. By default, Dynamics GP includes more zeros than you need in the sequence numbers. A seven-digit number with leading zeros is usually more than enough, because you will then have available 9,999,999 documents for each sequence. I also suggest that you include a short alphabetic prefix and a dash; you might use INV-0000001 for invoices. If you do not shorten the sequence numbers, then users will need to type in all those zeros to display documents, because Dynamics GP doesn't automatically fill in the zeros.

- ✔ **Options:** From the sales Order Processing Setup Options window that appears, you can set defaults concerning tax calculations, picking tickets, and purchase orders. You also can opt to allow markdowns, auto-assign lot numbers and serial numbers, and to allow users to enter non-inventoried items.

Entering a Sales Order Processing Document

You create all of the Sales Order Processing documents using the Sales Transaction Entry window — you simply change the document type to select the type of document you want to create. So, in this section, I show you how to create a sales order; later in the chapter, I show you how to transfer the sales order information to an invoice.

Sales orders help you manage promised goods. You create a sales order when a customer agrees to the transaction; when you deliver the goods or services to the customer, you then transfer the information from the sales order to an invoice. A sales order does not update the General Ledger; when you create the invoice, Dynamics GP updates the General Ledger.

To create a sales order, follow these steps:

1. **On the Menu bar, select Transactions⇨Sales⇨Sales Transaction Entry to display the Sales Transaction Entry window shown in Figure 6-3.**

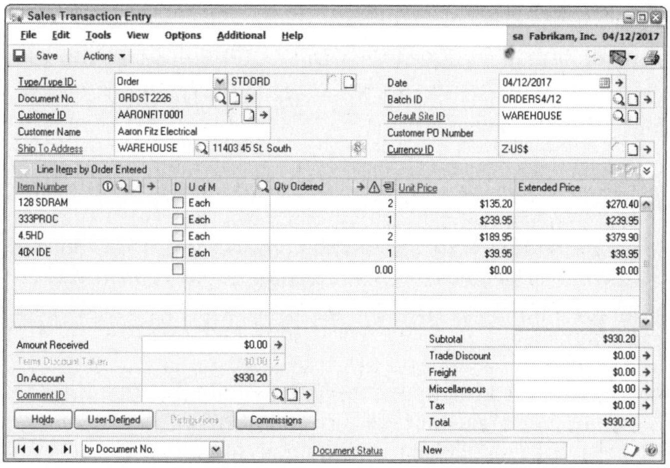

Figure 6-3: The Sales Transaction Entry window.

2. **From the Document Type list, select Order.**

   Dynamics GP fills in the Type ID using the information stored in the Receivables Setup Options window and the Sales Order Setup window.

3. **Click in the Document No. field, and Dynamics GP fills in the next available document number using the information stored in the Sales Order Processing Setup window.**

A word on storing free-form text

While it is generally OK to use free-form text fields to store information other than Dynamics GP intended, please keep in mind that Dynamics GP continues to refer to the field by its original name in the SmartList and on built-in reports. Even if you change the label on the Sales Transaction Entry window, Dynamics GP won't change the label on every window where this field appears, on the SmartList, or on built-in reports. Be aware that Dynamics GP enables you to define the names of true user-defined fields, such as the SOP header user-defined fields, in the appropriate setup window and Dynamics GP displays those field names automatically throughout the system. So, follow this rule of thumb: Use user-defined fields for free-form text until you exhaust all of those fields, and then start storing information in otherwise unused free-form text fields.

4. **In the Customer ID field, select a customer.**

    Dynamics GP fills in the customer's name, currency ID, default addresses, payment terms, shipping method, and tax schedule. If necessary, you can change any of these fields.

5. **In the Date field, enter a document date and select a Batch ID.**

    You must save sales orders in a batch; they will remain in the batch until you void, delete, or transfer them to another document.

6. **In the Default Site ID, select the site to which the merchandise should ship.**

7. **Use the Customer PO Number field to enter the customer's purchase order number if you have it.**

    This field is basically a free-form text field and you can use it to store some other information that is meaningful to your business.

8. **In the Line Items by Order Entered section, click in the first column on the first blank line.**

    You can use the Lookup button to select an item number; Dynamics GP fills in the unit of measure and a default quantity of 1, along with the unit price and the calculated price. If necessary, change the number in the Qty Ordered column; Dynamics GP updates the Extended Price column appropriately.

    You can click the Show Details button above the scroll bar in the Extended Price column to view detailed information for the item on the selected line.

9. **Repeat Step 8 for each item you want to add to the sales order.**

10. **In the Amount Received field, enter any deposit or payment the customer makes on the order.**

11. **If appropriate, change the trade discount, freight, miscellaneous, and tax amounts.**

12. **Click the Holds button to display the Sales Process Holds Entry window and enter hold information about the order.**

    See the section, "Placing Sales Order Processing documents on hold," later in this chapter, for more information.

13. **Click the User-Defined button to Sales User-Defined Fields Entry dialog box and enter information for user-defined fields.**

14. **If you are using sales people and sales territories and want to change the default commission information, you can click the Commissions button to display the Sales Commission Entry window.**

    From this window, you can change the sales person, territory, or commission percentage.

15. **In the Sales Transaction Entry window, click Save to save the sales order.**

Invoices should be posted, either individually or in a batch, generally after you print or electronically transmit them to the customer.

Some additional notes about entering Sales Order Processing documents:

✔ If your organization uses the Available To Promise feature and you want to view available to promise information about an item, click the expansion button beside the Qty Ordered field to open the Inventory Available to Promise Inquiry window.

✔ To remove an item from the document, select the item number and choose Edit➪Delete Row or click the Delete Row button above the Extended Price column.

✔ To change the shipping address for a single line item, select the item number, click the Show Details button on the scroll bar in the Extended Price column. Then, click the Lookup button beside the Ship to Address ID to select a different address or click the expansion button to open the Sales Ship To Address Entry window and change the address; Dynamics GP applies the address change only to the current line item.

✔ For fulfillment orders, invoices, and returns, you can click the Distributions button to change the default distributions for the document.

✔ If your organization uses the Extended Pricing feature and a promotion exists for an item you selected, Dynamics GP displays the Promotion Alert window; from this window, you can opt to apply the promotion to the line. If you accept a free item promotion, Dynamics GP automatically adds the free item to the order.

You can print sales documents as you enter them or, if you prefer to print them as a group, use the Print Sales Documents window; on the Menu bar select Transactions➪Sales➪Print Sales Documents.

Sales Orders and Purchase Orders

If you find that you don't have enough of an item in inventory to fill a sales order, you can back order the quantity for the item and create a purchase order using the back ordered quantity from the sales order instead of reentering the items on a purchase order in Purchase Order Processing.

When you try to include more of an item than you own on a sales order, Dynamics GP prompts you for an action. To generate a purchase order for an out-of-stock item, choose to include the item on a back order. Then, click the line on the sales order or on the back order that contains the item and choose Actions⇨Purchase. Dynamics GP displays the Purchase Orders Preview window shown in Figure 6-4, which displays a variety of information about the purchase order you can create. After you review the information, click Generate, and Dynamics GP creates the purchase order.

Figure 6-4:
The
Purchase
Orders
Preview
window.

Instead of creating a new purchase order for the back ordered items, you can link the sales line item to an existing purchase that you already have entered for the back ordered items; click the Item tab of the Purchase Orders Preview window and then click the Lookup button beside the PO Number field to select a purchase order that contains the item you want to order.

To link a sales line item to an existing purchase order, the following conditions must be true:

- ✔ The purchase order line item has an uncommitted quantity that is equal to or greater than the quantity needed for the sales document.
- ✔ The purchase order must allow commitments.

> ✔ The item numbers and site ID's must match.
>
> ✔ For drop-ship items, the ship-to address and shipping method on the sales order line item must match the ship-to address and shipping method on the purchase order line item.

Managing Sales Order Processing Documents

After you enter Sales Order Processing documents, you may want to make changes to the information. Or, you may want to use lines on one document to create lines on another document or to create an entirely new document. Or, you may want to transfer information from one Sales Order Processing document to another. You may need to delete documents from Dynamics GP because you won't be using them. And, you might want to place a hold on various Sales Order Processing documents.

You can make changes to all types of Sales Order Processing documents except invoices you have posted.

Modifying a Sales Order Processing document

To edit any SOP document, you can redisplay it in the Sales Transaction Entry window and make your changes.

You cannot edit an invoice or return after you post it; to make changes, you need to enter another transaction to reverse the original transaction.

To easily find the document you want to edit, click the Sales series button in the Navigation pane. From the list that appears above the Navigation pane buttons, click Sales Order Transactions. Dynamics GP replaces the Content pane with the Sales Order Transactions list (see Figure 6-5).

In the List area, select the transaction you want to edit by clicking the box in the left-most column beside the transaction. You can use the Filter area to narrow the number of visible documents, and you can click any column of any transaction to view basic details about the document in the Information pane.

Once you select a document, click Edit in the Action pane; Dynamics GP displays the document in the Sales Transaction Entry window.

Filter area

Action pane List Title drop-down menu

Look For field

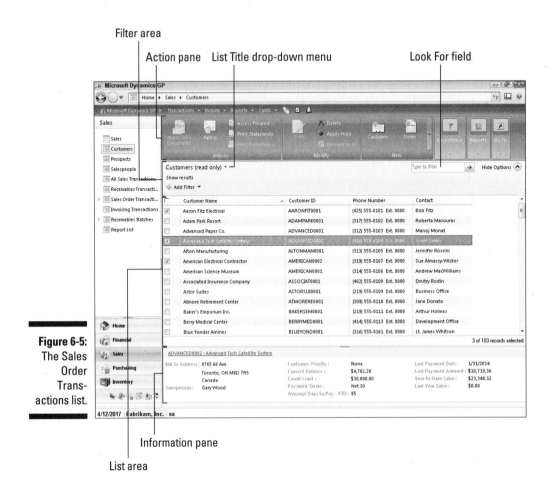

Figure 6-5:
The Sales
Order
Trans-
actions list.

Information pane

List area

Save data entry time — copy information

Suppose you've got a fairly lengthy quote already entered for one customer, and now you need to create a similar quote for another customer. Instead of redoing all the work involved to set up a new SOP document that contains everything you want, you can copy information from an existing SOP document and then add new items or delete lines.

1. **On the Menu bar, select Transactions⇨Sales⇨Sales Transactions Entry to display the Sales Transaction Entry window shown in Figure 6-6.**

2. **Start a new document by selecting the Type and letting Dynamics GP assign the Document Number. Or, you can display an existing document to which you want to add information in the Sales Transaction Entry window.**

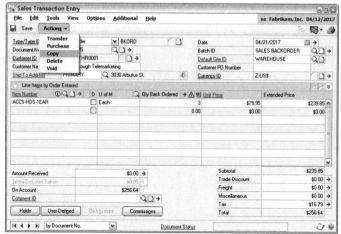

Figure 6-6:
Display the
document to
which you
want to add
information
in the Sales
Transaction
Entry
window.

You can find an existing document in the Sales Transaction Entry
window by selecting the Type/Type ID and the clicking the Lookup
button beside the Document No. field.

3. **Click Actions.**

4. **Click Copy.**

   Dynamics GP displays the Copy a Sales Order window (see Figure 6-7).

5. **Select the SOP document type and number containing the information
   you want to copy.**

6. **Use the Price Option drop-down list and the Use Price Level From
   Target Document options to specify the pricing you want to use for the
   information you copy.**

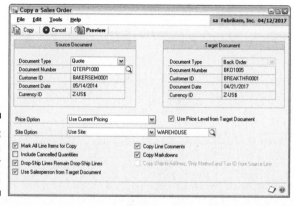

Figure 6-7:
The Copy a
Sales Order
window.

7. **Make a selection from the Site Option list box.**

If you select Use Site, select a site in the field that appears.

8. **Use the check boxes at the bottom of the window to select the copy options you want to use.**

9. **To view and, if appropriate, modify lines before you copy them, click the Preview button at the top of the window to display the Preview Line Items window shown in Figure 6-8.**

   You can select specific lines to include on the SOP document, and you can change the Order Quantity and Unit Cost. Click OK when you finish to redisplay the Copy a Sales Order window.

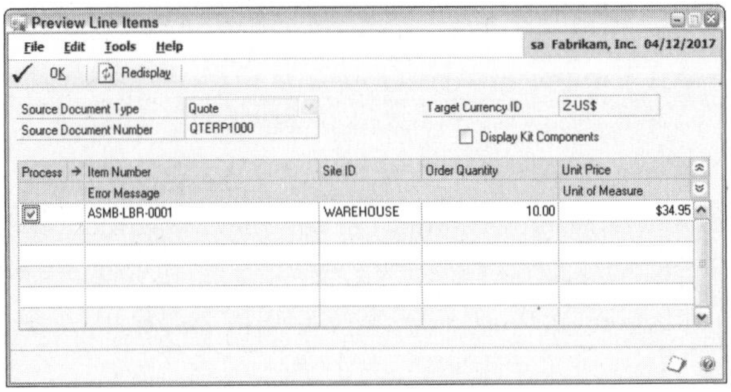

Figure 6-8:
The Preview
Line Items
window.

10. **Click Copy.**

    Dynamics GP displays the modified SOP document in the Sales Transaction Entry window.

As you might have noticed, you can copy information from any type of SOP document to any type of SOP document; you don't need to copy information from the same type of document that you are creating.

Transferring SOP documents

Transfers come in handy when, for example, you create a quote and the customer decides to buy. Instead of re-entering all the information from the quote onto a sales order or an invoice, you can transfer the information.

The settings you use when you establish your document ID's determine the types of transfers you can make. If you set up your document ID's to permit transfers, you can make the following types of transfers:

✔ Quotes to orders and invoices

✔ Orders to invoices and back orders

✔ Fulfillment orders to back orders

✔ Invoices to back orders

✔ Back orders to orders and invoices

You can transfer a single document to another single document or you can transfer multiple documents. Before a you transfer a document, you must verify that you have enough of each item to transfer to an order, invoice, or back order, and that you marked the appropriate transfer options for the document ID.

Dynamics GP won't transfer a document with partial quantities if you marked the Ship Complete Document option in the Sales Customer Detail Entry window. Similarly, if a document with the Ship Complete Document Option marked contains a line item that is discontinued and you override the quantity shortage, Dynamics GP cancels the quantity of the line item that can't be allocated.

To transfer a single document to a new type of document, follow these steps:

1. **Click the Sales series button in the Navigation pane.**

2. **From the list that appears above the Navigation pane buttons, click Sales Order Transactions.**

   Dynamics GP replaces the Content pane with the Sales Order Transactions list shown earlier in Figure 6-5.

3. **Find and select the document you want to transfer and click Edit in the Actions pane.**

   Dynamics GP displays the document in the Sales Transaction Entry window (see Figure 6-9).

4. **Select Actions➪Transfer.**

   Dynamics GP displays the Sales Transfer Documents window shown in Figure 6-10.

5. **Select the type of transfer you want to make and whether to include totals and deposits, if appropriate.**

6. **Use the list boxes at the bottom of the window to specify how you want Dynamics GP to handle shortages.**

   If you select Back Order All or Back Order Balance, Dynamics GP won't create the back order for these quantities when you complete the transfer. You need to open the document created by making the transfer and then transfer the back ordered quantity to a back order.

7. **You can click Preview to open the Sales Preview Transfer Quantities window to view the quantities that Dynamics GP will transfer.**

8. **Click Transfer.**

   Dynamics GP prints the Sales Transfer Log and you can review any errors that occur during the transfer process. In addition, Dynamics GP displays the newly created document in the Sales Transaction Entry window.

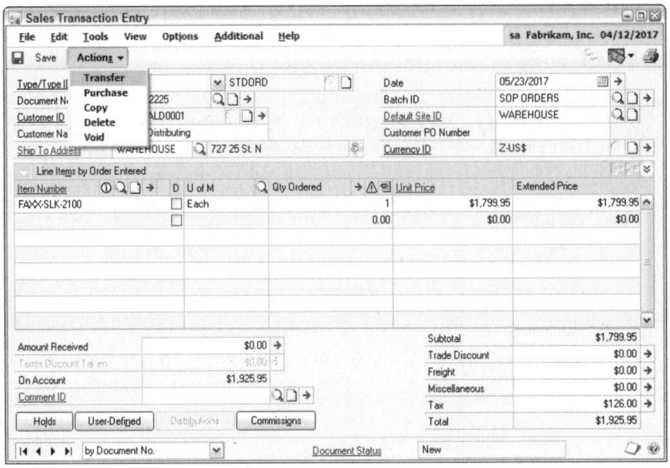

Figure 6-9:
The Sales
Transaction
Entry
window.

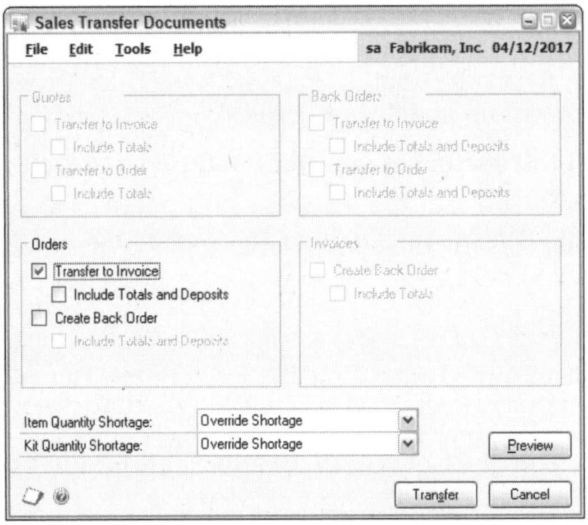

Figure 6-10:
The Sales
Transfer
Documents
window.

> If you have trouble transferring a document for a customer who is part of a national account, check the status of the credit checking and hold or inactive status options in the National Accounts Maintenance window.

You also can transfer a batch of documents at a time using the Sales Transfer Documents window. The batch you transfer can contain any combination of quotes, orders, invoices, back orders, and returns, and you can transfer all documents in the batch to a single type of document or to multiple types of documents. When you transfer a batch, Dynamics GP stores the new documents created by the transfers in the same batch as the original documents. You can transfer individual documents to a new batch by choosing the Document Number expansion button to open the Sales Document Detail

Entry window and assigning a new batch ID. Dynamics GP assigns the documents to the new batch after it completes the transfer.

To transfer a batch of documents, on the Menu bar select Transactions⇨Sales⇨ Sales Batches to display the Sales Batch Entry window (see Figure 6-11).

Figure 6-11:
The Sales
Batch Entry
window.

Select the batch containing the documents you want to transfer and click Transfer. Dynamics GP displays the Sales Transfer Documents window shown previously in Figure 6-10. Fill in the window, identifying the types of transfers you want to make and how to handle shortages. Then, click Transfer, and Dynamics GP prints the Sales Transfer Log and you can review any errors that occur during the transfer process.

If you're using sales fulfillment workflow, use the Sales Multiple Orders to Invoices Transfer window to transfer orders and back orders to invoices (on the Menu bar, select Transactions⇨Sales⇨Transfer Multiple Orders). Using this window, you can transfer groups of documents with the same characteristics, such as batch ID or requested ship date, instead of transferring one document at a time. Dynamics GP creates a separate invoice for each order or back order. You also can choose how to handle item quantity shortages and kit quantity shortages.

Deleting or voiding a Sales Order Processing document

If you set up the document ID you used to create the document to permit deleting, you can delete most documents, with the following exceptions:

✔ You cannot delete any document except a quote that you have printed. You must void documents that you have printed.

✔ You cannot delete any document that contains items that have been partially transferred to another document. You must void the document.

✔ You cannot delete any document assigned to a batch that is marked for posting. Deselect the batch to delete the document.

✔ You cannot delete any document that contains a posted deposit.

✔ You cannot delete any document containing a line item linked to a saved purchase order.

To delete a document, use the instructions in the section, "Modifying a Sales Order Processing document," earlier in this chapter, to display the document in the Sales Transaction Entry window. Then, click the Actions button and choose Delete.

The same rules apply to voiding a document. To void a document, display it in the Sales Transaction Entry window, click Actions, and then click Void.

Placing Sales Order Processing documents on hold

In Dynamics GP, you can put Sales Order Processing documents on hold at various stages of the sales cycle using a *process hold*. For example, your organization might require a manager's approval before you process a return. In this case, you might create the return but assign a process hold to it to avoid posting it until a manager approves it.

You can use process holds to restrict the transfer, fulfillment, printing, or posting of SOP documents. And, you can assign a process hold to an individual document or to groups of documents that use the same document ID.

To be able to assign a process hold, you must set up the process holds you want available; you use the Sales Process Holds Setup window (see Figure 6-12) to establish process holds. On the Menu bar, select Microsoft Dynamics GP⇨Tools⇨Setup⇨Sales⇨Process Holds.

Figure 6-12:
The Sales Process Holds Setup window.

Type a name and description for the process hold you want to establish. If you fill in the Password field, users must supply the password to remove a hold. In the Apply Hold To section, check the types of processes you want Dynamics GP to restrict when you apply this process hold. Click Save.

Once you set up a process hold, you can assign it to a single document or to all sales documents that use a particular document ID.

To assign a process hold to an individual document, you can display it in the Sales Transaction Entry window and click the Holds button to display the Sales Process Holds Entry window shown in Figure 6-13.

Click the Lookup button beside the Process Hold field and select a process hold. Then, click the Assign button; Dynamics GP displays the process hold in the Assigned Holds section. Click OK to redisplay the transaction in the Sales Transaction Entry window; the Holds button contains a stop sign icon, indicating that a hold exists for the transaction. To remove the hold, repeat the process to open the Sales Process Holds Entry window, select the hold, and click Remove. If necessary, supply the password.

If you prefer to work from the Action pane, click the Sales series button in the Navigation pane and then click the Sales Order Transaction list. Select the document you want to place on hold and click the down arrow beside the Edit button in the Modify group. From the menu that appears, click Apply Hold and, when Dynamics GP displays the Apply Holds Options window, select the appropriate hold and click Apply.

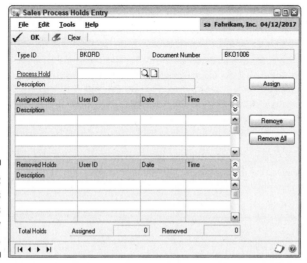

Figure 6-13:
The Sales Process Holds Entry window.

To assign a process hold to all sales documents that use a particular document ID, from the Menu bar select Microsoft Dynamics GP➪Tools➪ Setup➪Sales➪Sales Order Processing to display the Sales Order Processing Setup window. Then, click the Sales Document Setup button at the bottom of the window and choose Quote, Order, Back Order, Fulfillment Order/Invoice, or Return. In the window that appears, select a document ID and then click the Holds button. Dynamics GP displays the Sales Process Holds Assignments window for the selected document ID (see Figure 6-14).

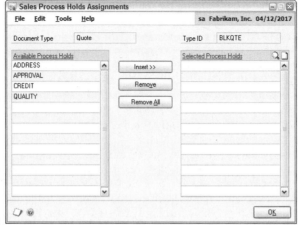

Figure 6-14:
The Sales
Process
Holds
Assign-
ments
window.

In the Available Process Holds column, select a hold and click Insert. You can add as many holds as you want. Click OK to save and close the window.

To remove a process hold from a document ID, reopen the Sales Process Holds Assignments window, and, in the Selected Process Holds column, select the process hold you want to remove. Then, click the Remove button.

In the Sales Process Holds Entry window, Dynamics GP displays, for each document, a complete audit trail that shows the user who added or removed a hold, and the date and time when the hold was added or removed. Sales Process Holds are an easy-to-set-up and handy feature to help control work-flow in the sales process.

Chapter 7

Cash Receipts and Collections

· ·

In This Chapter

▶ Recording payments from customers

▶ Sending statements to customers

▶ Reviewing outstanding balances for customers

▶ Tools you can use to aid in collecting money owed to you

· ·

*O*kay, here comes the fun part — collecting money from your customers! In this chapter, you read about the various time-saving techniques available in Microsoft Dynamics GP to help you collect the money your customers owe you.

Recording Customer Payments

In Dynamics GP, you use the Cash Receipts Entry window to enter payments of any type — cash, check, credit card, and so on — that you receive from customers. You need to apply each payment that you enter so that Dynamics GP can accurately reflect a customer's balance; you typically apply customer payments to invoices. In this section, you first read about the methods available in Dynamics GP to apply the payment to a customer's invoice. Then, I cover recording a customer payment. Finally, the section "Getting paid faster with lock boxes" presents an overview of how Dynamics GP handles lock box payments.

Saving time with Auto Apply

You need to apply customer payments that you enter to one or more invoices so that Dynamics GP can accurately track the customer's outstanding balance. You can opt to automatically apply payments or you can manually apply payments. And, you can apply payments as you enter them or after you enter them.

If you opt to automatically apply a payment, Dynamics GP applies the payment to as many documents as the payment amount allows, applying the payment first to the unpaid document with the oldest due date or document number, based on your selection in the Apply By Section of the Receivables Management Setup dialog box. If the payment amount exceeds the amount of the oldest unpaid invoice, Dynamics GP also applies the payment to the next oldest unpaid invoice.

If you selected Auto Apply to Finance Charges First in the Receivables Management Setup dialog box, Dynamics GP applies the payment amount first to finance charge documents and then to the oldest unpaid document.

If you prefer to manually apply a payment, you can select the documents to which you want to apply the payment. You also can divide the payment among several documents.

Entering a payment

To enter a payment, you use the Cash Receipts Entry window and you can enter payments individually or in batches. Any payments you enter automatically appear as receipts in the Bank Deposit Entry window if you're using the Bank Reconciliation module, enabling you to assign them to a bank deposit. You can read more about using the Bank Reconciliation module in Chapter 9.

If you use national accounts, make sure that you select the Allow Receipts Entry for Children of the National Account option in the National Accounts Maintenance window. Otherwise, you won't be able to record a cash receipt for a child customer of a national account.

To enter a customer payment, follow these steps:

1. **On the Menu bar, select Transactions⇨Sales⇨Cash Receipts to display the Cash Receipts Entry window (see Figure 7-1).**

Figure 7-1:
The Cash
Receipts
Entry
window.

2. **Enter or select a batch ID and a document date.**

   The document date is the date that appears in the Cash Receipts Entry window, and it controls the date Dynamics GP updates your Receivables Management records. Dynamics GP updates your General Ledger files using the date assigned to the batch if you assign the payment to a batch, assuming that you set up Cash Receipts to post by batch date rather than transaction date.

3. **Enter or select a customer ID.**

   Dynamics GP automatically displays the currency ID assigned to the customer card.

   Sometimes you know the invoice number the customer is paying but you aren't sure who the customer is; in that case, you can click the Lookup button beside the Locate Customer By Document field and select the document to which you intend to apply the payment.

4. **Select Check, Cash, or Credit Card to identify the type of payment.**

5. **In the Amount field, enter the amount of the payment.**

   - If you are entering a check, use the Checkbook ID field to enter or select the Checkbook into which you intend to deposit the check, and use the Check/Card Number field to store the check number.

   - If you are entering a cash payment, use the Checkbook ID field to enter or select the Checkbook into which you intend to deposit the cash.

   - If you are entering a credit card payment, use the Credit Card ID field to enter the customer's credit card number.

   If the customer is part of a national account, use the Auto Apply To box to select whether to apply the payment to the child customer displayed in the Cash Receipts Entry window or to the entire national account.

6. **Apply the payment to one or more unpaid sales documents using one of two methods:**

   Applying the payment as you enter it is optional, but recommended.

   - Click the Auto Apply button to automatically apply the payment. Dynamics GP applies the payment to the oldest unpaid documents.

   - Click the Apply button to open the Apply Sales Documents window (see Figure 7-2), and select the check box beside each transaction to which you want Dynamics GP to apply the payment. Click OK to redisplay the Cash Receipts Entry window.

   You can apply a payment to several documents without fully paying any of the documents by selecting each document and changing the amount in the Apply Amount field.

7. **Click the Save button or the Post button.**

Figure 7-2:
The Apply
Sales
Documents
window.

Applying payments after the fact

Suppose that you enter a payment or a credit but you don't apply it at the time you enter it. You use the Apply Sales Documents window to apply the payment or credit.

In this situation, you often don't know the unapplied payments and credits that exist and you don't know which customers have unapplied payments or credits. So, you may find the easiest way to apply these documents is to use the SmartList or the Navigation pane to find and apply them.

You also can use the Unapplied Documents report.

In the Navigation pane, click the Sales series button. From the list that appears above the series buttons, choose the Receivables Transactions list. Find the document you want to apply and select the check box beside it.

To easily find these documents, use the Filter area. In Figure 7-3, I clicked Add Filter and selected And. I then selected Document Type in the first list box that appears, Is in the second list box, and, in the third list box, I checked Credit Memo and Payments.

In the Manage group, choose Apply Sales Documents, which appears unavailable in Figure 7-3 because I opened the Filter list to show you options. Dynamics GP opens the Apply Sales Documents window you saw earlier in Figure 7-2. Fill in the window and click OK.

You can auto-apply from this window; click the Auto Apply button on the toolbar at the top of the window.

Manage group

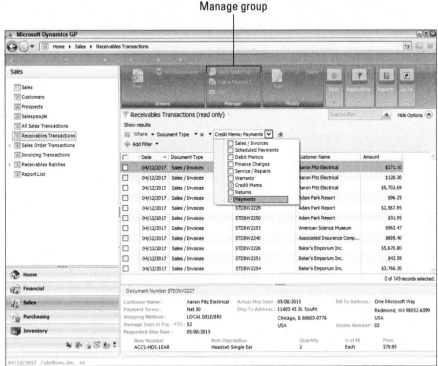

Figure 7-3:
Filtering the
list to find
documents
to apply.

If you entered any Terms Taken or Writeoff amounts, Dynamics GP might print a Receivables Apply Document Journal when you close the window, depending on the options you selected in the Posting Setup window.

Getting paid faster with lock boxes

If your company uses lock box services at any bank, you can automatically import into Dynamics GP the transaction files your banks supply to you; you won't need to enter each of the transactions individually in the transaction files into Dynamics GP.

Because I'm limited on space, I'm going to provide you with an overview of this process, so that you have a basic understanding of how it works. If you want more detail on this subject, see Chapter 18 of the Microsoft Dynamics GP Receivables Management manual.

In Dynamics GP, you specify import options for each bank that supplies you with lockbox transaction files, including the method you want Dynamics GP to use to apply the imported lockbox transactions.

You also set up an ID that profiles each lockbox transaction file you receive, specifying properties such as the checkbook associated with the lockbox transaction file and the format and location on your hard drive where you save the lockbox transaction file when you receive it from your bank. You also set up mapping specifications that identify the fields in Dynamics GP that correspond to the fields in each lockbox transaction file.

When you're ready to import a lockbox transaction file, you use the Lockbox Entry window shown in Figure 7-4.

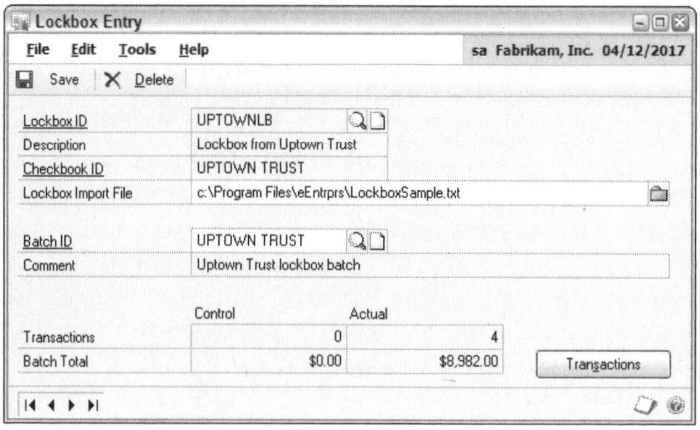

Figure 7-4:
The Lockbox
Entry
window.

The Lockbox ID is the profile you established for the lockbox file, and you select or enter a Batch ID. When you click Transactions, Dynamics GP imports the transactions in the lockbox transaction file and displays them in the Lockbox Transactions window. Dynamics GP displays an indicator beside each entry so that you can determine whether the transaction was fully applied, partially applied, not matched with a customer card, or is associated with national accounts. You can view detailed information about any transaction or assign or reassign a customer number to a transaction.

Keeping Customers in the Loop with Customer Statements

Many companies opt to send statements to their customers on some regular basis, such as monthly or quarterly. The statement shows all of the transactions processed for the customer's account. The statement can show both paid and unpaid transactions, and most companies opt to include unpaid and paid invoices along with the payments for paid invoices; this approach lets the customers see all of the activity on their accounts and ensures that you and your customers agree on the balance owed to you.

To make sure that statements show both paid and unpaid invoices, do not remove paid transactions prior to printing statements. The section "Removing paid transactions," later in this chapter, describes the process and explains its purpose.

Before you print customer statements, you should age your customer accounts to make sure that customer balances appear in the proper aging period. In addition, you may want to assess finance charges to customers with overdue balances.

Aging customer accounts

Dynamics GP doesn't automatically move transactions into new aging periods. Instead, you use a routine in Dynamics GP to age customer balances and ensure that customer balances appear in the correct aging periods. You can age customer balances as often as you like — daily, weekly, or once each month. You should, however, age customer balances before you print statements and also before you print the Aged Trial Balance Report described later in this chapter in the section "Working with the Aged Trial Balance Report." To age customer accounts, follow these steps:

1. **On the Menu bar, select Microsoft Dynamics GP⇨Tools⇨Routines⇨ Sales⇨Aging to display the Receivables Aging Process window shown in Figure 7-5.**

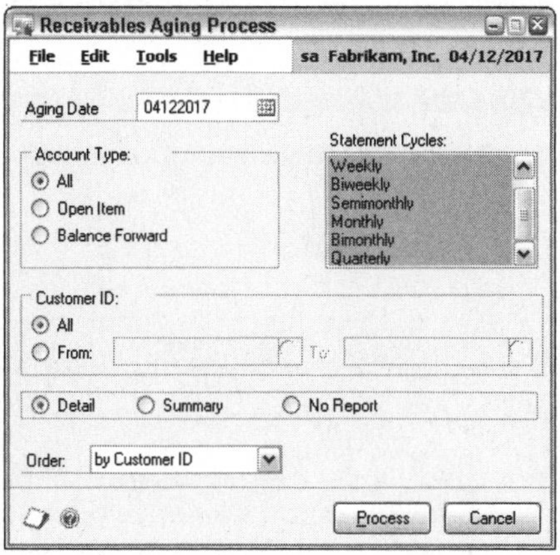

Figure 7-5: The Receivables Aging Process window.

2. **In the Aging Date field, select the date you want Dynamics GP to use to determine the age of a document.**

   Dynamics GP compares this date to either the due date or document date, depending on the option you selected in the Receivables Management Setup window.

3. **In the Account Type section, select whether to age all customers, open item customers, or balance forward customers.**

   When you age open item accounts, Dynamics GP calculates the age of each document and then transfers the documents to the correct aging period.

   When you age balance forward accounts, Dynamics GP calculates the age of each document in the current aging period, but doesn't actually move any documents to the noncurrent aging periods. Instead, Dynamics GP consolidates noncurrent balances after you remove paid transactions.

4. **Use the Statement Cycles list and the Customer ID section to select the customers you want to age.**

   Since you assign each customer card to a statement cycle, selecting particular cycles from the Statement Cycles list using Windows selections techniques — Shift+Click to select a contiguous range of cycles, or Ctrl+Click to select a non-contiguous range of cycles — limits the customers you age to only those customers assigned to the selected statement cycles.

   The Customer ID section enables you to select a range of customers.

   If you make choices in the Statement Cycles list and then select a range of customers, Dynamics GP ages only those customers in the range that are also assigned to the selected statement cycles.

5. **Choose Detail, Summary, or No Report to identify the type of report you want Dynamics GP to print after completing the aging process. Use the Order list box to specify the order of information on the report.**

6. **Click Process to begin aging the selected accounts.**

Assessing finance charges

You can use the Assess Finance Charges window to assign finance charges to a group of customers with past due balances. Many companies use finance charges as a means to encourage customers to pay in a timely fashion.

If you need to assess only one or two finance charges, consider using the Receivables Transaction Entry window to record a Finance Charge document.

To assess finance charges to a group of customers, follow these steps:

1. **On the Menu bar, select Microsoft Dynamics GP⇨Tools⇨Routines⇨ Sales⇨Finance Charge to display the Assess Finance Charges window (see Figure 7-6).**

The last date you assessed finance charges appears in the Last Finance Charge Date field; in the figure, finance charges have never been assessed.

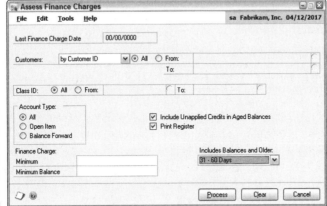

Figure 7-6:
The Assess
Finance
Charges
window.

2. **Select a range of customer cards.**

3. **In the Class ID section, you can restrict the customers for whom you assess finance charges by selecting only certain Customer Class ID's.**

4. **In the Account Type section, opt to assess finance charges for all, open item, or balance forward customers.**

5. **Select the Include Unapplied Credits in Aged Balances check box to ensure that you assess finance charges only for customers who owe you money.**

   If you don't select this box and Dynamics GP contains unapplied payments, you might accidentally assess a finance charge to a customer whose balance is really zero.

   The Include Unapplied Credits in Aged Balances check box is available only if you are assessing finance charges for open item customers and during a period other than the current period.

6. **Select the Print Register check box if you want Dynamics GP to print the Finance Charge Detail Report after assessing the finance charges.**

7. **In the Finance Charge Minimum field, enter the minimum finance charge you want Dynamics GP to assess.**

   If Dynamics GP would typically assess less than the amount you specify for a particular customer, then Dynamics GP assesses no finance charge for the customer.

8. **In the Minimum Balance field, enter the minimum balance that a customer must owe; Dynamics GP won't assess a finance charge for any customer owing less than the amount you enter.**

9. **Use the Includes Balances and Older field to select the earliest aging period for which you want Dynamics GP to assess finance charges.**

   Dynamics GP assesses finance charges on balances in that period and all older periods. If you don't change the default value shown in that field, which is the Current period, Dynamics GP will assess finance charges on all customers with a balance — current or overdue.

10. **Click Process.**

    Dynamics GP creates finance charge transactions and places them in a batch named RM FIN CHG. You can edit these transactions using the Receivables Transaction Entry window.

To ensure that the customer accounts reflect the finance charges, post the batch containing the finance charges.

Printing statements

After you age customers and, if appropriate, assess finance charges, you can print up-to-date statements. Statements list unpaid invoices and can also list paid invoices along with their payments if you don't remove paid transactions before printing statements. Statements show customers the total owed and break down the total to show the amount owed in each aging period.

I describe the process of removing paid transactions later in this chapter in the "Removing paid transactions" section.

When you print statements, you establish a set of options for Dynamics GP to use to print the selected statements. For example, you can opt to print statements only for open item customers with a past due balance. You can save options you set as a group using the Statement ID field; that way, in the future, you don't have to re-establish the options. Instead, you can simply select the appropriate Statement ID. Think of the Statement ID as a template of options that you save so that you can apply the options repeatedly when you print statements in the future for the same group of customers.

To set up Statement IDs and print statements, follow these steps:

1. **On the Menu bar, select Microsoft Dynamics GP⇨Tools⇨Routines⇨ Sales⇨Statements to display the Print Receivables Statements window shown in Figure 7-7.**

2. **In the Statement ID field, enter or select a statement ID and, if appropriate, use the Description field to enter a description.**

3. **In the Print section, choose Alignment Form to verify that the forms are positioned correctly in the printer. Choose Statements to print the actual statements.**

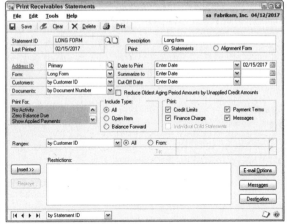

Figure 7-7:
The Print
Receivables
Statements
window.

4. **Use the Address ID field to select the address for your company that you want Dynamics GP to print on the statements.**

5. **From the Form list, select the form on which to print your statements.**

   Dynamics GP provides several different forms, each of which can be modified by your Dynamics GP consultant to, for example, add your company logo, include certain fields and not others, and use certain fonts.

6. **The Customers and Documents fields control the order in which the statements print and the method Dynamics GP uses — By Document Number, By Transaction Date, or By Due Date — to list entries on the statement.**

7. **Select dates in the Date To Print field, the Summarize To field, and the Cut-Off Date field.**

   The date you select in the Date To Print field appears on the statement.

   Dynamics GP summarizes transactions dated on or before the date you select in the Summarized To field and displays a total balance for those transactions. Dynamics GP displays in detail all transactions dated after the date in the Summarized To field.

   Dynamics GP includes transactions dated through the Cut-Off Date on the statements.

8. **Select the Reduce The Oldest Aging Period Amounts By Unapplied Credit Amounts option to ensure that Dynamics GP properly reflects unapplied payments on the statement.**

   This option is available only if you didn't mark Age Unapplied Credit Amounts in the Receivables Management Setup window.

9. **In the Print For list, select the customer groups for which you want to print statements and to specify how applied payments should appear on statements.**

10. **In the Include Type section, specify whether to print statements for all customers, open item customers, or balance forward customers.**

    Typically, most users opt to set up only open item customers, since they prefer to track receivables at the invoice level and don't want to lose detail at the end of each period.

11. **In the Print section, select the information you want to print on statements in addition to invoices and payments.**

12. **In the Ranges section, identify the customers for whom Dynamics GP should print statements. (If you select All, skip to Step 13.)**

    If you want to select a range of customers, use the Range list box to select a method to specify the range. Then, select the range and choose Insert. Dynamics GP considers a range a restriction — because you aren't printing statements for all customers — so, when you choose Insert, the range you selected appears in the Restrictions list.

    You can set up multiple restrictions using different options in the Ranges drop-down list, but you can enter only one restriction for each restriction type. For example, if you enter a restriction to print statements for customer ID's A through C, you can't enter another restriction for customer ID's D through G. To print statements for multiple ranges of customers, you must print statements for each range separately.

13. **You can use the E-mail Options button, the Messages button, and the Destination button to establish e-mail statement options, create specific messages for statements falling into various categories such as 90 Days Old, and specify output destinations — screen, printer, and file — for the statements.**

    See the next section for details on setting e-mail options.

14. **Choose Save to save the settings for the Statement ID for future printing.**

To print the statements, select the appropriate Statement ID and choose Print.

E-mailing statements automatically

When you set up customer cards, you had the option, in the Customer Maintenance Options window, to send statements by e-mail. If you set up any customers to receive e-mail statements, then you can use the E-mail Statements Options window to define your options.

To send customer statements by e-mail, you must use a MAPI-compliant e-mail service and have Adobe PDFWriter installed.

When you send a customer statement by e-mail, Dynamics GP creates the state-ment as a PDF file using Adobe Distiller or PDFWriter and attaches the PDF file to an e-mail message that you send to the customer. Dynamics GP stores the PDF statements in a folder within the Windows temp folder and automatically deletes the PDF statement after you send it as an e-mail attachment.

To set up options for e-mail statements, on the Menu bar select Microsoft Dynamics GP⇨Tools⇨Routines⇨Sales⇨Statements to display the Print Receivables Statements window shown previously in Figure 7-7. Select a Statement ID and then click the E-mail Options button to display the E-mail Statements Options dialog box shown in Figure 7-8.

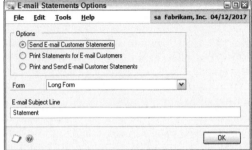

Figure 7-8:
The E-mail
Statements
Options
dialog box.

In the Options section, make a selection:

✔ **Send E-mail Customer Statements:** Select this option to send state-ments by e-mail to the Statement ID's selected customers for whom you marked Send E-mail Statements in the Customer Maintenance Options window.

✔ **Print Statements for E-mail Customers:** Select this option to print state-ments for the Statement ID's selected customers for whom you marked Send E-mail Statements in the Customer Maintenance Options window. Dynamics GP will neither create PDF files nor e-mail messages with attachments.

✔ **Print and Send E-mail Customer Statements:** Select this option to both print and send statements by e-mail to the Statement ID's selected cus-tomers for whom you marked Send E-mail Statements in the Customer Maintenance Options window.

Select the form to use for the e-mail statements and, in the E-mail Subject Line field, type the subject line you want to appear on the e-mail message the customers receive. Choose OK to close the e-mail Statements Options dialog box and, in the Print Receivables Statements window, choose Save to save your e-mail statement options. Choose Print to print or send e-mail customer statements.

After you send e-mail statements, Dynamics GP e-mails a status report to the e-mail address you specified in the Receivables Management Setup window, identifying the e-mail statements that were sent successfully and providing information about any errors that might have occurred during the process.

Working with the Aged Trial Balance Report

The Aged Trial Balance report lists the amount that each customer owes you and divides the amount into the aging periods you defined in the Receivables Management Setup window. Let's assume that you set up traditional aging periods of 0–30 days, 31–60 days, 61–90 days, and 91–120 days. When you view the Aged Trial Balance report, you can see how much a customer owes you and how much of the owed amount is current (between 0 and 30 days old), how much is 31–60 days old, and so on.

As you read earlier in this chapter, in the section "Aging customer accounts," Dynamics GP doesn't automatically move transactions into new aging periods. Instead, you use a routine in Dynamics GP to age customer balances and ensure that customer balances appear in the correct aging periods. You can age customer balances as often as you like — daily, weekly, or once each month. You should age customer balances before you print the Aged Trial Balance report.

You can print the Aged Trial Balance in detail, showing every transaction that affects each customer, or you can summarize it to simply view the totals. If you print the report in detail, you'll notice that Dynamics GP prints paid invoices, along with their payments. If the invoice is fully paid, the net amount is $0, so the customer's balance is correct. But you might be wondering why Dynamics GP prints paid invoices on the report.

Paid invoices remain open and appear on reports until you remove paid transactions. The process of removing paid transactions moves the transactions to history. Dynamics GP handles paid invoices in this way so that you can print customer statements that include both the original invoice and the customer's associated payments.

In the sections that follow, I'll show you how to remove paid transactions and then print the Aged Trial Balance report, both in summary and in detail.

Removing paid transactions

When you record a payment that pays an invoice in full, Dynamics GP doesn't automatically move the paid invoice to history. Instead, Dynamics GP continues to treat the paid invoice as an open transaction and displays it, along with its associated payment(s) on the Aged Trial Balance report. Dynamics GP handles paid invoices in this manner so that both the paid invoice and its associated payment(s) can appear on customer statements, giving your customers the opportunity to see that you recorded the invoice and its payment(s).

If you were to treat these documents as open documents forever, the Aged Trial Balance report would become very long and cumbersome to use. So, periodically — typically monthly — you use a routine to remove paid transactions. Removing paid transactions moves fully paid invoices and their associated payments to history; once in history, these transactions no longer appear on the Aged Trial Balance report.

To move paid transactions to history, follow these steps:

1. **On the Menu bar, select Microsoft Dynamics GP⇨Tools⇨Routines⇨ Sales⇨Paid Transaction Removal to display the Paid Sales Transaction Removal window (see Figure 7-9).**

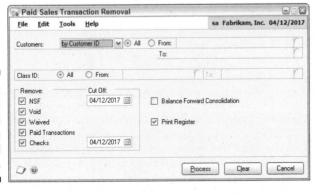

Figure 7-9:
The Paid
Sales
Transaction
Removal
window.

2. **Use the Customers list box and the options beside it to select a range of customer records for whom you want to remove paid transactions.**

3. **In the Class ID section, you can select a range of Class ID's to further restrict the customer records Dynamics GP should select.**

   Dynamics GP will remove paid transactions for customer records that fall within both the customer range and the class range.

4. **In the Remove section, select the types of paid transactions you want Dynamics GP to remove and enter a cutoff date.**

   Dynamics GP removes transactions that fall on or before the cutoff date.

Once you move checks to history, you cannot mark them as NSF checks. Therefore, you may wish to select a cutoff date for checks that is approximately one month earlier than the cutoff date you select for transactions.

5. **Select the Balance Forward Consolidation check box to have Dynamics GP summarize all documents for each balance forward customer and move their total from the current aging period to the noncurrent aging period.**

6. **Select the Print Register box to print a Removed Transaction Register that lists all removed transactions after Dynamics GP finishes removing the transactions; printing this report is optional.**

7. **Click Process to remove the selected transactions.**

Printing the report

Although you don't have to print statements or remove paid transactions before you print the Aged Trial Balance, I'm going to assume that you have, at a minimum, aged customer balances as described earlier in this chapter in the section "Aging customer accounts." And, I'll assume that you removed paid transactions if you have printed customer statements and don't want the Aged Trial Balance report to include paid invoices and their payments.

If you don't age customer balances before you print this report, the information on the report might not be accurate.

When you print any report in Dynamics GP, you establish and save a set of options that identifies the information Dynamics GP should include when printing the report as well as where to print the report — your screen, a printer, or a file. In the steps that follow, I'm going to print the Aged Trial Balance w/Options report, because, using this version of the Aged Trial Balance, you can best control what prints. For example, you can opt not to print customers with zero balances on the report. Follow these steps:

1. **Choose Reports⇨Sales⇨Trial Balance to display the Receivables Trial Balance Reports window shown in Figure 7-10.**

2. **Open the Reports list and select Aged Trial Balance w/Options.**

   Once you establish the report options, click the set of options you want to use in the Options list and click the Insert button. Then, click the Print button.

3. **If you haven't already set up options to print the Aged Trial Balance w/Options report, click the New button.**

   Dynamics GP displays the Receivables Trial Balance Report Options window shown in Figure 7-11.

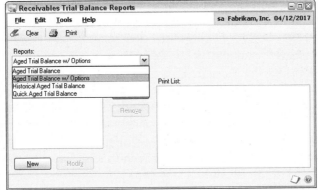

Figure 7-10:
The
Receivables
Trial
Balance
Reports
window.

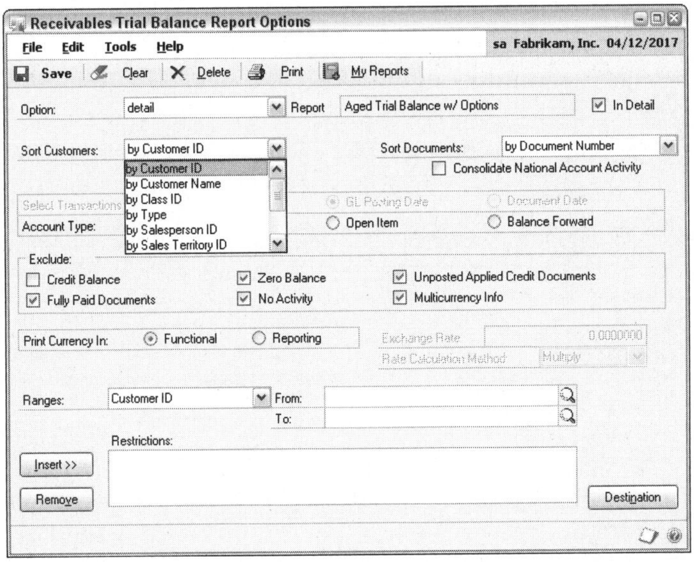

Figure 7-11:
The
Receivables
Trial
Balance
Report
Options
window.

4. **In the Option field, type the name you want to assign to this set of options; make it something that will help you remember the options you establish. Other users will be able to see, use, and possibly change these options.**

When you set report options, they apply to a specific report within a particular Dynamics GP company; they do not apply to all Dynamics GP companies.

5. **Select the In Detail check box to set up options that print each paid and unpaid invoice and any associated payment(s) for the selected customers.**

Do *not* select this option to print a summary version of the report that displays each customer's balance, divided up into aging periods.

6. **Use the Sort Customers list to select the way you want to sort the data on the report.**

7. **In the Exclude section, check boxes to exclude customers who meet those criteria; for example, if you check Zero Balance, Dynamics GP won't include any customers with a zero balance on the report.**

8. **Use the Ranges list box and the From and To fields to select only certain customers to appear on the report and then click the Insert button to restrict the report to display information only for the selected customers.**

9. **You can click the Destination button to specify where to print the report.**

10. **Click Save to redisplay the Receivables Trial Balance Reports window.**

11. **Click Print.**

Dynamics GP produces a report similar to the one shown in Figure 7-12.

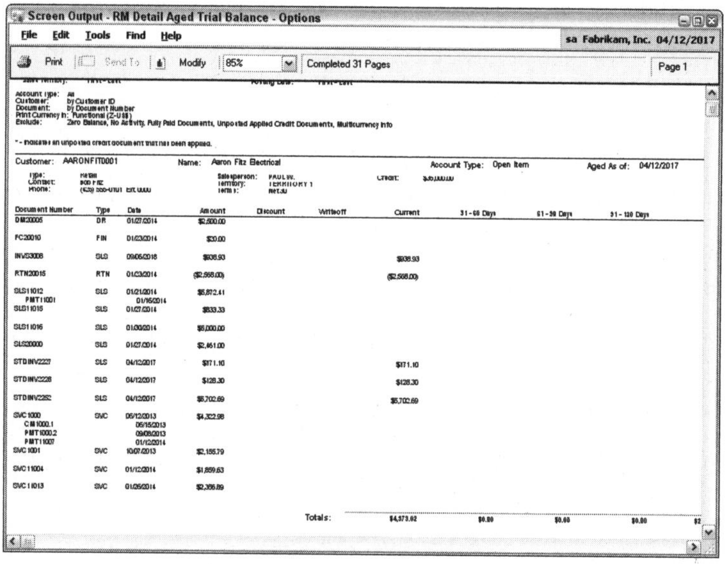

Figure 7-12:
A typical
Aged Trial
Balance
report.

If you want to control the options that appear unavailable in Figure 7-11, click the Sales series button in the Navigation pane and then click Report List from the list above the series buttons. Select the Aged Trial Balance w/Options report and then click the Edit Report Option button in the Modify group of the Actions pane. When the Receivables Trial Balance Report Options window appears, the options in the middle of the window will be available.

If you need to reconcile the Aged Trial Balance report to the Accounts Receivable account on your balance sheet, you may want to use the Historical Aged Trial Balance report, because you can print the Historical Aged Trial Balance report using a cutoff date based on the general ledger posting date as opposed to the document date. Using a cutoff date is handy in cases where you have documents dated one month but posted to the General Ledger in either a prior or subsequent fiscal period, such as an invoice dated March 31 that you posted to the General Ledger in a batch dated in the first week of April, and April begins a new fiscal period.

Collecting More Money Faster

Collecting money owed to you in a timely fashion can make or break your business. Sometimes, charging finance charges isn't sufficient motivation to entice customers to pay in a timely fashion, and you find that you need to designate staff members to make follow-up calls and send out letters to induce customers to pay.

In cases where cash flow is tight and you need to stay on top of your receivables, you might consider using the Collections Management module to help you track where you stand as you attempt to collect money owed to you. I'm going to provide you with an overview of the capabilities and functioning of the Collections Management module.

Using the Collections Management module, you can establish various staff members who are Dynamics GP users as "collectors" and assign various customer accounts to each collector. The *collectors* can create notes that identify each customer's status along with tasks for each customer that identify the steps that need to be taken to collect money due to you. Collectors also can create queries to help them do their jobs; for example, a collector may run a query daily that identifies customers with overdue balances as of that day. As customers pay, their names disappear from the list, while newly past-due customers appear on the list.

The Collections Management module also enables you to calculate the average sales per day and the average number of days that payments are outstanding in a rolling period.

Like other Dynamics GP modules, you need to do some setup work to establish the way the Collections Management module will function. For example, you establish the default overdue aging period, the types of collector notes that Dynamics GP should save, whether to age documents prior to running queries, and the default customer contact method. You also set up collectors, who are Dynamics GP users who can view information only from the Collections Management module. You can establish a range of customers for each collector, and you can restrict access to other collectors' notes. And, you enter collection information about your customers, such as the customer contact. Finally, you set up actions such as Dispute or Promise to Pay that collectors will be able to assign to notes they enter about customers. For example, suppose that a collector calls a customer regarding four outstanding invoices and the customer promises to pay the invoices by the end of the week. The collector can assign a promise to pay action to the invoices that includes a specified number of days for the customer to follow through on the promise. If the customer doesn't pay within the promised timeframe, Dynamics GP generates a collection task for the collector, and the collector can take the next appropriate action in the collection process.

Once you set up the Collections Management module, collectors can go to work, using the Collections Management Main Window shown in Figure 7-13 to complete most of their collection tasks.

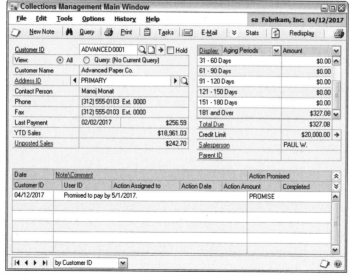

Figure 7-13: The Collections Management Main Window.

From this window, you can create notes, view financial information, and print letters, statements, and invoices or send them by e-mail.

Using the Collections Management Notes window shown in Figure 7-14, a collector can document a conversation with a customer and attach the note to one of the customer's invoices. The collector can also assign an action date to the note and, using the Collection Management Task List shown in Figure 7-15, monitor what actions the collector needs to take. You can open both windows from the Collections Management Main Window.

To analyze how your collections are going, you can use the Collections Management Build Query window to create a list of customers that meet criteria you specify; for example, you can build a query to help you generate a list of customers who need to be called about their overdue balances. Dynamics GP saves query results by Collector ID, so each collector can run his or her own queries and work with separate lists of customers. And, you can use the Collections Management Days Sales Outstanding window to calculate the average sales per day and the average number of days that payments are outstanding.

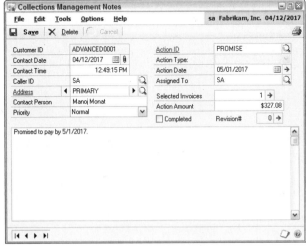

Figure 7-14:
The Collections Management Notes window.

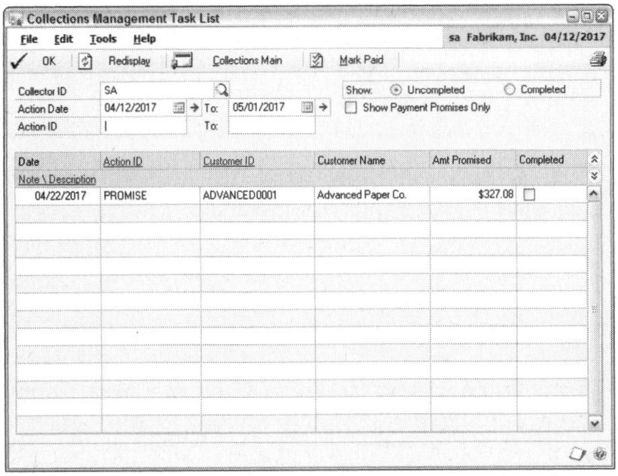

Figure 7-15:
The Collection Management Task List.

Finally, the Collections Management module comes with its own set of predefined collection letters that you can send to encourage customers to pay. You can add your own letters to the group, and you can send collection letters en masse via email from within the Collections Management module.

Chapter 8

All Roads Lead to the General Ledger

Typically, you use modules like the Purchasing module or the Receivables Management module to record your day-to-day transactions, and the process of posting transfers the effects of these transactions to the General Ledger module, which organizes your financial information by accounts. There are also transactions you need to record that affect your business but fall outside the realm of your day-to-day transactions, such as depreciation or accrued expenses. To enter these transactions, you work in the General Ledger module and enter journal entries. And, using the General Ledger module, you can set up budgets for your accounts so that you can compare your financial expectations to what actually happens in your business.

As with other modules in the Microsoft Dynamics GP series, you need to do a little setup work for the General Ledger module before you begin using it. After you set up the module, you begin the day-to-day business of using the General Ledger: You can make changes to accounts, record journal entries and, if you want, set up account budgets.

Setting Up Defaults

Before you set up the General Ledger module, you should set up options for your company, including account format, fiscal periods, posting, source documents, and audit trail codes. In Chapter 2 and in the System Setup Guide, you'll find more information about setting up these options. Later in this chapter, I'll talk about using source documents and audit trail codes to trace a document's history in Dynamics GP.

From the General Ledger Setup window, you can set a variety of options, including establishing the next journal entry number and indicating how Dynamics GP should display account balances in the General Ledger Account Maintenance as well as other Dynamics GP windows.

Follow these steps to set up defaults for the General Ledger module:

1. **On the Menu bar, select Microsoft Dynamics GP⇨Tools⇨Setup⇨ Financial⇨General Ledger to display the General Ledger Setup window shown in Figure 8-1.**

2. **In the Next Journal Entry field, type the number you want Dynamics GP to assign to the next journal entry number.**

3. **In the Display section, select whether you want Dynamics GP to display account balances as net change or period balance amounts.**

   If you choose Net Change, Dynamics GP displays the difference between each period and the preceding period. If you choose Period Balances, Dynamics GP displays the account's balance for each period.

   Dynamics GP uses the method you select throughout your company, but you can change the method in each window where account balances appear.

4. **In the Retained Earnings section, select the account your company uses for Retained Earnings and select the Close to Divisional Account Segments check box if your company tracks profit and loss for divisions.**

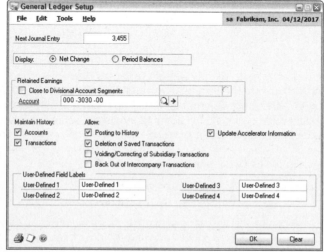

Figure 8-1:
The General
Ledger
Setup
window.

5. **Use the check boxes under Maintain History to specify whether Dynamics GP should keep account history, transaction history, or both.**

   If you opt to keep Account history, Dynamics GP stores account summary balances only. If you opt to keep Transaction history, Dynamics GP stores all transactions posted to an account. You can keep history for an unlimited number of years, and, during the year-end closing process, Dynamics GP changes current-year balances to previous-year balances.

   Most companies opt to keep both types of history to be able to print comparative financial statements and to calculate budgets based on information from a previous year.

6. **In the Allow section, select the following check boxes as appropriate:**

   - *Posting to History:* Select this option to enable users to post transactions to the most recent historical year; you will want to check this box to be able to post adjustments after you have closed the year. If you post to the closed year, Dynamics GP automatically creates a prior period adjustment entry to correct retained earnings.

   Initially, you might want to leave this option unchecked so that nobody accidentally posts to history; later, you can enable the option when you need it.

   - *Deletion of Saved Transactions:* Select this option to allow users to delete unposted transactions. If you don't select this box, users must void unposted transactions.

   - *Voiding/Correcting of Subsidiary Transactions:* Select this option to enable users to use the General Ledger module to void saved transactions that originate in other modules. Similarly, if you select this option, you enable users to use the General Ledger to back out or back out and correct posted transactions that originate in other modules.

   If a user voids or corrects a subsidiary transaction in the General Ledger module, Dynamics GP doesn't update the transactions in the subsidiary module. So, try to void or correct the transaction directly in the subsidiary module to allow the voiding and/or correcting journal entries to flow naturally from the subsidiary module to the General Ledger.

   - *Back Out of Intercompany Transactions:* Select this option to allow users to back out intercompany transactions.

   You back out a transaction to remove its effect from your company. When you back out a transaction, Dynamics GP creates a new transaction that reverses the debits and credits of the original transaction when you post the new transaction, ensuring a full audit trail. Dynamics GP does not allow you to delete or modify history directly.

7. **Select the Update Accelerator Information box if you use account ranges and wildcard characters in your financial statements and want to update row and column information on financial statements each time you modify the layout of an existing financial report using Advanced Financial Analysis.**

If you intend to write your financial statements using the FRx Report Writer as most consultants recommend, you won't use the Advanced Financial report writer feature, so this option is not important.

8. **In the User-Defined Field Labels section, establish labels for any user-defined fields you intend to use.**

You'll find free-form user-defined text fields on the General Ledger Account Card that can come in handy. For example, when migrating from another accounting system, if you revamp your chart of accounts in the process, you might want to store the legacy (old) account number in one of the user-defined fields.

9. **Click OK to save your choices.**

You may also want to set up transaction matching; see Chapter 1 of the General Ledger documentation for details. When you use transaction matching, you link related transaction distributions from different journal entries.

Building Your Chart of Accounts

In Chapter 2, I cover selecting the default chart of accounts when you set up your company. But, many users prefer to export the chart of accounts from their old systems, modify it in Microsoft Excel, and then have a Dynamics GP consultant import the chart of accounts using Integration Manager during the data conversion.

But, once your chart of accounts is in place, it isn't carved in stone; you will occasionally need to add, edit, or remove accounts.

Adding accounts to the Chart of Accounts

Your Dynamics GP Chart of Accounts can include three types of accounts: posting, unit, and allocation accounts.

You'll use *posting* accounts most often, and they get their name because you post transactions to them that reflect accounting events that occur in your business. Posting accounts track your company's assets, liabilities, revenue, expenses, and equity, and their balances appear on financial reports. Your Cash account, Accounts Payable account, and Telephone expense account are all posting accounts.

Unit accounts are similar to posting accounts in that you use them during transaction entry and Dynamics GP maintains both history and budget information for them. Unit accounts differ from posting accounts because unit accounts store quantities rather than dollars. Unit accounts are often used as the basis for an allocation; for example, you might allocate the rent expense to departments or cost centers based on head counts or square footage.

You can use *allocation* accounts to distribute percentages of a single transaction among several accounts. Dynamics GP supports two types of allocation accounts: fixed and variable. You use fixed allocation accounts to distribute fixed percentages of a single transaction among several accounts. You use variable allocation accounts in the same way, but only when you need to calculate the breakdown of the distribution using some factor besides a fixed percentage.

For more information on unit accounts, fixed allocation accounts, and variable allocation accounts, see Chapters 4, 5, and 6 of the Dynamics GP General Ledger documentation.

Since you use posting accounts more than any other type of account, follow these steps to add a posting account to the Chart of Accounts:

You can set up any of these account types by selecting the appropriate account type from the Cards⇨Financial menu.

1. **On the Menu bar, select Cards⇨Financial⇨Account to display the Account Maintenance window shown in Figure 8-2.**

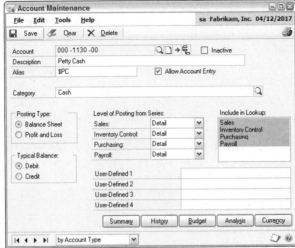

Figure 8-2:
The Account Maintenance window.

2. **In the Account field, enter a number.**

   Although you can enter any combination of letters or numbers, most people use only numbers when creating accounts.

3. **In the Description field, type a description for the account.**

   If you've set up account segments descriptions, you can leave the Description field blank, and Dynamics GP will create the account description by combining the account segment descriptions. For example, suppose that your chart of accounts has three segments: one each for region, department, and natural account. Suppose further that 01 represents the Southwest region, 100 represents the Marketing department, and 6200 represents the Salaries expense natural account. When you create the account 01-100-6200, Dynamics GP automatically fills in an account description of Southwest-Marketing-Salaries. You can override the description at any time. The Description field is 100 characters in length, so keep your segment descriptions short if you have a lot of segments.

   You can use the Alias field to enter a shorter name for the account to speed up data entry; you can use the account alias instead of the entire account number anywhere where you enter or select accounts.

4. **Select the Allow Account Entry check box to enable users to manually enter or select this account in transaction or distribution entry windows.**

5. **In the Category field, enter or select an account category to place the account in the proper group on financial statements.**

   For example, assign cash accounts such as Petty Cash, Operating, and Payroll to the Cash category.

   Dynamics GP's General Ledger module comes with 48 predefined account categories that you can use or modify; on the Menu bar, select Microsoft Dynamics GP⇨Tools⇨Setup⇨Financial⇨Category to display the Account Category Setup dialog box, scroll to the last line, and type the new category description.

   Since the FRx Financial Report Writer can read the Account Category as a basis for selecting accounts on financial statements, it's a good idea to create account categories that match your high level summary financial statement line item descriptions. In this way, you can specify the General Ledger Link Row format in FRx by using the Account Category, instead of using the account number, or account sets. When you add a new account in Dynamics GP, you simply assign it to the proper category, and it will automatically appear on your FRx report without any intervention on your part.

6. **In the Posting Type section, specify whether the account typically appears on the Balance Sheet or the Profit and Loss Statement.**

   Your choice in this section determines whether Dynamics GP will close the account at year-end.

7. **In the Typical Balances section, select Debit or Credit to indicate the account's typical balance.**

   Asset and expense accounts typically have debit balances, while liability, revenue, and equity accounts typically have credit balances.

8. **In the list boxes in the Level of Posting from Series section, select Detail to post a separate distribution amount to this account for each transaction in a batch or select Summary to post a summarized total for an entire group of transactions to this account.**

9. **In the Include in Lookup field, select the series where you expect to use this posting account; for each series you select, Dynamics GP makes the account appear in all Lookup windows.**

   Use standard Windows select techniques in this field; press Shift and click to select contiguous choices, or press Ctrl and click to select non-contiguous choices.

10. **In User-Defined 1 through User-Defined 4 fields, enter additional information about the posting account.**

    Dynamics GP displays this information on the Posting Accounts List and the Accounts List.

11. **Click the buttons at the bottom of the window to enter the following information:**

    • *Summary:* Select this button to open the Account summary window and view open-year summary information on a period-by-period basis for the account.

    • *History:* Select this button to open the Account History window to view and enter historical year summary information.

    • *Budget:* Select this button to open the Single-Account Budget Maintenance window and enter a budget for the account. You can set up a budget for the account now or wait until all accounts have been entered; for more information on budgeting, see the section, "Creating Budgets" later in this chapter.

    • *Analysis:* Select this button to open the Account Analysis Defaults window and enter default Multidimensional Analysis information. For more information, refer to the Microsoft Dynamics GP Multidimensional Analysis documentation. The Account Analysis feature is optional, and most Dynamics GP users do not need to use it.

    • *Currency:* Select this button if you're using Multicurrency Management to display the Select Account Currencies window and assign currencies to the account.

12. **Choose Save to save the account.**

When you don't need an account anymore

If an account has become obsolete and you're not planning to use it again, you can delete it from the Chart of Accounts if it meets certain criteria. If the account doesn't meet the criteria listed below, you can't delete it, but you can make it inactive.

To delete an account from the Chart of Accounts, it must *not*

- Have a balance
- Have activity for an open period
- Appear on any unposted transaction
- Be part of an allocation account
- Have any multicurrency data
- Have history amounts
- Be part of any transaction history records

When you delete an account, Dynamics GP also removes all budget information for the account.

You may find it more advantageous to make an account inactive instead of deleting it. You can't post to inactive accounts, but information for inactive accounts continues to appear on the financial statements if the inactive accounts have year-to-date activity. When you print other General Ledger reports, such as account lists, you can choose to include or exclude inactive accounts.

For details on deleting a unit account, fixed allocation account, or variable allocation account (or making one of these types of accounts inactive), see Chapters 4, 5, and 6, respectively, of the Dynamics GP General Ledger documentation.

To delete a posting account or make it inactive, on the Menu bar, select Cards⇨Financial⇨Account to display the Account Maintenance window. Then, using the Lookup button, select the account to display its information. To make it inactive, select the Inactive check box beside the Account number and then click the Save button. To delete it, click the Delete button on the toolbar.

Editing accounts

You can edit any single account by displaying it in the Account Maintenance window (on the Menu bar, select Cards⇨Financial⇨Account), making changes, and then clicking Save.

For information on editing unit accounts, fixed allocation accounts, or variable allocation accounts, see Chapters 4, 5, and 6, respectively, of the Dynamics GP General Ledger documentation.

You can copy, move, delete, inactivate, or update ranges of posting, unit, fixed allocation, and variable allocation accounts that you've already entered in your chart of accounts.

You might want to copy a range of accounts if, for example, you have created a set of accounts for one department that you would like to use for another department. During the process of copying the accounts, you can assign a new number to the segment that represents the department. When you copy accounts, Dynamics GP copies the typical balance, account type, series, and active/inactive information, but not the account balance. Dynamics GP creates account descriptions for the copied accounts by combining the descriptions of the account segments, leaving spaces in the account description for any segments that have a blank description.

You might want to move accounts if, for example, you change the responsibilities within your company and a different department now performs tasks associated with a range of accounts. During the process of moving the accounts, you can assign a new number to the segment that represents the department that now performs the tasks. When you move accounts, Dynamics GP creates descriptions for the new accounts by combining the descriptions of the account segments, leaving spaces in the account description for any segments that have a blank description. Dynamics GP allows you to move accounts *only if* they

- ✔ **Do not have a balance**
- ✔ **Do not have activity for an open period**
- ✔ **Do not appear on any unposted transaction**
- ✔ **Are not part of an allocation account**
- ✔ **Do not have any multicurrency data**
- ✔ **Do not have history amounts**
- ✔ **Are not part of any transaction history records**

You can update the level of posting for a range of accounts to, for example, change the level of posting from summary to detail so that you can track additional information for that range of accounts.

You can delete a single account or make a single account inactive using the technique described in the preceding section. But, you also can delete a range of accounts or make a range of accounts inactive.

To delete a range of accounts, they must meet the same criteria listed previously to move a range of accounts.

You use the Mass Modify Chart of Accounts window to copy, move, delete, inactivate, or update ranges of accounts. When you make mass changes to accounts, you can't "undo" the effects unless you restore a backup of your company. So, before you use the Mass Modify Chart of Accounts window, be sure to back up your company's data; see Chapter 14 for information on backing up. In addition, you might want to experiment with the sample company.

To modify a range of accounts, follow these steps:

1. **On the Menu bar, select Cards⇔Financial⇔Mass Modify to display the Mass Modify Chart of Accounts window shown in Figure 8-3.**

2. **From the Modify list, select the action you want to take.**

3. **In the Account section, select a range of accounts.**

4. **If you're copying or moving accounts, enter an account mask, using question marks to represent the portion of the account number that Dynamics GP *should not* change and supplying values for the portion of the account number Dynamics GP *should* change.**

   For example, suppose that your department number appears in the first segment and you want to create a similar set of accounts within the selected range for a new department. Supply the new department's number in the first segment and leave question marks in the other segments.

5. **If you're making a range of accounts inactive, select whether to include all accounts within the range or only those with zero balances.**

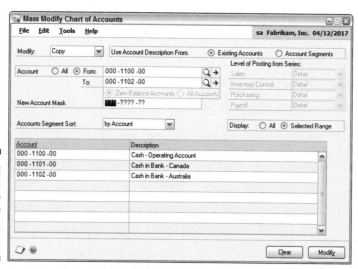

Figure 8-3:
The Mass
Modify
Chart of
Accounts
window.

6. If you're updating accounts, select the level of posting — Detail or Summary — for each series.

7. In the Display section, you can choose Selected Range to limit the accounts that appear in the Mass Modify Chart of Accounts window to only those that meet the criteria you establish.

8. Choose Modify.

Entering Journal Entries

Typically, you record a journal entry transaction only once. However, if you assign a journal entry to a recurring batch, you can post the entry periodically. To set up a batch of journal entries, on the Menu bar select Transactions⇨Financial⇨Batches. For details on setting up a batch, see Chapter 3.

To record a journal entry, follow these steps:

1. On the Menu bar, select Transactions⇨Financial⇨General to display the Transaction Entry window shown in Figure 8-4.

2. In the Journal Entry field, enter a journal entry number or accept the default number.

3. If appropriate, use the Batch ID field to enter or select a batch.

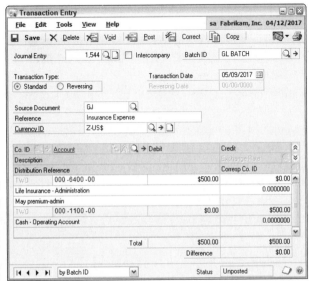

Figure 8-4:
The
Transaction
Entry
window.

4. **In the Transaction Date field, enter the date you want the posted transaction to affect your accounts.**

In the General Ledger, the Transaction Date is the posting date; there is no batch posting date for the General Ledger journal entries.

5. **In the Transaction Type section, select Standard or Reversing.**

A *standard* journal entry debits and credits the accounts you select.

If you select Reversing, the reversing date field will become enabled. When you post the *reversing* entry, in addition to the journal entry you entered, Dynamics GP automatically creates and posts a reversing entry using the reversing date you specified; both entries, the original and the reversing entry, post at the same time, but to different periods.

6. **In the Source Document field, select a source document code for the transaction.**

Typically, you would choose the default, which is GJ for General Journal.

7. **Use the Reference field to provide a description for the journal entry and, if appropriate, use the Currency ID field to select a currency for the transaction.**

8. **In the grid at the bottom of the window, enter accounts and debit and credit amounts.**

If the total debits do not match the total credits, you can save the journal entry in a batch and fix it later. You cannot post an unbalanced entry unless you are updating unit (non-financial) accounts. To update unit accounts, you can post one-sided journal entries.

You can include posting or unit accounts. Debits to unit accounts increase the account balance, while credits to unit accounts decrease the account balance.

You can use unit accounts to track non-financial amounts such as square footage.

You can click the expansion arrows at the right edge of the grid to view the account name along with the account number.

You can include a 30-character description in the Distribution Reference field below the account name to help you identify the purpose of the entry.

9. **Select Post or Save, depending on whether you selected a batch for the transaction.**

You cannot post transactions assigned to batches; you must post the entire batch.

You can print a report of journal entries by printing the Cross-Reference report. For details on setting up reports, see Chapter 12.

Déjà Vu: Reducing Keystrokes with the Quick Journal

Often, you make journal entries on a regular basis that use the same accounts but the amounts change. For example, if your company uses an outside payroll service to prepare payroll, you receive journal entries from the service for each payroll that you can use to update your books to reflect payroll. These journal entries almost always affect the same accounts but the amount per account varies. And, the list of accounts in the journal entry is lengthy.

Enter the Quick Journal Entry in Dynamics GP. You set up — one time only — the template for your journal entry. Then, you simply display the Quick Journal Entry in the Quick Journal Entry window and enter the correct amounts. All of the accounts you need appear automatically, and Dynamics GP automatically posts the difference between the sum of all debits and credits you enter to the offset account.

Use the Quick Journal Setup window and the steps below to create a Quick Journal Entry:

TIP

You also use this window to make changes and add accounts to an existing Quick Journal Entry or to delete a Quick Journal Entry that you have saved but not posted.

1. **On the Menu bar, select Microsoft Dynamics GP➪Tools➪Setup➪ Financial➪Quick Journal to display the Quick Journal Setup window shown in Figure 8-5.**

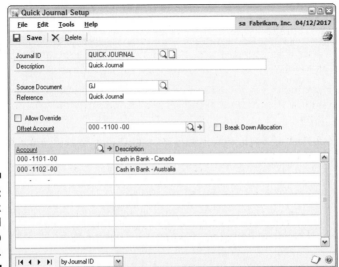

Figure 8-5:
The Quick
Journal
Setup
window.

2. In the Journal ID field, enter a journal ID; in the Description field, enter a description for the entry.

3. In the Source Document field, select a source document code, and, in the Reference field, enter a description of the Quick Journal Entry.

4. In the Offset Account field, select the offset account that Dynamics GP should use to post the entire offsetting amount for this quick journal.

   You cannot use a unit account as an offset account because unit accounts don't track financial information.

5. You can select the Allow Override option to permit users to override the default offset account when entering transactions.

6. Select the Break Down Allocation option if you want Dynamics GP to print breakdown allocations on the Quick Journal Edit List and Quick Journal Posting Journal.

7. In the grid at the bottom of the window, select the accounts you want to use when you record this Quick Journal Entry.

8. Choose Save.

When you're ready to record a Quick Journal Entry, follow these steps:

1. On the Menu bar, select Transactions⇨Financial⇨Quick Journal to display the Quick Journal Entry window shown in Figure 8-6.

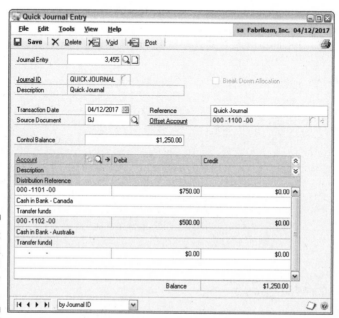

Figure 8-6:
The Quick Journal Entry window.

2. **In the Journal Entry field, enter a journal entry number or accept the default number Dynamics GP displays.**

3. **In the Journal ID field, select the ID of the Quick Journal Entry you want to record.**

   Dynamics GP fills in the Description, Reference, Offset Account, Source Document, and accounts you entered when you set up the Quick Journal Entry. If you select the Break Down Allocation option, Dynamics GP displays the breakdown of the allocations on the edit list and the posting journal. If you select the Allow Override option while setting up the Quick Journal Entry, you can select a different offset account.

   You can add or delete accounts to the Quick Journal Entry, but, to permanently change the Quick Journal Entry, you must use the Quick Journal Setup window.

4. **In the Transaction Date field, enter or accept the default transaction date.**

5. **If you want to confirm that the values you enter equal the amount you expect, use the Control Balance field to enter a control total.**

   Dynamics GP compares the control balance to the total of all debit and credit amounts you enter for the distribution accounts. If the two balances don't match, you won't be able to post.

6. **Enter debits and credits and double-check the balance.**

   You can click the expansion arrows at the right edge of the grid to display the account names and the Distribution Reference field; you can use the Distribution Reference field to provide a 30-character description of the entry to help you remember, at a later date, why you made the entry.

7. **Choose Save or Post.**

You also can save time creating journal entries by putting the journal entries in a General Ledger Batch that has a batch frequency set to something other than Single Use. Typically, when using the recurring batch feature, you set the batch frequency to Monthly. When you post this batch, Dynamics GP posts all the journal entries in the batch and then recreates them automatically with the individual posting date for each journal entry bumped up by one month; the recreated journal entries remain stored in the batch as unposted. You can then edit these entries in any way you see fit prior to posting. With a single use batch, the batch disappears after it's posted.

Creating Budgets

You can create one or more budgets for any or all of your Dynamics GP accounts using a variety of calculation methods that enable you to simply establish the amount you want to budget for each account and each period, or to base the amount on actual account balances of any open or historical year, or to base the amount on the budget amount you established in a different budget. You also can supply an annualized amount and let Dynamics GP divide the amount equally among the periods in your fiscal year.

Many people prefer to create budgets in spreadsheet programs like Microsoft Excel because of the analytical tools available while establishing the budget. With Dynamics GP, you don't have to worry about re-entering into Dynamics GP all the budget numbers you establish in Excel. Dynamics GP contains a wizard that helps you set up a budget in an Excel workbook that meets the formatting needs of Dynamics GP; then you can quickly and easily import the budget from Excel into Dynamics GP.

You also can export to Excel a budget you create in Dynamics GP so that you can modify it, and then import the budget back into Dynamics GP to update the budget stored in Dynamics GP.

Creating a budget in Dynamics GP

To calculate budgets for a single account, you can use the Single-Account Budget Maintenance window. You cannot calculate preliminary budgets using this window. To set up a budget for a single account using this window, see Chapter 2 of the General Ledger documentation.

To create a budget for a range of posting and unit accounts in Dynamics GP without using Excel, on the Menu bar select Cards⇨Financial⇨Budgets to display the Budget Selection window. Existing budgets that you can modify appear in this window. Click New on the window's toolbar and then click Using Microsoft Dynamics GP to display the Budget Maintenance window shown in Figure 8-7.

In the Budget ID field and the Description field, enter an ID and a description. Use the Based On list to specify whether Dynamics GP should base the budget on a fiscal year or a date range. If you choose Fiscal Year, select the fiscal year you want to use as the foundation for the budget. If you choose Date Range, specify a range that crosses one or more fiscal years. If you know you won't be making any changes to the budget information, choose Actual; otherwise, choose Preliminary.

To select the range of accounts for which you want to calculate budgets, click the Ranges button; in the Account Segment Ranges window that appears, select the Segment ID you want Dynamics GP to use when calculating the budget and then select a beginning number and an ending number for that Segment ID. Click Insert and then click OK to save the account range and redisplay the Budget Maintenance window.

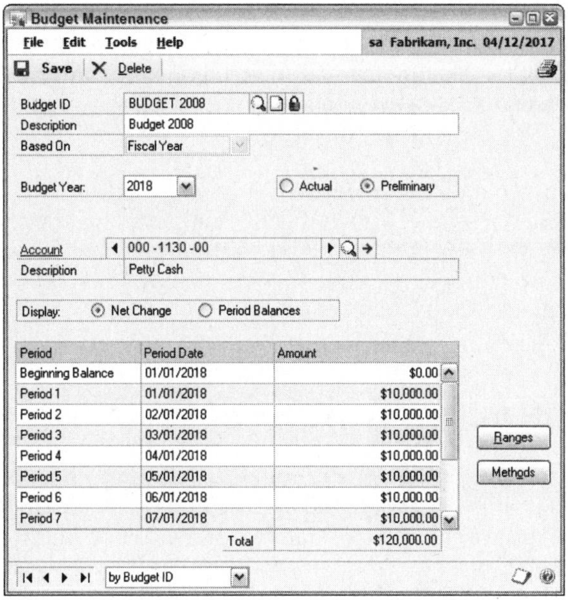

Figure 8-7:
The Budget Main-
tenance window.

Choose the Methods button to display the Budget Calculation Methods window shown in Figure 8-8.

Select a calculation method for the budget and then enter the necessary information for that calculation method. For example, select Other Budget Percent to copy amounts from an existing budget to the budget you're setting up and then calculate a specified percentage increase or decrease. If you select Yearly Budget Amount, you supply an annualized amount that Dynamics GP divides evenly among all selected accounting periods.

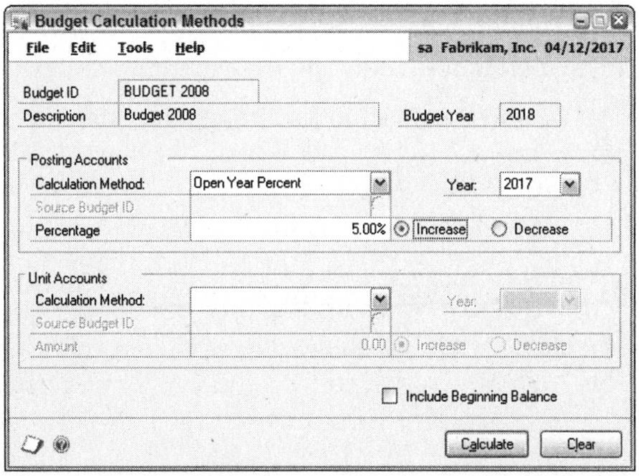

Figure 8-8:
The Budget Calculation Methods window.

Choose the Include Beginning Balance option if you want Dynamics GP to include beginning balance amounts in the budget. Then, select Calculate. Dynamics GP calculates the budget amounts; if you like what you see, select Save. If you don't like what you see, you can type over amounts for an individual account or recalculate the budget.

In the Budget Maintenance window, you can view the calculated budget amount one account at a time. In the Account field, use the Lookup button or the expansion arrow to select the account you want to view. Or you can click the scroll arrows on either side of the Account number to scroll forward or backward through accounts in sequential order.

Creating a budget in Excel

Creating a budget in Excel that you can quickly and easily import into Dynamics GP is a simple process if you use the Budget Wizard for Excel. This wizard helps you ensure that you format your worksheet properly and that you include all the information in the worksheet that Dynamics GP needs.

Using the Budget Wizard for Excel, you can create budgets that are percentages of actual amounts from open years, budgeted amounts, or actual amounts from historical years. You also can create a blank budget, which contains no values but formats the worksheet properly so that you can fill in the values and import the budget into Dynamics GP.

To create a budget in Excel that you can easily import into Dynamics GP, follow these steps:

1. **On the Menu bar, select Cards⇨Financial⇨Budgets to open the Budget Selection window.**

2. **Choose New and select Using Budget Wizard For Excel to display the opening window of the Budget Wizard for Excel.**

3. **Choose Next to open the New Budget Information window.**

4. **Enter a Budget ID and description for the budget and select the basis for the budget — Fiscal Year or Date Range. Then supply the fiscal year or date range for the budget.**

5. **Click Next to display the Budget Calculation Method window and select a calculation method: Open Year Percent, Other Budget Percent, Historical Year Percent, or Blank Budget.**

   The rest of the steps in this section assume that you select Open Year Percent.

The calculation method you choose determines what you see next and the information you need to supply. If you choose any method other than Blank Budget, you provide basically the same information as you finish walking through the wizard.

6. **Click Next and select an open year from which Dynamics GP can copy amounts. Also, identify the percentage by which Dynamics GP should increase or decrease the amounts (see Figure 8-9).**

If you choose Blank Budget in Step 5, you don't see the window described in this step, where you can identify a percentage by which to increase or decrease amounts Dynamics GP copies into the budget. Instead, skip to the next step.

7. **Click Next to display the Actual Amounts Selection window and select the years of data you want to include in the budget workbook.**

The Budget Wizard for Excel creates separate Excel worksheets for each year you select and places them in the order you select them.

8. **Click Next to display the Account Types window, where you can opt to include Balance Sheet accounts, Profit & Loss accounts, and Unit Accounts in your budget.**

For this example, I included only Profit & Loss accounts.

9. **Click Next to display the Accounts window, where you can select to include all or only some of the accounts for the account types you selected.**

If you include only selected accounts, select a segment for filtering the accounts, select the starting and ending segment numbers in the range, and choose Insert.

10. **Click Next to display the Account Verification window, where Dynamics GP lists the accounts it will include in the budget based on your selections.**

You can remove an account from the selection by removing the check that appears beside the account number (see Figure 8-10).

To add an account that doesn't appear in the list, choose Add Account to select the account from the Accounts Lookup window.

11. **Click Next to display the Workbook Selection window, where you can choose to create the budget in a new workbook or an existing workbook.**

In this example, I create a new workbook.

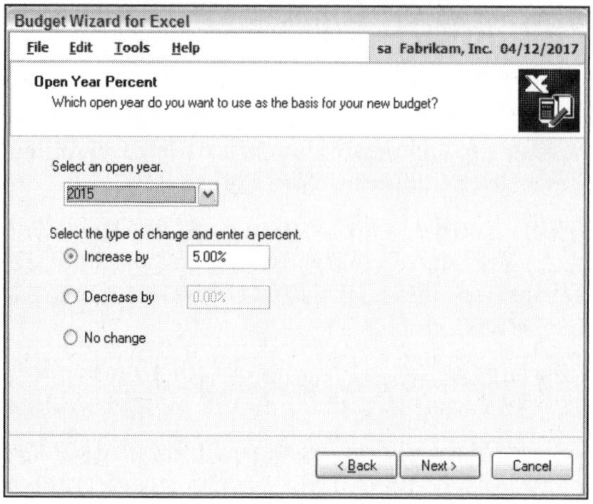

Figure 8-9:
Select the
year from
which
Dynamics
GP should
copy
amounts
and the
percentage
increase
Dynamics
GP should
apply to
those
amounts.

Figure 8-10:
Verify the
accounts to
include in
the budget.

12. **Click Next to display the last window of the Budget Wizard for Excel, where you can review your selections.**

13. **Click Finish.**

The wizard prompts you for a name for the new workbook it creates. After you save the workbook, the wizard builds a new budget worksheet and fills the columns with budget amounts from the accounts you selected, adjusted by the percentage you specified (see Figure 8-11).

Figure 8-11:
A typical
budget
workbook
created by
the Budget
Wizard for
Excel.

	Microsoft Excel - 2009 BUDGET.xls								

									2009 Budget
	Date Range	01/01/2017	to	12/31/2017					
		Beginning Balance - 2017	Period 1 - 2017	Period 2 - 2017	Period 3 - 2017	Period 4 - 2017	Period 5 - 2017	Period 6 - 2017	
Account	Description								
000-4100-00	Sales	0.00	0.00	0.00	0.00	0.00	0.00	
000-4110-01	US Sales - Retail/Parts	0.00	-2415.00	0.00	0.00	0.00	-3290.60	
000-4110-02	US Sales - Finished Goods	0.00	0.00	0.00	0.00	-367.19	-14929.85	
000-4111-01	Canadian Sales - Retail/Parts	0.00	0.00	0.00	0.00	0.00	0.00	
000-4111-02	Canadian Sales - Finished Goods	0.00	0.00	0.00	0.00	0.00	0.00	
000-4112-01	AustralAsian Sales - Retail/Parts	0.00	0.00	0.00	0.00	0.00	0.00	
000-4112-02	AustralAsian Sales - Finished Goods	0.00	0.00	0.00	0.00	0.00	0.00	
000-4114-01	Germany Sales - Retail/Parts	0.00	0.00	0.00	0.00	0.00	0.00	
000-4114-02	Germany Sales - Finished Goods	0.00	0.00	0.00	0.00	0.00	0.00	
000-4115-01	United Kingdom Sales - Retail/Parts	0.00	0.00	0.00	0.00	0.00	0.00	
000-4115-02	United Kingdom Sales - Finished Goods	0.00	0.00	0.00	0.00	0.00	0.00	
000-4116-01	South Africa - Retail/Parts	0.00	0.00	0.00	0.00	0.00	0.00	
000-4116-02	South Africa Sales - Finished Goods	0.00	0.00	0.00	0.00	0.00	0.00	
000-4117-01	Singapore Sales - Retail/Parts	0.00	0.00	0.00	0.00	0.00	0.00	
000-4117-02	Singapore Sales - Finished Goods	0.00	0.00	0.00	0.00	0.00	0.00	
000-4120-00	US Sales - Service Plans	0.00	-1729.63	0.00	0.00	0.00	0.00	
000-4121-00	Canadian Sales - Service Plans	0.00	0.00	0.00	0.00	0.00	0.00	
000-4122-00	AustralAsian Sales - Service Plans	0.00	0.00	0.00	0.00	0.00	0.00	
000-4124-00	Germany Sales - Service Plans	0.00	0.00	0.00	0.00	0.00	0.00	
000-4125-00	United Kingdom Sales - Service Plans	0.00	0.00	0.00	0.00	0.00	0.00	
000-4126-00	South Africa Sales - Service Plans	0.00	0.00	0.00	0.00	0.00	0.00	
000-4127-00	Singapore Sales - Service Plans	0.00	0.00	0.00	0.00	0.00	0.00	
000-4130-00	US Sales - Installation Charges	0.00	0.00	0.00	0.00	0.00	0.00	
000-4131-00	Canadian Sales - Installation Charges	0.00	0.00	0.00	0.00	0.00	0.00	
000-4132-00	AustralAsian Sales - Installation Charges	0.00	0.00	0.00	0.00	0.00	0.00	
000-4134-00	Germany Sales - Installation Charges	0.00	0.00	0.00	0.00	0.00	0.00	
000-4135-00	United Kingdom Sales - Installation Charges	0.00	0.00	0.00	0.00	0.00	0.00	
000-4136-00	South Africa Sales - Installation Charges	0.00	0.00	0.00	0.00	0.00	0.00	
000-4137-00	Singapore Sales - Installation Charges	0.00	0.00	0.00	0.00	0.00	0.00	

2009 BUDGET / Sheet1 / Sheet2 / Sheet3 /

Exporting and importing budgets

If you create a budget in Dynamics GP, you can export it to Excel to work on
it and then import it back into Dynamics GP. Similarly, if you create a budget
in Excel using the Budget Wizard for Excel, you can import the budget into
Dynamics GP.

To export a budget from Dynamics GP to Excel, follow these steps:

1. **On the Menu bar, select Cards⇨Financial⇨Budgets to display the
   Budget Selection window shown in Figure 8-12.**

   If an Excel icon appears beside a Budget ID, you have exported that
   budget to Excel at some time in the past.

2. **Select a budget and click the Excel button on the toolbar.**

3. **From the drop-down menu that appears, select Export to Excel to
   display the Export Budget to Excel window.**

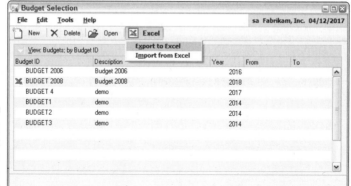

Figure 8-12:
The Budget
Selection
window.

4. **Select whether to create a new workbook or place the budget in an existing workbook.**

   In this example, I opt to use a new workbook. If you opt to store the exported information in an existing workbook, the Select An Existing Excel File dialog box appears so that you can select an existing workbook.

   Each time you export a budget, Dynamics GP assigns the Budget ID as the name of the workbook or the worksheet. If you have previously exported the budget and you don't change the name when prompted to save the exported information, Dynamics GP overwrites the workbook or the worksheet within an existing workbook with the same name. You cannot cancel the export process.

5. **Click OK to display the Save As dialog box if you opted to create a new workbook. If necessary, change the suggested filename; then click Save.**

   Dynamics GP exports the information and opens the appropriate Excel workbook.

Importing an Excel workbook that contains a Dynamics GP budget is simple if the workbook is formatted properly. If you created the workbook using the Budget Wizard for Excel, your workbook is automatically formatted correctly. If you created the budget workbook in Excel without using the Budget Wizard for Excel, I suggest you use the steps in the section "Creating a budget in Excel," earlier in this chapter, to create a skeleton worksheet that you can use as a model to format your worksheet before importing it into Dynamics GP.

To import a properly formatted budget stored in an Excel workbook into Dynamics GP, you use the Budget Wizard for Excel.

On the Menu bar, select Cards⇨Financial⇨Budgets to display the Budget Selection window and then click the Excel button on the toolbar. From the drop-down menu that appears, select Import From Excel to start the Budget Wizard for Excel. As you walk through the wizard, you

✔ **Decide whether the budget you are importing should be a new budget in Dynamics GP or replace an existing one.**

  • If you opt to create a new budget, you enter an ID and description for the budget, along with a basis — Fiscal Year or Date Range — for the budget.

  • If you opt to replace an existing budget, you select the existing budget's Budget ID.

✔ **Select the Excel workbook and worksheet within the workbook to import.**

When you click Finish, Dynamics GP imports the budget information.

Chapter 9

Bank Recs (Not Bank Wrecks)

You use the Bank Reconciliation module in Microsoft Dynamics GP to manage the balances of checkbooks you create in Dynamics GP and to reconcile the balances of those checkbooks with the balances on the statements you receive each month from your bank. For the most part, you don't need to enter transactions in the Bank Reconciliation module; the transactions you enter in other modules update the Bank Reconciliation module. There are a few exceptions to this rule of thumb, as you'll see when you read through this chapter.

Setting Up the Bank Reconciliation Module

As with other Dynamics GP modules, you can set up some default behavior for the Bank Reconciliation module. Dynamics GP does most of the work for you, establishing 1 as the starting number for bank transactions, receipts, transfers, and reconciliation adjustments and setting up default transaction types and codes. If you want to change these defaults, opt not to keep history, establish labels for user-defined fields, or establish a default checkbook, on the Menu bar select Microsoft Dynamics GP⇨Tools⇨Setup⇨Financial⇨Bank Reconciliation to display the Bank Reconciliation Setup window.

Before you can establish a default checkbook, you need to set it up; read the next section.

Working with Checkbooks

Checkbooks are not the same as cash accounts in Dynamics GP. You use checkbooks to track bank deposits and cash paid out so that you can reconcile each checkbook with your bank statements. Checkbooks are available throughout Dynamics GP, regardless of the other modules you purchased.

You should set up one checkbook for every General Ledger Cash account, and one General Ledger Cash account for every separate bank account number for which you receive statements from your bank.

Establishing the opening balance

Because you use checkbooks through Dynamics GP, the way you establish a checkbook's opening balance differs, depending on whether you start using Bank Reconciliation on the first day you use other Dynamics GP modules or whether you begin to use Bank Reconciliation at some point after you have used other Dynamics GP modules.

If you start using Bank Reconciliation along with all other Dynamics GP modules, you need to create your checkbooks, establish their opening balances, and register the Bank Reconciliation module by entering your registration key code before you post transactions in other modules.

If you start using Bank Reconciliation at some point after you use other Dynamics GP modules, you can set up checkbooks to use in Bank Reconciliation in two different ways:

- ✔ You can post all transactions you entered in other modules and establish the opening balances of your checkbooks before you register your Bank Reconciliation module, or

- ✔ You can create new checkbooks to replace existing checkbooks and then make existing checkbooks inactive. You won't have to post transactions entered in other modules before you begin to use the Bank Reconciliation module, but you will need to update your customers, vendors, and employees to make sure that their transactions post to the correct checkbook.

Whether you start using the Bank Reconciliation module along with or after other Dynamics GP modules, you establish the opening balance for your checkbooks using the same technique.

Outside Dynamics GP, reconcile your bank account using your old reconciliation system and enter the reconciled balance in the Last Reconciled Balance field of the Checkbook Maintenance window. Then, use Bank Reconciliation transactions — you can read about them in the section, "Understanding Bank Reconciliation Transactions," later in this chapter — to enter checks you have written and deposits you have made that did not appear on the last reconciled bank statement.

Creating a checkbook

You can set up as many checkbooks as you want to manage your company's cash, and you should set up a separate checkbook for each cash account in your Dynamics GP company. When you enter a transaction that uses a checkbook in a module such as the Payables module, Dynamics GP also updates the Bank Reconciliation module, making bank statement reconciliation an easy task.

As you set up a checkbook, you assign it to a single General Ledger Account. You can assign more than one checkbook to the same General Ledger Account; however, as a rule of thumb, you should set up one checkbook for every General Ledger Cash account, and one General Ledger Cash account for every separate bank account number for which you receive a separate, monthly, itemized bank statement.

By setting up a checkbook for each cash account, you can easily track and reconcile cash-related transactions because checkbook balances should then match cash account balances.

You create cards for each checkbook you intend to use; to create a checkbook, follow these steps:

1. **On the Menu bar, select Cards⇨Financial⇨Checkbook to display the Checkbook Maintenance window (see Figure 9-1).**

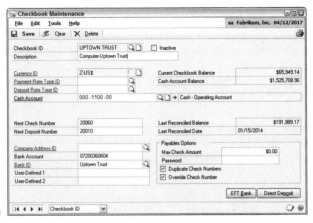

Figure 9-1: The Checkbook Maintenance window.

2. **In the Checkbook ID and Description fields, enter a checkbook ID and a name for the checkbook.**

If you're using Multicurrency Management, fill in the Currency ID, Payment Rate Type ID, and Deposit Rate Type ID fields. You can't change the Currency ID after you save the checkbook. The Currency ID lookup window displays only the active currencies available to your company.

3. **In the Cash Account field, select the cash account you want to associate with the checkbook.**

4. **In the Next Check Number and Next Deposit Number fields, enter a default value for the next check and deposit numbers. Be sure to include leading zeros so you don't run out of check and deposit numbers.**

By default, Dynamics GP assigns 00000000000000000001 as the Next Check Number and Next Deposit Number — and that's too many lead zeros! If you use the default number of leading zeros, you then need to enter them whenever you search for checks or deposits by number. I suggest that you limit both sequences — check numbers and deposit numbers to seven-digit numbers, which are easier to type and to read. A seven-digit number (one containing six leading zeros) gives you 9,999,999 numbers in the sequence, which is more than enough for the vast majority of situations.

5. **In the Company Address ID field, select the address at which you receive bank statements for this checkbook.**

6. **In the Bank Account field, enter the account number for the checking account at the bank.**

7. **In the User-Defined 1 and User-Defined 2 fields, enter any user-defined information.**

Dynamics GP updates the values that appear in the Current Checkbook Balance and Cash Account Balance fields; you cannot change these fields in this window. They might appear to be "out of sync" because receipts from the Sales series and the Bank Reconciliation module update the cash account but not the checkbook; you need to enter Deposit transactions in the Bank Reconciliation module to update the checkbook balance to reflect receipts. Read about Bank Reconciliation transactions later in this chapter.

8. **In the Last Reconciled Balance and Last Reconciled Date fields, enter the balance and date from the last bank statement you reconciled.**

See the previous section for details on determining the amount to enter into this field.

You can change the Last Reconciled Balance or the Last Reconciled Date fields until you reconcile your checkbook for the first time in Bank Reconciliation as described later in this chapter. However, the last reconciled balance is reflected in the checkbook balance; if you change the last reconciled balance, you might need to enter an adjustment transaction in the General Ledger to update the Cash account. Once you reconcile the checkbook, Dynamics GP updates the date and balance fields each time you reconcile, and you can't make changes to these fields.

9. **If you use the Payables Management module, supply the information in the Payables Options section.**

10. **Choose Save to save the checkbook.**

The EFT Bank button appears in the window if you have set up Company Options to enable electronic banking. You click this button to set up the electronic banking information for the checkbook.

Understanding Bank Reconciliation Transactions

Whenever you enter a transaction in another module that uses a checkbook, Dynamics GP updates the Bank Reconciliation module. Therefore, you should use the Bank Reconciliation transactions only to record those miscellaneous transactions, receipts, and deposits that you didn't record in another module.

In the Bank Reconciliation module, using various Bank Reconciliation module windows, you can record several types of transactions; in some cases, the transactions update both the checkbook and its associated cash account, while in other cases, the transactions update only the checkbook or only the cash account.

Use a Withdrawal transaction to record automatic deductions from the bank account, such as paychecks created by a payroll service. To enter this transaction in the Bank Transaction Entry window, on the Menu bar select Transactions⇨Financial⇨Bank Transactions. This transaction updates both the checkbook and the cash account.

Use the Check transaction to record a one-time payment to someone you don't want to set up as a vendor. Dynamics GP automatically generates a check in Bank Reconciliation each time you write a check in the Purchasing series. To enter a Check transaction in the Bank Reconciliation module, use the Bank Transaction Entry window; on the Menu bar select Transactions⇨Financial⇨Bank Transactions. This transaction updates both the checkbook and the cash account.

A note about general journal entries

Once you link a General Ledger Cash account to a checkbook, you should no longer record journal entries that debit or credit that Cash account because transactions flow *into* the General Ledger, but *never out* of the General Ledger. The General Ledger in Dynamics GP is the last stop. If you create a journal entry in General Ledger that effects cash, the journal entry will update only the General Ledger Cash account balance and not the checkbook balance, thereby causing a discrepancy.

Typically, you write checks in the Payables Management module, updating both the Payables Management subsidiary ledger and the checkbook, and simultaneously send a journal entry to the General Ledger that updates the cash account. Similarly, when you post cash receipts in the Receivables Management module, you update the Receivables Management subsidiary ledger and the General Ledger at the same time.

If you need to record a transaction affecting cash that was not part of the regular processing from other subsidiary modules, enter a Bank Reconciliation module transaction; doing so will update the checkbook and send a journal entry to the General Ledger. The same holds true for corrections; avoid making corrections to cash directly in the General Ledger. Instead, make the corrections in the other modules, because the other modules will send the correction journal entry to the General Ledger and update the subsidiary module's ledger at the same time.

Use the Increase or Decrease Adjustment transactions to record bank service charges or interest income. To enter this transaction in the Bank Transaction Entry window, on the Menu bar select Transactions⇨Financial⇨Bank Transactions. This transaction updates both the checkbook and the cash account.

You also can record these transactions during the reconciliation process; see the section "Reconciling a Checkbook," later in this chapter, for more information.

You can use the Receipts transaction to record miscellaneous amounts you collect, such as payments received from employees for employee stock purchases or proceeds on the sale of an asset. Dynamics GP automatically generates a receipt each time you record a customer payment in the Sales series, so, you need to enter this transaction in the Bank Reconciliation module only when you don't record the transaction in some other module. To enter a Receipt transaction in the Bank Transaction Entry window, on the Menu bar select Transactions⇨Financial⇨Bank Transactions. This transaction updates the cash account but does not update the checkbook. To update the checkbook, you assign receipts to deposits.

Although you can void transactions and receipts, use the originating module to void if the transaction was generated by another module. Void transactions or receipts in Bank Reconciliation only if you created the transaction or receipt in the Bank Reconciliation module.

Entering deposits

The Deposit transaction is a special breed of Bank Reconciliation transaction; unlike the other transactions in the Bank Reconciliation module, you use the Deposit transaction regularly to record bank deposits in Dynamics GP so that they will match the deposits that appear on your bank statement.

Often, you deposit several receipts simultaneously at the bank, and most banks record the sum of the receipts as the deposit amount instead of recording each receipt separately as a deposit. So, you use the Deposit transaction in Dynamics GP to record a transaction that represents the sum of multiple receipts; these Deposit transactions appear in the window when you reconcile your bank statement, but Receipt transactions do not.

You use the Bank Deposit Entry window shown in Figure 9-2 (on the Menu bar select Transactions⇨Financial⇨Bank Deposits) to record three different types of Deposit transactions in Dynamics GP. Use the Deposit With Receipts transaction type to match multiple receipts to a single deposit. Use the Deposit Without Receipts transaction type to record a deposit that isn't associated with any receipts; for example, you may want to record a Deposit Without Receipts if you're in a hurry to get to the bank and don't want to take the time to match the receipts to the Deposit. When you record a Deposit Without Receipts, you typically also record a Clear Unused Receipts transaction type to remove receipts from the Bank Deposit Entry window that you won't be associating with a deposit transaction.

The Clear Unused Receipts transaction type doesn't update either the cash account or the bank account; its sole purpose is to remove from view receipts you will never be attaching to a Deposit With Receipts transaction. The Deposit With Receipts transaction type and the Deposit Without Receipts transaction type both update the checkbook balance but not the cash account balance. Remember, receipts posted from the Cash Receipts module update the cash account balance, so, when you post a Deposit transaction type, Dynamics GP doesn't update the cash account to avoid double-posting and inflating the account balance.

As you enter a Deposit transaction, Dynamics GP displays available receipts in the bottom of the window if you select Deposit With Receipts or Clear Unused Receipts as the transaction type. For a Deposit With Receipts or a Deposit Without Receipts, you can click the Deposit Amount expansion button in the lower-right corner of the window to display the Deposit Totals window; in this window, you can break the deposit down into the totals for checks, credit cards, currency, and coin.

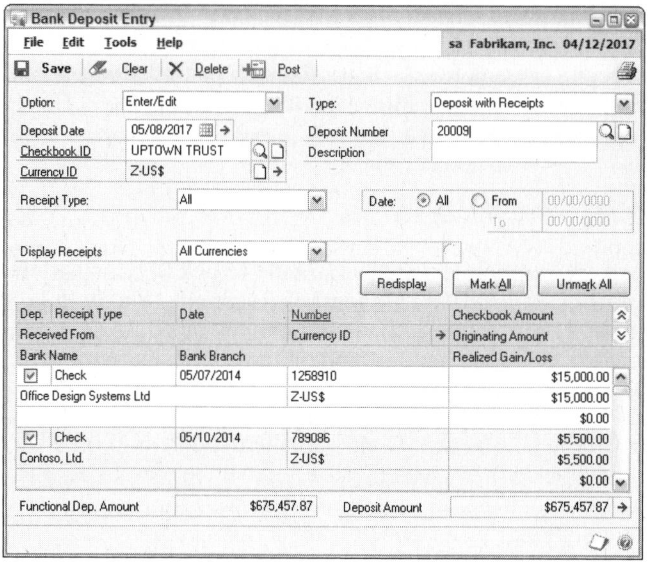

Figure 9-2:
The Bank
Deposit
Entry
window.

The Bank Reconciliation module is unusual in Dynamics GP because you can't post batches. The Bank Reconciliation module uses transaction-level posting; you must enter and post Bank Reconciliation transactions individually. You can save Bank Reconciliation transactions and post them at a later time, but you can save only one Clear Unused Receipts transaction or one Deposit With Receipts transaction at a time for each checkbook. If you enter and save a Clear Unused Receipts transaction, and then try to record either another Clear Unused Receipts transaction or a Deposit With Receipts transaction for the same checkbook, Dynamics GP displays the original Clear Unused Receipts transaction instead of letting you enter the new transaction. To enter a new Clear Unused Receipts transaction or a Deposit With Receipts transaction, you must first post or delete the existing deposit.

Transferring money between bank accounts

You can transfer money between checkbooks using the Bank Transfer Entry window; on the Menu bar select Transactions⇨Financial⇨Bank Transfers.

The process is straightforward; select the checkbook from which you want to transfer funds, the checkbook to which you want to transfer funds, and, in the Transfer From section, supply the amount to transfer. Click Post. When you transfer funds between checkbooks, Dynamics GP updates both the checkbook balances and the associated cash account balances.

Reconciling a Checkbook

You reconcile your bank statements with accounts in Dynamics GP to identify and resolve discrepancies that might exist between your Dynamics GP data and your bank statement.

To reconcile a Dynamics GP checkbook with a bank statement, you use the Select Bank Transactions window to identify transactions in Dynamics GP that also appear on the bank statement. If a transaction cleared the bank for an amount other than the one that appears in Dynamics GP, you can enter the difference and distribute the amount to the posting account of your choice.

During reconciliation, you also can enter adjusting entries to track interest income and service charges; this is particularly effective if you find an amount on the bank statement that you didn't notice until you started the reconciliation process. You don't need to stop the reconciliation to enter adjustment transactions in the Bank Transaction Entry window.

If you don't keep history, Dynamics GP deletes the reconciled transaction information after reconciling. If you keep history, Dynamics GP reclassifies the transactions you clear as historical records; these transactions appear on historical transaction reports after you reconcile.

To reconcile a bank statement with a Dynamics GP checkbook, on the Menu bar select Transactions➪Financial➪Reconcile Bank Statement to display the Reconcile Bank Statements window. Select a checkbook and enter the ending balance that appears on the bank statement, along with the ending date on the bank statement. You also can enter a cutoff date; Dynamics GP limits the transactions you can choose to clear based on the cutoff date. If you enter a cutoff date, Dynamics GP displays transactions with dates that fall on or before the cutoff date so that you can mark them as cleared if appropriate. If you don't enter a cutoff date, Dynamics GP displays all posted transactions that haven't been reconciled or voided.

After you complete the Reconcile Bank Statements window, click Transactions to display the Select Bank Transactions window (see Figure 9-3).

In the C column, check each transaction that appears on your bank statement to mark it cleared. When you finish, the Adjusted Bank Balance and the Adjusted Book Balance should be equal.

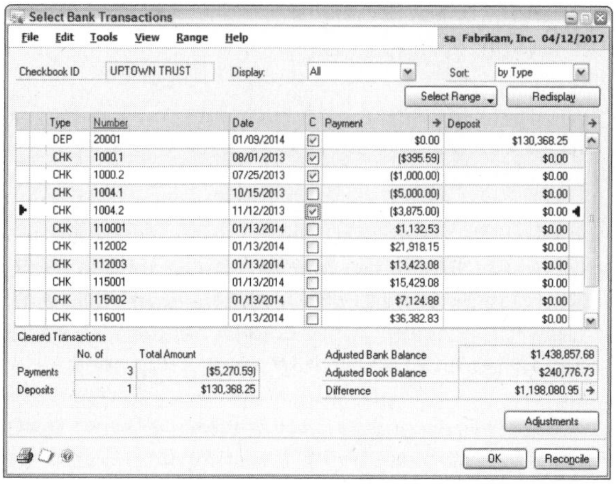

Figure 9-3:
The Select
Bank Trans-
actions
window.

If the Adjusted Bank Balance and the Adjusted Book Balance are not equal, you need to compare the amounts of each deposit and check in Dynamics GP with the amounts that appear on your bank statement. If you find a discrepancy, you can select the transaction with the differing amount in the Select Bank Transactions window and then choose the Payment or Deposit expansion button; Dynamics GP displays the Cleared Amount Entry window, where you can record the amount that appears on the bank statement. Click OK to redisplay the Select Bank Transactions window.

Next, click the Adjustments button to display the Reconcile Bank Adjustment window and identify the type of adjustment you want to record — Interest Income, Other Income, Other Expense, or Service Charge — and the amount. Click OK to redisplay the Select Bank Transactions window.

You really don't ever need to click the Adjustments button, because you can always enter a regular Bank Transaction such as an Increase Adjustment, Decrease Adjustment, or Withdrawal to record an adjustment.

When the Adjusted Bank Balance and the Adjusted Book Balance are equal, click Reconcile. Dynamics GP will not reconcile until the difference is zero.

Clearing Checks Automatically with Electronic Banking

If you use the Electronic Banking module, you can make electronic funds transfer (EFT) payments for Payables Management and Receivables Management, both inside and outside North America, as well as reconcile bank statements electronically. In this section, I'm going to describe briefly the process you go through to use the Electronic Reconcile portion of the Electronic Banking module to reconcile a bank statement.

To use Electronic Reconcile, you need to set up bank formats that match what comes in from your bank to Dynamics GP fields. Electronic Reconcile doesn't support all bank formats. If your bank format uses, for example, multiple transaction codes for several types of cleared checks, or if your bank uses the Bank Administration Institute (BAI) format, you won't be able to use Electronic Reconcile unless your bank is willing to supply a different format.

When you reconcile a bank statement electronically, you import statement information supplied by your bank into Dynamics GP. Once you download the information, you use the information I provided in the previous section; Dynamics GP uses the information you download to automatically clear transactions in the Select Bank Transactions window. Your job becomes making sure that the Adjusted Bank Balance and the Adjusted Book Balance are equal; if they aren't, you identify cleared differences and you make bank statement adjustments as necessary.

To use Electronic Reconcile, you need to set up one or more checkbooks for EFT transactions. After you set up the checkbook using the Checkbook Maintenance window as described earlier in this chapter, use the Checkbook EFT Maintenance window to specify a checkbook to use for EFT transactions. On the Menu bar, select Cards⇨Financial⇨Checkbook⇨EFT Bank.

Then, use the Electronic Reconcile Format Configurator window to create bank formats that define the files you'll be downloading from your bank. To open this window, on the Menu bar select Microsoft Dynamics GP⇨Tools⇨ Routines⇨Financial⇨Electronic Reconcile⇨Configurator. In this window, you specify a variety of information that describes the file you will import from your bank. See Chapter 5 of the Dynamics GP Electronic Banking manual for details on creating a bank format.

Setting up a bank format is a one-time process; once you create the format, you use it each time you want to download statement information from your bank.

When you're ready to reconcile a checkbook electronically, you use the Electronic Reconcile Download Transactions window to download information. On the Menu bar, select Microsoft Dynamics GP⇨Tools⇨ Routines⇨Financial⇨Electronic Reconcile⇨Transactions Download to display the window and select the appropriate bank format. Then, select Download and Dynamics GP goes to work, downloading your data. For details, see Chapter 10 of the Dynamics GP Electronic Banking manual.

Chapter 10

Getting Inventory Under Control

. . . .

In This Chapter

▶ Setting up the Inventory Control module

▶ Working with items

▶ Understanding inventory transactions

▶ Reporting on inventory

. . . .

*M*anaging inventory is critical to businesses that sell goods. If you don't have enough on hand, you might lose a sale. If you have too much on hand, you tie up dollars in inventory that you must maintain, and owning that inventory has a cost for your business. You can use the Inventory Control module to help you track your inventory.

You also can use the Inventory Control module to create item cards for services, miscellaneous charges, and non-stock items, and you can create pricing schemes for all these items.

Setting Up the Inventory Control Module

As with other modules in Microsoft Dynamics GP, you need to do some setup work for the Inventory Control module before you begin to use it. Because the Inventory Control module can integrate with Invoicing, Sales Order Processing, Purchase Order Processing, Bill of Materials, and General Ledger, be sure to coordinate the setup procedures for all of these modules.

To set up preferences and default entries for the Inventory Control module, follow these steps:

1. **On the Menu bar, select Microsoft Dynamics GP⇨Tools⇨Setup⇨ Inventory⇨Inventory Control to display the Inventory Control Setup dialog box shown in Figure 10-1.**

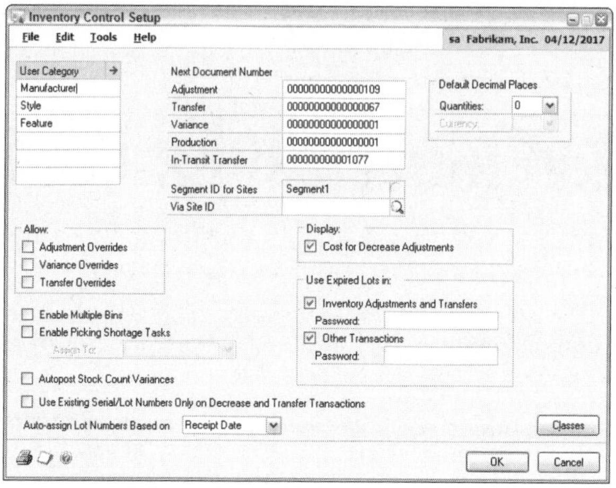

Figure 10-1:
The
Inventory
Control
Setup dialog
box.

2. **Use the User Category fields to create up to six user-defined text fields to classify related items.**

   The User Category is not a free-form field; the user selects from a list of values that you define. User categories provide a way for you to group your inventory and analyze trends in purchases and sales. Click the expansion arrow beside the User Category field to display the Item Category Setup dialog box, where you can create item categories.

   You can view the User Categories in the SmartList and on various reports. You supply a name for each of the User Category fields and that name will appear throughout the system as the label for that field. It is generally recommended that you take advantage of this useful feature.

3. **In the Next Document Number fields, supply the next document number for adjustment, transfer, variance, and in-transit transfer transactions.**

   Later in this chapter, in the section, "Understanding Inventory Transactions," I'll describe these transactions.

   The numbers you enter determine the number of unique document numbers available. If you use a five-digit number, you'll be able to record 99,999 unique transactions.

4. **In the Segment ID for Sites field, enter or select a General Ledger account segment ID to represent inventory sites.**

   The account segment ID corresponds to the accounts you set up in the Account Segment Setup window to track items by site. Once you've entered this information and moved the pointer out of the field, you can't change it.

Sites are inventory warehouse locations. Typically, you select the account segment that denotes either geographic location, product line, department, or division; you can only choose one. When posting inventory transactions, you can swap the segment value associated with the inventory site into the General Ledger distribution; in this way, you create a General Ledger distribution mapping between inventory sites and some segment of the General Ledger account number. This is an optional behavior; you can leave the segment field on the individual site cards blank and the swapping behavior will not occur.

5. **Use the Via Site ID field to enter or select the Site ID that serves as the interim location for items as you move them from one site to another using an in-transit transfer transaction.**

   Setting the Via Site ID ensures that the items aren't sold before they reach their destination.

   You can leave the Via Site ID field blank and enter a Site ID when entering new in-transit transfer transactions.

6. **In the Default Decimal Places section, open the Quantities list and enter or select the number of decimal places to use by default for item quantities when you create new item records.**

7. **If you're not using Multicurrency Management, open the Currency list box and enter or select the number of decimal places to use by default when Dynamics GP displays currency amounts associated with items.**

   If you're using Multicurrency Management, this field won't be available.

8. **In the Allow section, select the overrides you want to allow.**

   If you allow overrides, you can allocate quantities that are greater than the quantity available.

9. **Check the Enable Multiple Bins option to use multiple bins at each inventory site.**

   If you select this option, Dynamics GP requires bin information for transactions.

   You need to do more than just select this option, so you might want to postpone selecting the option until you have done things like create the bins at each site and specify default bins for each site and for each item-site combination. In addition, this option affects stock count records if you use the stock count feature. Refer to the information concerning multiple bins and stock counts in Chapters 3, 13, and 17 of the Inventory Control manual.

10. **Select the Enable Picking Shortage Tasks option and select a user if you want to be able to create a task when a shortage occurs in the Sales Order Fulfillment Entry window or the Manufacturing Component Transaction Entry window.**

    You can use the task to create a stock count or to locate the missing quantities.

11. **Select the Autopost Stock Count Variances option to automatically post stock-count variances.**

12. **Select the Use Existing Serial/Lot Numbers Only on Decrease and Transfer Transactions option to limit lot numbers and serial numbers on decrease and transfer transactions to existing lot numbers and serial numbers.**

13. **Use the auto-assign Lot Numbers Based On list box to specify whether Dynamics GP should automatically assign lot numbers to transactions by receipt date or expiration date in Sales Order Processing, Microsoft Dynamics GP Bill of Materials, and Invoicing.**

14. **In the Display section, select the Cost for Decrease Adjustments option if you want Dynamics GP to display costs for decrease adjustment transactions.**

15. **In the Use Expired Lots In section**

    a. *Select the Inventory Adjustments and Transfers option to enable using expired lots when entering inventory adjustments and transfers.* If you want to limit the users who can use expired lots, enter a password in the Password field.

    b. *Select the Other Transactions option to enable using expired lots when entering transactions in Bill of Materials, Purchase Order Returns, Sales Order Processing, Invoicing, and Manufacturing.* If you want to limit the users who can use expired lots, enter a password in the Password field.

16. **Choose OK to save your changes.**

In addition to setting up the Inventory module itself, you also do any of the following to make processing easier in your company's environment:

✔ **Create unit of measure schedules.** If you buy and sell items in different units, you can use *unit of measure schedules* to identify the various equivalents. For example, you might purchase lumber by the yard and sell it by the foot or the inch. You can read more about unit of measure schedules in Chapter 4 of the Inventory Control manual.

✔ **Establish lot categories with lot attributes.** *Lot categories* enable you to group lot-numbered items by shared characteristics called lot attributes. For example, flooring tile is often assigned to lot categories so that you can track all tiles produced with certain sets of colors or patterns. Lot attributes describe the characteristics of the lot; you use the lot attributes when you enter an increase adjustment to identify the lot-numbered item you receive or when you need to decrease a particular lot because you're selling product to a customer who needs to match a previous purchase. You can read about lot categories and attributes in Chapter 6 of the Inventory Control manual.

✔ **Set up Dynamics GP to track items in multiple bins.** By default, Dynamics GP tracks items within inventory sites. If you enable multiple bin processing, you can track item quantities in bins that reside within each site. Dynamics GP processes bin quantities and displays them in the item's base unit of measure. You can identify default bins for transaction types at each site and for a particular item and transaction type at a site. For example, if you always use a certain bin when you sell Item A from the North Street warehouse, you can set up that bin as the default sales order bin for the item at the North Street warehouse. In most cases, if you haven't established a default bin for the item-site combination or the site, you can enter a bin as you enter the transaction. And, you can transfer items from one bin to another. For more information on tracking items in multiple bins, see Chapters 3 and 13 of the Inventory Control manual.

✔ **Create stock count calendars and cycle counts.** After you create an item, you can specify how often the item should be counted. You can set up a *stock count calendar* that Dynamics GP uses to determine when next to count the item. See the section "Performing a physical inventory," later in this chapter, for more information.

Maintaining Your Items

There's more to setting up items than, well, setting up items. First, there are different types of items you can set up. And, for each item, you need to define the valuation method your company uses to calculate the item's value in inventory.

You also can set up item classes in Dynamics GP, and I recommend that you use item classes because they make setting up items much easier. After you create items, you need to establish beginning balances for items currently on-hand unless you are just starting out in business and have no items in inventory — not the typical case.

And then there's pricing; you have to identify how much you typically charge customers for each item. So, let's get started.

Understanding item types

You assign each item you create to an item type. Dynamics GP supports the following six types of items:

Once you assign the item type to an item and save the Item Card, you cannot change the item type. If you need to change the item type, you would need to create a new item with the different item type. However, you can, at any time, change the item type of a Sales Inventory item to a Discontinued item.

- ✔ **Sales Inventory:** Use the Sales Inventory item type to track on-hand stock quantities; think of this item type as the classic inventory item. For the Sales Inventory item type, Dynamics GP tracks quantities, and you can enter both increase and decrease adjustment transactions. Amounts posted to the Inventory and Inventory Offset accounts appear on the Distributions Breakdown Register. Posting from Purchase Order Processing affects the Inventory account and either the Accrued Purchases account or the Accounts Payables account. Posting from Sales Order Processing affects the Inventory account, the Cost of Goods Sold account, and either the Cash account or the Accounts Receivables account.

- ✔ **Discontinued:** A Discontinued item is a Sales Inventory item that you no longer plan to use going forward. Discontinued items can be automatically removed from the system during the Inventory year-end closing. For the Discontinued item type, Dynamics GP tracks the same information as it tracks for Sales Inventory items. You can enter adjustments for this type of item, and you can delete an item of this type when the quantity reaches zero. Posting updates the Inventory and Inventory Offset accounts. Posting from Sales Order Processing affects the Sales, Cash, Cost of Goods Sold, or Accounts Receivables accounts. If you don't want to sell discontinued items, be sure that you don't select the Allow Sale of Discontinued Items option in the Sales Order Processing Setup Options window.

- ✔ **Misc Charge:** The Misc Charge item type, Services item type, and Flat Fee item type are very similar in that Dynamics GP doesn't track any on-hand stock quantity; therefore, you can use any of these three item types for services, charges, and fees. However, Dynamics GP doesn't track current cost for the Misc Charge item type, but does for the Services and Flat Fee item types. Once you assign an item to this item type, you can't change the item type. Posting updates the Sales account and either the Cash account or the Accounts Receivable account.

- ✔ **Kit:** A Kit is a group of items that are bundled, priced, and sold together as one product. Using kits can speed up data entry and make pricing schedules easier to create and maintain. For the Kit item type, Dynamics GP doesn't track the on-hand stock quantity of the kit, but does track the quantities of the components based on their individual item types. Depending on the item type, posting updates the Inventory and Cost of Goods Sold accounts you specify for each component. Posting from Sales Order Processing affects the Inventory and Cost of Goods Sold accounts and either the Cash account or the Accounts Receivables account.

- ✔ **Service:** For the Services item type, Dynamics GP tracks current costs but not quantities. You can sell items assigned to the Services item type individually or as part of a kit. Posting updates the Sales account and either the Cash account or the Accounts Receivable account.

> ✔ **Flat Fee:** Dynamics GP handles the Flat Fee item type very much the same way it handles the Services item type; Dynamics GP tracks current costs but not quantities; you can sell items assigned to the Flat Fee item type individually or as part of a kit; and posting updates the Sales account.

FIFO, LIFO, and all that jazz

The valuation method you choose for an item determines how Dynamics GP calculates the cost of the item. Dynamics GP supports five different valuation methods.

If you choose the FIFO Perpetual valuation method, Dynamics GP assumes that items you purchased first are the ones you sell first; *FIFO* stands for First In, First Out. Dynamics GP maintains detailed information about the cost of all items, calculates the value of inventory at its actual cost, and sets the current cost for items equal to the cost of the item the last time you bought it. This is the most popular method of costing.

If you choose the LIFO perpetual valuation method, Dynamics GP assumes that items you purchased last are the ones you sell first; *LIFO* stands for Last In, First Out. Dynamics GP maintains detailed information about the cost of all items, calculates the value of inventory at its actual cost, and sets the current cost for items equal to the cost of the item the last time you received it.

The Average Perpetual valuation method is actually a moving average. To calculate the current cost of items assigned to this valuation method, Dynamics GP totals the cost of items with the same item number and calculates the average of the total cost. Dynamics GP revalues the average cost of an item throughout the period as you enter increase transactions for items valued using this method. The formula follows: (Current units × current moving average cost) + (New units × purchase price) / (Current units + new units).

If you choose the FIFO Periodic valuation method, Dynamics GP assumes that items you purchased first are the ones you sell first, but Dynamics GP values the items at their standard cost. At the end of the year, you can adjust the standard cost to the current cost.

If you choose the LIFO Periodic valuation method, Dynamics GP assumes that items you purchased last are the ones you sell first, but Dynamics GP values the items at their standard cost. At the end of the year, you can adjust the standard cost to the current cost or the cost of the item the last time you received it.

If you choose to track items by serial number, Dynamics GP uses a costing method known in accounting jargon as "specific identification." To track by serial number, set up the item as a Sales Inventory item type and let the costing method default to FIFO Perpetual on the Item Card; the costing method you choose will not come into play since the system costs each unique serialized item. Choose the Options button on the Item Card to open the Item Maintenance Options window; in the Track list box, select Serial Numbers.

You track cost variances, which can result with any of the valuation methods, in the General Ledger using the Inventory Variance account.

Setting up item classes

Conceptually, *item classes* enable you to group items according to common characteristics. The beauty of item classes revolves around the time they save you. When you define an item class, you provide basic default information about all items that you will assign to the class, such as the valuation method, the price group, the General Ledger account mapping, and the sales tax option. When you assign items to the class, Dynamics GP automatically assigns default information of the class to the items, making it quicker and easier to define new items. Also, using item classes, you can make changes to many items at once; you change the item class information and then Dynamics GP "rolls down" the changes to items that belong to the class. Item classes also are a common sorting option on reports.

Dynamics GP uses the information on the item card, not on the item class, when setting default information as you enter transactions for an item; the Item Class is a handy way to default information as you create the Item and to make mass changes to items.

To set up an item class, on the Menu bar select Microsoft Dynamics GP➪Tools➪Setup➪Inventory➪Item Class to display the Item Class Setup window shown in Figure 10-2.

Enter a Class ID and Description and select an Item Type and a Valuation Method. Use the Track list box to specify whether items in this class will have serial numbers or lot numbers.

Identify a Sales Tax Option and, if appropriate, select a tax schedule for the item class, and specify whether to allow back orders for this item class. If you selected Sales Inventory or Discontinued for the Item Type and LIFO Perpetual, FIFO Perpetual, or Average Perpetual for the Valuation Method, you can use the Revalue Inventory for Cost Variance option to specify whether Dynamics GP should revalue purchase receipts for items in this class when cost variances exceed a percentage you specify in the Tolerance Percentage field.

In the Maintain History section, specify the types of history you want to maintain for items assigned to this item class.

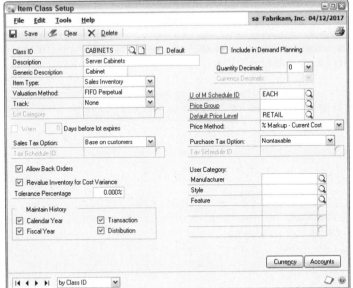

If appropriate for the items in this class, use the Quantity Decimals list box to specify the number of decimal places Dynamics GP should make available. Assign a unit of measure schedule and, if you use standard pricing, enter a price group, the price level, and a price method you use most often for items in this class.

Use the Purchase Tax Option to specify the way Dynamics GP should handle taxes for items in this class, and if appropriate, select User Category information for items in this class.

You can click the Accounts button to display the Item Class Accounts Setup dialog box, where you can select the posting accounts for items in this class. I recommend that you set the default General Ledger accounts at the Item Class level so that you can roll down the accounts to the individual Item Cards associated with the Item Class; that way, sales of different classes of inventory items can update different revenue and/or Cost of Goods Sold accounts.

Creating items

You create items to represent the things you sell. Items don't have to be physical things; for example, your landscaping company may sell plants as well as various maintenance service packages.

You might store all your inventory in one central warehouse, or you might sell items from a variety of warehouses; when you set up your items, you can specify the warehouse in which you store each item.

If your company uses multiple locations to store inventory and fill orders, you should set up sites that represent these locations. You can then assign each inventory item to its proper site. You also can, if appropriate, create bins for each site. See Chapter 13 of the Inventory Control manual for details on creating sites and bins.

You also can specify items that can substitute for other items; that way, a salesperson can avoid losing a sale if you're currently out of stock for the requested item.

To create an item, follow these steps:

1. **On the Menu bar, select Cards⇨Inventory⇨Item to display the Item Maintenance window shown in Figure 10-3.**

2. **In the Item Number field, enter a number that can be a combination of letters and numbers.**

Use the same number of characters for each item you set up. Also, consider including leading zeros in your item numbers to ensure that enough item numbers will be available to add new items and that item numbers will sort appropriately in reports and scrolling windows.

3. **In the Description field, enter a description for the item. You can use the Short Description and Generic Description fields to enter alternate description information for the item.**

Click the *i* button beside the Description field to open the Internet Information window and supply Internet information for the item.

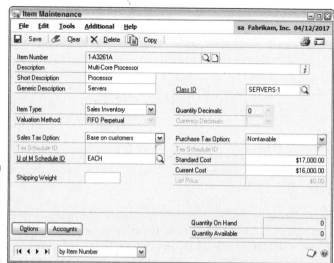

Figure 10-3:
The Item Maintenance window.

4. **Use the Class ID field to enter or select an item class.**

   Dynamics GP fills in the Item Type, Valuation Method, Sales Tax Option, Purchase Tax Option, U of M Schedule ID, and Quantity Decimals fields with default information stored in the item class; you can make changes as needed.

5. **In the Shipping Weight field, you can enter shipping weight information; enter the weight in the base unit of measure for the item.**

6. **In the Standard Cost field, you can enter the item's standard cost information if you use standard costing or intend to base price schedules on a markup of standard cost. If you use don't use Multicurrency Management, you can also enter a List Price.**

   You can base price schedules on a percentage of a List Price. If you use Multicurrency Management, you need to enter a List Price for each active currency.

   The Current Cost field is updated automatically by the system each time you record a receipt or an invoice for the item, so it will show the last cost.

   You can click the Options button to display the Item Maintenance Options dialog box and supply additional information about the item, such as two substitute items and user category information.

7. **Click Save.**

You can copy item information to help you create new items quickly. Display Item Maintenance window and enter a new Item ID. Then, click the Copy button to display the Item Copy window. Select the item from which you want to copy information and select the attributes to copy. Click Copy, and Dynamics GP displays the copied information in the Item Maintenance window where you already established the new item number. Make any necessary changes and save the new item.

Entering beginning balances

You enter adjustment transactions to enter On Hand beginning item quantities for Sales Inventory and Discontinued items; you can use the general steps provided to record transactions in the section, "Understanding Inventory Transactions," later in this chapter, to enter the adjustment transactions.

When you enter beginning balance transactions, however, it's important to make sure that the transactions don't update the General Ledger; if you allow them to update the General Ledger, you inflate the value of the inventory account. To avoid updating the General Ledger with beginning balance transactions, include all the adjustment transactions in a single batch that you create using the steps below.

Before you enter beginning balances, make sure that you have defined any sites containing inventory and that you have assigned items to sites. If you use multiple bins, make sure you create bins before you enter beginning balance transactions. If you use Invoicing or Sales Order Processing, Dynamics GP automatically updates history information in Inventory Control for items for which you keep calendar, fiscal, or transaction history. If you use Purchase Order Processing and Dynamics GP Bill of Materials, Dynamics GP updates only transaction history.

1. **On the Menu bar, select Transactions⇨Inventory⇨Batches to display the Inventory Batch Entry window (see Figure 10-4).**

2. **In the Batch ID and Comment fields, enter an identifier and brief description for the batch.**

3. **Open the Origin list and choose Transaction entry.**

4. **Deselect the Post to General Ledger option to avoid updating the General Ledger with duplicate entries.**

5. **Choose Transactions to open the Item Transaction Entry window.**

6. **Enter adjustment transactions as described in the section, "Understanding Inventory Transactions," later in this chapter.**

After you post the beginning quantity information, repeat Steps 1 through 4 to select the Post to General Ledger option for future batches, ensuring that your daily transactions update the General Ledger.

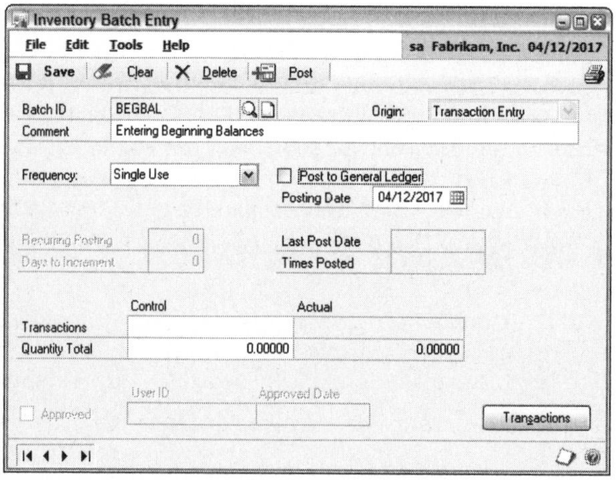

Figure 10-4:
The Inventory Batch Entry window

Standard pricing versus extended pricing

Dynamics GP supports using two different pricing schemes: standard pricing or extended pricing. You can choose to use one or the other but not both, and you can create fairly complex pricing structures with either. The pricing scheme you choose depends on the way your company does business; as a rule of thumb, you need extended pricing if you require date-sensitive promotional pricing, otherwise stick with standard pricing because it is considerably easier to set up and maintain.

Standard pricing

If you use standard pricing, you can define price levels and price groups to use in conjunction with price lists. A *price level* is a pricing tier that you can assign to items, customers, and prospects. For example, you might create a Regular price level and a Top Customer price level — and then assign the Top Customer price level to customers with whom you do lots of business and want to provide special pricing.

You can use *price groups* to identify items that have similar pricing structures that you might want to update as a group. For example, suppose that you sell the same T-shirt in several colors. If the price of one changes, the price of all of them will probably change. In this case, you can assign them all to the same price group and when prices change, you can update the price lists for all those items at once.

Price lists contain the actual prices you want to assign to items. You enter the percentage or price for each price level you create. It's generally a good idea to base the price on either a markup of standard cost or a percentage of list price, rather than a currency amount. In this way, when prices change, you only need to update the standard cost on the item card or the list price, and Dynamics GP automatically sets all the various tiers of price levels and volume discounts. If you choose to set prices by a flat currency amount and you to change pricing, then you will need to manually change the dollar amounts in all the lines of the various schedules themselves. Choosing a markup of actual cost is usually not the preferred approach since actual costs can fluctuate too much and cause unpredictable pricing. Whether you choose to allow users to override the price or lock the price down in Sales Order Transaction Entry might also affect your decision to use actual cost as the basis of price. If you lock down the price, you have more reason to not use actual cost.

You can create price levels and price groups without knowing item prices; you only need item prices when you create price lists.

For details on setting up standard pricing, see Chapter 10 of the Inventory Control manual.

Extended pricing

If you use extended pricing, you set up price groups, price sheets, and price books. You use *price groups* to identify and group items for which you calculate pricing in the same way. Typically, you set prices for all items in the group; if necessary, you can override the group price.

A *price sheet* is a list of prices that you use during a particular period. You can create each price sheet for different combinations of items, price groups, or both. Dynamics GP calculates prices as long as every item has a net price on a price sheet or is part of a price group that has a net price on a price sheet.

A *price book* is a collection of price sheets. You can assign only one price book to any particular customer, but you can assign the same price book to multiple customers. In addition to assigning price sheets to price books, you can assign a price sheet to a customer or a prospect.

You can create a promotional price sheet that contains special offers for individual products.

Dynamics GP automatically creates a base price book called, appropriately, BASEBOOK. Dynamics GP takes prices from the base price book if Dynamics GP can't find a price anywhere else in the pricing hierarchy. Dynamics GP does not automatically add prices to the base price book; you must assign net price sheets to this book.

To use extended pricing, you enable it in the Sales Order Processing module; refer to the Sales Order processing manual for details on enabling the option. For details on setting up extended pricing, see Chapter 11 of the Inventory Control module.

Understanding Inventory Transactions

You can enter four different inventory-related transactions for items with an item type of Sales inventory or Discontinued:

- ✔ **Adjustment:** There is really no difference in the way Dynamics GP treats an adjustment transaction and a variance transaction; effectively having both transactions gives you two different numbering schemes for transactions that have the same effect on your Dynamics GP data. You typically use adjustment transactions for write-offs of inventory, discrepancies discovered outside of a physical count, and so on. Generally, increases to inventory occur in the Purchase Order module during a Receiving Transaction Entry, and decreases to Inventory occur in the Sales Order module when you post a Sales Order Invoice, but there may be times when you want to manipulate inventory quantities directly in the Inventory Control module, and in these situations, you use the adjustment transaction.

- ✔ **Variance:** You use variance transactions when a stock count produces a different on-hand quantity than you find recorded in Dynamics GP.

✔ **Transfer:** You use transfer transactions when you want to move items from one site to another or change items from one quantity type to another.

✔ **In-transit transfer:** You can use in-transit transfer transactions to track the location of items being moved from one site to another while in transit; in-transit transfer transactions help you prevent the accidental sale of items in transit.

Follow these steps to record an inventory adjustment or variance transaction:

1. **On the Menu bar, select Transactions➪Inventory➪Transaction Entry to display the Item Transaction Entry window shown in Figure 10-5.**

2. **Open the Document Type list and select the appropriate document type: Adjustment or Variance.**

3. **In the Number field, enter a document number or accept the default document number.**

4. **In the Date field, enter a transaction date.**

   If this transaction is part of a batch, the date you enter here is the date that Dynamics GP updates your Inventory Control records. The posting date — the date when Dynamics GP updates your General Ledger records — is assigned to the batch. If this transaction is not part of a batch, you can assign the posting date by choosing the expansion button in the Date field.

5. **In the Batch ID field select or enter a batch number.**

Figure 10-5:
The Item
Transaction
Entry
window.

6. **In the Default Site ID field, select the site to which most of the lines on the transaction apply.**

The Default Site ID is optional. If you select a Default Site ID, Dynamics GP automatically fills in the Site ID on each line of the transaction using the Default Site ID, and you can change the Site ID if necessary. If you don't select a Default Site ID, you need to select a Site ID on each line of the transaction.

7. **Click in the Item Number column and click the lookup button to select an item number.**

When you enter the item number, Dynamics GP displays the unit cost and unit of measure.

8. **In the Quantity column, enter the quantity for the transaction. To enter an adjustment that decreases the quantity, enter a negative number.**

If you use multiple bins, you need to specify a bin to keep bin quantity information up to date; selecting a bin doesn't affect posting.

9. **In the Site ID column, accept the Default Site ID or select another site.**

If your company uses the Available To Promise feature, you can view available to promise information about the item by clicking the Quantity Available link to open the Inventory Available to Promise Inquiry window.

10. **As you finish a line entry, another window might open where you can supply lot number, serial number, or bin quantity information as needed.**

11. **Repeat Steps 7 through 10 to add more lines to the transaction.**

12. **Choose Save.**

You can move items with an item type of Sales Inventory and Discontinued from one site to another using a transfer transaction. As soon as you enter a transfer, Dynamics GP updates the allocated quantity of the item at the site where the item was originally stored (the "from" site) but doesn't update the on-hand quantity of the item at the site where you are moving the item (the "to" site) until you post the transaction.

To enter a transfer, follow these steps:

1. **On the Menu bar, select Transactions⇨Inventory⇨Transfer Entry to display the Item Transfer Entry window shown in Figure 10-6.**

2. **In the Number and Date fields, enter a document number and date.**

3. **If the transaction is part of a batch, use the Batch ID field to enter or select a batch.**

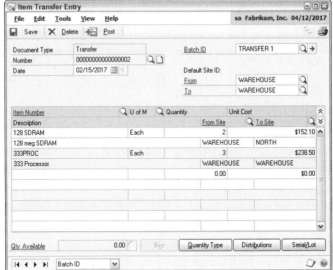

Figure 10-6:
The Item
Transfer
Entry
window.

4. In the Default Site ID section, select default From and To sites that apply to most of the lines on the transaction.

Dynamics GP will automatically display in the From Site and To Site fields on each line of the transaction; you can change the Site ID's on the transaction lines as needed.

5. Click in the Item Number field and then click the lookup button to select an item number to transfer.

When you enter the item number, Dynamics GP displays the unit cost and unit of measure.

6. In the Quantity field, enter the number of items you want to transfer.

7. Verify the From Site and To Site fields.

If your company uses the Available To Promise feature, you can view available to promise information about the item by clicking the Quantity Available link to open the Inventory Available to Promise Inquiry window.

8. As you finish a line entry, another window might open where you can supply lot number, serial number, or bin quantity information as needed.

9. Repeat Steps 5 through 8 to include additional items on this transactions.

10. Save or post the transaction.

When you transfer items from one site to another, you may want to use an interim location that Dynamics GP calls a *via site*. Using a via site, you can prevent accidental sale of the items while they are in transit to the destination site. You can use the In-Transit Transfer Entry window to enter in-transit transfer transactions to account for the location of items you move from one site to another. Once the original location fulfills and ships the items to the via site, you post an inventory transfer transaction, creating a purchase receipt for the goods in the via location.

1. **On the Menu bar, select Transactions⇨Inventory⇨In-Transit Transfer Entry to display the In-Transit Transfer Entry window shown in Figure 10-7.**

2. **In the document Number field, select a document number or choose New and accept the default document number Dynamics GP displays.**

3. **In the Order Date field, enter or accept the default date.**

4. **In the Promised Date field, enter the date you expect the merchandise to arrive at the destination site.**

5. **In the From Site ID field, enter or select the originating site from which you are shipping the merchandise.**

6. **In the Via Site ID field, enter or select the interim location to represent the location of the item while it is in transit.**

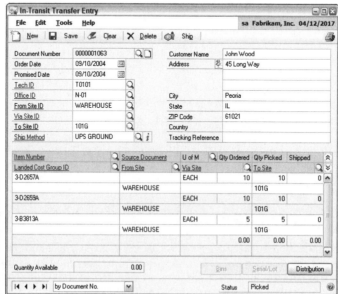

Figure 10-7:
The In-Transit Transfer Entry window.

7. **In the To Site ID field, enter or select the destination site for the merchandise.**

   Dynamics GP displays the To Site ID's address information in the Customer Name and Address fields after the insertion point leaves the To Site ID field. This address appears when you print the packing slip.

8. **In the Ship Method field, enter or select a shipping method.**

9. **Click in the Item Number field and enter or select the item number you are transferring.**

   Dynamics GP fills in the default unit of measure, the From Site, the Via Site, and the To Site.

10. **In the Qty Ordered field, enter the quantity of the item to transfer.**

11. **In the Qty Picked field, enter the quantity to be picked from inventory.**

    You can enter a quantity that is less than but not more than the quantity ordered.

12. **As you finish a line entry, another window might open where you can supply lot number, serial number, or bin quantity information as needed.**

13. **Repeat Steps 9 through 12 to enter additional items to transfer.**

    If you track lot or serial numbers for an item, select the item and choose Serial/Lot to open windows where you can view or select lot or serial numbers. If you are using multiple bins, you also can enter bin numbers for the serial or lot number.

14. **Choose Save.**

Finding Out About Your Stuff

You can run a variety of reports and inquiries concerning inventory items; in this section, I touch on just a few.

The Back-Ordered Items Received report

As you fill orders from customers, you may find that you're out of a particular item. So, you order the item and the customer agrees that you should ship the back-ordered item as soon as you receive it. You need to identify back-ordered items that you receive so that you can make sure that you ship them to the customer.

Enter the Back-Ordered Items Received report. Because you typically use purchase orders to order back-ordered items, Dynamics GP classifies this report as a Purchase Order Processing report. The Back-Ordered Items Received report shows receiving information for sales documents that were linked to purchase orders as well as updated costs and quantities successfully allocated and fulfilled on sales orders.

The report also shows sales documents that were not linked to purchase orders.

To print the Back-Ordered Items Received report, follow these steps:

1. **On the Menu bar, select Reports⇨Purchasing⇨Analysis to display the Purchasing Analysis Reports window shown in Figure 10-8).**

2. **From the Reports list, select Back-Ordered Items Received.**

3. **Choose New to open the Purchasing Analysis Report Options window.**

4. **Enter an option name and create a report option to sort and restrict the report.**

5. **Select Destination to specify a printing destination.**

6. **Select Print.**

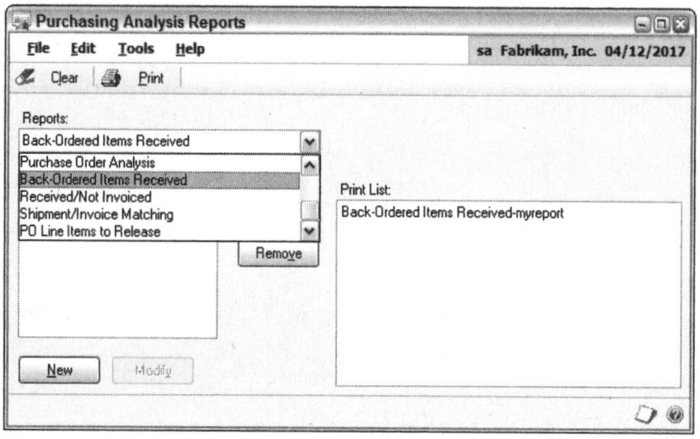

Figure 10-8: The Purchasing Analysis Reports window.

Purchasing Analysis Reports		sa Fabrikam, Inc. 04/12/2017

File   Edit   Tools   Help

Clear   Print

Reports:

Back-Ordered Items Received

Purchase Order Analysis
Back-Ordered Items Received
Received/Not Invoiced
Shipment/Invoice Matching
PO Line Items to Release

Print List:

Back-Ordered Items Received-myreport

Remove

New   Modify

The Stock Status report

The Stock Status report provides you with up-to-date information on each item; the report includes the following fields for each item:

- ✔ **Quantity on Hand**
- ✔ **Quantity on Order**
- ✔ **Quantity Back Ordered**

✔ **Quantity Requisitioned**

✔ **Quantity Allocated**

✔ **Current Cost**

✔ **Inventory Value**

You can print this report by using the Menu bar and selecting Reports➪ Inventory➪Activities, and then selecting Stock Status from the Reports list. Click the New button to create a set of options and set the destination where the report should print. As you set options, you can include additional information, such as serial and lot numbers, and you can limit the report to sites you specify. You can use this report to obtain the detail needed to reconcile the inventory values in the Inventory Control module with the General Ledger and/or on the Balance Sheet.

Item Inquiry

You can use inquiry windows to view inventory-related transactions. For example, use the Item Transaction Inquiry window to view any posted transaction for an item from any module, including but not limited to Inventory Control.

You can limit the transactions you view to just Inventory Control transactions if you use the Inventory Transaction Inquiry window. If your organization uses multiple bins, you also can view information about the bins used for a transaction.

You can use the In-Transit Transfer History Inquiry window to view in-transit transfers.

But the Purchase Receipts Inquiry window is your window into the FIFO Layers. From this window, you can view all the purchase receipts that exist for a particular item. For example, you might use this window to find out the actual costs and quantities on a specific receipt, particularly if you suspect that an item cost was entered incorrectly.

To view purchase receipt information, follow these steps:

1. **On the Menu bar, select Inquiry➪Inventory➪Receipts to display the Purchase Receipts Inquiry window shown in Figure 10-9.**

2. **In the Item Number field, enter or select an item number.**

3. **In the Site ID field, enter or select a site.**

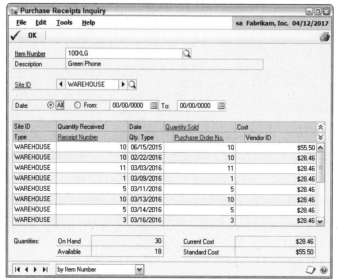

Figure 10-9:
The
Purchase
Receipts
Inquiry
window.

4. Use the Date section to limit the transaction information that Dynamics GP displays.

Dynamics GP displays the receipts for the specified item and location.

You can view additional information for a specific transaction if you select the transaction and click the Receipt Number link, Purchase Order No. link, or the Quantity Sold link. Dynamics GP opens a window with detailed information.

Performing a physical inventory

You can use cycle stock counting and the stock count calendar to help you manage your inventory. Typically, cycle counting means that your inventory personnel are counting a few items each day instead of relying on an annual inventory count. Using this approach, you can help ensure that you don't experience out-of-stock conditions because you can count items most critical to your business with a frequency you specify. You also can keep a close eye on expensive items. When you use cycle counting, you spread stock counts evenly over a cycle. For example, if you set up a 30-day cycle count, you spread the counts over the 30 days.

Dynamics GP uses a stock count calendar to determine when next to count an item. A *stock count calendar* identifies the days when a stock count can and cannot be performed. For example, if your employees don't work weekends, you might choose to designate all Saturdays and Sundays as days when a stock count cannot be completed. If you use the stock count calendar in conjunction with cycle counting, Dynamics GP spreads the suggested count dates over the length of the cycle.

To set up the stock count calendar, on the Menu bar select Microsoft Dynamics GP⇨Tools⇨Setup⇨Inventory⇨Stock Calendar to display the Stock Calendar Maintenance window. In the Company-side Down Day Settings section, you can identify weekend days by selecting Sundays Only or Saturdays and Sundays. In the calendar portion of the window, select other days that nobody works at your company, such as legal holidays. Click OK when you finish.

When you set up a cycle count, the window you use depends on whether you want to set up a cycle count for a single item or for groups of items. To set up a cycle count for a single item, on the Menu bar select Cards⇨Inventory⇨ Quantities/Sites to display the Item Quantities Maintenance window. Select an Item Number and a Site ID number and choose Stock Count to open the Item Quantities Stock Count window (see Figure 10-10).

Figure 10-10: The Item Quantities Stock Count window.

Fill in the Last Stock Count Date and Time and, in the Stock Count Interval Days field, enter the number of days between stock counts. Dynamics GP schedules the first stock count for the item at this site based on the date and the stock count interval.

You should consider non-working days when you set the stock count interval. For example, if you want to count an item every Wednesday and your stock count calendar indicates Sundays as non-working days, the stock count interval should be 6.

Click OK to close the Item Quantities Stock Count window and then click Save in the Item Quantities Maintenance window.

To set up a cycle count for a group of items, on the Menu bar select Cards⇨Inventory⇨Count Cycle Assignment to display the Stock Count Cycle Assignment window. In the Stock Count Interval Days field, enter the number of days between counts. If appropriate, change the date and time that appear in the Date And Time to Start Counting fields.

Use the Restrictions section to select the items you want to count using this frequency. If appropriate, insert additional restrictions. To remove items from the resulting list, choose Details to open the Cycle Assignment Details window, where Dynamics GP displays each item that met your criteria. To remove an item from the count cycle, remove the check that appears beside the item number in the Include column. When you finish identifying items to include in the count, click Process in the Stock Count Cycle Assignment window. Dynamics GP prints the Stock Count Cycle Assignment Report so you can verify your entries.

Finally, you can print the Physical Inventory Checklist shown in Figure 10-11 to help inventory employees record count information. On the Menu bar, select Reports⇨Inventory⇨Activity to display the Inventory Activity Reports window. From the Reports list, select Physical Inventory Checklist. In the Options section, click New. Then, set up options for the report and select a report destination.

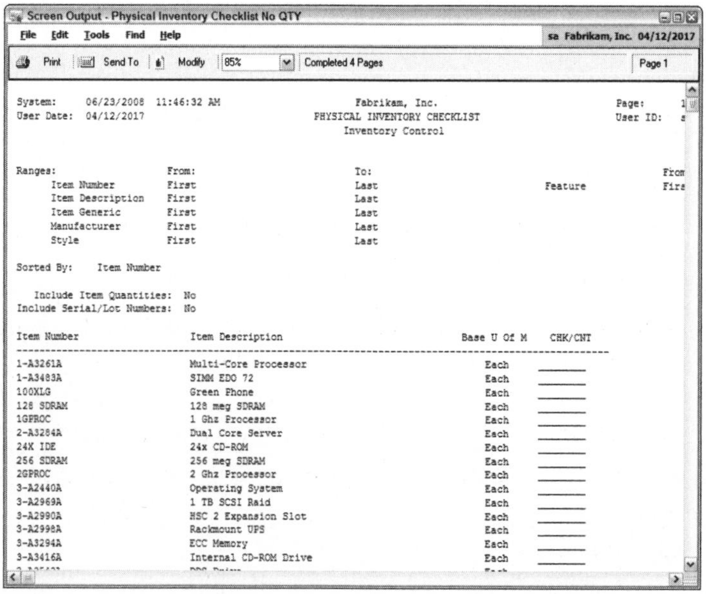

Figure 10-11: The Physical Inventory Checklist report.

After inventory personnel count the items in a stock count schedule, you enter stock count results. Dynamics GP compares those results to the captured quantities for each combination in the stock count schedule, and then calculates default variance amounts that you can use to create and post transactions. Dynamics GP doesn't create any transactions until you process the stock count.

When you process a stock count, several things happen:

✔ **Dynamics GP creates variance transactions and, if you select the Autopost Stock Count Variances option, Dynamics GP also posts the transactions.** Dynamics GP bases the cost information for variance transactions on the cost of the items at the time of the stock count.

✔ **Dynamics GP calculates new Next Stock Count Dates for the items in the stock count schedule.**

✔ **Dynamics GP stores history information of the results of the stock count.**

✔ **If you opted not to reuse the stock count, Dynamics GP deletes it; otherwise, Dynamics GP clears the stock count results and sets the status of the count to Available.**

✔ **Dynamics GP prints the exceptions report for processing a stock count, which lists any problems that prevent the stock count information from being processed.** The report lists variance transactions and the batch number and variance transaction numbers used.

You use the Stock Count Entry window to enter and process the results of a stock count, based on information recorded on the stock count forms. Follow these steps:

1. **Choose Transactions⇨Inventory⇨Stock Count Entry to display the Stock Count entry window.**

2. **In the Stock Count ID field, enter or select a stock count ID with a status of Started or Entered. Dynamics GP displays the combinations included in the stock count in the scrolling window.**

3. **Accept or change the default document date and the default count date; by default, Dynamics GP sets both dates using the user date.**

4. **In the Sort By field, select the sorting order for the scrolling window.**

5. **In the scrolling window, enter the counted quantity for each item using the item's base unit of measure.**

   You can enter counts in other units of measure; refer to the Dynamics GP Inventory Control module manual, Chapter 22.

When you move out of the field in the scrolling window, Dynamics GP automatically calculates the variance quantity, updates the Count Date and Count Time fields using the default count date and time, and marks the Verified option.

If you track the item by lot or using serial numbers, you must enter information about the lot or serial numbers of the items that were counted. See Chapter 21 in the Dynamics GP Inventory Control module manual for details.

6. **Repeat Step 5 for each combination.**

After you enter a counted quantity for an item in the scrolling window, Dynamics GP makes available the options for Autopost Stock Count Variances and Reuse Stock Count. The default setting for the Autopost Stock Count Variances option comes from the Inventory Control Setup window. The default setting for the Reuse Stock Count option comes from the Stock Count Schedule window.

With the insertion point on any line in the scrolling window, you can click Distribution to view the distribution accounts for each combination in the scrolling window and make changes, if needed.

7. **Click the Unposted Trx button and the Trx History button to view unposted transactions and transaction history for any stock count result that has a variance.**

8. **Save or process the stock count information.**

If you choose Process, Dynamics GP creates and, if you selected the Autopost Stock Count Variances option, posts inventory variance transactions. If you choose Save, Dynamics GP doesn't post transactions, and you'll be able to enter more stock count results for this stock count schedule later. To post the transactions, use the Inventory Batch Entry window.

Part III
Stuff You Do from Time to Time

The 5th Wave   By Rich Tennant

"Look-what if we just increase the size of the charts?"

In this part . . .

This part focuses on tasks you don't do daily but you perform on some less frequent basis. Read about closing your company's books, saving report criteria, and using utilities to find and correct data discrepancies.

Chapter 11

Closing the Books

In This Chapter

▶ Reviewing common period-end tasks

▶ Closing the year

M icrosoft Dynamics GP enables you to keep data for an unlimited number of open and historical years, but you can post transactions to only one historical year and any number of open years. So, you need to be able to close fiscal and calendar years.

In addition, you can close fiscal periods in Dynamics GP to make sure that users don't post transactions to periods for which work has been completed.

In this chapter, you read about the things you do to close the books.

Period-End Stuff

First, you need to understand that Dynamics GP doesn't require you to do anything at the end of a fiscal period. What you choose to do is really up to you.

Most people create customer statements and, if appropriate, assess finance charges at the end of each fiscal period. But some companies use a rolling technique for customer statements. These companies divide their customers into groups that match the working days of each month and then send statements daily, but only to that day's group of customers. Each customer receives only one statement each month but the company actually creates statements daily. Similarly, some companies print the Aged Trial Balance once each month and age prior to printing, while other companies age and print the report daily.

See Chapter 7 for details on aging, preparing customer statements, and assessing finance charges.

Depending on your company's industry, you might take inventory at the end of a period to reconcile stock on hand with stock recorded in Dynamics GP; most inventory-based companies perform a physical inventory at least once each year and often twice each year.

Many people print a series of reports at the end of each fiscal period for each Dynamics GP module; you can create a report group for your period-end reports to make this process easier. See Chapter 12 for details.

Many companies close fiscal periods when they determine that processing for that period is complete. Closing a fiscal period helps ensure that no users accidentally post transactions to that period. Closing a period isn't a "final" action; that is, if you later discover transactions that should be posted to a closed fiscal period, you can reopen that period, post the transactions, and then close the period again.

If you don't want to close a fiscal period for an entire module, you can select particular windows to close for a particular period using the Mass Close Fiscal Periods window.

To close a fiscal period, follow these steps:

1. **On the Menu bar, select Microsoft Dynamics GP➪Tools➪Setup➪Company➪Fiscal Periods to display the Fiscal Periods Setup window shown in Figure 11-1.**

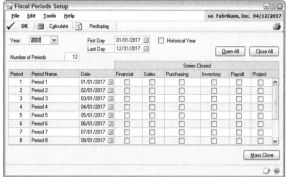

Figure 11-1:
The Fiscal Periods Setup window.

2. **In the Year list box, enter or select a year.**

3. **In the Series Closed grid, select the check boxes that correspond to the series and period you want Dynamics GP to close.**

Reconciling to the General Ledger

Dynamics GP users typically process thousands of transactions during the normal course of business. When you consider the volume of transactions, you realize that it's probable and even likely that users accidentally don't follow standard procedures or make and post unintended entries. As a result, you might discover that the payables or receivables balances on a General Ledger Trial Balance report don't match the corresponding balance on Aged Trial Balance reports from the Payables Management or Receivables Management modules. The balances won't match, for example, if a user posts a transaction to but not through the General Ledger and then deletes the transaction or changes its amount before posting it in the General Ledger.

You can use the Reconcile to GL window (on the Menu bar, select Microsoft Dynamics GP⇨Tools⇨Routines⇨Financial⇨Reconcile to GL) to generate a Microsoft Excel spreadsheet that can help you match transactions in the General Ledger with the originating transactions in Payables Management and Receivables Management and help you identify adjusting transactions that you need to make to reconcile any discrepancies.

When you close a period for a series, Dynamics GP no longer permits posting to that period from any window in that series. You can close only certain windows in a module by clicking Mass Close to display the Mass Close Fiscal Periods window; click the check box in the Closed column beside the window and period you want to close.

4. Click OK to close the window and save your entries.

Closing the Year

Closing the year in Dynamics GP transfers all current-year information to history if you keep history records and prepares the accounting system for a new fiscal year. When you close subsidiary modules such as Receivables Management, closing resets all year-to-date totals to zero.

In Receivables Management and Payables Management, you actually perform two year-end closing processes: calendar year closing and fiscal year closing.

You can enter transactions for a new year before closing the current year by entering the transactions in separate batches for the new year that you do not post until you close the current year.

Closing inventory

When you close the year in inventory, Dynamics GP transfers all summarized current-year quantities, costs, and sales information to transaction history. Dynamics GP also updates the Beginning Quantity of each item to be the On Hand quantity at each site and resets the Quantity Sold field for each item to zero.

Depending on the options you select when you close, Dynamics GP might also update the standard cost of each item using the FIFO Periodic or LIFO Periodic valuation methods to the current cost and might remove

- ✔ **Purchase receipts of items that have been completely sold**
- ✔ **Cost change history information**
- ✔ **Discontinued items that have been completely sold**
- ✔ **Lot attributes of items tracked by lot numbers that have been completely sold**

Before you close the year in the Inventory module, make sure that you do the following:

- ✔ **Enter and post all transactions for the following modules if you use them to ensure that historical information is accurate and that Dynamics GP updates year-to-date amounts correctly: Sales Order Processing, Invoicing, Purchase Order Processing, Inventory Control, and Bill of Materials.**
- ✔ **Reconcile inventory quantities as described in Chapter 34 of the Dynamics GP Inventory Control manual.**
- ✔ **Print the Physical Inventory Checklist and complete a physical inventory. Then, post any inventory adjustments needed.**
- ✔ **Print reports such as the Stock Status report for your permanent records.**
- ✔ **Back up your company data (see Chapter 15 for details).**

To close the year in the Inventory module, follow these steps:

1. **On the Menu bar, select Microsoft Dynamics GP⇨Tools⇨Routines⇨Inventory⇨Year-End Close to display the Inventory Year-End Closing window shown in Figure 11-2.**

2. **In the Remove section, identify records to remove.**

Figure 11-2:
Inventory
Year-End
Closing
window.

Dynamics GP doesn't remove discontinued items if they are assigned to kits, if they are components of bills of materials, or if they have bills of materials of their own.

Select Item's Standard Cost in the Update section to update the standard cost information for items with FIFO Periodic or LIFO Periodic valuation methods. Dynamics GP adjusts the standard cost of each item to the amount you most recently paid for the item.

3. Choose Process to close the year.

Microsoft Dynamics GP closes the year; you won't be able to post inventory transactions or batches, reconcile quantities, change valuation methods, or change decimal places.

After closing the year, you might want to close fiscal periods for inventory. See the section "Period-End Stuff," earlier in this chapter.

Closing the tax year

For Receivables Management and Payables Management, you may also want to use the Tax Year-End Closing window to prepare your tax records for a new year. When you close the tax year, Dynamics GP clears the accumulated year-to-date tax totals in the Tax Detail Maintenance window (on the Menu bar, select Microsoft Dynamics GP⇨Tools⇨Setup⇨Company⇨Tax Details) and moves them to last year's tax totals. If you close the tax year, you can separate year-to-date tax totals for each year.

Closing a tax year affects all the tax details you entered. Complete this procedure only once every year after you close any Sales and Purchasing series years and before posting any documents to the next year. On the Menu bar, select Microsoft Dynamics GP⇨Tools⇨Routines⇨Company⇨Tax Year-End Close to display the Tax Year-End Close window. Select the Close Year box, make sure a check appears in the Print Report box, and click Process.

Closing the Sales series

When you close the Sales series, Dynamics GP transfers current-year balances to last year's balance and sets the current-year balances to zero. For Receivables Management, you close both the fiscal year and the calendar year, even if you use only fiscal periods.

Before you close either the calendar year or the fiscal year, make sure that you post all transactions for the current year and back up your data; see Chapter 14 for details.

You should close the calendar year after you print the last set of statements for the year you intend to close. When you close the calendar year, Dynamics GP updates information that appears in the Customer Finance Charge Summary window shown in Figure 11-3 (on the Menu bar, select Cards⇨Sales⇨Summary and click the Finance Charges button). Dynamics GP updates

 ✔ **The Calendar Finance Charges field to display the date you closed the calendar year**

 ✔ **The Current Year Amount field to display total finance charges for the new calendar year**

 ✔ **The Last Year amount field to display totals for the year you closed**

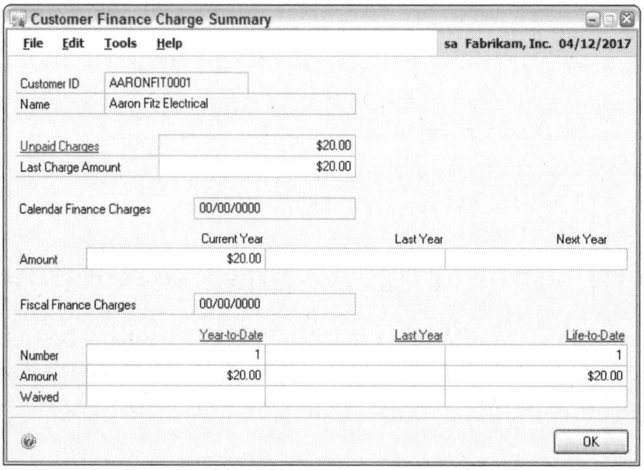

Figure 11-3:
The
Customer
Finance
Charge
Summary
window.

When you close the fiscal year, Dynamics GP updates the information that appears in the Customer Summary window (on the Menu bar, select Cards⇨Sales⇨Summary) when you open the Summary View list box and select Amounts Since Last Close. Dynamics GP updates the numbers in the Year to Date column and the Last Year column to display, respectively, totals for the new fiscal year and the year you close.

Dynamics GP also updates information that appears in the Customer Finance Charge Summary window (refer to Figure 11-4) so that you can print finance charge totals on December and January statements for tax reporting purposes. Dynamics GP updates the Fiscal Finance Charges field to display the date you closed the fiscal year. Dynamics GP also updates the amounts in the Year to Date column and the Last Year column to display, respectively, totals for the new fiscal year and for the year you close.

To close the Calendar year, follow these steps:

1. **On the Menu bar, select Microsoft Dynamics GP➪Tools➪Routines➪Sales➪Year-End Close to display the Receivables Year-End Closing window shown in Figure 11-4.**

Figure 11-4:
The
Receivables
Year-End
Closing
window.

2. **In the Year To Close section, choose Calendar.**

   If your fiscal year coincides with the calendar year, you can close both at the same time by choosing All.

3. **Make sure a check appears in the Print Report box.**

4. **Click Process.**

You close the fiscal year using the same steps; select Fiscal in Step 2.

After you close the fiscal year, you may want to close fiscal periods for all or some windows in Receivables Management. See the section "Period-End Stuff," earlier in this chapter.

Closing the Purchasing series

Like the Receivables Management module, you close both the calendar year and the fiscal year in the Payables Management module. When you close the calendar year, Dynamics GP transfers the current year's 1099 amounts to last year's balance for all vendors. When you close the fiscal year, Dynamics GP transfers all current-year balances other than

1099 balances to last year's balances. You can view the amounts that Dynamics GP updates in the Vendor Yearly Summary window; on the Menu bar, select Cards⇨Purchasing⇨Summary, select a vendor, and click the Yearly button.

Make sure that you post all transactions for the year you intend to close before closing the year. And, be sure to back up your data before closing; see Chapter 14 for details.

To close the calendar year in the Payables Management module, follow these steps:

1. **On the Menu bar, select Microsoft Dynamics GP⇨Tools⇨Routines⇨ Purchasing⇨Year-End Close to display the Payables Year-End Closing window.**

   This window looks just like the Receivables Year-end Closing window; refer to Figure 11-4.

2. **In the Year To Close section, choose Calendar.**

   If your fiscal year coincides with the calendar year, you can close both at the same time by choosing All.

3. **Make sure a check mark appears in the Print Report box.**

4. **Click Close Year.**

Printing 1099 forms

At the end of the year or early into a new year, most companies print 1099 statements for vendors who qualify to receive them. Dynamics GP enables you to print 1099 statements at any time and for a year other than the current year. Chapter 3 describes how to designate a vendor as a 1099 vendor. To print 1099's, follow these steps:

1. On the Menu bar, select Microsoft Dynamics GP⇨Tools⇨Routines⇨Purchasing⇨Print 1099 to display the Print 1099 window.

2. In the Address ID field, select your company's address.

3. In the Payer's Federal ID Number field, type your company's Federal ID number.

4. In the 1099 Year box, type the year for which you want to print 1099 statements.

5. From the 1099 Type list box, select Miscellaneous, Dividend, or Interest.

6. From the Form Type list box, select Continuous or Select Single Feed.

7. By default, Dynamics GP suggests that you print 1099 forms for all vendors, but you can select a range of vendors for whom to print 1099 forms.

8. In the Print section, select 1099 Form.

9. From the Order list box, select the order in which you want the forms to print: Vendor ID, Vendor Name, Vendor Class, or Type.

10. Choose Print.

You close the fiscal year using the same steps; select Fiscal in Step 2.

After you close the fiscal year, you may want to close fiscal periods for all or some windows in Payables Management. See the section, "Period-End Stuff," earlier in this chapter. You may also want to close the tax year; see the side-bar, "Closing the tax year," Earlier in this chapter.

Closing the General Ledger (the important one)

Closing the year automatically does the equivalent of manually preparing and posting closing entries to the general ledger. Dynamics GP transfers all current-year information for each account in the Chart of Accounts to account and transaction history if you keep history, preparing the accounting system for a new fiscal year.

In addition, during the year-end closing process, Dynamics GP

- ✔ **Reconciles and summarizes the General Ledger balances that have accumulated throughout the year**
- ✔ **Removes inactive accounts with zero balances**
- ✔ **Transfers open-year profit and loss amounts to the Retained Earnings account and zeros all profit and loss account balances**
- ✔ **Summarizes balance sheet accounts, bringing the balances forward as the accounts' beginning balances in the new fiscal year**

  Dynamics GP creates beginning balances for the new year after completing the year-end close process. Therefore, financial statements for the new year, whether printed from Advanced Financial or from FRx, will reflect only current year activity until you close the prior year. To get around this limitation, you can create calculated columns in FRx to make financial statements look like the balances have been brought forward during the time you are waiting to close last year's books.

- ✔ **Brings the balance of unit accounts forward to the new fiscal year**
- ✔ **Prints the Year-End Closing Report**

Before you close a year, complete the following tasks:

- ✔ **Post final transactions in all modules except the General Ledger and complete month-end and period-end procedures for all modules except General Ledger.**
- ✔ **Print a year-end detailed trial balance.**
- ✔ **Print any year-end financial statements you need.**

✔ After posting all transactions, complete year-end procedures for Inventory, Receivables Management, and Payables Management, in that order.

✔ Post final adjusting entries in the General Ledger.

✔ Optionally, use the Fiscal Periods Setup window to close the last period of the current fiscal year. See the section, "Period-End Stuff," earlier in this chapter, for details.

✔ VERY IMPORTANT: Print an Account List to double-check the posting type for the posting accounts.

Dynamics GP uses the posting type to identify the accounts to close retained earnings and the accounts for which balances should be brought forward to the next year. To print an Account List, on the Menu bar select Reports⇨Financial⇨Accounts to open the Chart of Accounts Report window and select All Accounts in the Reports list or use a SmartList. If you find an incorrect posting type, change it in the Account Maintenance window (on the Menu bar, select Cards⇨Financial⇨Account).

If you close the year and accounts exist that should have been tagged as Balance Sheet but were tagged as Profit and Loss (or vise versa), then Dynamics GP won't bring the balance forward properly; this is not a simple matter to correct. You'll find a technical article on CustomerSource in the Knowledge Base that explains the steps you would need to take to correct such an error. Not fun, so, doublecheck the posting type for your accounts before closing the year.

✔ If you want to keep historical records, check the General Ledger Setup window (on the Menu bar, select Microsoft Dynamics GP⇨Tools⇨ Setup⇨Financial⇨General Ledger) to confirm that checks appear in the Maintain History section beside Accounts and Transactions.

✔ Check links for all Financial tables and back up your company data; see Chapter 14 for details.

✔ Set up a new fiscal year using the Fiscal Periods Setup window. See the section, "Period-End Stuff," earlier in this chapter.

To close the fiscal year, follow these steps:

1. **On the Menu bar, select Microsoft Dynamics GP⇨Tools⇨Routines⇨ Financial⇨Year End Closing to display the Year-End Closing window (see Figure 11-5).**

2. **In the Retained Earnings Account field, enter or select the retained earnings account you want Dynamics GP to use to close the year's profit or loss.**

If you are closing divisional retained earnings, enter or select one of the divisional retained earnings accounts.

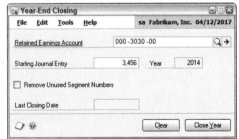

Figure 11-5:
The Year-
End Closing
window.

In the General Ledger setup window (on the Menu bar, select Tools➪Setup➪General Ledger), you can indicate whether you want to post dollars to a single Retained Earnings account or split dollars among several Retained Earnings accounts based on the divisional segment of your General Ledger account number. If you wish to split dollars among Retained Earnings accounts, you must create Retained Earnings accounts for each division. Dynamics GP will not create the accounts for you; it will, however, calculate the amount to post to each account and create the closing journal entry for you. In the General Ledger setup window, you can specify any one of the Retained Earnings accounts you establish; Dynamics GP will know to swap out the divisional segment based on the segment that you indicate as the division.

3. **In the Starting Journal Entry field, enter a starting number for Dynamics GP to use as the first journal entry number in the new fiscal year.**

4. **Select the Remove Unused Segment Numbers option to have Dynamics GP remove unused account segment numbers.**

5. **Select Close Year.**

It's possible that the progress window might seem to stop at 50 percent; don't try to close Dynamics GP or restart your computer. As long as your hard drive is processing, let the process continue. When something like this happens, Dynamics GP is usually processing the details of accounts with large transaction volumes like Cash or Accounts Payable.

When Dynamics GP completes the closing process, it prints the Year-End Closing Report, which lists the accounts Dynamics GP closed and the transactions Dynamics GP created to close them.

At this point, consider closing all fiscal periods for all series using the Fiscal Periods Setup window (refer to the section, "Period-End Stuff," earlier in this chapter) to prevent users from posting transactions from any module to any period in the year you closed.

Finally, adjust budget figures for the new year using the Budget Maintenance or Single-Account Budget Maintenance windows and print financial statements. See Chapter 8 for details on working with budgets.

Chapter 12

Analyzing Information through Inquiries, SmartLists, and Reports

• •

In This Chapter

▶ Using inquiries to analyze information

▶ Using SmartLists to analyze information

▶ Printing reports

• •

*I*t would be most disheartening to put information into a computer and not be able to get it back out again. This chapter describes the various tools built into Microsoft Dynamics GP that you can use to analyze information:

✔ **You can make inquiries.**

✔ **You can use SmartList.**

✔ **You can print reports.**

You'll find inquiry windows available for every Dynamics GP module you have installed; *inquiry windows* provide access to information in a quick, efficient manner.

SmartList is an easy-to-use ad hoc query and reporting tool that you can use to find and print information and, if you want, export it to Microsoft Excel for further analysis. You create customized SmartList queries that you can save and reuse whenever you want.

And, of course, *reports* provide you with a way to print financial information to your screen, to paper, or to a file.

 You also can use the lists that appear in the Navigation pane above the Navigation pane buttons to help you find information. In Chapter 7, I used one of the lists to help me apply payments after the fact.

Making Inquiries

Using inquiry windows is a quick and easy way to view both summary and detailed information about any Dynamics GP module. You can use an inquiry window to view all transactions — work, open, historical, or a combination of those transaction types — for a vendor. Or, you can use an inquiry window to view a yearly summary of a customer's activity. Or, you can use an inquiry window to track down the documents that contribute to the balance of a general ledger account, as I demonstrate in this section.

There are tons of inquiry windows available in Dynamics GP; I urge you to explore them, as they provide an easy and powerful way for you to find information.

All inquiry windows are available from the Inquiry menu; you then point to the series associated with the inquiry you want to make, and Dynamics GP displays the list of inquiry windows available to you.

Suppose that you want to view the breakdown of your cash account by period; on the Menu bar, select Inquiry⇨Financial⇨Summary to display the Summary Inquiry window shown in Figure 12-1.

Summary Inquiry				
File Edit Tools View Help			sa Fabrikam, Inc. 04/12/2017	
Clear				
Account	000 -1100 -00			
Description	Cash - Operating Account		Year:	2017
Period	Debit	Credit	Net Change	Period Balance
Beginning Balance	$0.00	$0.00	$0.00	$0.00
Period 1	$0.00	$0.00	$0.00	$0.00
Period 2	$56,583.42	$2,994.59	$53,588.83	$53,588.83
Period 3	$33,422.79	$96,695.26	($63,272.47)	($9,683.64)
Period 4	$185,714.22	$12,945.09	$172,769.13	$163,085.49
Period 5	$0.00	$50.00	($50.00)	$163,035.49
Period 6	$0.00	$0.00	$0.00	$163,035.49
Period 7	$0.00	$0.00	$0.00	$163,035.49
Period 8	$0.00	$0.00	$0.00	$163,035.49
Period 9	$0.00	$0.00	$0.00	$163,035.49
Period 10	$0.00	$0.00	$0.00	$163,035.49
Period 11	$0.00	$0.00	$0.00	$163,035.49
Period 12	$0.00	$0.00	$0.00	$163,035.49
Totals	$275,720.43	$112,684.94	$163,035.49	$163,035.49
				Currency
◄ ◄ ► ►I by Account				

Figure 12-1:
The Summary Inquiry window.

Select an account — in this example, I select the Cash account — using the lookup button, and Dynamics GP displays the period balances for the account for the year specified in the Year list box in the top-right corner of the window. You can change the year to view period balances for the account for open years.

You can use the History Summary Inquiry window to view period balances for historical years.

You cannot change any information that appears when you work with inquiry windows; they are "view-only" windows.

As you review the information, you become curious about the values in a particular period; for this example, let's focus on Period 2. To view the values that make up the period, click the period and then click any of the column heading links: Debit, Credit, Net Change, or Period Balance. Dynamics GP displays the Detail Inquiry window for the selected account if you click any of these links (see Figure 12-2).

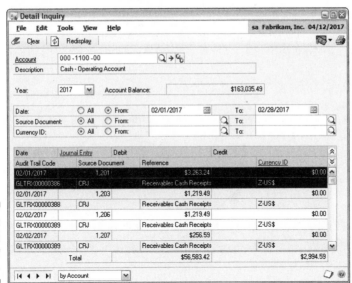

Figure 12-2:
The Detail Inquiry window.

The period balance appears at the bottom of the window on the Total line; note that you can see total Debits and total Credits. If you click the Show Details icon at the right edge of the grid area, Dynamics GP displays the details for each transaction, including its audit trail code and source document code.

You can view the actual journal entry — and the accounts to which the amounts were distributed — if you click the line of the transaction and then click the Journal Entry link. Dynamics GP displays the Transaction Entry Zoom window shown in Figure 12-3.

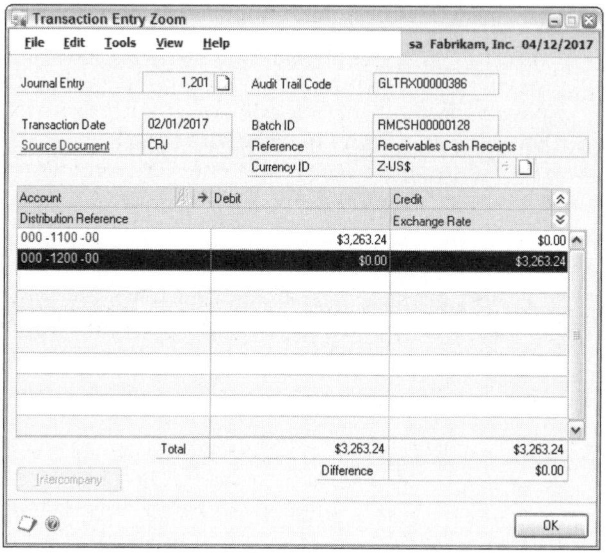

Figure 12-3:
The
Transaction
Entry Zoom
window.

As you review the debits and credits of the transaction, you can view the document that generated the journal entry. Click the Source Document link to display an Inquiry Zoom window associated with the type of transaction that generated the journal entry. In this example, you see the Cash Receipts Inquiry Zoom window (see Figure 12-4), because the journal entry was generated when a user recorded a customer's payment.

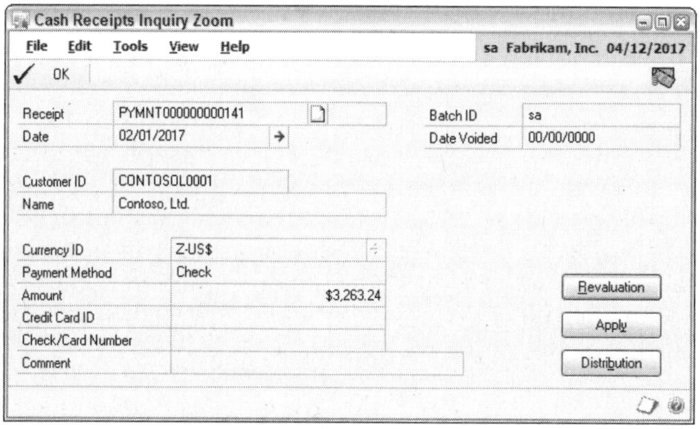

Figure 12-4:
An Inquiry
Zoom
window.

The Cash Receipts Inquiry Zoom window identifies the document number and date, along with the name of the customer who made the payment.

While viewing the Detail Inquiry window, I selected a transaction that debited a cash account; most often, customer payments result in a debit to a cash account. If I had selected a transaction that credited the cash account and then clicked the Journal Entry link followed by the Source Document link, in all probability, Dynamics GP would have displayed the Payables Payments Zoom window, because credits to a cash account are most often generated when you write a check to pay a vendor.

Getting Information at Your Fingertips with the SmartList

SmartList is a built-in tool that you can use to easily create custom queries to find and print information in any Dynamics GP module and, if you want, export the information to Microsoft Word or Excel. You can save the customized SmartList queries that you create and reuse them whenever you want. For example, suppose that you want to monitor urgent sales orders. You can create and store the transactions in a batch you name "URGENT" and then create a SmartList called "Urgent Orders" that uses a search criterion to display transactions in the URGENT batch.

You can open the SmartList window shown in Figure 12-5 by using the Menu bar and selecting Microsoft Dynamics GP⇨SmartList.

Available SmartList queries, called *Favorites,* appear in the tree on the left side of the window; click any plus sign to display the SmartList favorites available in a particular category. When you click a particular SmartList favorite, the data associated with that SmartList favorite appears in the right portion of the SmartList window.

You can print the results of any SmartList query; simply click the Print button on the SmartList window toolbar. If you prefer, you can export the SmartList query results to Word or Excel by clicking either the Word button or the Excel button on the SmartList window toolbar. In addition, you can select another destination by clicking the Go To button in the SmartList. You can change the default Go To behavior for each SmartList using the SmartList Options window; on the Menu bar, select Tools⇨Setup⇨System⇨SmartList Options. And, you can view on-screen the details of any card or transaction that appears in a SmartList query result window just by double-clicking anywhere in that row.

The Go To button

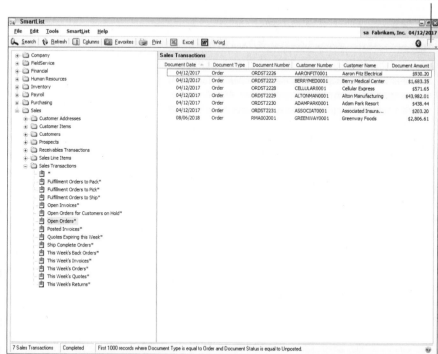

Figure 12-5:
The
SmartList
window.

Dynamics GP comes with a series of predefined favorites, and you can modify them or, better still, create your own SmartList favorites. You can identify a predefined favorite by the asterisk that appears beside it. In Figure 12-5, I clicked the Open Orders favorite; note that the name of the SmartList favorite includes an asterisk.

In addition to the favorites you find in Dynamics GP, a number of products that integrate with Dynamics GP also include SmartList favorites that allow you to search for data associated with those applications.

Selecting columns to display

Suppose that you view a favorite and like most of what you see, but decide that you really don't need to see some information, and you'd like to see the columns presented in a different order. For example, the Open Orders displays the Document Date, Document Type, Document Number, Customer Number, Customer Name, and Document Amount. After viewing the Open Orders favorite, you decide that you don't need both the Customer Number and the Customer Name. You can edit the appearance of the favorite by following these steps:

1. **On the Menu bar, select Microsoft Dynamics GP⇨SmartList to display the SmartList window.**

2. **Click the plus sign (+) beside a SmartList category and select the SmartList you want to modify.**

   Dynamics GP displays the SmartList information in the right pane of the SmartList window.

3. **Click the Columns button on the SmartList window toolbar to display the Change Column Display dialog box shown in Figure 12-6.**

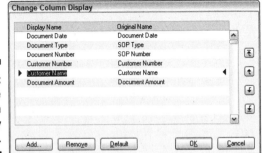

Figure 12-6:
The Change
Column
Display
dialog box.

4. **Click each column you want to hide and then click the Remove button.**

5. **To reorder columns, select a column you want to move and click the Up or Down arrows on the right side of the Change Column Display dialog box.**

   Moving a column up in the dialog box moves the column to the left when you view the SmartList on-screen.

6. **Click OK when you finish.**

   Dynamics GP redisplays the SmartList, incorporating your changes.

You can expand the capabilities of SmartList if you purchase the additional product, SmartList Builder. With SmartList Builder, you can add subtotals and formulas to a SmartList, extend the SmartList to use any table in Microsoft Dynamics GP, and control work flow.

Saving your own version of a SmartList

If you decide you really like your own version of the SmartList better than the default version, you can save it. While viewing your version, click the Favorites button on the SmartList window toolbar to display the Add or Remove Favorites window shown in Figure 12-7.

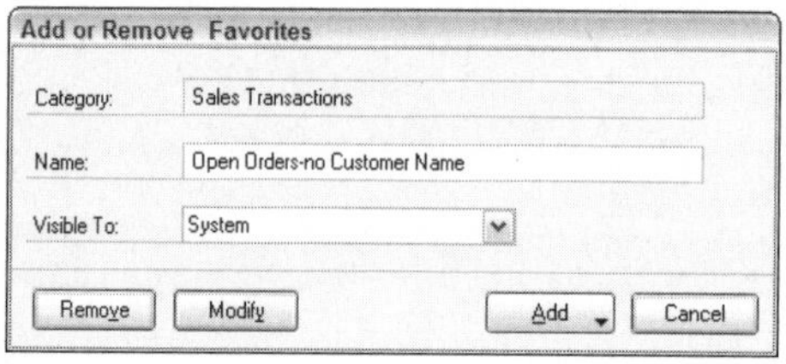

Figure 12-7:
The Add
or Remove
Favorites
window.

Add or Remove Favorites	
Category:	Sales Transactions
Name:	Open Orders-no Customer Name
Visible To:	System

Remove   Modify   Add ▾   Cancel

Supply a new name for the favorite and use the Visible To list to decide which Dynamics GP users can use your SmartList. Then, click the Add button and choose Add Favorite.

It's a good idea to leave the view of the original predefined favorite unchanged and save your own version under a different name, so that you can always display the original view. After you've made your own favorite, you may wish to make further changes down the road; to save your changes to an existing favorite, select the Favorites button again and then press the Modify button to save your changes.

You also can click Add Favorite and Reminder to add a customized Reminder as you save the SmartList if you want a reminder for the SmartList to appear on your Dynamics GP home page.

Setting search criteria for a SmartList query

Once again, suppose that you're working with an existing SmartList favorite and you want to modify the data that appears. For example, you decide that you need an Urgent Orders SmartList, and the Open Orders SmartList contains much of the information you want to include; you need, however, to make sure that your Urgent Orders SmartList displays only those orders stored in the URGENT batch. You can modify the criteria of the SmartList query's search and then save it.

Display the SmartList to modify or use as a foundation for a new SmartList by clicking it in the left pane of the SmartList window. Then, click the Search button on the SmartList window toolbar to display the Search Sales Transactions window shown in Figure 12-8.

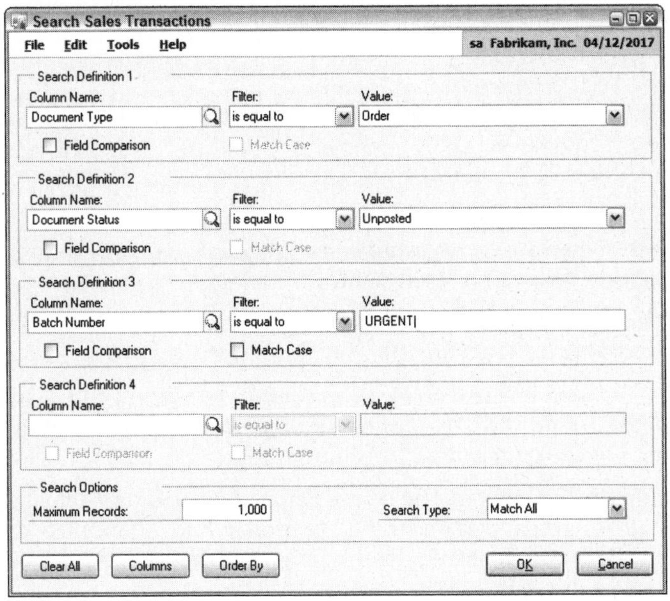

Figure 12-8:
The Search
Sales
Trans-
actions
window.

You can set up to four search criteria, and the Open Orders SmartList already has two search criteria established; one that sets the Document Type to Order, and another that sets the Document Status to Unposted.

You set the search criteria by specifying definitions for columns. To add a search criterion that displays only transactions stored in a batch named URGENT, follow these steps:

1. **Click the lookup button beside the Column Name field of an available Search Definition to display the Columns dialog box shown in Figure 12-9.**

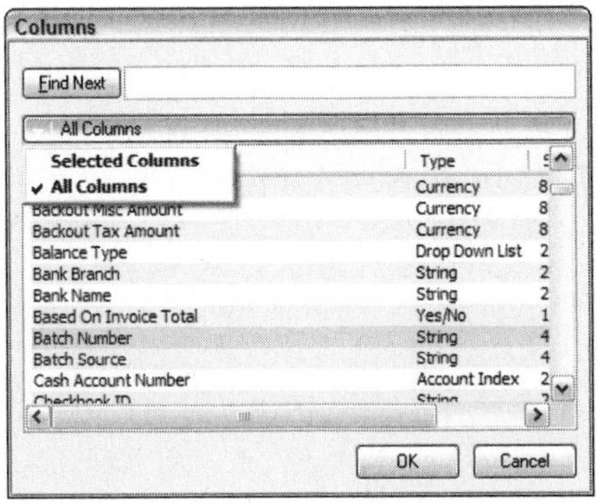

Figure 12-9:
The
Columns
dialog box.

2. **Select the column on which you want to base your definition and click OK to redisplay the Search window; for this example, I selected Batch Number.**

   If the column you want to use as the basis for your search definition doesn't appear in the Columns dialog box, click the carat above the Field Name box and select All Columns. Then, scroll to find the column you want to use.

3. **Open the Filter list box and select a comparison operator; for this example, I selected "is equal to."**

4. **Open the Value list box and select the value appropriate for your definition; for this example, I typed URGENT.**

5. **You can use the Search Options section to control the maximum number of records Dynamics GP displays when you use the SmartList query and to determine the Search Type.**

   Using the Search Type field, you can specify whether Dynamics GP should match all your search definitions or any combination of your search definitions when determining whether to display a record as a result of the search.

6. **Click OK to display the SmartList using your criteria.**

   The criteria you establish for the SmartList appear at the bottom of the SmartList window when you view the SmartList results.

Printing Standard Reports

Using the Great Plains Report Writer that comes with Dynamics GP, you can print hundreds of standard reports. And, if you find that you print the same set of reports on some regular basis, you can create a report group for those reports; then, you can print the reports as a group instead of individually.

When you print a report in Dynamics GP, you create report options that define the information you want to include on reports and the way in which you want the information sorted. As part of your report options, you also define where you want Dynamics GP to print the report — to your screen, to a printer, or to a file, and you can print the report to all three places.

To print any standard report, on the Menu bar select Reports, point to the series associated with the report, and then click the report. In Figure 12-10, you see the window that appears when you choose Reports➪Purchasing➪Check Information. For every standard report, a window very similar to this one appears when you select the report.

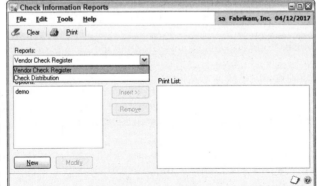

Figure 12-10:
The Check
Information
Reports
window.

If the window contains a Reports list box, you can open it to see the variations of the report available for you to print. Any report options you previously established appear in the Options list; to print the report, you must select a set of options and click the Insert button.

To create a set of options, click the New button in the lower-left corner of the window.

Setting up report options

When you click the New button, Dynamics GP displays the report options window associated with the report you selected; each report options window is different because each report displays different information. Figure 12-11 shows the Check Information Report Options window.

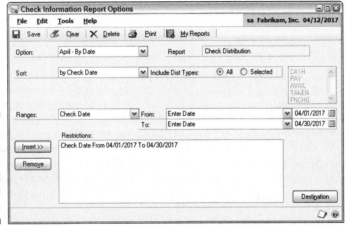

Figure 12-11:
The Check
Information
Report
Options
window.

In the Option field, type a name for the options you're going to set; use a name that will help you remember the options you establish.

Open the Sort list box and select a method by which to sort the report.

If appropriate, use the Ranges section to restrict the information that Dynamics GP prints on the report; use the list box to select the type of restriction you want to establish and then use the From and To boxes to enter the values associated with the restriction. Click the Insert button to store the restriction.

Other options will appear in other report options windows; the options that appear are specialized for the report you opted to print.

Selecting report destinations

You need to set up the destination for each set of options you create. Click the Destination button to display the Report Destination dialog box shown in Figure 12-12.

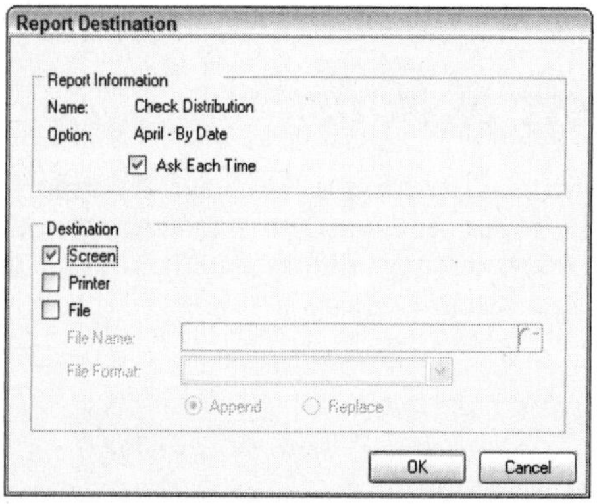

Figure 12-12:
The Report
Destination
dialog box.

In the Report Information section, select the Ask Each Time check box if you want the opportunity to choose where the report will print each time you print it. In the Destination section, select the check boxes associated with where you want the report to print; you can select all of the boxes. If you select the File check box, click the folder beside the File Name field to select a folder where Dynamics GP can store the file and to assign a name to the file. Then, from the File Format list, select the format you want Dynamics GP to use when creating the file: Text File, Tab– Delimited, Comma– Delimited, or HTML file.

TIP

You can set a default destination for new report options in the User Preferences window. Choose Microsoft Dynamics GP⇨User Preferences.

TIP

Keep in mind that, if you are primarily trying to export data in electronic format, you might be better off using a SmartList, because not all Dynamics GP Report Writer reports line up the columns and rows of data as you might expect.

Click OK to redisplay the report options window, where you click Save to save all the report options settings you selected, including the destination options.

When you close the report options window by clicking the X in the upper-right corner, the first window for the report appears; in this example, refer to Figure 12-10. In the Options list, click the options you created and then click Insert. To print the report, click the Print button on the window's toolbar. Dynamics GP prints the report to the destination you selected, using the options you specified (see Figure 12-13).

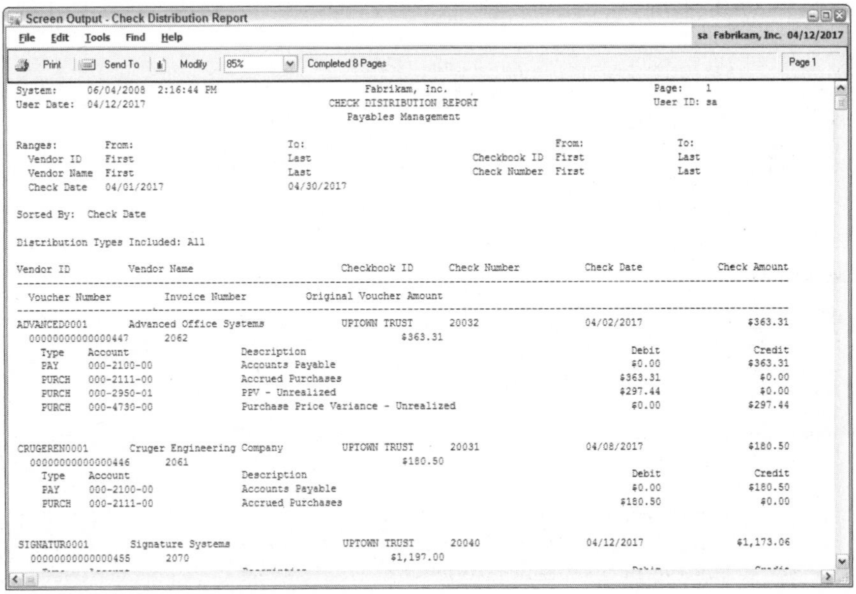

Figure 12-13: A sample report.

TIP

If you select Screen as a destination for your report and you use a MAPI-compliant mail system such as Microsoft Outlook, you can e-mail the report. If you have Acrobat Distiller or PDFWriter installed, you can e-mail the report in PDF format. Click the Send To button in the toolbar of the Screen Output window. You can purchase Acrobat Distiller or PDFWriter from Adobe Systems.

If the report doesn't look exactly the way you'd like — say you'd like to add information to the report — you can edit the report in GP Report Writer. From any of the report windows, including the Screen Output window, select Tools⇨Customize⇨Report Writer. Dynamics GP prompts you to open the report writer software — the dialog box you see suggests Dynamics GP and that's the option you should select. A new window opens, where you can view available reports, along with data types, fields, and tables. For details on using the Dynamics GP Report Writer to modify a report, select Help⇨Contents while viewing the Report Writer window. You can return to Dynamics GP by selecting File⇨Microsoft Dynamics GP.

External reporting tools

In addition to the standard reports discussed here, you have several other ways to produce and print reports from Dynamics GP:

✔ **You can use Advanced Financial Analysis, a basic reporting tool that you can use to create and modify financial statements.** Because Advanced Financial Analysis comes as part of Dynamics GP, you might want to use it if you don't have extensive reporting needs. You can use it to modify the four standard financial statements in Dynamics GP: the Balance Sheet, the Profit and Loss Statement, the Statement of Retained Earnings, and the Statement of Cash Flows. For more information, see the Advanced Financial Analysis documentation.

✔ **To schedule reports to print, you can use Report Scheduler and Reports Catalog.** *Report Scheduler* installs automatically when you install Dynamics GP, and you can use it to schedule and publish your Report Writer reports in a flexible and secure way. After you schedule reports using Report Scheduler, you publish reports to the *Reports Catalog.* If you use Business Portal, you also can assign reports to Business Portal center pages and roles. For more information, refer to the Report Scheduler guide that's included on your Dynamics GP CD.

✔ **If your organization uses Distributed Process Server, you can process some reports on your computer and send other, long reports to a designated process server on the network so that you can continue working while the reports are being created.** You'll find more information about using the Distributed Process Server in the System Administrator's Guide.

✔ **You can print many Dynamics GP reports to a Microsoft Excel file so that you can view, analyze, and print your reports.** As you read in Chapter 8, you can create and modify Dynamics GP budgets in Excel.

✔ **If you use Business Portal, you can use the Data Connection wizard in Excel to access data stored in an external source, such as Microsoft SQL Server, which is the database that Dynamics GP uses to store your company information.** The wizard makes it easy to create customized queries for information stored in Dynamics GP, including information about customers, vendors, transactions, and items. You can save and rerun frequently used queries rather than create them each time. For more information about using the Data Connection wizard, see the Excel documentation.

✔ **If you need more extensive financial reporting than Advanced Financial Analysis can provide, you can use FRx Financial Reporting, Dynamics GP's preferred financial report writer, to create customized financial statements.** You also can use FRx to extract information from your general ledger and combine it with information from an Excel spreadsheet. For more information about FRx, see the FRx documentation.

✔ **You can use Crystal Reports to create reports and customized queries using your Dynamics GP data.** Crystal Reports can be delivered over the Web using Business Objects. You can import data from multiple sources and publish reports to several standard formats, including XML, PDF, and ODBC. Crystal Reports also integrates with Microsoft Office applications, such as Excel and Word. For more information, refer to the Working With Crystal Reports guide on your Dynamics GP CD, or refer to the documentation for the Crystal Report product.

✔ **You can use Microsoft SQL Reporting Services (SRS) to create custom reports.** SRS is a powerful report writer, but somewhat less user-friendly than Crystal Reports at this stage of its development. SRS reports can be delivered on the Business Portal. Both Crystal and SRS are full-featured report writers that can easily access the SQL Server database that stores your Dynamics GP data. In addition, you can use any report-writing software product that can access SQL Server to create reports of Dynamics GP data; Crystal Reports and SRS are simply the most popular.

✔ **If you are using Business Portal, you can create key performance indicators to help monitor current performance, indicate when performance is within specific alert ranges, and compare current performance to past performance.** You also can use query pages and result viewer Web Parts to create customized queries about your Dynamics GP customers, vendors, transactions, and items. For more information, refer to your Business Portal documentation.

✔ **You can use Microsoft Analysis Cubes to analyze and report financial data and share information across your organization.** You can customize report packages to include only the information that is relevant for each recipient. For more information, refer to the Dynamics GP Analysis Cubes documentation.

Working with report groups

Suppose that, at the end of each month, you print a set of standard reports in each series that you haven't customized. You always print the same reports using options you have already established. You can save yourself the trouble of displaying all those windows to print each report individually if you create a report group for them.

When you create a report group, all of the reports in the group must belong to the same Dynamics GP series. But, after we go through these steps, I'll show you how to create a report group of report groups so that you can easily print reports from several series.

Before you create a report group, make sure that you have set up the options for each report you intend to include in the group. To create a report group for reports in a single Dynamics GP series, follow these steps:

1. **On the Menu bar, select Reports, then a series, and then select Groups to display a Report Groups window (see Figure 12-14).**

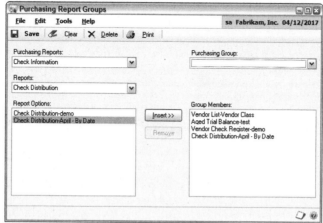

Figure 12-14: A Report Groups window.

2. **From the series Reports list, select the report category.**

3. **From the Reports list, select the report.**

4. **In the Report Options list, click a set of options and then click Insert.**

   Dynamics GP displays the report in the Group Members list.

   You can add up to 32 report options to a single group.

5. **Click the Save button on the window's toolbar to save the group, and, when Dynamics GP prompts you to enter a name for the group, supply one.**

6. **Click the Print button to print the group.**

The next time you open this window, you will be able to select the group from the group list box in the upper-right corner of the window; Dynamics GP will automatically add all of the reports in the report group to the Group Members list.

To create a report group of report groups, follow these steps:

1. **On the Menu bar, select Reports⇨Combined Group to display the Combined Report Group window.**

2. **From the Series list box, select a series.**

3. **From the Groups box, select the report groups you want to include in the combined group and choose Insert.**

   Dynamics GP displays the report group in the Combined Group Members box.

4. **Repeat Steps 2 and 3 for each series and report group to include all the report groups in the combined report group.**

5. **In the Combined Groups box, type a name for the combined group.**

6. **Choose Save.**

To print a combined report group, select it from the Combined Groups list box and click the Print button on the toolbar of the Combined Report Group window.

Setting up quick financial statements

For other Dynamics GP reports, you need to set up display options before you can print the report, but you don't need to set up the report's layout. For financial statements, however, you need to set up report layouts as well as report options.

You can use the Quick Financial Setup window to define the layout for financial statements. When you define a financial statement layout, you define the columns that will appear on the report; Dynamics GP automatically defines the rows in the financial statement, using General Ledger account categories to group the accounts on the statements.

Each financial statement includes a number of required columns, which automatically appear in the window when you select the type of financial statement you want to create. In addition to these required columns, you can insert optional columns for each financial statement.

The Quick Financial Setup window has some limitations. For example, you can add optional columns only after required columns; you can't insert an optional column between two other optional columns or before the required columns.

For more flexibility, you can edit a report layout you create in the Quick Financial Setup window using the Advanced Financial Report Layout window. From this window, you can add report columns or move columns to new locations.

If you modify an existing quick financial statement and close the window, an alert message will appear and ask if you want to save your changes. If you choose Delete, the entire financial statement will be deleted.

You must set up at least one Profit and Loss Report before you can set up any Balance Sheet, Statement of Retained Earnings, or Statement of Cash Flows report because these three reports all depend on a Profit and Loss Report to supply a net income or net loss amount.

To set up a quick financial statement:

1. **On the Menu bar, select Reports⇨Financial⇨Quick Financial to display the Quick Financial Setup window (see Figure 12-15).**

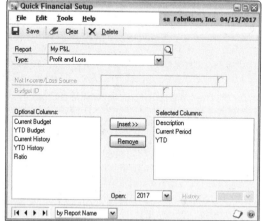

Figure 12-15:
The Quick
Financial
Setup
window.

2. **In the Report field, enter or select a financial statement name.**

3. **In the Type field, select a statement type.**

4. **If you select Balance Sheet, Statement of Cash Flows, or Statement of Retained Earnings in Step 2, use the Net Income/Loss Source list to identify the Profit and Loss report that will provide the net income or net loss source amount for the statement.**

5. **Required columns for the report appear in the Selected Columns list. To add a column shown in the Optional Columns list, click it and then click Insert. To remove an optional column from the layout, select it and choose Remove.**

   If you include a budget column, enter a Budget ID; similarly, if you include a history column, enter or select an open year and a historical year.

   You can include up to five required and optional columns for a Balance Sheet and up to six columns on a Profit and Loss Statement, Statement of Retained Earnings, and Statement of Cash Flows. You cannot control the order of the columns and you cannot add more than one budget or history year from the Quick Financial Setup window; to change column order or add years, use the Advanced Financial Reports window (on the Menu bar, select Reports⇨Financial⇨Advanced Financial).

6. **Choose Save.**

Printing financial statements

After you set up financial reports, you can print them using the Financial Statement Report window, but you must set up report options, as you do for other standard reports.

If you want to enter a prior period adjustment when printing a Statement of Retained Earnings, on the Menu bar select Reports⇨Financial⇨Prior Period Adjustments to display the Prior Period Adjustments window. Enter a description and amount for the adjustment; the description and amount of the adjustment appears as an adjustment to the beginning balance of the Retained Earnings account when you print the statement.

To print a financial statement, follow these steps:

1. **On the Menu bar, select Reports⇨Financial⇨Financial Statements to display the Financial Statement Report window, which closely resembles the window shown earlier in Figure 12-10.**

2. **From the Report list, choose the report you want to print.**

3. **Click New to open the Financial Statement Report Options window; this window closely resembles the window shown earlier in Figure 12-11.**

4. **In the Option field, type a name to describe the report options.**

5. **Use the Amounts list to specify the level of detail to print for the report amounts.**

   If you choose Detail with Rollups, Summary, or Summary with Rollups, select First Account or Category/Row in the Description section to specify whether Dynamics GP should print the first account description or the account category description for the report's rows.

6. **In the Include section, select Zero Balances and Unit Accounts to include these types of accounts on the report. If you are updating the accelerator file and want to use this updated information when printing this financial statement, select the Use Accelerator check box in the Include section.**

7. **To print only a range of accounts, use the Segment ID field to select or enter a Segment ID.**

   If you select a Segment ID, you can select the Individual Report box to print an individual report for each segment within the range you define. If you don't select the Individual Report box, Dynamics GP produces a single report that includes all accounts in the selected range.

If you select Individual Report and your financial statement displays ratio columns based on user-defined calculations, you can choose to base the calculation on the individual report or on all accounts in the defined range. For more information, see the Advanced Financial Analysis documentation.

You can click Adjust to make a temporary adjustment to the financial statement; Dynamics GP removes the changes when you close the Financial Statement Report window. You can click Revert if you made a temporary column adjustment and want to remove it before printing.

8. **Choose Destination to select a printing destination.**

9. **Click Save to save the report options.**

Once you set up the report options for the financial statement, you can print it the same way you would print any other report; from the Financial Statement Report window, select the report to print, select the options and click Insert, and then click the Print button on the window's toolbar.

Reprinting journals

I've mentioned several times that you can reprint posting journals; to reprint a posting journal for the General Ledger, use the Menu bar and select Reports⇨Financial⇨Cross-Reference. Set up report options, select them, and then click Print.

To reprint a posting journal for any other series, choose Reports, point at the series, and click Posting Journals. You will find several different posting journal reports listed; select the appropriate one, select report options, and then click Print.

Chapter 13

Using Utilities and the Professional Services Tools

*U*tilities exist for each Microsoft Dynamics GP module; these utilities help you perform a variety of functions. In this chapter, I show you how to use the reconciliation utilities in three different modules. When you reconcile, Dynamics GP compares summary information to detail information and makes changes to bring your data in line, if necessary. The reconciliation process can take a long time, depending on how much history you have stored in the Dynamics GP database and how powerful your hardware is, so you may want to start the process on a Friday afternoon.

I also introduce the Professional Services Tools Library module, a powerful set of tools originally created by the Dynamics GP consulting team and ultimately turned into a module in its own right. Using the Professional Services Tools Library module, you can perform a variety of functions not otherwise available in Dynamics GP. For example, using tools in the Professional Services Tools Library module, you can change the ID numbers for customers, vendors, items, employees, or accounts.

Reconciling Sales Orders

When you reconcile sales documents, Dynamics GP verifies item quantities and totals on sales documents and recalculates quantities and totals as needed. During reconciliation, Dynamics GP updates the following information if necessary:

- ✔ Document item quantities
- ✔ Canceled item quantities
- ✔ Transferred item quantities
- ✔ Fulfilled item quantities for serial- and lot-numbered items
- ✔ Quantities linked to purchase orders
- ✔ Remaining item quantities
- ✔ Amount remaining
- ✔ Document subtotals
- ✔ Batch information

You should reconcile Sales Order Processing and Purchase Order Processing before reconciling Accounts Receivable, Accounts Payable, or Inventory. You use the same basic steps provided below to reconcile Purchase Order Processing; to open the Reconcile Purchasing Documents window, use the Menu bar and select Microsoft Dynamics GP➪Tools➪Utilities➪Purchasing➪ Reconcile Purchasing Documents, then select the range of documents to reconcile, and click Process.

As a precaution, Microsoft urges you to make backups prior to running Utilities or Professional Services Tools. However, you don't need to make a backup if your organization makes regularly scheduled backups as part of an SQL Server Database Maintenance Plan. See Chapter 14 for details on backing up your Microsoft Dynamics GP company.

1. **On the Menu bar, select Microsoft Dynamics GP➪Tools➪Utilities➪ Sales➪Reconcile-Remove Sales Documents to display the Reconcile-Remove Sales Documents window shown in Figure 13-1.**

Figure 13-1: The Reconcile-Remove Sales Documents window.

2. **In the Documents section, select a range of documents to reconcile.**

3. **In the Options section, select Reconcile Sales Documents.**

You can select the Print Report Only check box to print a report that provides information about the selected documents before you reconcile them. If you select this option, Dynamics GP prints the report but does not reconcile the documents.

4. **Click the Process button.**

When reconciliation finishes, Dynamics GP prints the Reconcile-Remove Sales Document Report, which lists the sales documents that were reconciled.

From the same window, Dynamics GP can also remove completed sales documents that you haven't moved to history; completed sales documents are those with no remaining quantities. Follow the steps above, but, in Step 3, select Remove Complete Documents.

Reconciling Payables Management

When you reconcile payables accounts, you can reset the totals in the Vendor Credit Summary window for unapplied payments, unpaid finance charges, and current balances to reflect the posted payments and transactions. You might reconcile a current year to ensure the amounts on an aged trial balance report match the amounts on vendor lists.

You can reconcile the summary amounts, fiscal-year amounts, or calendar-year amounts. If you reconcile summary amounts, Dynamics GP reconciles unapplied payments, unpaid finance charges, current balance totals, and on-order amounts for the range you select. If you reconcile fiscal year amounts or calendar year amounts, Dynamics GP reconciles fiscal-year or calendar-year period summary information for the year you enter. If you reconcile calendar year amounts, you can choose to reconcile all amounts, only 1099 amounts, or all amounts except 1099 amounts.

If you reconcile data after removing transaction data for the selected year or for a range for which you don't keep history, your data might become inaccurate. Similarly, your data might become inaccurate if you reconcile a voided payment that crossed calendar years and was applied to an invoice with a 1099 amount.

To reconcile payables accounts, follow these steps:

1. **On the Menu bar, select Microsoft Dynamics GP⇨Tools⇨Utilities⇨ Purchasing⇨Reconcile to display the Reconcile Payables Accounts window (see Figure 13-2).**

2. **In the Range section, use the Range list box to specify how you want to select a range of vendors; then choose All or select a starting and ending vendor to filter the vendors being reconciled.**

3. **In the Reconcile section, select Summary, Fiscal Year, Calendar Year, or Batches.**

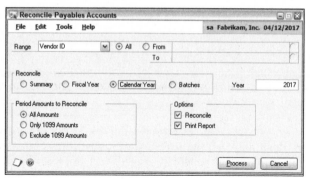

Figure 13-2:
The
Reconcile
Payables
Accounts
window.

If the vendor has no transaction history or open records, Dynamics GP zeroes the vendor's period summary information.

4. **If you select Fiscal Year or Calendar Year in Step 3, enter the year for which you want Dynamics GP to reconcile summary information against detail information.**

5. **If you select Calendar Year in Step 3, use the Period Amounts to Reconcile section to specify whether Dynamics GP should reconcile all amounts, only 1099 amounts, or all amounts except 1099 amounts.**

6. **In the Options section, select Print Report to print a Reconcile Balances Report, which lists the vendor records and the unapplied payments, unpaid finance charges, and current balances that Dynamics GP reconciles during the process.**

   If you select this option without selecting the Reconcile option, Dynamics GP prints the report but makes no changes.

7. **In the Options section, select Reconcile to reconcile the amounts for the vendors you selected.**

8. **Click the Process button to print the Reconcile Balances Report, reconcile amounts, or both.**

Reconciling Inventory

On occasion, it's helpful to reconcile inventory quantities. For example, if your data has been damaged, or if you change the number of decimal places you want to track for an item, you should reconcile inventory. When you reconcile inventory, Dynamics GP recalculates inventory quantities for the range of item numbers you specify and resets those quantities to match purchase receipt and serial number or lot number quantities.

If your Dynamics GP company is set up to use multiple bins, you can set up reconciliation so that Dynamics GP adjusts the quantities in the bins to match the quantity for the site. But, Dynamics GP doesn't reconcile the allocated quantities for bins to the allocated quantities for the site. Instead, Dynamics GP reconciles the allocated quantities for bins to the allocated quantities in unposted transactions because you can allocate items at the site level before allocating them at the bin level. Generally, items are allocated at the site level at the instant the allocation occurs, but items are allocated at the bin level when you fulfill the allocation.

When you enable multiple bins, you should reconcile inventory records. Reconciliation creates a bin for every item-site quantity that you haven't already assigned to a bin. For more information about what happens when you reconcile inventory after marking the options, refer to Handling Existing Quantities for Multiple Bins on page 20 of the Inventory Control Manual.

If your Dynamics GP company uses serial numbers or lot numbers, then Dynamics GP assigns new serial numbers or lot numbers during reconciliation when these numbers are missing.

If you don't want to use the numbers that Dynamics GP adds, you can enter decrease transactions to remove the effects of those changes and then enter increase transactions for the correct numbers in the Item Transaction Entry window.

Dynamics GP reconciles items entered on drop-ship purchase orders or on lines of drop-ship blanket purchase orders to the Drop-Ship PO quantity in Inventory Control. Dynamics GP doesn't reconcile the on-order quantities for items on a drop-ship purchase order or a drop-ship blanket purchase order. Dynamics GP reconciles the remaining on-order quantity of released and change purchase order line items and blanket line items to the on-order quantity for all sites and each item-site combination of an item.

If you use Purchase Order Processing or Sales Order Processing, reconcile these modules before reconciling inventory quantities because Dynamics GP might alter purchasing and sales information during reconciliation; you want Dynamics GP to use the altered information when reconciling quantities for inventoried items. See the section, "Reconciling Sales Orders," earlier in this chapter, for details on reconciling sales documents. To reconcile purchasing documents, use the Menu bar to select Microsoft Dynamics GP⇨Tools⇨ Utilities⇨Purchasing⇨Reconcile Purchasing Documents. Select the range of documents to reconcile and click the Process button. You use the same general procedure to reconcile both Accounts Receivable and Accounts Payable; see the section, "Reconciling Payables Management," earlier in this chapter, for information.

To reconcile inventory, follow these steps:

1. **On the Menu bar, select Microsoft Dynamics GP⇨Tools⇨Utilities⇨ Inventory⇨Reconcile to display the Reconcile Inventory Quantities window (see Figure 13-3).**

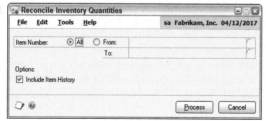

Figure 13-3:
The
Reconcile
Inventory
Quantities
window.

2. **In the Item Number section, enter or select the range of item numbers you want to reconcile.**

3. **Select the Include Item History check box if you're reconciling inventory because you've changed the number of quantity decimals for an item.**

   Selecting this check box tells Dynamics GP to update the item's history records as well as current records.

4. **Click the Process button.**

   Dynamics GP compares actual quantities and the quantities resulting from posted transactions and adjusts quantities if necessary; when reconciliation finishes, Dynamics GP prints the Reconcile Report.

Taking Advantage of Professional Services Tools

The Professional Services Tools Library was developed by the Dynamics GP consulting team over a number of years; the tools proved to be so useful that they were made available as a module for Dynamics GP. Many clients find these tools extremely useful to correct problems with existing data.

Among the more popular tools available in the Professional Services Tools Library, you can change account numbers, item numbers, customer numbers, employee numbers, or vendor numbers, and you can merge accounts, customers, items, or vendors.

You can install the Professional Services Tools Library using your Dynamics GP CD, and, due to the nature of the changes you can make with the Professional Services Tools Library, you might want to limit the users who have access to the tools; you can do so by establishing a security role. See Chapter 14 for details.

To use the Professional Services Tools Library, in many instances, you need to be logged in to Dynamics GP as the system administrator (the sa login) and be the only user logged in to Dynamics GP.

Changing the previously unchangeable

You can't change item, customer or vendor ID numbers using the Maintenance windows in Dynamics GP, and, without the Professional Services Tools Library, your only option is to delete an existing ID number and create a new record — and often, you can't delete an existing record because transactions are tied to it.

Using the Professional Services Tools Library, you can change these ID numbers; you can change a single ID number or a group of ID numbers. The tool goes through all cards, work, open, and history files and changes the ID everywhere, keeping everything in synch so that you won't know the ID had ever been anything but the ID you specify.

Changing a single ID number

Changing a single ID number requires no preliminary preparation on your part; in the steps that follow you see how to modify an inventory item number:

1. **In the Dynamics GP Navigation pane, click the Home button.**

2. **From the list that appears above the Home button, click Professional Services Tools Library.**

   The Professional Services Tools Library window appears (see Figure 13-4).

3. **In the Inventory Tools section, click Item Number Modifier and click Next.**

   The Item Number Modifier window appears (see Figure 13-5).

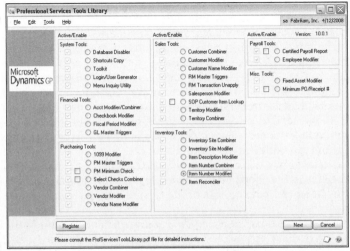

Figure 13-4:
The Professional Services Tools Library window.

4. **In the Starting Item Number field, enter or select an item ID number.**

5. **In the New Item Number field, enter the new number for the item.**

6. **Click Convert.**

   The tool prompts you to make a backup of your database.

7. **After the backup finishes, click Continue.**

   The tool notifies you when the process finishes.

8. **Choose OK and close the Item Modifier window.**

   A Report Destination window appears so that you can select a report destination for the Converted Item Number(s) report.

You can change customer ID numbers using the Customer Modifier option in the Professional Services Tools Library window, sales person ID numbers using the Salesperson Modifier option, and vendor ID numbers using the Vendor Modifier option.

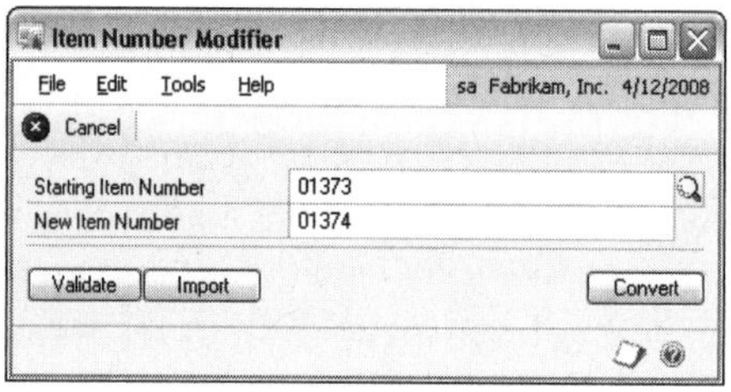

Figure 13-5:
The Item
Number
Modifier
window.

Changing a group of ID's

You can use the Professional Services Tools Library to change ID numbers for a large collection of accounts, items, customers, or vendors. For example, suppose that you want to change 2500 current item numbers to 2500 new item numbers. You import a two-column spreadsheet using the Item Number Modifier tool to accomplish the change.

To set up the data you want to use to make the change, enter existing system data — such as the item numbers — in the first column of data in the spreadsheet. In the second column of the spreadsheet, enter the new number. For account numbers, be sure to include dashes. Then, save the spreadsheet as a tab-delimited text file in Microsoft Excel.

Then, follow these steps; in this example, I use the Vendor Modifier window, but the steps apply regardless of the type of number you want to change:

1. **In the Dynamics GP Navigation pane, click the Home button.**

2. **From the list that appears above the Home button, click Professional Services Tools Library.**

The Professional Services Tools Library window appears (refer to Figure 13-4).

3. In the Purchasing Tools section, click Vendor Modifier and click Next.

The Vendor Modifier window appears (see Figure 13-6).

Figure 13-6:
The Vendor
Modifier
window.

4. Click the Validate button.

The tool prompts you to select a file to validate.

5. Select the spreadsheet file containing the information you want to import and choose Open.

When the validation process finishes, a Report Destination window appears so that you can select a report destination for the report that verifies the validity of the information in your spreadsheet. If any of the data on the report appears to be invalid, fix the spreadsheet and repeat the validation process until all of the data is valid.

6. Click the Import button.

The tool prompts you to select a file to import.

7. Select the spreadsheet file you validated in Step 5.

When the tool finishes importing the data, it alerts you with a message.

8. Click OK, and close the Vendor Modifier tool.

A Report Destination window appears so that you can select a report destination for the report that identifies the data changed by the tool.

Merging customers, items, or vendors

It happens — you set up a customer and then accidentally set up the same customer again, with a different customer ID. But, the worst part is that you don't realize you've set up the customer twice until you've recorded transactions using both customer ID's.

In this situation, you want to combine the two customers into one customer. And, using the Professional Services Tools Library, you can merge the customers; follow these steps:

You can use the same approach to combine item numbers, vendor numbers, or account numbers using the Item Number Modifier tool, the Vendor Modifier tool, or the Acct Modifier/Combiner tool. You also can merge groups of data using the approach described in the previous section.

1. **In the Dynamics GP Navigation pane, click the Home button.**

2. **From the list that appears above the Home button, click Professional Services Tools Library.**

   The Professional Services Tools Library window appears (refer to Figure 13-4).

3. **In the Sales Tools section, click Customer Combiner and click Next.**

   The Customer Combiner window appears (see Figure 13-7).

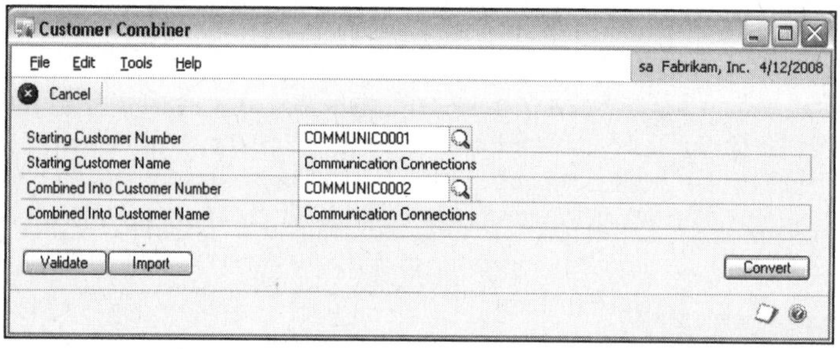

Figure 13-7:
The
Customer
Combiner
window.

Customer Combiner	□ ⊡ ⊠
File Edit Tools Help	sa Fabrikam, Inc. 4/12/2008
⊗ Cancel	

Starting Customer Number	COMMUNIC0001
Starting Customer Name	Communication Connections
Combined Into Customer Number	COMMUNIC0002
Combined Into Customer Name	Communication Connections

Validate	Import		Convert

4. **In the Starting Customer Number field, enter the number of the customer you want to stop using in Dynamics GP.**

5. **In the Combined Into Customer Number field, enter the customer number you want to continue using in Dynamics GP.**

6. **Choose Convert.**

   The tool prompts you to make a backup of your database.

7. **After the backup finishes, click Continue.**

   The tool notifies you when the process finishes.

8. **Click OK and close the Customer Combiner window.**

   A Report Destination window appears so that you can select a report destination for the Combined Customer Numbers report.

Part IV
Administering and Extending Your Dynamics GP System

The 5th Wave   By Rich Tennant

"I started running 'what if' scenarios on my spreadsheet, like, 'What if I were sick of this dirtwad job and funneled some of the company's money into an off—shore account?"

In this part . . .

Your financial data is important information, and you should protect it and control who has access to it. In this part, you find out how to manage these tasks, and you can read about many of the ways you can customize Dynamics GP.

Chapter 14

Safeguarding Your Database

- -

In This Chapter

▶ Setting up security

▶ Safeguarding the database

- -

*W*hen you expend significant time and effort in recording information into any computer program, the health and welfare of that data becomes critical. You need to protect your Microsoft Dynamics GP data both from unauthorized use and from events beyond your control, such as flood or fire.

In this chapter, you read about much of the security available to you for your Dynamics GP data. In addition, I describe techniques you can use to try to repair damaged data.

Establishing Security for Your Dynamics GP Database

You can set security in Dynamics GP at several different levels. For example, you need to set up records that identify each user of the Dynamics GP company. You can also set up security tasks that identify work that needs to be done, and then you can assign security tasks to a security role. You then can assign security roles to users so that you, effectively, limit a user's use of Dynamics GP to only those tasks he or she needs to accomplish. Fortunately, Dynamics GP comes with dozens of predefined security roles that you can tweak if need be, so setting up security is as easy as adding users, assigning them access to one or more companies, and then assigning them to one or more predefined roles.

You can take security a step further by establishing account-level and even field-level security. When you establish account-level security, you limit the accounts any particular user can use to only those accounts assigned to the user. Using field-level security, you can limit access to a window, field, or form using a password as opposed to limiting access to windows or forms based on the user's security roles.

Setting up account-level or field-level security is certainly not required; you need to judge whether the added security layer you want to gain is truly worth the time needed to maintain the additional security settings. Users may get locked out of fields and accounts that they need to access, and sorting out the security setting may prove to be time consuming. On the other hand, these added security levels can be quite powerful when properly implemented in cases where they are truly needed.

Setting system security

Dynamics GP won't enforce any security settings unless you select the Security option in the Company Setup window; on the Menu bar, select Microsoft Dynamics GP⇨Tools⇨Setup⇨Company⇨Company and confirm that the Security checkbox is selected. With this option enabled, Dynamics GP's default security settings become effective; Dynamics GP creates some default security roles and one security task, and the default settings allow all users to open only the windows and forms used to log in to the application.

In addition, you need to set a system password that controls access to security settings so that only a limited number of people can change security settings once you establish them. To establish a system password, use the Menu bar to select Microsoft Dynamics GP⇨Tools⇨Setup⇨System⇨System Password to display the System Password Setup dialog box. In the New Password field, enter a password; then reenter it in the Reenter New Password field and click OK.

The Dynamics GP system password is not the same as the Microsoft SQL Server sa (system administrator) password; however, you can use the same password to make remembering them easier.

If you are changing the System password, you must enter the existing password in the Old Password field and then fill in the other two fields.

Setting up users

Before anyone can use Dynamics GP, you need to create users. You can create as many user records as you want, but the number of users who log in to simultaneously use Dynamics GP cannot exceed the number of users allowed per your registration keys. After you create users, you need to grant access to Dynamics GP companies; otherwise, the users won't be able to open any Dynamics GP companies.

Creating a user record

Dynamics GP automatically creates two user records for you by default: the user record with the ID of sa (system administrator) and the record with the ID of DYNSA. The sa user has access to the entire system. To create other users, follow these steps:

Creating a Dynamics GP user also creates an SQL login.

1. **On the Menu bar, select Microsoft Dynamics GP⇨Tools⇨Setup⇨System⇨User to display the User Setup window shown in Figure 14-1.**

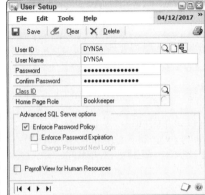

Figure 14-1:
The User
Setup
window.

2. **In the User ID field, enter an ID.**

3. **In the User Name field, enter the person's full name.**

4. **In the Password field, enter the password this user will use when starting Microsoft Dynamics GP.**

5. **In the Class ID field, you can assign the user to a class.**

If you plan to enable account-level security, you need to set up user classes and assign each user to a class. User classes come into play when you establish organizational structures for your company to segregate, for example, various divisions; you can assign a user class to each division and then, by assigning users to a user class, you create a relationship for a group of users with a particular division. For details on setting up organizational structures, user classes, and enabling account-level security, see Part 5 of the System Setup manual that comes with Dynamics GP.

6. **In the Home Page Role field, assign the user to a user role.**

   The user role determines the content that appears by default on the user's Dynamics GP Home page.

7. **If you use SQL Server 2005 or later on Windows Server® 2003 or later, you can**

   - *Enforce Password Policy Mark:* Select this option to force users to adhere to the same password policies that have been established on the Windows Server domain.

   - *Change Password Next Login:* Select this option to force users to change their passwords the next time they log in to Microsoft Dynamics GP. This option is available if you also select the Enforce Password Policy option.

   - *Enforce Password Expiration:* Select this option to force users to change their passwords after the number of days defined by the Windows Server domain password policies. This option is available if you also select the Enforce Password Policy option.

8. **Click Save to save the user record.**

Granting access to Dynamics GP companies

Each time you create user records or create a new Dynamics GP company, you need to grant users access to appropriate Dynamics GP companies. Follow these steps:

1. **On the Menu bar, select Microsoft Dynamics GP⇨Tools⇨Setup⇨System⇨User Access to display the User Access Setup window shown in Figure 14-2.**

2. **In the Users list, select a user ID.**

   All existing Dynamics GP companies appear in the Company Name list.

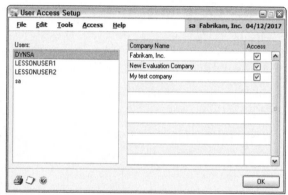

Figure 14-2:
The User
Access
Setup
window.

3. In the Access column, select the companies you want the user to be able to open.

4. Repeat Steps 2 and 3 for each Dynamics GP user.

5. Click OK to save your settings and close the window.

Creating security tasks

You set up security tasks to grant access to windows, reports, files, and other Dynamics GP resources that users need to complete a task. For example, you might set up a security task that grants access to the windows needed to print customer statements. By default, Dynamics GP creates one security task for you called DEFAULTUSER that grants access to windows, forms, and reports that most users need while working in Dynamics GP.

Once you create security tasks, you can then create security roles, which are a collection of security tasks. See the next section, "Creating security roles," for more information.

To create a security task, follow these steps:

1. On the Menu bar, select Microsoft Dynamics GP⇨Tools⇨Setup⇨ System⇨Security Tasks to display the Security Task Setup window shown in Figure 14-3.

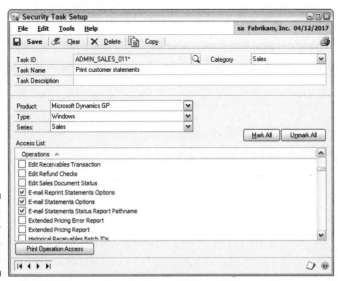

Figure 14-3:
The Security Task Setup window.

2. **In the Task ID field, enter a task ID.**

    You can copy all security settings from an existing security task. Click Copy. The Copy Security Task window appears; enter an existing Security Task ID and click OK. The Copy Security Task window closes and the Security Task Setup window reappears, displaying the security settings of the task that you copied.

3. **In the Task Name and Task Description fields, enter a name and description for the new security task.**

4. **Open the Category list and select a category for the security task; categories correspond to series in Dynamics GP.**

5. **From the Product list, select Microsoft Dynamics GP.**

    If you use integrating products with Dynamics GP, they appear in the list in addition to Microsoft Dynamics GP and you can select one of the integrating products.

6. **From the Type list, you can select the type of item to which you want to limit access.**

    For example, you can limit access to windows or reports.

7. **Open the Series list and select the series to which you want to set access.**

    For example, to grant access to a window, report, or other resource in Receivables Management, select Sales.

8. **In the Access list, select the items to which you want to grant access and make sure that no check mark appears beside any item to which you don't want to grant access.**

    You can double-click a window or report in the Access List to view it.

9. **Repeat Steps 6 through 8 to set security for the selected task for all series.**

10. **Click Save to save your changes.**

Creating security roles

You use security roles to group a series of security tasks and then you assign the security role to a user. That way, the user has access to all the security tasks he or she needs to do a job.

Dynamics GP creates some security roles for you by default. For example, you'll find that the Accounting Manager security role is made up of security tasks that allow any user assigned to this role to view General Ledger account information, enter journal entries, enter bank transactions, and perform other tasks that an accounting manager might perform. If you decide to use only the predefined security roles, you can skip this step.

1. **On the Menu bar, select Microsoft Dynamics GP⇨Tools⇨Setup⇨ System⇨Security Roles to display the Security Role Setup window shown in Figure 14-4.**

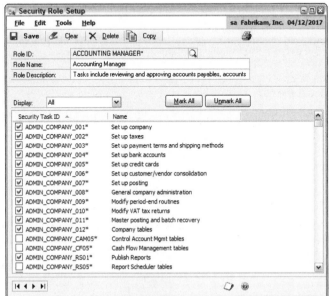

Figure 14-4:
The Security
Role Setup
window.

2. **In the Role ID field, enter a role ID.**

   You can copy all security settings from an existing security role. Click Copy. The Copy Security Role window appears; enter an existing Security Role ID and click OK. The Copy Security Role window closes and the Security Role Setup window reappears, displaying the security settings of the role that you copied.

3. **In the Role Name and Role Description fields, enter a name and description for the new security role.**

4. **From the Display list, select a category to display the security tasks available for that category.**

5. **Select the security tasks to which users assigned to the role you are creating should have access.**

   You can double-click a security task to view information about that task.

6. **Repeat Steps 4 and 5 to set security for all categories for this security role.**

7. **Click Save to save your changes.**

Assigning users to security roles

After you create security tasks, security roles, and user records, you can assign users to one or more security roles. Since the security role is made up of one or more security tasks, assigning a user to a security role can limit what the user can do in Dynamics GP.

In addition, you assign security roles to users on a company-by-company basis. In one company, a user might have access to General Ledger information but in another company, the same user might have access only to Sales series information.

When you created this company, you had the option to copy security access information from another Dynamics GP company. If you selected that option, you don't need to establish user security for the current company; instead, you can use the steps below to modify security settings.

To assign a user to one or more security roles, follow these steps:

1. **On the Menu bar, select Microsoft Dynamics GP⇨Tools⇨Setup⇨ System⇨User Security to display the User Security Setup window shown in Figure 14-5.**

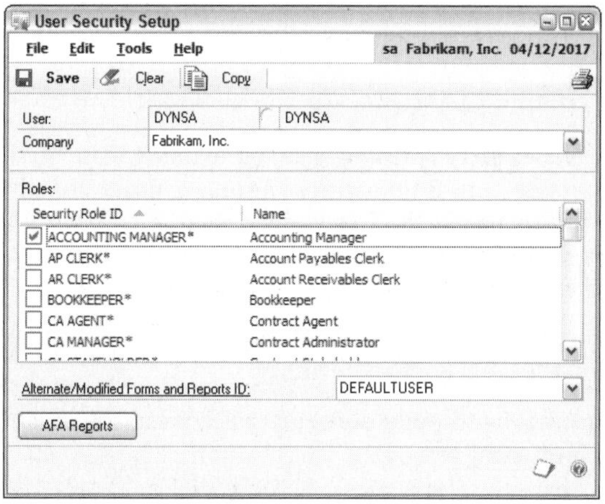

Figure 14-5:
The User
Security
Setup
window.

User Security Setup							sa Fabrikam, Inc. 04/12/2017

2. **In the User field, select the user ID of the person for whom you want to set security.**

In the Company list, Dynamics GP displays the list of the companies to which the user has access.

3. **In the Company list, select a company.**

   Dynamics GP displays all available security roles.

4. **Select each role to which you want to assign the user.**

5. **You can use the Alternate/Modified Forms and Reports ID drop-down list to identify the alternate or modified forms and reports to which the user should have access.**

You can click the AFA Reports button to open the Advanced Financial Analysis Reports Security window where you can select the Advanced Financial Analysis reports to which the user should have access. By default, Dynamics GP grants users access to all Advanced Financial Analysis reports. Remember, though, that users can view an Advanced Financial Analysis report only if they also have access to the Advanced Financial Analysis windows associated with that report.

You can assign the same role to the user in other companies; choose Copy to open the Copy User Security window and display a list of companies to which the selected user has access. Select the companies to which you want to copy this user's security settings and click OK to save your changes and redisplay the User Security Setup window.

6. **Click Save.**

If you haven't activated security in the Company Setup dialog box, use the Menu bar and select Microsoft Dynamics GP⇨Tools⇨Setup⇨Company⇨Company, then select the Security check box.

Setting field-level security

You can hide or assign a password to any field, window, or form in Dynamics GP using field-level security; in this way, you can make fields, windows, or forms available to only those users who know the password.

You create field-level security ID's and, if appropriate, define passwords to make a window, form, or field available only to those who know the password. Then, you assign the field level security ID's to users and user classes.

1. **On the Menu bar, select Microsoft Dynamics GP⇨Tools⇨Setup⇨ System⇨Field Level Security to display the Field Level Security window.**

2. **Click the Add button to open the Field Security Maintenance window.**

3. **In the Field Security ID and Description fields, enter the ID and a description.**

4. **Click the lookup button beside the Product Name field to open the Resource Explorer window shown in Figure 14-6.**

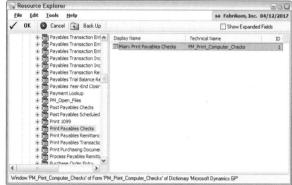

Figure 14-6:
The
Resource
Explorer
window.

5. **Use the left side of the Resource Explorer window to select a window, form or field.**

The type of object that appears in the right side of the Resource Explorer window depends on what you select in the left portion of the window.

6. **Click OK to redisplay the Field Security Maintenance window.**

7. **From the Security Mode list box, select a security mode:**

- *Password Before:* You must enter a password to make the field available.

- *Password After:* You must enter a password to save any changes you make.

- *Warning Before:* Dynamics GP displays a warning and denies access to the field.

- *Lock Field:* Dynamics GP displays the field, but you cannot tab or click into it, so you cannot change the value.

- *Disable Field:* Microsoft Dynamics GP displays the field but the field and its label appear gray, and you cannot tab or click into the field, so you cannot change its value.

- *Hide Field:* Dynamics GP doesn't display the field.

- *Password Window:* You must enter a password to display the window.

- *Disable Window:* Only the system administrator's password opens the window.

- *Password Form:* Users or classes must enter the correct password to display the form.

- *Disable Form:* Only the system administrator's password displays the form.

8. **Use the Password ID field to enter or select a password ID if the security mode you selected requires a password.**

9. **Click Save.**

You can now use the Field Level Security window to apply this field security ID to users and user classes. In the Field Level Security dialog box, select a user or user class, select the Field Security ID, and click the check box beside either the user or the Field Security ID. Microsoft Dynamics GP selects both the user or user class and the Field Security ID. Click Apply. After Dynamics GP makes the assignment and you finish assigning Field Security ID's, click OK.

Safeguarding Your Database

When you expend significant time and effort in recording information into any computer program, the health and welfare of that data becomes critical, and the data you store in your Dynamics GP company database is no different.

Databases can become scrambled if, for example, your building experiences a power failure. Hard drives, where you store your data, fail. Or become damaged in a flood or a fire. Or get stolen, along with the rest of the computer.

If you care for and maintain your company database, you can minimize your exposure to negative events like these that are often beyond your control.

Checking table links

On occasion, unexpected things happen that can damage the tables in your Dynamics GP company database. You can check table links to examine the data in related tables and, if possible, repair damaged data.

If you want to learn about the structure and behavior of the SQL tables that make up your company database, see Chapter 3 of the System Administrator Guide that comes with your Dynamics GP software.

If you suspect a damaged table in the System or Company series, see the Help topic Reconciling Tables.

To check links, follow these steps:

1. **Make sure that no one is using Dynamics GP.**

   To identify the users in Dynamics GP, use the Menu bar and select Microsoft Dynamics GP➪Tools➪Utilities➪System➪User Activity.

2. **Make a backup.**

   See the next section, "Making a backup," for details.

3. **On the Menu bar, select Microsoft Dynamics GP➪Maintenance➪Check Links to display the Check Links window.**

4. **From the Series list box, select the Dynamics GP series you want to check.**

   If you know the name of the damaged table, but aren't sure of the series to which it belongs, use the Menu bar and select Microsoft Dynamics GP➪Tools➪Resource Descriptions➪Tables to display the Table Names dialog box. From the Series list box, select a series and then scroll through the list or click the Find button, type the name of the table, and click Find.

5. **Select each table you want to check and choose Insert.**

   You can check tables from different series by changing the series and selecting tables.

6. **Click OK.**

   Dynamics GP checks links in the selected tables in the background; you can perform other tasks in the meantime. When Dynamics GP finishes checking links, it produces the Check Links Report; you have the opportunity to set a destination for the report. Because the report could be very large, print it first to the screen and then, if necessary, print it to paper and to a file.

As a result of checking links, you may find that you need to re-enter information. You can use the Table Descriptions window (on the Menu bar, select Microsoft Dynamics GP➪Tools➪Resource Descriptions➪Tables) to view information for the table you checked, and then use a window that accesses the table to re-enter information.

Making a backup

Checking links can't solve all problems. There may be times when you need to restore a backup of your company data. And, of course, to be able to restore a backup, you need to make backups.

To protect your Dynamics GP data, you should establish and maintain strict procedures for backup. Please consult with your computer network administrator and make sure that a sound backup plan is in place and is being followed.

There are basically two types of backups: the backup of the SQL databases, which is called a Database Maintenance Plan in SQL Server, and the backup of the server's hard drives. If the server computer itself fails, you can go to the server's hard drive backups, which are often stored on some kind of tape device.

Many organizations rely on tape backup units or back up by copying data to a remote location using the Internet. These techniques are fine as long as you test them to ensure that you can restore whatever you back up. To test, make a backup of your Dynamics GP data using your preferred method and then restore the backup to a different folder on your computer or to a different computer altogether. If the restored data performs properly, you're all set and don't need to follow the steps provided here to back up or restore your Dynamics GP company.

Dynamics GP data is stored in the Microsoft SQL Server Database. The designers of Dynamics GP have designed the posting routines using database-stored procedures which use transaction rollback in the event of a power failure. So, even if your PC shuts down in the middle of posting, you should be able to recover the batch using the Batch Recovery feature without experiencing data corruption, because transaction rollback ensures that unless the entire batch completes all steps in the posting routine, the entire process will be reversed out of the database.

Nonetheless, if you experience a severe problem with the data inside one of your Dynamics GP company databases, even if nothing is wrong with the hardware, it is possible to restore that company database from a SQL Server database backup, which typically is made by the Database Maintenance Plan on the previous night. All your GP company databases, along with the system database, called DYNAMICS, should be backed up every night automatically by the SQL Server SQL Agent; this is your SQL Server Database Maintenance Plan.

Point in Time Recovery is a SQL Server feature which uses transaction logging to allow you to restore to a specific time of day in the past. In my experience, many Dynamics GP sites use the Simple Data Recovery Model as opposed to the Full Data Recovery Model. The Simple Data Recovery Model doesn't create transaction logs, but instead creates just one nightly full database backup; that is typically sufficient. Check with your network administrator to discuss the various options for SQL Server backup strategies.

The location where you store your backups is very important. Storing backups on a hard drive that subsequently fails doesn't do you much good. Similarly, storing backups in your office won't help you if your office is robbed, flooded, or damaged by fire. For complete safety, make two copies of each backup; store one on-site and one off-site. Many companies store an off-site backup at the boss's house, in a bank vault, or use online services that store backups in a remote location that may be in a different state.

Ideally, your Dynamics GP data should be backed up by a Database Maintenance Plan that uses an SQL Agent Job to automatically start the backup process and verify the backup when the process finishes; your network administrator creates this Database Maintenance Plan directly within the SQL Server Database. If you do not have a Database Maintenance Plan in place already, Dynamics GP makes it easy for you to create one using a feature within Dynamics GP which, in turn, creates the SQL Server Database Maintenance Plan. To do this, you must log on as the system administrator and nobody else can be using Dynamics GP. Follow these steps:

1. **On the Menu bar, select Microsoft Dynamics GP⇨Maintenance⇨Backup to display the Back Up Company window.**

2. **From the Company Name list, select the company you want to back up.**

   To back up all companies, select System Database.

   Dynamics GP displays the path and file name where the backup file will be stored.

3. **If necessary, click the folder beside the Select the Backup File field and change the backup path and file name.**

4. **Click OK.**

   Dynamics GP makes the backup and displays a message when the backup is complete.

You can click the Schedule button in the Back Up Company dialog box to create a schedule that starts a backup automatically at the time and on the days you specify.

Recovering from a disaster

Occasionally, hard disk failures, power surges, power losses, floods, fire, and other problems can damage or destroy data. And, because you understand that you can't predict the factors that cause data damage, you make backups regularly.

So, when the time comes and you suffer a data loss, you reach for your latest backup and restore it — and, because you've faithfully made regular backups, the impact on your business is minimal.

Because the information in your Dynamics GP database is so interrelated, you should restore the entire database; don't try to restore only damaged tables.

In the rare event when you wish to restore a company from backup, please consult with your network administrator, who can perform the restore either from within SQL Server or from tape media or a mirrored or redundant hard drive using the appropriate backup software. Alternatively, you can initiate a database restore yourself from within Dynamics GP; to do so, follow these steps:

1. **Log into a company other than the one you want to restore.**

2. **On the Menu bar, select Microsoft Dynamics GP⇨Maintenance⇨Restore to display the Restore Company window.**

3. **From the Company Name list, select the company you want to restore.**

4. **Click the folder beside the Select The File To Restore From field and navigate to the location of the backup file you want to restore.**

5. **Click OK.**

   Dynamics GP restores the backup.

Chapter 15

Extending Dynamics GP's Functionality with Modifications & Customizations

- -

In This Chapter

▶ Creating reminders

▶ Working with lists

▶ Customizing and extending Microsoft Dynamics GP

- -

*T*here are many ways you can customize the way that you use Microsoft Dynamics GP. The customization options fall into these broad categories:

✔ **Out-of-the-box options and features**

- *Setup options*

- *Report options*

- *Built-in features such as Reminders, Lists, and SmartLists*

- *User preferences*

✔ **Customization tools**

- *Modifier module with VBA*

- *Extender module*

- *Dexterity customizations*

✔ **Third-party products**

- *Add-on products written in Dexterity (Dynamics GP's native language)*

- *Other products that work with Dynamics GP*

Out-of-the-box options and features involve simply changing the setup options which will alter the software's behavior. You customize report options to save the criteria, sorting, grouping, and destination options for built-in reports so that the next time you run the reports you will same time. You can use the Task feature to create tasks and reminders so that you don't let things you need to do in Dynamics GP slip through the cracks. You also can take advantage of the Lists feature; lists group similar records in one place. And, while you view a list, you can work with the records in the list, making changes to them or using them to complete activities; for example, you can select customers and send statements to them. You can sort and customize lists to make them easy to use.

You can use the Modifier module to make changes to Dynamics GP windows. For example, you can hide fields, make fields required, add fields, and change the labels for fields. You also can create new windows, and a programmer can add a layer of Visual Basic custom programming to command buttons and other objects within the window to create additional functionality. Use the Modifier module if you have complex functionality changes that are likely to require custom programming; otherwise, you may wish to use the Extender module, which does not require any custom programming.

Using the Extender module, you can add custom fields. The Extender module adds a new window that contains the extended fields; you link these extended fields to a built-in object such as the Customer Card or Inventory Item Card. The new fields that you add can be text, date, or currency types of fields, and you can make these fields available on SmartLists and other reports.

Dexterity is the native language of Dynamics GP. Often called DEX, *Dexterity* is a programming language that was developed in C++ specifically for the original Windows-based version of Great Plains. Most third-party products written specifically for Dynamics GP were developed in Dexterity, so they mimic the exact look and feel of Dynamics GP. If you have very extensive customization requirements, you may consider having a custom third-party product written in Dexterity specifically for your company; many Dynamics GP consulting practices have Dexterity programmers on staff. However, you should exhaust your other customization possibilities before considering Dexterity customizations as they tend to be harder to code and maintain.

You also can import and export Dynamics GP data using Excel and SmartList, and you can exchange data with external data sources using Integration Manager and eConnect. Unfortunately, I don't have enough room to cover all of these topics, but you can discuss any and all of them with your Dynamics GP consultant.

In this chapter, I show you how to create reminders, work with lists, and use the Modifier module to change an optional field to a required field.

Creating Reminders

You can set up reminders for overdue invoices, payables due, recurring batches of transactions that you need to post, and SmartList favorites that meet conditions that you specify. Dynamics GP automatically creates predefined reminders that you can enable to notify you of overdue invoices, payables due, recurring General Ledger batches, recurring Receivables batches, recurring Payables batches, items due for stock count, and lots due to expire. And, you can create your own reminders. For example, you can set up a customized reminder to alert you when a SmartList favorite meets the conditions that you specify.

To set up predefined reminders and create custom reminders, follow these steps:

1. **On the Menu bar, select Microsoft Dynamics GP▷User Preferences to display the User Preferences window.**

2. **Select Reminders to open the Reminder Preferences window shown in Figure 15-1.**

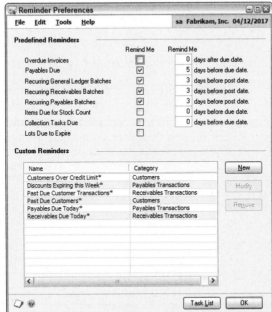

Figure 15-1:
The
Reminder
Preferences
window.

The options displayed in this window depend on the modules you have installed and registered.

3. **In the Predefined Reminders section, select the Remind Me check box beside each event for which you want to see a reminder and enter the number of days preceding the event that Dynamics GP should display the reminder.**

4. **To create a new custom reminder, click the New button; Dynamics GP displays the Custom Reminder window shown in Figure 15-2.**

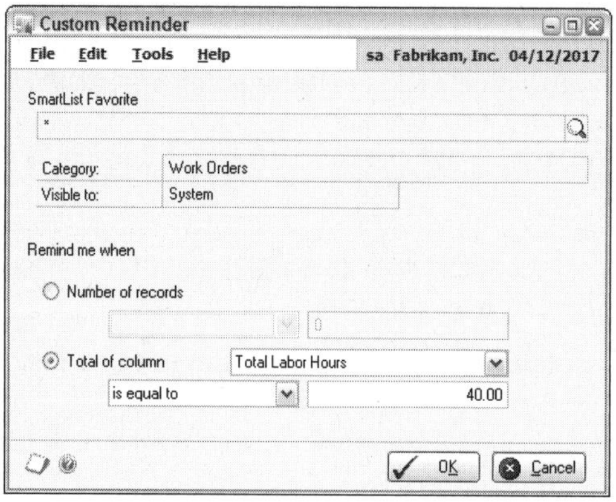

Figure 15-2:
The Custom
Reminder
dialog box.

5. **From the SmartList Favorite field, select a SmartList favorite.**

Dynamics GP fills in the Category and Visible To information.

6. **In the Remind Me When section, select an option to specify the condition that must exist for Dynamics GP to display the reminder.**

7. **Choose OK to save your changes and redisplay the Reminder Preferences window, where your new custom reminder appears.**

Working with Lists

Lists group similar records in one place; while viewing any list, you can work with the records in the list, making changes to them. The available lists appear in the Navigation pane above the Navigation pane buttons; to see the lists for any particular series, click that series button. To view a particular list, click the name of the list; Dynamics GP displays the list in the content pane area of the application window (see Figure 15-3).

Using a list, you can view similar records, select one or more records, and then simultaneously perform actions for all of the selected records. For example, in the Customers list, shown in Figure 15-3, you can select multiple customer records and then print statements for the selected customers.

Filter area   List Title drop-down menu

Action pane   Look For field

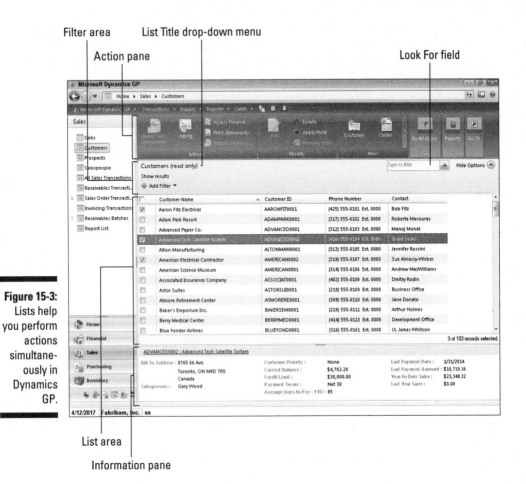

Figure 15-3:
Lists help
you perform
actions
simultane-
ously in
Dynamics
GP.

List area

Information pane

You select the action you want to take in the Action pane of the List window. You can filter the list using the Look For field and the options in the Filter area. The records in the list appear in the List area, and you check various records to take actions on them. The details for any record you highlight — regardless of whether you select the list element — appear at the bottom of the List window in the Information pane.

Dynamics GP supports two types of lists:

✔ **Primary lists** are the ones that come with the product; you can easily identify them because they are the top-level lists that appear in the Navigation pane. When you display a primary list, the words "read only" appear beside its name. You can personalize primary lists, but you cannot customize them. Some primary lists have arrows beside them; the arrows indicate that the primary list was used to create a list view.

✔ **List views** are the ones that you or someone in your organization creates; they appear beneath the primary lists in the Navigation pane. You click the arrow beside a primary list to view and use the list views. You can both personalize and customize a list view.

Personalizing a list

You can personalize both primary lists and list views in the following ways:

✔ **You can sort by any column heading that appears in the list; just click the column heading.**

✔ **You can resize the width of the columns, and you can drag and drop columns to re-order them.**

✔ **You can resize the information pane vertically by dragging the top border up or down.**

✔ **You can hide or show the Action pane, the Filter Options pane, or the Information pane by opening the list title drop-down menu, pointing at Show, and clicking the appropriate option.**

Any choices you make to personalize a primary or list view are visible only to you and not to other users. In addition, Dynamics GP remembers the choices you make when personalizing a primary list or a list view and displays the list using those choices each time you open the list.

Creating and customizing a list view

If you have proper security privileges, you can create list views that contain just the information you want to view and you can customize those list views. Follow these steps to create and customize a list view:

1. **In the Navigation pane, select the primary list or an existing list view entry to serve as the foundation for the new list view.**

2. **Open the list title drop-down menu and choose Save As.**

3. **In the Save As dialog box that appears, type a name for the new list view and click OK.**

   Dynamics GP displays your new list view in the Content pane.

4. **Open the list title drop-down menu and choose Customize to display the List View Customization window shown in Figure 15-4.**

5. **Use the Visible In list box to select the companies in which the list view should appear.**

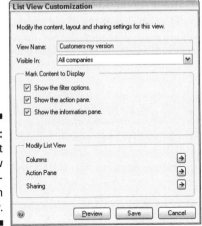

6. **In the Mark Content to Display section, select options to hide or display filter options, the action pane, and the information pane.**

7. **In the Modify List View section, select the expansion arrow beside**

   - *Columns* to select the columns you want to display in the list view

   - *Sharing* to select users or roles who can view the list view

   - *Action Pane* to display the Action Pane Details dialog box, where you can add, remove, and reorder the groups that appear in the Action pane and the actions in each group

8. **In the List View Customization window, you can click Preview to see the results of the choices you made; when you're satisfied, click Save.**

You can export list information to Excel; click the Go To button and select Send to Excel from the menu that appears.

Customizing and Extending Dynamics GP

There are many ways in which you can customize Dynamics GP and extend its functionality. For example, each user can customize the way Dynamics GP appears on his or her workstation by setting user preferences. You also can use the Modifier module to add or move fields and change the appearance of Dynamics GP windows in other ways. Programmers can use Visual Basic for Applications (VBA) to create custom windows, add fields to windows, and set default values for fields.

Most third-party add-on applications for Dynamics GP have been written, to date, in Dexterity, a form of C++ and the language used to create Dynamics GP. Although programmers can create custom extensions in Dexterity, there is a general movement away from Dexterity and toward a more traditional Microsoft language, such as VBA.

In this section, I introduce you to the Modifier module. To work in the Modifier module, you must have security access. If the Modifier command appears gray and unavailable, either you haven't registered the module or you don't have security privileges to use it. Your Dynamics GP registration keys must indicate that your company is licensed to use the Modifier module if you want to write Modifier customizations directly to your Dynamics GP installation. If your company is not licensed to run Modifier, you need the Customization Site License; this license is somewhat less expensive that owning the Modifier module and means that Dynamics GP consultants can code Modifier customizations on their systems and then load the customizations onto your system. Owning the Modifier module, rather than just the Customization Site License, is often the preferred approach. Using the Customization Site License, all the aspects of your system would need to be duplicated on a test or development system to efficiently code the customizations.

Customizations with the Modifier module

You can use the Modifier module to change the appearance of individual windows, make changes that will appear throughout Dynamics GP, and add new fields to windows. Artfully configuring Dynamics GP is better than extensive customization; using the Modifier module, a Dynamics GP consultant often can help you configure Dynamics GP to achieve your goal without writing special applications to interface with Dynamics GP.

The Modifier module recognizes windows as exactly what you'd expect — the things that pop up as you choose menu commands. While working in Dynamics GP, you enter and edit information in windows.

The Modifier module also recognizes *forms* as a collection of windows, tables, and menus that work together. For example, two windows — the Main_Reports window and the Options window — and several tables work together to produce the Aged Trial Balance report for Receivables Management. The Modifier module groups these resources together in a form called RM_Trial_Balance_Reports.

The Modifier stores changes and additions you make in the forms dictionary, which is separate from the dictionary that stores the resources that come with Dynamics GP. Using a separate dictionary maintains the integrity of the accounting system.

Let's walk through an example of using the Modifier module to change a field from an optional one to a required one. Suppose that you want to ensure that users enter a generic description in the Item Maintenance window. You can make the field a required field; follow these steps:

1. **Open the window you want to modify and then use the Menu bar to select Microsoft Dynamics GP⇨Tools⇨Customize⇨Modify Current Window.**

   For this example, I opened the Item Maintenance window by choosing Cards⇨Inventory⇨Item.

   The Modifier module copies the form to the forms dictionary, displays the Form Definition window in the background and, in the foreground, displays the layout for the window you selected; the layout consists of the window and the Toolbox (see Figure 15-5). For this example, the IV_Item_Maintenance window appears, along with the Toolbox.

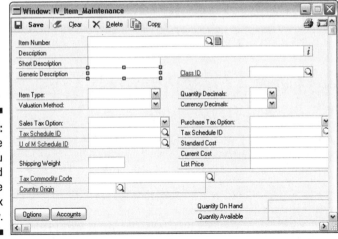

Figure 15-5:
The window you selected and the Toolbox window.

2. **Select the field you want to modify; for this example, I selected the Generic Description field.**

3. **Select Layout⇨Properties to display the Properties window (see Figure 15-6).**

4. **In the list, find and select the Required property.**

5. **Toward the top of the box, open the list and select True.**

6. **Click the X in the upper-right corner of the layout window to close it, and the Modifier module prompts you to save your changes.**

7. **Select File⇨Microsoft Dynamics GP to close the Modifier module and redisplay Dynamics GP.**

Figure 15-6:
The
Properties
window.

The Modifier QuickStart manual that comes with Dynamics GP contains a series of lessons you can walk through and become familiar with the various actions you can take using the Modifier.

Seeing what's installed and what's been customized

You can identify what's been installed by viewing the `Dynamics.set` file; you can view this file, shown in Figure 15-7, by choosing Microsoft Dynamics GP➪Tools➪Setup➪System➪Edit Launch File.

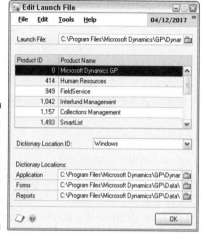

Figure 15-7:
The
Dynamics.
set file
shows you
what's been
installed.

To view a complete list of the Dynamics GP windows that have been customized, use the Customization Maintenance window (see Figure 15-8). On the Menu bar, select Microsoft Dynamics GP⇨Tools⇨Customize⇨Customization Maintenance.

You also can open Customization Maintenance window from any Dynamics GP window; select Tools⇨Customize⇨Customization Maintenance.

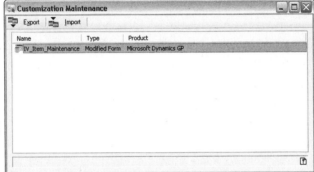

Figure 15-8:
The
Customization
Maintenance
window.

Part V
The Part of Tens

"Your database is beyond repair, but before I tell you our backup recommendation, let me ask you a question. How many index cards do you think will fit on the walls of your office?"

In this part . . .

*E*very For Dummies book contains a Part of Tens, and this one is no different. In the Part of Tens, you read about common implementation pitfalls and Microsoft Dynamics GP's most useful features.

Chapter 16

Implementation Pitfalls

. . . .

In This Chapter

▶ Though this be madness, yet there is methodology in it

▶ Rewriting history (or leaping forward to the past)

▶ When exceptions are the rule

▶ To-be or not to be as-is

▶ Template of doom (or the dog ate my homework)

▶ Nine pregnant women in a room for a month

▶ Going over budget without going overboard

▶ The phone book syndrome

▶ Back office is the cart, not the horse

▶ Bridges to vaporware

. . . .

As I describe in Chapter 1, setting up and using Microsoft Dynamics GP isn't a simple operation; it's a large-scale project that can affect your entire organization. As such, implementing the use of Dynamics GP falls into the realm of Enterprise Resource Planning (ERP).

The term Enterprise Resource Planning (ERP) has been in use for more than a decade. Back when I started out, we simply installed accounting software. The marketing people moved away from the term accounting software because, as more and more modules were added, the term became too limited and, therefore, misleading. Today, accounting software includes modules for human resources management, sales lead tracking, contact management, self service web portals, field service management, manufacturing, and on and on. ERP software is aimed at bringing all of the company's functions under one roof, one shared unified database, accessed by a suite of integrated modules. The benefits that arise from such full-scale integration are, indeed, enormous and include

  ✔ **Elimination of re-keying**

  ✔ **Elimination of custom interfaces**

  ✔ **Comprehensive reporting**

How many companies re-key the same customer address two, three, or even six separate times in different, disconnected departments? This wastes time and results in errors. Mismatched names, duplicate customer accounts, and address discrepancies result in frustrated employees and angry customers (or, perhaps I should say, former customers).

Custom interfaces, intended to electronically bridge the gap between disconnected systems, are a step beyond re-keying; nonetheless, they are often a source of the greatest pain, and sometimes not much better than re-keying. They cost a lot of money to develop, and even more money to maintain. Maintaining these interface programs is often a mixture of prayer, voodoo, real-time code changes slapped directly into production, manually tweaking immense text files, and hiring people to watch over error logs because you've come to expect the system to hiccup. These interfaces started out as a twinkle in the eye of a business analyst or software salesperson who drew a line between two circles on a white board one day, never realizing that the cost of that one single line would surpass the cost of the entire suite of off-the-shelf modules.

Believe it or not, to this day, the most widely-used method of generating comprehensive enterprise-level reports is to cut and paste into Excel, sometimes re-keying from a stack of hardcopy reports. Talk about pain. Excel is also widely used as a database, a practice never intended for a spreadsheet program. Microsoft Access is used to track all sorts of things outside the system. The problem is that these Excel and Access files contain crucial data needed for comprehensive reporting. People start using Microsoft Office to do what they think the ERP system can't do because they just don't realize how to configure the ERP system to handle those functions because of a lack of training, a lack of configuration, or a lack of effort to get people to change their old bad habits.

The days will soon be over when a business can afford to have a hodge-podge of Excel files, Access databases, industry-specific verticals running on obsolete operating systems, disconnected back office accounting packages, custom "spaghetti" interfaces, and "rubber band" stop gap measures tying it all together.

The promise of ERP is simply this. Information is keyed or captured electronically once. It then flows through a suite of seamlessly interconnected modules and into a data repository where comprehensive reporting is possible at the touch of a button.

Since Dynamics GP is a true ERP solution, I have compiled a list of the top 10 ERP implementation pitfalls. Study this list carefully. It was compiled from interviews conducted with dozens of veteran ERP implementers from the top consulting firms in the world. These are people I have had the great pleasure of working alongside during my stints with some of the globe's largest and most prestigious top-tier consulting firms. This list is based on more than twelve years of "in the trenches" ERP implementations, including the largest single-site Microsoft Business Solutions project in North America.

Though this be Madness, Yet There is Methodology in it

Classic ERP project management methodology calls for the following phases:

1. Gap Analysis

2. Business Requirements Gathering

3. Functional Design

4. Technical Design

5. Build (Install, Setup, Configuration, and Custom Coding)

6. Testing

7. Training

8. Go "Live"

9. Post Implementation Support

10. Continuous Improvement

Following an established, time-tested methodology makes perfect sense. And there is no way a large complex IT project, such as implementing Dynamics GP, is going to be successful without the organizing framework of a good methodology. However, please be warned: Methodologies alone do not ensure or predict, do not reduce risk, and when applied incorrectly, are largely to blame for hampering many creative, intelligent, and productive IT professionals, and breeding a cancerous negativity that spreads throughout project teams to undermine morale and derail ERP projects.

Is methodology the enemy? Of course not. But, unfortunately, many times it seems that way. And there are times when you would actually be better off without a methodology at all, as crazy as that sounds. The problem is not with the methodology itself, which contains sound principles and steps that are both logical and proper. The problem is in how the methodology is applied to individual projects. The three classic mistakes in applying a methodology to an ERP project are

✔ **Neglecting to size the methodology to the project**

✔ **Not allowing the phases to overlap (non-iterative or waterfall approach)**

✔ **Serving the methodology, rather than the methodology serving the project team**

Project management methodologies promise to remove the human element from the picture; that is, we can ensure success, as long as we faithfully follow the methodology. Anyone, theoretically, can manage and deliver an on-time and under budget ERP project. We can order any robot to follow the methodology, and they will instantly be a great implementer.

Hogwash. The methodology can be misapplied. So then, why not create and enforce a methodology for correctly applying your methodology? Surely, we can figure out how methodologies are misapplied, discover scientific principles and establish systematic solutions to methodology misuse, and solve the problem of misapplied methodologies once and for all by creating a "methodology methodology." But of course, this is more nonsense. We run into an endless regression, like looking at yourself looking into a mirror. Who is going to control the controllers? Who is going to spy on the spies?

There is no substitute for the human element: spontaneous creativity, natural intuition, and sound yet flexible judgment born of real-world experience. Methodologies are useful and essential tools, and in the right hands work wonders in reducing implementation risk.

Size matters

Keep in mind that the need for standard IT project methodologies arose from "out of control" spiraling costs on very large complex engagements. Most established methodologies were developed by Tier One consultancies tackling huge multinational projects. The methodologies were designed to be all-encompassing, global in scope, and thorough enough to handle the building of the international space station. However, many times all we are doing is setting up accounting software for a small business, not planning to send astronauts to land on Mars. The methodology needs to be streamlined and simplified in order to be effective. Phases can be collapsed together. Status reporting requirements can be relaxed. Status meetings can be held monthly instead of daily. Naming conventions can be dropped. Documentation standards can be made more flexible. Traceability requirements that seek to tie the original requirements gathered to the final detailed design, often requiring a complex numbering scheme and time-consuming documentation, can be eliminated. Use cases and test scripts can be combined into the training classes.

By rigidly holding to the requirements of a methodology that was originally designed to control immense projects, the danger is that, on a mid-size or small-scale project, there will not be enough hours in the budget to cover the mind-numbing array of methodology activities. The project manager may be afraid to be lax in the application of the methodology, for fear of being criticized for not following it, and so he or she will not remove enough of the onerous methodology requirements. The project then becomes a sham, in which people are hurriedly rushing through steps that they know are overkill. No ERP project has the time to waste on such charades.

Iterative approach

Some would argue that the *waterfall* approach, which calls for a definitive clear-cut end to each phase of the project, can work well in some instances, and I don't disagree. I will point out, however, that, more often than not, an iterative approach in which the phases sort of bleed into one another is more effective. The greatest danger of a non-iterative approach is that the project team can become split into two warring camps: the business analysts and client subject matter experts or users (the functional folks) against the geeks (the programmers, the technical folks). The split occurs during the end of the functional design phase and beginning of the technical design phase. You can end up with a battle of wills. The techno-geeks can stonewall by constantly complaining that they do not have the business rules specified in sufficient detail. Instead of just rolling up their sleeves, making a few phone calls, and figuring out the answers, they start playing an "us against them" e-mail game, sending "flame mails" back and forth, arguing endlessly about who is doing their job properly. Or, you get the functional people assuming a dug-in position of "if it's in the business requirements, you had better build it or we will get you, and I don't care how difficult you say it is now, it's already been approved." The worst-case scenario for an ERP project occurs when each side stonewalls the other, the camps are totally polarized, and project paralysis sets in.

Ideally, programmers (the builders) should be involved in the early stages of the project: the gap analysis, requirements gathering, and functional requirements. Often these IT resources are concluding other projects, or perhaps they have not been hired or assigned yet. However, a lead technical architect should be involved early in the project. To design a solution without consulting the technical folks (the ones who are actually going to be responsible to build that solution) is very unwise. Often a totally unfeasible and unrealistic or ill-conceived solution has been worked out in detail only to have to be completely re-worked at a later point by the technical folks, causing delays in meeting project due dates and potentially sparking a battle between the functional and technical team members.

Methodology masters and slaves

A *methodology master* is a project manager who uses the methodology as a weapon to beat people over the head. He or she uses the methodology requirements to exert power just for the sake of proving the project manager is in control. These types of project managers mistakenly believe that, if they can force everyone to follow the methodology to the letter, the methodology will carry everyone along to victory due to its inherent power. Wrong. The methodology is a collection of related guidelines that includes a logical sequence of recommended actions and does not prohibit, excuse, or exempt a person from using common sense, common decency, and a human brain.

A *methodology slave* is a truly pathetic and despicable creature. This is some-one who is in total C.Y.A. mode. The methodology slave is cowed by the great and terrible methodology and does not serve the users or the project objectives. The methodology slave serves the methodology. By filling out all SharePoint status reports on time (who cares about the content?), following correct documentation naming conventions (who cares about the feasibil-ity?), and filing the sign-offs (who cares about the strategy?), the methodol-ogy slave hides behind the methodology. If the project fails horribly, the methodology slave will forward along an e-mail that clearly shows all the methodology rules were followed and his or her behavior on the project was impeccable and completely without blame. The methodology slave won't speak out when common sense and accumulated experience tells him or her that the project has a flawed strategy, unrealistic due dates, a bad choice of programming tools or software modules, or other serious problems.

The project team must remain unified in purpose and vision. The shared goal must be to put an ERP system in place that serves customers by allowing users to provide better service to their customers. The methodology must serve the team by providing a flexible framework within which to collaborate successfully.

Rewriting History (or Leaping Forward to the Past)

I find it odd that one of the most pressing concerns clients have when moving to a new system is their desire to move all the data from the old system into the new system. The reason they are changing their system is often because the data is bad. So now they get the chance to start out fresh, and the first thing they want to do is load all this garbage into their nice, new, pristine system. Yuck!

Obviously, we don't want to lose any real information. And you certainly don't want to lose the history of what your customers have purchased from you in the past. But most people don't realize that loading the historical inventory transactions, purchasing activity, and sales orders from their old system into Dynamics GP is extremely expensive and often pure folly. There are just too many database tables involved to make it work right. In importing a customer record, you may need to update upwards of five tables, but importing invoice history with the attached inventory movements, tax details, salesperson details, linked purchase orders, and so on, can involve literally hundreds of tables. Yes, there are import utilities, but those utilities typically will import only into an unposted batch, not directly into history, making you try (in vain) to recreate years of posting activity — a time-consuming, error-prone process that is completely unnecessary.

Instead, move the history to a data warehouse. Why? Because, you can transfer only the relevant data and toss out the rest, reducing your cost to a small fraction of the cost to import the data into Dynamics GP. The users will have quick and easy read-only access to that historical data using a simple reporting tool or basic front-end query tool. Retrieval will be fast and painless. Best of all, you can pull the plug on the old system. Remember, typically, the users only need read-only access to a listing of what was sold to whom over the last five years or so; they don't need you to recreate the entire transactional history of an accounting system including all the audit trails, sales tax historical calculations, accounting distributions, and so on. However, to import the information into the new system, you would, by necessity, have to re-create all that minutia because that minutia constitutes required fields. The problem is non-trivial. In fact, if your implementation project plan calls for a data conversion of sub-ledger transactional history, you are probably in for a load of trouble. As that data conversion misses its due dates, the project will fall behind schedule and exceed its budget. The training schedule will suffer, and you may end up going "live" during busy season.

The data warehouse idea has only one down side: You will not be able to get comparative prior year data on your Dynamics GP reports until one year down the road, as you build up a new history in the new ERP. So, if you want to create prior year comparison reports during the first year you use your new system, you will need to cut and paste information or move the new data into the data warehouse, or use some other workaround. However, keep in mind that you will often be comparing apples and oranges anyway, because when you put the new system in place, you may very well also be re-engineering the business processes, changing item numbers, revamping the product categories, and so on. So, more often than not, comparing data from the old and new systems won't make sense anyway and, therefore, is not worth doing.

That said, there is data you will want to import from your old system. Typically, you will want to import the master files, such as the chart of accounts, and the customer, vendor, and inventory item lists. If you can keep the same customer, vendor, and inventory item numbers, then keep them. Don't change ID numbers and confuse everyone who has used those numbers for years unless there is a valid business reason to make those changes. Too often, people change numbers for no reason, and the users get really uptight, confused, and angered.

The basic rule of thumb is that importing the General Ledger detail history is usually a good idea, whereas importing historical sub-ledger detail is usually a very bad idea. Importing the General Ledger detail is not too difficult as long as your chart of accounts does not change between your old system and your new system, or as long as you maintain a good map between old account numbers and new account numbers. Consolidating more than one old account number into one new account number is typically not problematic. But, splitting old account numbers into two or more new account numbers typically doesn't work unless you set up a general account for the history. For example, suppose that Cash in your old system was account number 1000 and, in your new system, you intend to set up Cash–Checking using account number 1010 and Cash–Money Market using account number 1020. In this case, you will need to move all the history to the 1010 account or create yet another account — perhaps Cash with an account number of 1000 — and store historical transactions in that account.

The other data conversions that may make sense to do, in order of likelihood, are the open accounts receivable (A/R), open accounts payable (A/P), and open purchase orders (P/O). Typically, you can import open A/R as a simplified one-line invoice without taxes, inventory items, posted partial payments, and so on, that is valued at the remaining open balance; this is the preferred approach. Once open A/R balance is imported, you can run an A/R aging report and compare it to the Balance Sheet to make sure that the A/R subsidiary ledger matches the General Ledger. Then, you can apply cash receipts going forward. For A/P, it is often possible to "pay down" the legacy system and avoid the data conversion completely. P/O's are often difficult to convert due to their complexity; they often contain many lines of inventory item detail. Also, some companies opt to re-key open P/O's into the new system instead of converting them electronically; this approach is often used as a training exercise to help users learn how to enter purchase orders in the new system.

When Exceptions are the Rule

In business, every rule has several exceptions. There are those special customers (or vendors) who get special treatment. Often these special customers make up only a small percentage of your overall sales revenue, and yet, they might take up a disproportionate amount of time and energy in your finance, administrative, and customer service departments. These "problem children" are not only a problem to your day-to-day operations, but they can easily kill an ERP implementation project. You can spend 90 percent of your time designing, coding, and testing special features to handle these exceptional customers, only to find that you have missed your due dates, and then, to add insult to injury, those customers stop buying or change their requirements. The same kind of thing happens with vendors.

You cannot have a "one size fits all" mentality when designing an ERP system. You need to build into the system the flexibility to deal with a variety of situations; however, you must do some math first. You should come up with key metrics to measure the materiality of programming in special algorithms to handle exceptions. Questions you should be asking *before* approving customizations to handle exceptions to the rule are these: How many customers (customers, vendors, employees, or whatever) does this exception affect? How many times did this happen last month? What is the total dollar volume each month for these exceptional transactions? Why can't we just contact the customer and insist that they follow our new standard procedures? How can we influence the customer, vendor, or employee to adopt the new standard procedures?

Every project has at least one nudnik who delights in pointing out how every proposed new feature will fail because it doesn't account for this or that exception. When asked how often the exception occurs, this person retorts with vague answers such as "lots of times" or "often enough." Folks like these can't see the forest for the trees. The only way to combat them is to force them to use objective metrics and then calculate an agreed-upon percentage materiality threshold. For example, you can say that if the exception pertains to less than 5 percent of revenue, it will be handled in a later phase.

Remember, even if the exception happens to only one customer only one time per year, the IT development effort to handle that exception will be exactly the same as if that feature were invoked 100 percent of the time for all your customers. Understand and abide by materiality considerations and use key metrics to back up your claims. Shelve exception handling features to later phases such a post implementation continuous improvement.

To-Be or Not to Be As-Is

Often called the *as-is* process, the best way to get started implementing an ERP system is to study what the users actually do today in the normal course of business. The as-is process is followed by the design of the to-be process. The as-is process should be flowcharted and documented in sufficient detail, before doing anything else. This approach, although part of classic IT methodology, is sometimes criticized or underemphasized by well-intentioned folks who go around saying things like "We don't want to recreate the mess we have now!" and "Just because that's how you did it in the past, doesn't mean we need to continue perpetuating the same old bad habits." Unfortunately, these forward thinkers are famous for using their zeal for process re-engineering as an excuse to gloss over and ignore what has been going on day to day in a company for years and years. As a result, they never get a grip on reality; they never understand how the system needs to operate in the real world.

The fact will always remain that the so-called silly and inefficient processes that the supposedly unsophisticated users have followed blindly for years are, in actuality, intricate processes that evolved over time due to very pressing and very real business demands. Process re-engineering is rarely a no-brainer. More often that not, people are doing something a certain way because they have found, after several years, that that's the best way to do it. Users aren't stupid.

Now, even if you have all these grandiose notions about streamlining to the point where you can reduce your workforce by half, the fact remains, that you need to establish a base line of the minimum functionality required to keep the business up and running. To understand what those minimum business requirements are, you need to understand what the users are doing now, in reality, as opposed to what some middle managers are imagining they should be doing in some future utopian pipe dream. Too often, designers start with the wish list, focus on the wish list, and then wind up designing something totally impractical; the implementation fails miserably.

But even if you don't make the mistake of ignoring the as-is process, you can fall into another trap: The idea that you've really studied the as-is process just because somebody drew up a bunch of neato "swim lane" diagrams using Visio. The diagrammatic approach to understanding business flow, with all its arrows and boxes and yes/no decision points, will not even begin to approximate the complex reality, with its nearly infinite variety of exceptions, ripples, nuances, and human-brain-powered flexible decision-making that occurs everyday. You cannot create an accurate model of business processes in Visio, nor will the ERP system itself accurately model reality. In other words, you cannot ever have enough data elements in your database to describe the infinite variety of reality. So what do you do?

There is an art to describing the as-is process at a sufficient level of detail, using both diagrams and clear and ample prose. There is an art to separating the wheat from the chaff and documenting only those special points of interest in the intricate puzzle that require discussion. **These special points of interest occur where the business process intersects with a feature of the ERP system that needs to be configured in a special way.** A good analyst observes what users do today with a very special mindset — a future-oriented mindset. He or she is looking for opportunities to process re-engineer the business based on an intimate knowledge of the built-in capabilities of the base ERP package, along with a good idea of how much it would take to customize that package for a specific purpose.

You often waste both time and money when you have general purpose business analysts study the as-is process. "General purpose" business analysts are not programmers, they typically are not very technical, and they usually are not functional experts in the ERP package. But, many project managers use them with the idea in mind to study the process without any bias about the particular software that is being used or proposed to solve the problem. These project managers feel the business requirements gathering should be pure and unhindered by any ugly technical limitations of specific systems and specific solutions, so they believe a generic business analyst will suffice. You can summarize the approach of these project managers in the following way: "We are first merely documenting everything about the business, then in a later phase, we will decide how to change it and make it better." But that kind of approach doesn't work well, because it's like a doctor examining a patient without any knowledge of what drugs and surgical procedures he has available to cure the patient. They simply don't know what to look for, they don't know what is relevant, so they end up reporting very obvious things, or worse yet, they diagram very intricate but totally unimportant processes. Should you really be paying someone over a hundred dollars an hour to draw little boxes with sayings inside them like "Print the Invoice" or "Stamp the invoice with today's date" or an arrow labeled "Send to Shipping Dept?"

Generally, it is a waste of time and money to diagram business processes, unless you are doing so to illustrate a point about some significant action required to successfully implement the system. Consider the models to be tools to illustrate relevant points, such as process bottlenecks, or additional needs, such as a third-party software add-on that was not part of the original software purchase, that will eventually become a chunk of work during the build phase or a business decision to be made by management.

Template of Doom (or the Dog Ate My Homework)

Some well-meaning ERP consultants try to get the users involved in the implementation by giving them "homework" in the form of templates that need to be filled out. These templates are boiler plate Microsoft Word or Excel documents that outline the configuration parameters of the ERP package for the modules being implemented. The idea is to hold the users accountable for each and every setup option, force them to make decisions about all features, and to offload as much of the project work as possible from the consultants to the clients. Clients like this approach because they reason that the fees will be reduced because they can get salaried employees to do the consultant's work. They feel the consultants should only be doing what is absolutely necessary, such as installing the software or running the data conversion utility. The users can certainly figure out how they want to "flip the switches" in the module setup screens; they can certainly decide on coding schemes for inventory items, charge codes, SKU's, customer ID's and the like. The consulting firms like this approach because, down the road, they believe that if the client complains about anything, they can just point to the fancy template that the client approved and say "Look, you approved it. See, you wanted it set up that way!"

Enter reality. Oops, the users have full-time jobs. They are constantly handling production issues and end up neglecting their "homework" and leaving the templates blank. The project drags on and falls behind schedule. Those delays end up being costly to everyone involved. Suppose that the users do fill out the templates; because they are not experienced ERP consultants, the users may fill out the templates only partially or incorrectly. The coding schemes that users create independently may try to put too much information in one field, because the users are unaware of other fields and features available in the software. In short, the users need help. The users need to be involved — very involved — but they need guidance from an experienced ERP consultant. Yes, that costs money, in the short run, but saves money in the long run.

There are many setup options that the consultant is better off just setting and forgetting, without consulting the user. The experienced Dynamics GP consultant knows which features need to be brought to the attention of users. *Danger Will Robinson*: if your Dynamics GP consultant is telling you to fill out a form in a Word document for the entire collection of setup screens for all your modules, he or she is clueless.

Nine Pregnant Women in a Room for a Month

Implementing an ERP solution takes time and cannot be rushed. Once due dates start to slip, you cannot simply throw bodies at the problem and expect to meet the original due dates which have become unrealistic. Thus the old adage, "You cannot put nine women who are one month pregnant in a room and get a baby."

ERP project managers need to have the skills to accurately assess progress. Too often, especially on large complex engagements, there are not enough objective deliverables or milestones set early on, so that the consulting team is able to coast along for months and months without having to deliver the goods. Bad apples are not weeded out until the worm has eaten it to the core.

If the milestones are merely paper deliverables, watch out. Business requirements, functional specifications, and technical specifications are usually long, boring documents that people neglect to scrutinize properly. Often a boiler plate "fluff" document passes for a deliverable. Sometimes the deliverables are excruciating in their complexity, so project management has a false sense that all is well, when in fact, the document is written at too low a level of detail, pertaining to only one tiny facet of the project, and there is no comprehensive, documented solution for the project. Project managers can reduce implementation risk and identify weak or underperforming team members early by adopting a phased approach and by insisting on short-term milestones and deliverables that evidence tangible progress. Milestones can take many forms, including actual working code, migrated data, interactive prototypes, interim solutions, and pilot projects.

A phased approach is usually the best approach for several reasons. It forces the consultants to deliver early on, flagging the bluffers and rewarding the doers. It allows the consulting firm to have a quick win, which builds confidence with the client's staff. For a project to be successful, the users must be excited and feel positive about the change (Change Management 101). Let's face it, ERP clerical users are some of the most pessimistic and skeptical folks on the planet. They have seen highly-touted million-dollar projects scrapped; they have endured vaporware training sessions reminiscent of a Dilbert cartoon, and they have been kept in the dark while upper management and their consultancy partners battled in conference rooms and courtrooms. So, showing the users that you are here to deliver a good, realistic, working system is paramount, and you can most easily demonstrate your intent by setting some modest first-phase goal with a relatively short time frame and then making sure that you deliver that initial phase on time and to specifications.

Going Over Budget without Going Overboard

How could an ERP implementation project possibly go over budget? What went wrong? How could this situation have been avoided? Surely, this is the worst catastrophe imaginable. Not! Boy, I know I sound like a consultant, but think about it. The worst thing imaginable is not going over budget, it's going over budget without a plan.

Some client-side project managers insist on sticking to budget and sticking to deadlines, no matter what. They stake their reputation (and perhaps their personal incentive plan bonuses) on meeting due dates and being on or under budget. However, in the absence of other metrics to measure user satisfaction and return on investment, being on time and on budget is meaningless. Any fool can slap in a broken, ill-designed system on a predetermined arbitrary date and force users to suffer through the consequences, while trying to spin the story that the project was a huge success because it was "completed" (and I use the term loosely) on time. And, of course, if the project was on time it will be on budget (because after all, time is money; you pay by the hour). It is so much better to go over budget and wait to go live until the system is truly ready than to disrupt the operations of a company by releasing an unstable system. The customers and employees you lose during a time of system chaos may never return and are expensive to reacquire. These costs are seldom considered, but they should be.

ERP projects can go over budget for a vast array of reasons:

✔ Employee illness

✔ Unforeseen network issues

✔ Unforeseen hardware problems

✔ Unrelated human resource changes

✔ Organizational changes

✔ Legitimate and wise decisions to change strategy in response to changing business needs

✔ The client changes the project's scope

✔ The consulting firm sends rookies to do a senior's job

✔ The weather

The list is endless. So how to deal with it? You need a plan. That doesn't mean you plan to fail. It just means you've been around the block and are wise enough to know that ERP projects sometimes do go over budget.

A graduated rate reduction schedule is a great way to deal with overages. Using a graduated rate reduction schedule, the consulting firm's rates are reduced the moment the budgeted hours are exceeded with two or three additional reductions as hours exceed pre-defined thresholds. Finally, after a very large number of hours, the rate returns to the standard rate. Notice I said reduced, not eliminated. Many clients mistakenly believe that it is good practice to simply stop paying bills, consider the estimate to be a fixed-price project with a cost ceiling, and then to just badger the consultants for more and more free hours. "Fix it on your dime." Fixed price ERP implementations are generally a bad idea not only for the consulting firm but for the client as well. If the project goes over schedule and budget, the consultants will hate being on a losing project. They will try to get off the project, and they will not perform well. The situation will be tense, and most people do not perform well under tense circumstances. In the worst-case scenario, these kinds of projects end up in a legal battle in which everyone loses (except the lawyers).

Instead, if the rate is lowered, it provides an incentive for the consulting firm to move on to the next project (not to milk this one client to death), and an incentive for the customer to limit the hours as well (since they are paying for each hour). This scheme works well when the graduated rate reduction schedule is agreed upon before the project ever begins, avoiding the tense and very uncomfortable situation of negotiating rate reductions or write-offs while everyone is upset and pointing fingers as the project is struggling and behind schedule. The work simply proceeds, albeit at a lower rate; costs are managed, the client doesn't feel cheated, and the consulting firm doesn't feel squeezed. The job gets done.

Too many IT projects do not have a contingency plan for cost overages. When you consider that the majority of IT projects do go over budget, this would seem to be such an obvious part of an IT project plan; yet, it is a part most often left out, because people are afraid to admit they aren't perfect, for fear that others will lose confidence in them. This false pride can kill an ERP project.

Implementing complex computerized business systems is difficult. The final cost is hard to estimate accurately, because the number of features is so very vast and the cost of implementing each and every little feature would have to be known with an exactitude that is impossible to attain. A doctor can estimate the cost of laser eye surgery; it is a procedure that is performed in a standard way each time. A caterer can estimate the cost of a wedding by knowing the head count and the names of the dishes to be served. An ERP consultant cannot simply list the modules and the number of users and know the exact cost, because there is an infinite variety of ways to configure those modules; there are too many unknowns. A seasoned ERP veteran can come very close using a combination of experience, instinct, and most importantly, a detailed up-front business analysis; however, the graduated rate reduction schedule provides just enough flexibility to keep both client and consulting firm working together toward their shared goals and objectives. Rule of thumb: Try your hardest to come in on budget by planning, analyzing, and managing the project using a proven methodology, but, at the same time, have a plan in place just in case you go over budget.

The Phone Book Syndrome

Revamping the chart of accounts is usually a good idea any time you implement a new ERP system, since you have the opportunity to start fresh and eliminate a lot of deadwood, to simplify and streamline. Unfortunately, too many over-zealous CFO's use it as an opportunity to ensure that every possible combination of business measurements is introduced into the Chart of Accounts. They envision being able to hit a button and get virtually any report directly out of the General Ledger in any dimension, be it departmental, cost center, region, product line, brand, customer type, manager, employee, or project code. It's a nice dream, but the reality is that they can't get this fine level of granularity in their numbers today, and they have no concrete plan as to how to get such highly detailed numbers in the future. It's time to raise the red flag if you are setting up segments for account numbers that don't currently exist without first planning how you'll ever manage to use those numbers going forward. And, even if you do believe you can produce those more detailed numbers in the future, you'll still need to undertake a cost/benefit analysis that accounts for the difficulty of producing those details and the cost of reconciling them each month. You must ask yourself, "Is the increased reporting flexibility worth the increased administrative and/or IT overhead?" Often the answer is no, but people tend to underestimate or, worse yet, ignore altogether the administrative or IT overhead cost incurred to gather and maintain financial data. They behave as though the numbers are going to just magically appear. "If I build the chart of accounts, the numbers will come." NOT!

Unfortunately when you deal with a "segment freak," you end up with an account number that's longer than a credit card number and has too many segments, most of which will never be used. The clerks will end up getting carpel tunnel syndrome keying in long strings of meaningless zeros for years to come. But worst yet, the Chart of Accounts will expand exponentially until it's the size of the Las Vegas Yellow Pages. Do the math: If you have just three segments for department, region, and product line in addition to the base account number, and your company has ten departments, ten regions, and ten product lines, with only 1000 account numbers, you still get one million accounts in your Chart of Accounts! Although you may say that you don't need to create every combination of account, department, region, and product line, don't underestimate the task of figuring out which combinations you do need to create, and what convoluted business logic you'll need to apply in your determination.

If you make project code a segment, then every time your company embarks on a new project, you have the task of expanding your Chart of Accounts even more, and as projects are retired, you end up with a lot of inactive accounts; what a mess! You should also avoid the dreaded sub-account which masquerades as a segment. A sub-account is really nothing more than an extension of the account. You can simply use a longer account number or, better yet, renumber your accounts. For example, suppose that your Cash is 1000, and you're using the sub-account to specify the type of cash account; Checking is 1000-100 and Petty is 1000-200. Why not renumber the account numbers so that 1010 would be Checking, and 1020 would be Petty. Sub-accounts are confusing because they look like departments, but they're not. People often end up using the sub-account segment for multiple purposes, sometime as a sub-account, sometimes as a cost center or department. Try to avoid using a segment to mean different things in different areas of the Chart of Accounts; you'll just create a confusing mess for no reason. Instead renumber your account numbers to represent what you want.

Avoid numbering accounts sequentially such as 1001, 1002, 1003; this numbering scheme provides no wiggle room. Instead use 1010, 1020, and 1030, leaving space to insert additional accounts later. Use a four- or five-digit account number. A six- or seven-digit account number will just cause you to spend more time keying, and you'll get bleary-eyed looking at the numbers. Do the math: A five-digit number, if you start the numbering with 10000, will yield 90,000 possible account numbers, a six-digit number will yield 900,000 account numbers. That's just crazy. Usually a four-digit number is enough, yielding 9000 possibilities.

Back Office Is the Cart, Not the Horse

During the late nineties, in the rush to get on the Web, companies hired web page design firms to create web sites. Many of these web sites allowed customers to browse items and place orders. After the web sites had been designed, built, and launched, and thousands, if not millions of dollars, had been spent, and everyone agreed that the web site looked really cool and super-nifty, it suddenly dawned upon everybody that they had no way to process the web orders. Too many managers underestimated the difficulty of electronically linking the web site to a sales order processing, inventory control, accounts receivable, and general ledger system. The web site did not talk to the back office. Worse yet, they did not even speak the same language. The inventory items on the web site used different codes than those used in the order entry system, and different yet again from those used in the purchasing department. Nothing agreed, nothing was in synch. The unfortunate answer was to print out web orders to paper (or route them to e-mail, and then print them out to paper), and hand-key the orders into the accounting system.

The web site should have been designed on top of a stable, full-featured, fully integrated ERP system. Unfortunately, too many web sites are created in a vacuum, with the assumption that they will be tied into the ERP in the future using custom interfaces. Those custom interfaces need to contain a great deal of data transformation logic, because the web site was not developed using the standards already established in the ERP system. As a result, the interfaces are error-prone, costly to maintain, and difficult, if not impossible, to upgrade.

Any company considering establishing their first e-commerce system or planning to overhaul or revamp their existing e-commerce system should bear in mind that the back office (ERP) system is the infrastructure on which to build a web site, which will be a seamless external extension of the ERP. Rule of thumb: Put in the ERP first, then extend it to include an e-commerce–enabled Web site.

Bridges to Vaporware

Large complex organizations typically have several IT initiatives going on concurrently; therefore, projects may have dependencies on other projects. The problem is that your team may not have any control over related projects. You may be told to interface your solution to some other team's solution and to design your solution to meet the specifications of the other solution. It can be very frustrating to find out that the other team has failed and they are scrapping their project after you have invested so much of your time, energy, and talents into tailoring your solution to fit their *vaporware* (promised code that has not been designed, developed, and sufficiently tested).

The rule of thumb here is to remain cautiously optimistic about nascent systems with which you need to interface. Have a contingency plan that takes into account that related dependent system development may lag behind or be scrapped. Be prepared to continue to interface with the legacy system, just in case the new system is not quite ready on time (or never materializes). There is no reason that your project should fail because of another team's mismanagement.

Never assume that the other system will be ready on time. Never assume that a software vendor will have a promised interface ready on time. Never assume that a third-party developer will have its code ready for the new version of the base package. Have a contingency plan in place for all vaporware.

Chapter 17

Most Useful Features

In This Chapter

▶ SmartLists

▶ Recurring batches

▶ Transaction-level notes and attachments

▶ Originating master names and ID's

▶ Classes

▶ Company posting setup options

▶ FRx transaction-level reporting

▶ FRx Trees

▶ Excel-based budgeting

▶ SOP document types

*I*n this chapter, you can read about my "top ten" list of most useful Microsoft Dynamics GP features. Many of them save time or keystrokes or both.

SmartLists

SmartLists provide users with an easy way to quickly extract information from Dynamics GP and send it directly into Excel. With no programming experience, a user can design ad-hoc queries, deciding the columns to extract and how to filter and sort the information. After you set up a SmartList, you can save it as a favorite and share it with other users. The SmartList window appears in Figure 17-1.

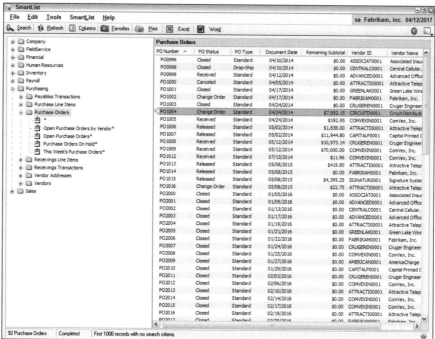

You can use SmartLists to control workflow by having users monitor a SmartList as if it's a queue of work to be performed. For example, you can create a SmartList that you might call "Urgent Orders" that would display all transactions users save to a batch number called "URGENT." The user can monitor the SmartList to quickly identify and fill a list of urgent orders. By double-clicking any item that appears in the SmartList, the user can instantly navigate to that card or transaction and work the items on the list.

You can read more about SmartLists in Chapter 12.

Recurring Batches

The Recurring Batch feature is available in any module but most useful in the General Ledger to help you close a period. You can enter the journal entries needed to close a month in a recurring batch. After you post this recurring batch, Dynamics GP makes the recurring batch available again, incrementing the posting date of all the journal entries in the batch by a month — or whatever time period you select for the recurring batch frequency. You can then edit the transactions in the recurring batch to change the dollar amounts, or add or delete lines. When you have lengthy journal entries that contain the same accounts, period after period, but change in dollar amounts, the recurring batch is an enormous time saver.

Transaction-Level Notes and Attachments

You can attach notes and Excel, Word, or PDF files to any transaction in Dynamics GP so that other users can see the supporting documentation for a transaction without having to go to a physical file cabinet to research. In a note, you can describe why you made a certain adjustment, correction, or unusual entry. It's a good habit to document inside the system instead of leaving yellow sticky notes outside the system on your desk or in the file cabinet.

You also can attach notes to cards and even to windows. Some companies attach notes to windows to document what the company is doing uniquely with that particular window; for example, if your company uses the comment field in a particular window to store certain types of information, you can attach a note to the window that helps users remember what to put in the comment field.

Originating Master Names and ID's

Suppose that you post a transaction, such as a payables voucher, from a subsidiary ledger, and that transaction flows in detail to the General Ledger. The Dynamics GP General Ledger detail table contains several fields, called *originating master fields*, that store the vendor ID, the vendor name, the invoice number, and the invoice date. These originating master fields help accountants easily perform account analysis since you can display these fields on reports and in a SmartList; from the SmartList, you can send them directly to Excel.

Classes

Using classes, you can establish default general ledger accounts and other settings to make the average user's job easier when creating customers, vendors, or items. If you establish classes and then train the average user to select a class when creating the customer, vendor, or item, Dynamics GP will automatically assign all of the default information to the new record. Classes are also a good way to tag cards for sorting and filtering purposes on reports. And, if you use classes, you can easily make mass changes to all cards based on a particular class by changing the class. When you change the class, Dynamics GP prompts you to "roll down" the change to all cards based on the class.

It's a good idea to limit the number of classes you create. If you create too many classes, you'll need to change too many classes to make the "roll down" feature effective.

Company Posting Setup Options

The Posting Setup window, shown in Figure 17-2, enables you to control the behavior of Dynamics GP so that it performs the way you want. Working from this window, you can set options to, for example, post automatically to the General Ledger, post individual transactions or batches, require approval for batches using a password prior to posting, and identify the reports to print when you post a transaction or batch. You can set these options differently for different series and, within a particular series, you can treat some transactions in one way while you handle other transactions in other ways.

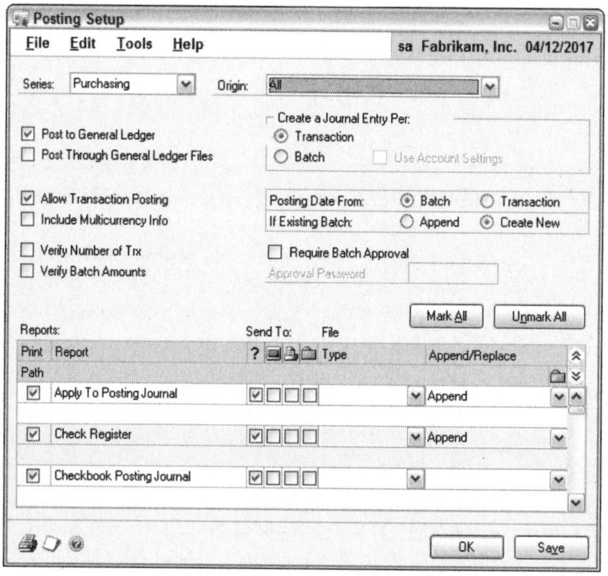

Figure 17-2:
The Posting
Setup
window.

You can open this window by using the Menu bar and selecting Microsoft Dynamics GP⇨Tools⇨Setup⇨Posting⇨Posting.

FRx Transaction-Level Reporting

Because you can include the originating master fields, such as Vendor ID, Vendor Name, Invoice No., and Invoice Date on reports, including FRx Financial Statements, you can drill down from a summarized line on a financial statement to view the details behind it.

For example, while viewing an income statement in the FRx Drill Down Viewer, you can double-click the Telephone expense line and see the individual general ledger accounts, such as cell phone expense and land line expense, that make up the total of telephone expenses. You can then double-click the cell phone expense line to identify the vendor, invoice number, and date of each expense charged to the cell phone expense account. Users who have profit and loss responsibility can take advantage of this feature to examine financial statements down to the individual invoice level without calling the Finance Department to ask for detailed information concerning a line item on the financial statements.

FRx Trees

Using the FRx Tree feature, you can build one or more organizational trees that you can use to filter financial reports based on a segment of the chart of accounts. In this way, you save report building and maintenance time, because you only need to build and maintain one report to report on any of the organizational units — divisions, departments, or regions — in your company.

Excel-Based Budgeting

Many companies like to create company budgets in Excel for a number of reasons. For example, in Excel, you can use complex formulas and even link to supporting worksheets to generate budget figures. In addition, many companies find it easy and effective to e-mail Excel workbooks containing budget information to managers for update or review prior to finalizing the numbers.

The Excel-Based Budgeting feature in Dynamics GP enables you to import budget information from Excel workbooks directly into the General Ledger module's budget table, making generation and revision of budgets a breeze.

Read more about Excel-based budgeting in Chapter 8.

SOP Document Types

The Sales Order Processing (SOP) Module is very flexible, and creating different types of SOP documents is one of the best ways to control the behavior of the module. You can create an unlimited number of document types for each of the various documents that SOP contains — Quote, Order, Invoice, Back Order, and Return. Suppose that you have separate lines of business that function in different ways. You can use document types to create a Quote, Order, and/or Invoice for each line of business that is completely different in appearance. SOP document types also control function; for example, in one line of business, you might want to check for on-hand inventory quantities at the time you enter the order into the system, while, in another line of business, you may not need that scrutiny.

You can read more about SOP document types in Chapter 6.

Appendix

Microsoft Dynamics GP Modules

Microsoft Dynamics GP is a modular product, with separate modules to cover various aspects of accounting for business transactions. You don't need to purchase particular modules to make the software work. Instead, you can purchase only those modules you feel you need. For example, if you sell inventory items but you don't assemble any items, you don't need to buy the Bill of Materials module. Similarly, if your company doesn't track costs for jobs, you don't need to buy the Job Costing module. Some people buy only the General Ledger module and use other software packages to handle other aspects of their business accounting because those other software packages meet some customized or specialized need. Dynamics GP enables you to purchase the modules you want to use. And, you don't need to purchase everything at one time; you can purchase some modules now and others later.

In this appendix, you'll find brief descriptions of each Dynamics GP module available for sale. In addition, you'll also find descriptions of the various licensing plans available to you.

While you purchase modules separately, when you work in Dynamics GP, you don't select a particular module. Instead, you select tasks to perform that correspond to business functions such as creating an invoice for a customer or paying a vendor bill. The modules installed are transparent to you and Dynamics GP lets you work in a way that makes business sense instead of "computer" sense. You can read more about performing these task-related business functions in Part II.

Getting What You Need with the Modular Approach

There are many modules available to meet a wide variety of business needs. In Table 1, you'll find the module name and a brief description of its function. These descriptions aren't intended to give you a comprehensive picture of the functions you can perform with any particular module. Instead, they give you an overview of the module. For more details, visit www.microsoft. com/dynamics/gp/product/default.mspx and search for Fact Sheets.

Table 1	Modules Available for Microsoft Dynamics GP
Module	*Description*
Advanced Distribution	Advanced Distribution helps you maintain control over your distribution channels, improve processes, and provide excellent customer service. You can create user-defined sales fulfillment workflows, define process holds, and ensure that all drop-ship line items meet requirements before shipping.
Advanced Picking	Using this module, you can reduce handling and increase accuracy for both single and multi-site warehouse operations and tailor picking routines to meet your business requirements, bin or bay sequence, or method of operation, lowering overhead, reducing handling, and improving accuracy.
Analysis Cubes for Excel	Using this module, you can produce analytical views of sales trends, customer buying patterns, and other values that help you better understand your business and plan for the future. Using Microsoft SQL ServerTM 2000 and SQL ServerTM 2005, this module creates Analysis Cubes that enable you to view information in familiar pivot tables in Microsoft Office Excel. In addition, you can automate report building to reduce the time spent on administrative work and increase the time spent analyzing information.

Module	Description
Analytical Accounting	Use this module to help you analyze financial data by including or restricting whatever data you want. You can organize data hierarchically for multi-level reporting and find and analyze transactions across Dynamics GP General Ledger, Receivables, Payables, Inventory, Sales Order Processing, Purchase Order Processing, Grant Management, and Bank Reconciliation. Using transaction dimension codes, you can classify, report, and analyze financial transactions based on your specific business needs, such as Cost Center, Profit Center, Region, and Hours. Transaction dimension codes eliminate the need to analyze transactions on the basis of account segments.
Audit Trails	This module helps you track changes made to transactions, recording the date, time, user who made the change, and details of the change. You can control the tables and the fields monitored by the Audit Trails feature.
Available to Promise	Using this module, you can quickly view how much of each product you have on hand and how much is committed, and you can quickly find the earliest date that you can supply an item to a customer while still meeting all existing commitments. You can view forward-looking inventory projections that include outstanding sales and purchase orders, unposted inventory, bills of materials, and manufacturing transactions, so you can make accurate commitments to customers.
Bank Reconciliation	Using this module, you see on-screen summaries that include adjusted bank balance, adjusted book balance, and cleared payments. The details that appear include deposit number, transaction number, type, payment amount, and description, and you can drill down into any transaction when you need even greater detail. You can sort transactions by type or date, and mark single or entire ranges of transactions for further attention. You can easily resolve discrepancies by viewing the bank transactions that make up your checkbook balance for a specified date and drill down to view the cleared status of any transaction. If you manage multiple check books, you don't need to finish the reconciliation for one check book before you start the next one.

(continued)

Table 1 *(continued)*

Module	Description
Bill of Materials	Using the Bill of Materials module, you can maintain an active bill of materials for each item to track components currently in use and manage bills in production. In addition to manufacturing bills of materials, you can create other types of bills that meet the specific needs of your products. For example, you can create engineering bills of materials that make visible the effects of engineering change orders on costs.
Business Portal	Using this module, you can provide role-tailored access to information and processes from a single Web-based portal using SharePoint Services. Because you can create privileges that you can assign to people who fill a particular role, you can make appropriate information available to employees, customers, and vendors.
Cash Flow Management	The Cash Flow Management module provides you with forecasting capabilities you can use to monitor, predict, and manage cash inflows and outflows, helping you improve your cash flow.
Collections Management	Using the Collections Management module, you can reduce bad debt expense and improve your cash flow. The module provides the customizable information views and automated bad debt management tools that generate correspondence, e-mail notices, statements, and invoices to customers.
Crystal Reports	Crystal Reports is a full-featured report writer that can pull data from any table in your Dynamics GP company. Using this module, you can control report logic, formatting, and data selection and turn your Dynamics GP data into interactive Web documents and presentation quality reports in Excel, Word, and other Office applications.
Customization	Using this module, developers can integrate data from external sources or from legacy applications into Dynamics GP and modify your Dynamics GP solution to fit the most exacting business requirements.
Demand Planner	With the Demand Planner module, you can forecast sales and materials requirements; these forecasts can include corporate trend and seasonality factors and estimate margins of error.

Module	*Description*
eBanking	Using this module, you can manage and reconcile bank accounts electronically. You can transmit payables to the bank after you've processed them. Dynamics GP conforms to U.S. bank industry electronic funds transfer (EFT) standards with support for automatic clearing house (ACH) format and most Canadian formats, while also allowing customers to create and map the EFT file format structure. You also can transfer sales batches with associated payments and automatically generate an electronic file of payments to transfer to your bank.
eExpense	With the eExpense module, employees can submit expense reports in a browser-based environment that consists of simple checklists and templates with pre-populated data that use pre-configured or custom cost centers mapped to General Ledger accounts.
Electronic Document Delivery	Using the Electronic Document Delivery module, you can organize and schedule the e-mail message delivery of invoices, credit memos, and other sales documents to your customers in XML, HTML, Excel, or PDF format.
Encumbrance Management	This module, which integrates with Purchase Order Processing and was designed specifically for not-for-profit and public sector organizations, helps you easily locate and track budget information, query current or historical encumbrances, and streamline period-end and year-end reporting processes.
Engineering Change Management	The Engineering Change Management module helps manufacturers organize and manage changes requested by customers to processes or components.
Enterprise Reporting	The Enterprise Reporting module offers you an efficient reporting solution for complex, distributed environments. You can import data from multiple data sources into the Enterprise Reporting database, reducing the need for redundant data entry. Using a Web browser, you can view, modify, and analyze business data and remotely process or schedule report packages for distribution in a variety of formats, including print or e-mail attachments.

(continued)

Table 1 *(continued)*

Module	Description
Field Service	If you run a service business, the Field Service module can help you manage service calls, administer contracts, forecast purchasing and scheduling requirements based on product time in service or usage, and coordinate open service requests with upcoming preventive maintenance calls. You also can generate return authorizations, track repair and return status, and properly credit customer invoices for returns.
Fixed Asset Management	Using the Fixed Asset Management module, you can capture the information you need about your assets for tax or reporting purposes. You also can perform depreciations, averaging, or comparisons across assets.
General Ledger	The General Ledger module helps you manage the financial heart of your business. Using the General Ledger module, you can design an accounting structure to suit your business and create unique structures for each company in your organization up to 66 characters long and up to 10 segments of any length, and customizable General Ledger fields. You also can create definable fiscal periods and make prior-year adjustments with full audit control.
Grant Management	Using the Grant Management module, you can automate many of your grant management processes to track funds, demonstrate accountability, and help attract future funding.
HR Management Self-Service Suite: Canada and HR Management Self-Service Suite: United States	A web-based portal, the HR Management Self-Service Suite for Microsoft Business Portal integrates human resources and payroll data and helps provide accurate, current information across your organization. Access to information is controlled by assigning role-tailored permissions to each user.
Human Resources Management	Use the Human Resources Management module to manage every aspect of your organization's employees. You can record, track, and maintain employee data, including attendance; salaries and promotions; trainings, classes, certifications and skills; health and wellness data; performance reviews, merits, demerits, and disciplinary plans; and government compliance. You also can automatically produce injury reports.

Module	Description
Integration	The Integration module contains tools that help your developers connect your organization's applications and data so that you can easily share data, integrate processes, and manage change. The Integration module enables you to import data from almost any database or desktop application, including comma- and tab-delimited text files, XML, and most open database connectivity (ODBC) data sources.
Inventory Management	Using the Inventory Management module, you can track items across multiple locations, track a single inventory item across multiple bins, set item prices on a customer-by-customer basis, track serialized items, and use controls and automated alerts to avoid selecting expired lots for distribution. You also can choose default entries for classes of items, such as color, style, and manufacturer, and rank your inventory items by usage value, actual or project usage quantity, on-hand inventory value, or unit cost.
Job Costing	If your business focuses on jobs, as most manufacturing concerns do, you can use the Job Costing module to capture all costs when they occur and consolidate them into one location to gain a detailed understanding of costs, identify costs at any point in a job, and automatically calculate variance between estimated and actual costs.
Key Performance Indicators (KPIs)	The Key Performance Indicators modules is a web-based portal that you can use to define and make available key performance indicators such as profitability, debt-to-equity, and gross margin to specified individuals. Each person can view key performance indicators relevant to his or her area to monitor and act on business performance.
Manufacturing Order Processing	The Manufacturing Order Processing module helps manufacturers track production costs in detail and manage work orders, routings, and outsourcing.
Materials Requirements Planning	The Material Requirements Planning module helps you plan production effectively. Using forecasts and sales orders allows for detailed analysis of recommendations generated by the Material Requirements Planning module, including "what-if" scenarios. In addition, you can convert Material Requirements Planning suggestions to purchase orders.

(continued)

Table 1 *(continued)*

Module	Description
Microsoft Forecaster	Use the Microsoft Forecaster module to create, monitor, and execute accurate and realistic budgets. You can budget employees in multiple scenarios with salary planning worksheets and flexible salary and bonus designations. You can import both General Ledger and non-General Ledger data into the Forecaster module.
Microsoft FRx Professional	The Microsoft Business Solutions for Analytics–FRx Professional helps you produce comprehensive, highly customizable financial and management reports from the General Ledger to report on both budget and actual amounts.
Multicurrency Management	If yours is a multinational organization, you can use the Multicurrency Management module to comply with international currency standards and work with international clients and vendors using numerous currencies. This module helps you maintain current exchange rates and define new ones for specific customers or contracts as needed.
Order Management	The Order Management module provides a web-based portal that your customers can use to place and update orders. You provide protected access to online information using this out-of-the box, business-to-business portal.
Payables Management	Using the Payables Management module, you can improve your control over business expenses. This module provides you with up-to-the-minute information about your payables and management of your vendors, and automates many routine or complex tasks.
Payroll: Canada and Payroll: United States	The Payroll module helps you manage and control all of the functions associated with paying your employees. Among other features, the Payroll module provides setup checklists to help ensure that the functionality you want is installed and available; calculates taxes, deductions, and benefits; produces detailed records of pay, benefits, and deductions to help you comply with government reporting obligations; processes salary and hourly pay automatically for groups of employees; and offers direct deposit options.

Module	Description
Process Server	Using the Process Server module, you can move processor-intensive tasks off the computers your employees use every day and onto dedicated process servers, improving computer performance and enabling your employees to get more work done in the same amount of time.
Project Accounting	If your business is project-oriented, the Project Accounting module can help you connect project activities with company financials and ensure accurate accounting and billing processes throughout project life-cycles with its extensive reporting capabilities.
Project Time and Expense	The Project Time and Expense module is web-based and enables project team members and managers to capture, review, and approve project time and expense data so that you can promptly and accurately invoice customers and reimburse out-of-pocket employee expenses.
Purchase Order Processing	Using the Purchase Order Processing module, you can set up long-term purchasing agreements — blanket purchase orders — with vendors that help to simplify the ordering process. You also can automate purchase order processes; for example, you can automatically map purchase order line numbers to line items. And your shipping options are flexible: you can record shipments and invoices separately or together, assign different Ship To addresses for each line item on a purchase order, and have vendors drop ship orders to customers.
Quality Assurance	In a manufacturing environment, the Quality Assurance module helps you start with the quality of raw materials your manufacturing process needs. Using this module, you can design testing procedures of incoming materials so that you produce quality products the first time around and reduce manufacturing delays, rework, and scrap.
Receivables Management	Using the Receivables Management module, you can track invoices, process receipts from customers, and analyze customer activity to reduce the risk of uncollectible receivables.

(continued)

Table 1 *(continued)*

Module	*Description*
Report Pack	The Report Pack module uses Microsoft SQL Server 2000 Reporting Services and provides a number of commonly used reports. In addition, the SQL Server Reporting Services wizard helps you create additional commonly needed reports quickly and easily.
Report Writer	Use the Report Writer module to modify existing reports or create entirely new ones using multiple fonts, colors, sizes, and graphics. You can pull data from multiple locations, create restrictions to pinpoint specific information, perform calculations on data, and sort the information to view it the way you want.
Requisition Management	In environments where you need extensive control over the purchasing process, you can use the Requisition Management module to enable employees to enter purchase requisitions online for manager approval; approved requisitions are automatically transferred to the Purchase Order Processing module.
Sales Forecasting	With the Sales Forecasting module, you can create forecasts for a range of items or salespeople and combine multiple forecasts into one master forecast. If you integrate the Sales Forecasting module with the Material Requirements Planning module, both sales and manufacturing managers can evaluate the influence of various economic or environmental events on production and prepare for possible scenarios before they occur.
Sales Order Processing	Using the Sales Order Processing module, you can enter and process orders, back orders, invoices, and returns quickly and accurately. You can assign priority ranks to customers to direct allocations to customers based on their priority ranking. You also can route quotes and other documents for approval before they're processed or shipped and automatically populate purchase orders with information from corresponding sales orders.
Security Management	Using the Security Management module, you protect your data by assigning security to tasks based on the role of the user in your Dynamics GP environment. You set security in an easy-to-use interactive format, and you can control access to data, applications, and tools.

Module	Description
SmartList Builder	You can use the SmartList Builder to create your own SmartLists with the information that you want to view and analyze. Link tables and add calculated fields to, for example, analyze profits or calculate commissions. Summarize information using functions such as sum, count, minimum, or maximum.
System Manager	You use the System Manager module, always included with the purchase of any Dynamics GP module, to configure Dynamics GP to help you work as productively as possible and effectively share information. You'll find helpful tools like setup checklists, and you can customize the Home page for your role.
Web Services	Use Extensible Web Services to help your developers enable real-time information sharing and connect people, systems, and devices to integrate processes for Dynamics GP users.

Getting More Modules for Your Money with Business Ready Licensing

The Dynamics GP modules you'll need depend on the type of business you run and the current and future software needs your company might have. You can choose from two editions of pre-selected modules available for Dynamics GP, and then add other functionality as needed.

In addition to licensing an edition, you license the users who need to use it. You can choose between full or partial access user licenses, depending on your needs.

Full access user licenses

A full access user license allows one user to access all functionality within the edition at any one time. You only pay for the people accessing the system at any one time. If you have 30 people who need to use the system, but no more than 10 of them will use the system simultaneously, then you only pay for 10 full access user licenses.

Partial access user licenses

You also can choose from several types of partial access user licenses. A partial access user license is priced lower than the Full Access user license and enables you to extend access to your Dynamics GP solution to many more people across your organization.

Business Essentials Edition

This edition focuses on providing core financial management needs and functionality, including but not limited to

- ✔ **General Ledger, analytical accounting, multicurrency management, and bank reconciliation**
- ✔ **Accounts receivable via the Receivables Management module**
- ✔ **Accounts payable via the Payables Management module**
- ✔ **Fixed Asset Management**
- ✔ **Sales Order Processing**
- ✔ **Purchase Order Processing and encumbrance management for non-profit organizations**
- ✔ **Inventory Management**
- ✔ **Microsoft FRx Desktop (1 user)**

In addition to the modules, this edition includes one full access user license, and you can purchase additional full and partial access user licenses. You also can license additional modules, such as payroll modules, for this edition.

Advanced Management Edition

This edition includes all of the functionality of the Business Essentials edition along with the following functionality:

- ✔ **Cash management.**
- ✔ **Collections management.**
- ✔ **Advanced business intelligence and reporting.**
- ✔ **Grant management for non-profit organizations.**

- ✔ **Customer relationship management, including Microsoft Dynamics CRM Professional Server.** To use this product, you must purchase at least one user license for it. The Microsoft Dynamics Advanced Management edition does not include user access for Microsoft Dynamics CRM.

- ✔ **Manufacturing functionality, including manufacturing bill of materials, manufacturing order processing, production scheduling, and material requirements planning.**

- ✔ **Supply chain management functionality, including bill of materials, order management, purchase order generation, and requisition and returns management.**

- ✔ **FRx-related functionality.**

In addition to this functionality, the Advanced Management edition includes one full access user license, and you can buy additional full and partial access licenses. You also can license other modules separately to enhance the functionality of the Advanced Management Edition.

Index

• *N* •

• T •

• U •

Notes

Notes

Notes

USINESS, CAREERS & PERSONAL FINANCE

ounting For Dummies, 4th Edition*
-0-470-24600-9

okkeeping Workbook For Dummies†
-0-470-16983-4

mmodities For Dummies
-0-470-04928-0

ing Business in China For Dummies
-0-470-04929-7

E-Mail Marketing For Dummies
978-0-470-19087-6

Job Interviews For Dummies, 3rd Edition*†
978-0-470-17748-8

Personal Finance Workbook For Dummies*†
978-0-470-09933-9

Real Estate License Exams For Dummies
978-0-7645-7623-2

Six Sigma For Dummies
978-0-7645-6798-8

Small Business Kit For Dummies, 2nd Edition*†
978-0-7645-5984-6

Telephone Sales For Dummies
978-0-470-16836-3

USINESS PRODUCTIVITY & MICROSOFT OFFICE

cess 2007 For Dummies
-0-470-03649-5

cel 2007 For Dummies
-0-470-03737-9

fice 2007 For Dummies
-0-470-00923-9

tlook 2007 For Dummies
-0-470-03830-7

PowerPoint 2007 For Dummies
978-0-470-04059-1

Project 2007 For Dummies
978-0-470-03651-8

QuickBooks 2008 For Dummies
978-0-470-18470-7

Quicken 2008 For Dummies
978-0-470-17473-9

Salesforce.com For Dummies, 2nd Edition
978-0-470-04893-1

Word 2007 For Dummies
978-0-470-03658-7

DUCATION, HISTORY, REFERENCE & TEST PREPARATION

rican American History For Dummies
8-0-7645-5469-8

gebra For Dummies
8-0-7645-5325-7

gebra Workbook For Dummies
8-0-7645-8467-1

t History For Dummies
8-0-470-09910-0

ASVAB For Dummies, 2nd Edition
978-0-470-10671-6

British Military History For Dummies
978-0-470-03213-8

Calculus For Dummies
978-0-7645-2498-1

Canadian History For Dummies, 2nd Edition
978-0-470-83656-9

Geometry Workbook For Dummies
978-0-471-79940-5

The SAT I For Dummies, 6th Edition
978-0-7645-7193-0

Series 7 Exam For Dummies
978-0-470-09932-2

World History For Dummies
978-0-7645-5242-7

OOD, GARDEN, HOBBIES & HOME

ridge For Dummies, 2nd Edition
8-0-471-92426-5

oin Collecting For Dummies, 2nd Edition
8-0-470-22275-1

ooking Basics For Dummies, 3rd Edition
8-0-7645-7206-7

Drawing For Dummies
978-0-7645-5476-6

Etiquette For Dummies, 2nd Edition
978-0-470-10672-3

Gardening Basics For Dummies*†
978-0-470-03749-2

Knitting Patterns For Dummies
978-0-470-04556-5

Living Gluten-Free For Dummies†
978-0-471-77383-2

Painting Do-It-Yourself For Dummies
978-0-470-17533-0

EALTH, SELF HELP, PARENTING & PETS

nger Management For Dummies
8-0-470-03715-7

nxiety & Depression Workbook or Dummies
8-0-7645-9793-0

ieting For Dummies, 2nd Edition
8-0-7645-4149-0

og Training For Dummies, 2nd Edition
8-0-7645-8418-3

Horseback Riding For Dummies
978-0-470-09719-9

Infertility For Dummies†
978-0-470-11518-3

Meditation For Dummies with CD-ROM, 2nd Edition
978-0-471-77774-8

Post-Traumatic Stress Disorder For Dummies
978-0-470-04922-8

Puppies For Dummies, 2nd Edition
978-0-470-03717-1

Thyroid For Dummies, 2nd Edition†
978-0-471-78755-6

Type 1 Diabetes For Dummies*†
978-0-470-17811-9

INTERNET & DIGITAL MEDIA

AdWords For Dummies
978-0-470-15252-2

Blogging For Dummies, 2nd Edition
978-0-470-23017-6

Digital Photography All-in-One Desk Reference For Dummies, 3rd Edition
978-0-470-03743-0

Digital Photography For Dummies, 5th Edition
978-0-7645-9802-9

Digital SLR Cameras & Photography For Dummies, 2nd Edition
978-0-470-14927-0

eBay Business All-in-One Desk Reference For Dummies
978-0-7645-8438-1

eBay For Dummies, 5th Edition*
978-0-470-04529-9

eBay Listings That Sell For Dummies
978-0-471-78912-3

Facebook For Dummies
978-0-470-26273-3

The Internet For Dummies, 11th Edition
978-0-470-12174-0

Investing Online For Dummies, 5th Edition
978-0-7645-8456-5

iPod & iTunes For Dummies, 5th Edit
978-0-470-17474-6

MySpace For Dummies
978-0-470-09529-4

Podcasting For Dummies
978-0-471-74898-4

Search Engine Optimization For Dummies, 2nd Edition
978-0-471-97998-2

Second Life For Dummies
978-0-470-18025-9

Starting an eBay Business For Dumm 3rd Edition†
978-0-470-14924-9

GRAPHICS, DESIGN & WEB DEVELOPMENT

Adobe Creative Suite 3 Design Premium All-in-One Desk Reference For Dummies
978-0-470-11724-8

Adobe Web Suite CS3 All-in-One Desk Reference For Dummies
978-0-470-12099-6

AutoCAD 2008 For Dummies
978-0-470-11650-0

Building a Web Site For Dummies, 3rd Edition
978-0-470-14928-7

Creating Web Pages All-in-One Desk Reference For Dummies, 3rd Edition
978-0-470-09629-1

Creating Web Pages For Dummies, 8th Edition
978-0-470-08030-6

Dreamweaver CS3 For Dummies
978-0-470-11490-2

Flash CS3 For Dummies
978-0-470-12100-9

Google SketchUp For Dummies
978-0-470-13744-4

InDesign CS3 For Dummies
978-0-470-11865-8

Photoshop CS3 All-in-One Desk Reference For Dummies
978-0-470-11195-6

Photoshop CS3 For Dummies
978-0-470-11193-2

Photoshop Elements 5 For Dummie
978-0-470-09810-3

SolidWorks For Dummies
978-0-7645-9555-4

Visio 2007 For Dummies
978-0-470-08983-5

Web Design For Dummies, 2nd Edit
978-0-471-78117-2

Web Sites Do-It-Yourself For Dumm
978-0-470-16903-2

Web Stores Do-It-Yourself For Dumm
978-0-470-17443-2

LANGUAGES, RELIGION & SPIRITUALITY

Arabic For Dummies
978-0-471-77270-5

Chinese For Dummies, Audio Set
978-0-470-12766-7

French For Dummies
978-0-7645-5193-2

German For Dummies
978-0-7645-5195-6

Hebrew For Dummies
978-0-7645-5489-6

Ingles Para Dummies
978-0-7645-5427-8

Italian For Dummies, Audio Set
978-0-470-09586-7

Italian Verbs For Dummies
978-0-471-77389-4

Japanese For Dummies
978-0-7645-5429-2

Latin For Dummies
978-0-7645-5431-5

Portuguese For Dummies
978-0-471-78738-9

Russian For Dummies
978-0-471-78001-4

Spanish Phrases For Dummies
978-0-7645-7204-3

Spanish For Dummies
978-0-7645-5194-9

Spanish For Dummies, Audio Set
978-0-470-09585-0

The Bible For Dummies
978-0-7645-5296-0

Catholicism For Dummies
978-0-7645-5391-2

The Historical Jesus For Dummies
978-0-470-16785-4

Islam For Dummies
978-0-7645-5503-9

Spirituality For Dummies, 2nd Edition
978-0-470-19142-2

NETWORKING AND PROGRAMMING

ASP.NET 3.5 For Dummies
978-0-470-19592-5

C# 2008 For Dummies
978-0-470-19109-5

Hacking For Dummies, 2nd Edition
978-0-470-05235-8

Home Networking For Dummies, 4th Edition
978-0-470-11806-1

Java For Dummies, 4th Edition
978-0-470-08716-9

Microsoft® SQL Server™ 2008 All-in-One Desk Reference For Dummies
978-0-470-17954-3

Networking All-in-One Desk Reference For Dummies, 2nd Edition
978-0-7645-9939-2

Networking For Dummies, 8th Edition
978-0-470-05620-2

SharePoint 2007 For Dummies
978-0-470-09941-4

Wireless Home Networking For Dummies, 2nd Edition
978-0-471-74940-0

OPERATING SYSTEMS & COMPUTER BASICS

Mac For Dummies, 5th Edition
978-0-7645-8458-9

Laptops For Dummies, 2nd Edition
978-0-470-05432-1

Linux For Dummies, 8th Edition
978-0-470-11649-4

MacBook For Dummies
978-0-470-04859-7

Mac OS X Leopard All-in-One
Desk Reference For Dummies
978-0-470-05434-5

Mac OS X Leopard For Dummies
978-0-470-05433-8

Macs For Dummies, 9th Edition
978-0-470-04849-8

PCs For Dummies, 11th Edition
978-0-470-13728-4

Windows® Home Server For Dummies
978-0-470-18592-6

Windows Server 2008 For Dummies
978-0-470-18043-3

Windows Vista All-in-One
Desk Reference For Dummies
978-0-471-74941-7

Windows Vista For Dummies
978-0-471-75421-3

Windows Vista Security For Dummies
978-0-470-11805-4

SPORTS, FITNESS & MUSIC

Coaching Hockey For Dummies
978-0-470-83685-9

Coaching Soccer For Dummies
978-0-471-77381-8

Fitness For Dummies, 3rd Edition
978-0-7645-7851-9

Football For Dummies, 3rd Edition
978-0-470-12536-6

GarageBand For Dummies
978-0-7645-7323-1

Golf For Dummies, 3rd Edition
978-0-471-76871-5

Guitar For Dummies, 2nd Edition
978-0-7645-9904-0

Home Recording For Musicians
For Dummies, 2nd Edition
978-0-7645-8884-6

iPod & iTunes For Dummies,
5th Edition
978-0-470-17474-6

Music Theory For Dummies
978-0-7645-7838-0

Stretching For Dummies
978-0-470-06741-3

Get smart @ dummies.com®

- **Find a full list of Dummies titles**
- **Look into loads of FREE on-site articles**
- **Sign up for FREE eTips e-mailed to you weekly**
- **See what other products carry the Dummies name**
- **Shop directly from the Dummies bookstore**
- **Enter to win new prizes every month!**

Separate Canadian edition also available
Separate U.K. edition also available

Available wherever books are sold. For more information or to order direct: U.S. customers visit www.dummies.com or call 1-877-762-2974.
U.K. customers visit www.wileyeurope.com or call (0) 1243 843291. Canadian customers visit www.wiley.ca or call 1-800-567-4797.

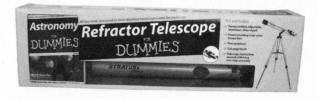